The Gourmands' Way

Julia Child · M.F.K. Fisher
Alexis Lichine · A. J. Liebling
Richard Olney · Alice B. Toklas

THE
GOURMANDS' WAY

*Six Americans in Paris and
the Birth of a New Gastronomy*

JUSTIN SPRING

Farrar, Straus and Giroux   New York

Farrar, Straus and Giroux
18 West 18th Street, New York 10011

First edition, 2017

Library of Congress Cataloging-in-Publication Data
Names: Spring, Justin, 1962– author.
Title: The gourmands' way : six Americans in Paris and the birth
of a new gastronomy / Justin Spring.
Description: New York : Farrar, Straus and Giroux, [2017] |
Includes bibliographical references and index.
Identifiers: LCCN 2017001319 | ISBN 9780374538019 |
ISBN 9780374711740 (ebook)
Subjects: LCSH: Food writers—United States—Biography. | Cooks—
United States—Biography. | Food writing—France—Paris.
Classification: LCC TX649.A1 S675 2017 | DDC 641.5092 [B] —dc23
LC record available at https://lccn.loc.gov/2017001319

Designed by Jonathan D. Lippincott

Our books may be purchased in bulk for promotional, educational, or business use.
Please contact your local bookseller or the Macmillan Corporate and Premium
Sales Department at 1-800-221-7945, extension 5442, or by e-mail at
MacmillanSpecialMarkets@macmillan.com.

www.fsgbooks.com
www.twitter.com/fsgbooks • www.facebook.com/fsgbooks

P1

Frontispiece: Photograph by Paul Child
(Courtesy of the Schlesinger Library, Radcliffe Institute, Harvard University)

For

A.D.K.

twenty-five years of adventure, at home and abroad

Every man has two countries—France and his own.
—John F. Kennedy, on his state visit to Paris, 1961

De toutes les passions, la seule vraiment respectable me paraît être la gourmandise.
—Guy de Maupassant, "Amoureux et Primeurs"

Contents

The Gourmands' Way

Introduction

The three women and three men in this book are a lively, sensual, fractious, and deeply opinionated group. They come from all walks of life and all levels of the socioeconomic spectrum, and include an artist, a homemaker, a businessman, a journalist, a novelist, and a woman of letters. Some of them were rich, and some were poor; some were happily married, while others had passionate affairs and multiple partners, and still others lived mostly alone. They are A. J. Liebling, the finest war correspondent, sportswriter, and man-on-the-street reporter of his generation; Alice Toklas, life partner of Gertrude Stein, who reinvented herself, at age seventy-five, as a cookbook author and memoirist; M.F.K. Fisher, a sensualist storyteller and fabulist; Julia Child, who evolved from a pleasure-loving newlywed to America's greatest television food celebrity; Alexis Lichine, a wildly ambitious wine merchant and connoisseur; and Richard Olney, an expatriate artist who evolved (but only reluctantly) into a cookbook author and wine expert writing for both French and American readerships. My goal in this book is to describe some very specific moments and experiences that seem to me to have shaped their characters and careers, but in doing so I will also look at a particular historical period during which France and its cooking briefly captured the American popular imagination. Along the way

I will observe how that American fascination with French food first bloomed; how profusely it flourished; and then how quickly it faded—all through the epicurean adventures of six hungry *bons viveurs*.

While this book is primarily about writers and their writing, it is also about Paris. Cherished by generations of Americans for its beauty, sensuality, and luxury, the French capital emerged from World War II relatively unscathed (at least compared with Europe's other leading cities) and during the boom years that followed the war, it became once again a world center for fashion, philosophy, and the arts. More important to this book, it also renewed its reputation as the world capital of gastronomy. Understandably, many Americans who came to Paris during these years made fine dining a prime concern. In doing so, they benefited enormously from the strength of the postwar dollar and the virtual collapse of the European market for luxury food and drink—circumstances that allowed them, for a brief while, to enjoy the world's greatest wines and most celebrated cuisine at what today seem like rock-bottom prices.

In looking at the Parisian experiences of these six innovative writers, I hope to demonstrate how much of their excitement about food and wine came to them not only through adventurous eating and drinking, but also through French gastronomic literature (and, by association, through French literary culture)—for while few Americans realize it, much of what these writers wrote came out of (or in some cases was appropriated from) writing on food and wine by the French. Up to now, few of their biographers have looked at the lively writing on food and wine taking place among the French during the period 1900 to 1975. But even as I juxtapose French and American food writings and food experiences of the past century, I intend to show how truly daring and innovative these six Americans actually were in what they wrote—for none of them was simply presenting readers with a "translated" account of French gastronomic literature. Rather, they were attempting to explain the nature of French culinary awareness through their own particular experiences, circumstances, backgrounds, and personal ambitions. And ultimately each did so in a way that was neither a part of the existing French tradition nor the evolving American. Rather, each took a new, more relaxed, and relatively informal approach to food awareness that suited the changing times in which they lived. This new sort of writing appealed strongly to readers back home—where, thanks to changing social conditions, literate Americans were suddenly forging new, more thoughtful, and ultimately more intimate relationships with their kitchens.

For each of these writers, the key to their success as writers lay in presenting French food and wine through the simplifying lens of the self, and in doing so, offering American readers a new, easy-to-grasp way of acquainting themselves with French food and wine. They were, in that way, charismatic tour guides specifically for Americans who might otherwise have been overwhelmed by the complexity of French cuisine and French foodways. And thanks to their passion for their subject, these writers skillfully communicated the French preoccupation with food quality, food freshness, *terroir*, and seasonality—four crucial French concepts that are today centrally important to the contemporary American understanding of eating and drinking well.

Although each of these six writer-adventurers wrote accounts of their experiences in France, their Parisian exploits are often only minimally or fragmentarily documented. But all arrived in Paris with a lively curiosity about what the French ate and drank, and all had experiences in Paris that shaped the course of their later lives. They had much in common, and often crossed paths: frequenting the same well-known Paris restaurants and cafés, admiring the same French writers and chefs, living in the same little neighborhoods, reading the same great books, enjoying the same great French foods and wines, and even taking the same road trips to celebrated wine regions and Michelin-starred restaurants.

More important, like the expatriate American writers, artists, and composers of the Lost Generation, they all came to Paris seeking a better way of living and being. And ultimately they were united in a common endeavor: the broadening of American cultural awareness about food appreciation, preparation, and enjoyment. During a moment in American history when food preparation was focused largely on convenience and economy, these writers found in France something entirely different: a sense of the importance (and pleasure!) of good food and wine to everyday life. They engaged, each in his or her own way, in a cross-cultural exchange of ideas about eating well—and the knowledge they brought home has continued to inform American food awareness and food enjoyment ever since.

Each of these writers gave America a new way of thinking about food and wine—and these very different ways of thinking all have their own validity and significance. Together they seem to me to have initiated an American cultural dialogue on food that has continued (in an equally fractious, contentious, cacophonous manner) up to the present day—a gastronomic dialogue that involves not only cookbook authors, memoirists, and food journalists, but also restaurateurs and reformers, fabulists and home economists, hucksters and raconteurs and entrepreneurs too. Like a number of other contentious dialogues that evolved among Paris-based American expatriates of the 1950s and 1960s—including dialogues about gender and racial equality, sexual freedom, political dissent, and the right to free speech and artistic expression—the food-and-wine dialogue that was begun by these gourmands has helped establish a new way of thinking about eating well in the United States: one that was not about economy or convenience, but about pleasure, balance, restraint, and, ultimately, about well-being. The stories, guides, and information they presented so appetizingly to their readers may have been considered by their literary contemporaries as not much more than instruction manuals, diversion, and light entertainment. However, anyone who cares to look back in time can now clearly see that through these writers' combined efforts, French gastronomical knowledge, wisdom, and excitement became part of American culture. Through them, the age-old French dialogue surrounding food, wine, and the table started to become an American dialogue as well.

ONE

Liebling and the Lion of Belfort

When the Allied forces entered Paris on August 25, 1944, war correspondent A. J. Liebling (or "Joe") was right there with them. Thanks to his high-level connections in the U.S. Third Army, he had been attached to its First Infantry Division since its campaign in North Africa, filing stories for *The New Yorker* throughout the war. He had not been allowed to accompany them across the Channel on D-day, but three weeks later, he had been shipped over and given his own jeep and driver to facilitate his reporting on the aftermath of the Allied invasion. It had been a busy couple of months. Then, at summer's end, the Allies had marched on Paris, and five days of heavy fighting brought them to the outskirts of the city. Liebling followed behind, keeping as close to the action as he could, but getting up to Paris was not easy. There was continuing resistance from the Germans. Many bridges, buildings, and roads had been sabotaged along the way, and there had been blockades, traffic jams, and random gun- and artillery fire as well. But at last Liebling's driver reached the southern entry into the capital, the Porte d'Orléans.

Liebling had last seen Paris four years and two months earlier, just hours before the arrival of the Nazis, and now he was one of the first Allied journalists to return. The city had been much on his mind throughout the war: from boyhood onward, it had been his favorite place on earth. His father, a self-made New York furrier, had regularly taken the Liebling family to Europe, ostensibly so that his *zaftig* wife might lose weight at a German spa. But these health-related journeys had always included a stop or two in Paris, during which time the entire family ate grandly and to their hearts' content. Liebling's earliest memories of the place, which dated from the years before World War I, had been of military parades, fantastically curvaceous, full-figured women of the Lillian Russell type, and a seemingly endless array of elaborate desserts and iced pastries. The elegance of the city, of its residents, and of its restaurants was all so different from anything he had known at home.

Liebling spent most of his boyhood on the outskirts of New York, in the little beach community of Far Rockaway, where he was brought up on the plain, eat-it-it's-good-for-you cooking of the household's equally plain German *Fräuleins*. As boyhood gave way to adolescence, he developed a passion for military history, a talent for writing, and a predilection for trouble. Though he didn't quite fit in with them, he liked to hang out with tough guys and hoods. And he liked to break rules. After he got booted out of Dartmouth College, he talked his father into sending him to Paris, saying he would spend the academic year of 1926 to 1927 completing his education at the Sorbonne. His father only reluctantly agreed, but he nonetheless provided Liebling with a two-thousand-dollar letter of credit, one that enabled his son to spend the better part of the following school year skipping classes, strolling the boulevards, and eyeing pretty girls, or else whiling away the hours in restaurants and cafés, reading, smoking, and learning hands-on all about French wine and French food.

The Sorbonne may have bored him, but French literature and culture did not: Liebling immersed himself that year in various French novels, histories, and memoirs, and he read all kinds of French newspapers and magazines as well. At one point, his lifelong love for the racier French classics led him to translate the pornography of Nicolas-Edme Rétif, hoping he might use his new French to pick up girls. At the end of that glorious year (having successfully picked up a number of them), he was entirely broke and without prospects, and upon returning to the United States penniless he was forced to take a job as a local news reporter in dreary Providence, Rhode Island. "If I had compared my life to a cake," he later noted, "the sojourns in Paris would have represented the chocolate filling. The intervening layers were plain sponge."[1]

Now, on this day of liberation, as his jeep rumbled into Paris, the most brilliant and widely read bad-boy reporter of his generation was struck yet again by the attractiveness of the Parisian women, who seemed to have grown even more desirable through their years of wartime hardship. They "wore long, simple summer dresses that left their bodies very free . . . their bare legs were more smoothly muscled than Frenchwomen's before the war, because they had been riding those bicycles or walking ever since taxis vanished from the streets of Paris, and their figures were better, because the *pâtissiers* were out of business." He was now thirty-nine years old and desperate for a taste of real female company—not just the pay-and-get-out services of the whores who followed the army. As the beautiful young Parisiennes on their bicycles bore down upon the oncoming jeeps, all smiles and waves, he was overwhelmed by a rush of desire. "I understood how those old Sag Harbor whalers must have felt," he wrote afterward, "when the women of the islands came swimming out to them like a school of beautiful tinker mackerel."

The sight of the beautiful city—and of the beautiful welcoming women on their bicycles, of the jubilant crowds rushing out to meet the advancing Allied troops, some of them offering up fresh fruit and sandwiches and bottles of wine to the liberators—was suddenly more than Liebling could bear, and he wept. "There were thousands of people, tens of thousands, all demonstratively happy," he wrote of the moment. "In any direction we looked, there was an unending vista of cheering people. It was like an entry into Paradise."

❧

All summer had been building to this moment. Liebling could not have been more delighted with the location for the D-day landings, for he knew Lower Normandy well: he had taken several long hiking tours there in the fall of 1926, walking an average of fifteen miles a day, quenching his thirst with pint after pint of hard cider as he went, and punctuating each of his daylong rambles with an enormous Norman meal. As a result, he recalled much of the gently rolling landscape from memory—and he recalled the menus too. Most important, he knew that the rich food of Normandy, based on butter and cream, might well have overwhelmed his digestion had he not had easy access to Calvados, taking shots of it not only between courses (as the traditional *trou normand**), but also at the meal's conclusion, as a hefty, tumbler-size *digestif*. Eighteen years had passed since those heady student days, but Liebling remembered every detail of the food and drink of *la région Basse-Normandie* as clearly as if he had eaten there the day before. In fact, the whole place made him feel uncannily at home—as he put it, as if "I had landed on the southern shore of Long Island and drive[n] inland toward Belmont Park."[2]

Since disembarking on June 24, he had been interviewing Frenchmen about their experiences of the German occupation and the D-day landings, composing brilliant and moving stories about the invasion and its aftermath for *The New Yorker*. Much of what he wrote about was horrible, and even weeks after the invasion the smell of death lay all around—the human corpses and cow carcasses were everywhere. One of his favorite small towns, Vire, in the Calvados, had been virtually obliterated, and Caen, its capital, had been reduced to smoking rubble. Nevertheless, he was used to death and destruction by now, and he was feeling more exhilaration than despair, because the Allies had the Nazis on the run.

Moreover, thanks to the season, Normandy was just then at its most beautiful and welcoming. Summer brought with it sunny afternoons, salt breezes, and the gentle scent of dog roses blooming in the *bocages*. The fine flat sandy beaches had water warm enough for swimming, and everywhere one looked there were broad open vistas of gray sea, green pasture, and blue sky. So long as Liebling kept filing his stories—and as he liked to boast, he could "write better than anyone

---

*Literally "the Norman hole," *le trou normand* is a custom of taking Calvados, an apple brandy made from hard cider, between courses, both to facilitate the digestion and to renew the appetite.

who could write faster, and faster than anyone who could write better"—he was free to go anywhere and do anything he liked: tour the local sights, visit with army acquaintances and journalist friends, and seek out the finest available Norman food and drink. Which was, in fact, easy enough to do since, now that the Germans had been routed and all transport lines had been blocked or destroyed, Norman farmers were rich in delectable foodstuffs and eager to turn these perishable goods into cold, hard cash. As a result, Liebling had ready access to more choice produce and top-quality artisanal foods than anyone in the army had seen in four long years.[3]

There was also some great drinking to be done—and not just of the local *cidre, pommeau*,* or Calvados either. During the liberation of Cherbourg, while covering the surrender of Fort de Roule, Liebling and a group of fellow journalists stumbled upon an underground storage room holding a mind-boggling Nazi treasure trove of brandy, Cointreau, Bénédictine, and Champagne. Since the Allied army had not yet secured the place, the journalists quickly trundled all they could out to their waiting jeeps and trucks. "Joe [Liebling] advised us on our choice of liqueurs," one of them later recalled. "We . . . stored them in the jeep just before the MPs placed guards at the entrance of the fort [and] that supply of booze liberated at Cherbourg lasted us almost all the way to Paris."[4]

Whether he was interviewing French civilians or American GIs, Liebling always kept a bottle of Calvados handy for sharing, for this fine apple brandy was, he found, a great way to loosen up tongues. And it wasn't difficult to obtain either, since Norman farmers had been selling it on the black market throughout the Occupation—both as a form of organized resistance and as a way of providing for their families. Those Americans and Brits who had the freedom to move about and speak to the locals at will—journalists mostly—were quick to take advantage of this Norman bounty, and those fluent enough in French to parse the *Guide Michelin* did even better. Ernest Hemingway set up for a while at the Hôtel de la Mère Poulard on Mont-Saint-Michel.

---

* *Cidre* is hard cider. *Pommeau* is a traditional mixture of apple juice and Calvados, usually taken as an aperitif.

The famed inn on the monastery-island was not exactly the most convenient place from which to file a story, but its restaurant was legendary: though specializing in omelets, it was strong on a number of gourmet dishes based on prized local ingredients. Liebling made his way there too, and visited with war photographer Robert Capa over a long and leisurely lunch. The hotel's menu featured not only its famed soufﬂéd omelet cooked over an open fire, but also oysters from Cancale just to the west, lobsters from the English Channel, and delicate salt-marsh-raised lamb from Avranches to the immediate east.

Not long after that meal at La Mère Poulard, Liebling brought two fellow journalists to another fine little restaurant he had found north of the Mont, halfway up the Cotentin peninsula. After a lively negotiation in French with the *patron*,* he had secured his buddies a festive lunch of *sole bonne femme* and *tournedos, sauce Choron*.† Unfortunately their dessert was cut short by an emergency call, as they were summoned to witness the Eighth Corps cleaning out a pocket of German resistance at La-Haye-du-Puits, twelve miles away. The journalists then came under fire on a roadside strewn with German corpses and rotting cows—a situation that proved highly compromising to their digestions.[5] When the last of the Germans had been wiped out, Liebling recalled, "We stayed around awhile, rather at a loss for conversation, then left, feeling that we had atoned for our good lunch."[6]

Liebling had truly been in his element in Normandy, for war and gastronomy were the two great loves of his childhood, when he would lie in bed reading biographies of Napoleon while munching candy bars. Covering the invasion of Normandy was therefore a dream come true, not only because it marked a great turning point in the war, but also because Norman cuisine is among the richest and best in all of

---

*The French name for a restaurant proprietor, one who is in many instances both owner and chef.
† *Sole bonne femme* is sole cooked simply, as a "good wife" (*bonne femme*) might. The Julia Child–Simone Beck version calls for poaching the folded filets in a combination of butter, white wine, fish stock, and sautéed mushrooms and shallots, then straining off the liquid, thickening it with a roux, and adding a final enrichment of heavy cream. In *tournedos, sauce Choron*, the sauce is a variation on *sauce béarnaise* featuring a small amount of tomato paste; it is named after chef Alexandre-Étienne Choron (1837–1924) of the celebrated Paris restaurant Voisin.

France.* Liebling certainly thought so, for he liked rich food and strong drink, and he liked to eat until it hurt. After so many months in war-ravaged England, where the rations had been meager and the cooking dreary, he was beside himself at being back among people who understood intrinsically what it was to eat richly and well. In fact, he was half-convinced he had a Norman soul. As he later explained to his readers, "The Norman takes his vegetables in the form of animals—herbivores eat grass [and the Norman] Man, a carnivore, eats herbivores. . . . [Likewise] the Norman takes his fruit in the form of cider and its distillate, Calvados."

Liebling loved all Norman food, but he particularly adored the region's rich, ripened, full-fat cheeses: Pont l'Évêque, Neufchâtel, Camembert, and the pungent Livarot, to name just a few. A fellow journalist later recalled coming upon him in their shared tent one very warm afternoon in late June, to find Liebling lying on his cot in his undershorts, a classic French novel propped up on his hairy chest, "and on his rounded belly . . . an open box of ripe Camembert, which he dipped into occasionally with a finger."[7] Open-minded about flavors, textures, and scents, Liebling also went out of his way to secure large quantities of *andouillette de Vire*, a massive sausage made entirely of smoked pig intestines. Its heavy barnyard odor was enough to send most Americans reeling, but Liebling loved its excremental funk. He had always been the most fearless of eaters. Even after contracting typhoid from sewage-contaminated oysters in childhood, no food had ever scared him or put him off. Split sheepsheads, *tête de veau*, tripe, brains, chitterlings—nothing could deter this gastronomic commando.

But during the summer of 1944, Liebling was eating only the finest—having waited four long years to return to France, he was now ready to lay down any cash necessary for the best French food that money could buy. "I am still of the opinion that Lower Normandy has the best sea food, the best mutton (from the salt meadows of the Avranches region), the best beef, the best butter, the best cream, and

---

* Alice Toklas later recalled the delights and limitations of Norman cooking: "At Duclair everything was cooked in cream: chicken, cabbages, indeed all vegetables and most meats. We stayed there several days before this bored us. At nearby Rouen butter replaced the cream" (*Alice B. Toklas Cook Book*, p. 74).

the best cheese in Europe," he later wrote in his masterpiece, *Normandy Revisited*. His idea of a good Norman lunch, he continued, was "a dozen *huîtres de Courseulles*, an *araignée de mer* . . . with a half pint of mayonnaise on the side, a dish of *tripes à la mode de Caen*, a partridge Olivier Basselin, poached in cream and cider and singed in old Calvados, a *gigot de pré-salé*, a couple of *biftecks*,* and a good Pont l'Évêque."[8]

♣

Liebling's coverage of the war had begun with similarly extravagant restaurant meals taken in Paris during the winter and spring of 1939 to 1940. Like many journalists, he had lived most of his life on the fly, eating irregularly and badly, but covering the outbreak of World War II in Paris had briefly changed all that. He arrived in France to cover the war for *The New Yorker* in October, at age thirty-five, having lobbied hard with his editors for the coveted spot. (The magazine's well-established Paris correspondent, Janet Flanner—"Genêt"— unexpectedly needed to return to the United States to look after her dying mother.) There was little to keep Liebling in New York: his pretty young Irish-American wife had suffered a mental breakdown shortly after their marriage, and she had been institutionalized ever since, with no hope of recovery. As a result Liebling had no home life, no love life, and no prospect of children.[9] Being a lifelong fan of Frenchwomen, French literature, French military history, and French cuisine, he had pushed hard to be sent back to Paris on assignment, sensing he would surely be happier there, even if the Nazis invaded. "I spent several man-hours of barroom time impressing St. Clair McKelway, then managing editor, with my profound knowledge of France," Liebling later remembered, adding that since McKelway spoke no French he was in no position to judge Liebling's (which was only so-so). McKelway then suggested Liebling's name to the magazine's editor in chief, Harold Ross, proposing

---

* *Huîtres de Courseulles* are oysters from the Norman village of Courseulles-sur-Mer. *Araignée de mer* is an edible form of spider crab. *Tripes à la mode de Caen* is a slow-baked casserole of cow stomach, enriched with a calf's foot and flavored with Calvados. Olivier Basselin was a fifteenth-century poet and composer of many famous Norman drinking songs. *Gigot de pré-salé* is a roast leg of lamb made from lamb raised on the grasses of Norman salt marshes. *Bifteck* is the French word for "steak" (adapted from the English "beefsteak").

that Liebling might cover the war from the human-interest angle.* Ross grudgingly agreed, but only on the stipulation that Liebling keep away from stories of Parisian "lowlife"—he knew all too well Liebling's predilection for booze, gambling, and whores, and he was committed to keeping *The New Yorker*, as he put it, "a family magazine."

Upon arrival, Liebling found the city "looked much as it had [when I was a college student there] in 1927 except for the strips of paper pasted across shop windows to keep the glass from flying in case of a bombardment." He was older now, though, so instead of taking cheap student rooms in the Latin Quarter, he checked into the Hôtel Louvois, "a second-class, comfortable pile favored by traveling salesmen." The Louvois was situated not on the Left Bank but the Right, just up the street from the Palais-Royal, which had been a center of Parisian vice for more than a century. He soon discovered that the hotel had a number of good, expense-account-type restaurants close by, as well as a substantial population of streetwalkers who made a specialty of catering to visiting businessmen. But he had chosen the hotel primarily because it was so close to the government offices in the First Arrondissement, Liebling's new beat.

Liebling's job for *The New Yorker* was to file good stories as often as possible—but doing so was not going to be easy, because after the invasion of Poland in September and the subsequent declaration of war, nothing much happened. And in fact it would be seven months until the Germans invaded, a period now remembered as the "phony war." Liebling spent this seven-month *"sitzkrieg"* (as he called it) chatting up every Frenchman he could, and doing so whenever possible over a good meal that could be charged up against his expenses. "I don't want to give the impression that I covered Paris for *The New Yorker* entirely from cafés and brothels," he later recalled. "I took the responsibilities of my new career so seriously that I joined the American Press Association of Paris and went at least once a week to [press briefings at] the Hotel Continental."[10]

---

*In fact, during this first year in Paris, Liebling was inventing a new form of reporting, "the lower-key, more sociological reportage that papers like *The New York Times* have subsequently adopted as the standard business of their foreign staffs" (Sokolov, *Wayward Reporter*, p. 133).

Liebling loved Paris, loved the French, and loved filing his stories as the invasion loomed—particularly since, thanks to Paris's few remaining tourists and many top-notch restaurants, he was suddenly eating and drinking better than anyone ever could have imagined, and he never had a problem getting a reservation. Back in New York, his financial situation had been made doubly difficult by his wife's costly institutionalization, and as a result, Liebling had lived in a state of perpetual debt there, borrowing from the magazine against articles not yet delivered, a predicament that would ultimately keep him chained to his desk for the better part of his life. But quality reporting and writing is difficult and labor intensive, and quality reporting and writing was the only kind Liebling cared to do. So he had long since resigned himself to living in debt, dining modestly, and working round the clock. Desire for literary fame was the carrot that tempted him ever onward, and debt the highly effective stick.

But in the Paris of 1939 to 1940, all his costs were being covered by his *New Yorker* expense account. And those few items he could not write off—such as nights out at Parisian brothels—were being picked up by his public relations contacts in the Champagne business, who were also happy to treat him to as much of their bubbly as he cared to imbibe. As a result, he was now pretty much living in good restaurants, and when not taking a meal, he was walking the streets in a state of perpetual, if mild, intoxication. Thirteen years earlier, when he had survived on a small monthly student allowance, he was often too short of funds to eat or drink during the last days of each month. Now the dollar was strong, his pockets were deep, and everyone was eager for his custom—a twist of fate that enabled Liebling not only to indulge in *haute cuisine* to his heart's content but also to chat at length with various *patrons*, waiters, wine captains, and *maîtres d'hôtel*.

And chat they did, freely and openly, for Liebling had a genius for drawing people out. Balding and bespectacled, his round face had "a look of sheer benignness and good humor [that] made him attractive to everyone," as his friend and editor Katharine Angell (later Mrs. E. B. White), would later remember.[11] His ability to quote effortlessly from French literature—particularly from those rakes Villon,

Rabelais, Rétif, and Balzac—made even the most reserved of Frenchmen warm to him. The fact that he tipped like a maharajah also helped.

✤

Being flush with cash did not mean, however, that Liebling had for-
saken his taste for the simple life. As a student he had learned a great
deal about French cuisine at a small, well-run restaurant near the
École des Beaux Arts. There, for many evenings of his year abroad, he
had pondered the daily specials *sur l'ardoise* ("on the blackboard") and
agonized over how to spend his very limited funds: on a good wine
and a budget cut of meat—or, alternately, on a mediocre wine but a
very good steak? In retrospect, he felt the impecuniousness of his
1926 to 1927 year at the Sorbonne actually helped him understand
French cooking, because, as he later wrote, "the first requisite for
writing well about food is a good appetite, [and] the second is to put
in your apprenticeship as a feeder when you have enough money to
pay the check but not enough to produce indifference to the size of
the total."[12] Here, in Liebling's opinion, the average rich man was at a
distinct disadvantage, for

> Even in Paris, one can dine in the costly restaurants for years
> without learning that there are fish other than sole, turbot,
> salmon (in season), trout, and the Mediterranean *rouget* and
> *loup de mer.* The fresh herring or sardine *sauce moutarde*; the
> *colin froid mayonnaise*; the conger eel *en matelote*;* the small
> fresh-water fish of the Seine and the Marne, fried crisp and
> served *en buisson*;† the whiting *en colère*‡ (his tail in his mouth,
> as if contorted with anger); and even the skate and the
> *dorade*—all these, except by special and infrequent invitation,
> are out of the swim. . . . All the fish I have mentioned have
> their habitats in humbler restaurants, the only places where the
> aspirant eater can become familiar with their honest fishy tastes

---

* A way of preparing fish (usually freshwater fish) in a sauce of red wine, onions, and mushrooms.
† Trans.: "in the shape of a bush."
‡ *En colère* means "angry."

and the decisive modes of accommodation that suit them. . . .
The consistently rich man is also unlikely to make the acquaintance of meat dishes of robust taste—the hot *andouille* and
andouillette, which are close-packed sausages of smoked tripe,
and the *boudin*, or blood pudding, and all its relatives that
figure in the pages of Rabelais and on the menus of the market restaurants. He will not meet the *civets*, or dark, winy
stews of domestic rabbit and old turkey. . . . And [of course]
the world of tripery is barred to the well-heeled, except for
occasional exposure to an expurgated version of *tripes à la
mode de Caen.*[13]

In seeking out such robust, earthy, regional cuisine, Liebling
needed an ally, since eating alone night after night was simply too
sad—and while he could invite along any number of reporter companions, not everyone understood or appreciated the rustic (and occasionally off-putting) foods of the poor. Luckily he had recently met
and befriended a newspaperman who had been living and working
in Paris for more than a decade, and whose passion for French food,
wine, and spirits rivaled his own: Waverley Root. Root "was a very
good eating companion," Liebling later recalled, for "he knew a lot of
small restaurants that were not well known and that had a faithful
clientele that all weighed over 100 kilos."[14] The genial, bewhiskered
journalist, the future author of *The Food of France* (1958), had been
working as a stringer for the Paris edition of the *Chicago Tribune* (and
eating his way steadily through the restaurants and brasseries of Paris)
since his arrival there in 1926. Although the two men were often in
disagreement about the nature and origin of various dishes (and
would remain so throughout their lives, particularly after Root published his controversial book), these arguments were really just a way
of chewing the fat. And together they chewed a good deal of it: Liebling
routinely devoured double or triple the food of anyone else in the restaurant. ("I used to be shy about ordering a steak after I had eaten a
steak sandwich," he later noted, "but I got over it.")
    Massive overeating of this sort was already taking a toll on his
body. His feet were chronically inflamed with gout—not only at the

toes, but also at instep, ankle, and heel—and he had gout-related arthritis in his knees and elbows. He also suffered from shortness of breath, sleep problems, depression, lethargy, mood swings, and high blood pressure. Being unable to run very far (or even walk very far) was going to be dangerous for him when the war began, he knew; but his answer to the problem was simply not to think about it and to get on with his meal. He came from a family of hearty eaters and was going to eat as much as he liked, no matter what anyone advised to the contrary.

The day the German invasion of Paris began, Liebling was resting his gouty feet in the bar of the Hôtel Lotti, a block from the Place Vendôme, sipping a Champagne aperitif. (He would have preferred a cocktail, but the government had recently put liquor restrictions in place—so like his fellow Parisians, Liebling had to settle for sparkling wine.) The roar of the German bombers overhead and the *ack-ack-ack* of the French antiaircraft guns were both very disturbing; but since there was nothing anyone could do about either of them, and since there was nothing yet to write about, and since he was already feeling pretty darned good, Liebling chose to stay on for lunch. The waiters closed the metal shutters to protect their diners from bomb blasts and the service began. After the aperitif there were the *entrée*, the *plat*, and the *dessert*—each with its own wine. Then coffee, and finally a cigarette.[15]

By June 14, 1940, the French ground forces to the north and west had been overwhelmed by the Luftwaffe and by superior German ground forces, leaving Paris open and defenseless to the advancing Germans. The French government, after considering its options, retreated in disarray to the Loire Valley, and was regrouping there at Tours. Liebling and Root, facing capture or detainment in Paris, decided to follow the French government south—thinking there was probably still some good reporting to be done on that side, and any number of possible escape routes to the sea. They drove south in Root's sputtery little Citroën 11, taking with them another American newspaperman who had broken his ankle and couldn't manage the train. Liebling then spent three days chasing down stories in crowded, chaotic little Tours, after which the French government packed up and withdrew to Bordeaux. So too did Liebling and Root.

Despite the fine food and drink available in both of these legendary wine-producing regions, and despite the sensationally good meals on offer at nearly every place they stopped along the road, the two men could not find much pleasure in their eating. France was in a state of collapse; Paris was lost; Hitler and his thugs were preparing to overrun all of Europe—and from what Liebling could tell, the French government couldn't do anything more to stop it. All around them, meanwhile, the French were envisioning the horrors of 1870 and 1914 all over again: the death, starvation, and destruction were for many of them all too recent memories. "There was a climate of death in Bordeaux, heavy and unhealthy like the smell of tuberoses," Liebling wrote of his last miserable days in France, which he spent mostly in high-end restaurants. "Men of wealth, heavy-jowled, waxy-faced, wearing an odd expression of relief from fear, waited for a couple of hours for tables and then spent all afternoon over their meals, ordering sequences of famous claret vintages as if they were on a *tour gastronomique* instead of being parties to a catastrophe."[16]

But then, even in times of crisis, one still had to eat and drink; and with his own departure from France looming, Liebling resolved to drink the best of the wine while it was still available to him, knowing he would not see its like for some time.

❧

Now, four years later, after filing war stories from Algeria, Tunisia, and England—and having survived most of it on army chow and K rations—Liebling was on the road back to Paris. The drive from Normandy into the Île-de-France, the region immediately surrounding the city, proved complicated because of the fighting: his driver needed to dip down south to Rambouillet forest before turning northeast again. Only in midafternoon did they reach the Porte d'Orléans. There Allied officers warned them that hostile fire continued throughout the city, and that Hitler had almost certainly ordered Dietrich von Choltitz, his *Kommandant von Gross-Paris*, not to surrender, but to blow up all the bridges and burn the city to the ground.

As Liebling and his driver cautiously made their way up through the Left Bank toward the Seine, the two men wondered which way to go, for they could hear small-cannon fire coming from the direction of the Invalides, and more from the Gare d'Orsay. Rather than risk being killed in a massive explosion at one of the Seine crossings, Liebling told his driver to go "back to the Gare [Montparnasse] to ask at Division [Headquarters] if there was a safe route across." The driver wheeled around and headed back toward the vast old train station.

Leaving the jeep at its entrance, Liebling walked up a long flight of stairs toward the waiting room to ask his question—and there, to his complete astonishment, he came upon the scene of a lifetime—von Choltitz himself, surrounded by his officers, surrendering the city to General Leclerc. "It wasn't until I saw th[os]e glum krauts in custody," Liebling wrote after, "that I was sure we and Notre Dame and the festive crowds wouldn't all go up in a cloud of black smoke."[17]

The formal surrender was complete by five p.m., with only Liebling and two other reporters* there to witness the scene. As the room emptied, the three journalists packed up their notebooks and made their way by jeep down the boulevard du Montparnasse and the boulevard Raspail to the hotel that had been designated for *la presse étrangère*—the Hôtel Néron, just a few hundred feet from the massive Lion de Belfort statue on Place Denfert-Rochereau.† Bartholdi's great bronze Lion,‡ sculpted to commemorate the heroic three-month-long resistance to the Prussian siege of Belfort in the War of 1870, had always been a favorite landmark for Liebling, who loved all things noble, grand, and military. Besides, its sculptor was the same man who had sculpted New York's Statue of Liberty. This afternoon its simple inscription, "*À la Défense Nationale*," had never seemed more poignant.

Liebling then turned his attention to the hotel. He thought the

---

* They were Paul Gallico of *The Saturday Evening Post* and Harold Denny of *The New York Times*.

† Place Denfert-Rochereau, formerly known as Place d'Enfer ("Place of Hell"), was once a main entry gate into Paris. A junction of three boulevards, three avenues, and three streets, it is also the site of a train station, the Gare Denfert-Rochereau, and the entry point to the catacombs of Paris, which contain the bones of more than six million Parisians.

‡ After the original, which Bartholdi had sculpted in sandstone just below the fortress of Belfort in the Franche-Comté.

Néron "an appetizingly wicked name;* a good orgy would be appropriate on such a night." But the modest little hotel bore no hint of vice. In fact there were no women of any sort to be found there, only "young men in berets, shirt sleeves, and pistol belts bounding up the stairs three at a time."[18] The chubby reporter, exhausted after his long day, signed in, got his room key, and lugged his typewriter, bedroll, and knapsack upstairs on swollen, achy feet. Once there, he took a quick bath—there was no hot water—and put on the only clean clothes he had left, a pair of socks. He'd had nothing to eat all day apart from K rations, and now it was dinnertime.

Here was a tough situation that called for a creative solution, for all Paris was essentially in lockdown. "I went into a bar and had one of those sticky red *apéritifs* that partly refute the notion that the French have sensitive palates," he wrote in his later remembrance of the day. "It cost a hundred francs, which was two dollars then. I was getting hungry . . . [but nothing] was open; the reports of a food shortage in Paris were evidently well founded. . . . [And] by now, it was beginning to be really dark. From the direction of the Luxembourg [Gardens] came the sound of steady firing—small-cannon as well as machine-gun."[19] Liebling remembered the area around the Néron pretty well, though, for during his student year at the Sorbonne he had taken boxing instruction close by, at the American Baptist Center, after which he would often take a vermouth-cassis† at the Closerie des Lilas. Surely it was still there; a legendary gathering place for France's great writers and artists, the comfortable café-restaurant also had a long-standing reputation for good, solid, affordable cooking. Liebling had in fact passed many a happy evening there, and while there was no guarantee it would be open, it was only a short walk away.

As he walked past the noble Lion of Belfort—a tribute to the bravery of Colonel Denfert-Rochereau and his long-suffering men— Liebling saw only a few lights in the windows. The shops were closed, but several bars remained open for those brave enough to celebrate.

---

* "Néron" is the French rendering of "Nero," the debauched Roman emperor.
† A large and refreshing cold drink, served over ice, consisting of two parts dry vermouth, one part crème de cassis, and soda water.

Random memories of his year at the Sorbonne kept coming back to him as he continued down the avenue—memories of long walks on the boulevards, of hearty meals, of cheap, sturdy wines. Those fine young working-class girls who had been willing to share his table and his bed with him in exchange for a little something at the end of the night. Their friendly and matter-of-fact openness to such an exchange. The friendly openness of just about everyone, back then. Tonight Paris may have been swallowed up in darkness, but it was bright with memories of a happier time, and possibly more lovable than ever, for as he later noted, "any liberated place acquires a special charm, like a kitten recovered from the town dump."

He was relieved to see a light on at the Closerie des Lilas, which "stood by itself, with gravel and trees all around it; quiet and cool, it had a touch of class."[20] As he drew closer, though, he realized that the restaurant held no customers—just the *patron*, his wife, the barman, and a waitress. Nonetheless Liebling ambled in and, in his best French, began with his usual small talk, speaking as rapidly and genially as possible on a succession of topics. He described how he had come to the Closerie during his student days; how he had attended the "celebration at this very bar of Lindbergh's safe arrival in Paris in 1927"; and how, just today, he had experienced innumerable perils on the road up from Normandy with the army. He finished by praising the outstanding character of General Leclerc. He half-expected to be shown the door, because the restaurant was clearly not serving. But his repartee made the desired impression. In Liebling's words, "It took." After smiles all around, he was invited to join them in their meal: "As the waitress brought in a great terrine of potato soup, the boss asked me if I had eaten. I magnanimously consented to join them, even though his wife warned that there would be nothing to follow but an omelet and a salad. . . . The *patronne*, it was plain, had never sampled a k-ration."[21]

As they began to eat, Monsieur Colin, the *patron*, informed Liebling that he was the first American to set foot in the Closerie since the taking of Paris in June 1940. "At the moment of [that] debacle," Colin went on, "when the future looked blackest, I set aside two bottles against the arrival of the first American customer to return here. One is a bottle of the *véritable* Pernod and the other contains Black and

White [scotch]. . . . I have never opened either. Which bottle will you drink?"

"I chose the whisky," Liebling later wrote, "because I knew I could drink more of that." Colin nodded, and the meal continued. After they had finished their soup, their omelet ("big as an eiderdown"), their salad, and their wine, Colin brought out the bottle of scotch, opened it, and poured Liebling a glass. "It was the only trophy or award I won during the war," Liebling remembered, "and I wouldn't have traded it for the DSO."*[22]

As they drank and talked, Liebling found himself growing increasingly melancholy, for he was remembering a working-class girl he had brought here from the Latin Quarter back in 1927. Angèle had lived with him for a while in his student digs, accepting meals and drinks and small gifts of money in return for her pleasant company and sexual favors. "Angèle was of a steady, rough good humor [and] she was a solid drinker," he remembered. "All her appetites were robust. In bed she was a kind of utility infielder."† Their arrangement had been merely friendly, with no expectations and few illusions. But Liebling treasured something she had once said to him, something that had remained with him ever since. She had told him: *"Tu n'es pas beau, mais t'es passable."* ‡ It hadn't been much of a compliment, but it hit the mark. "My brain reeled under the munificence," he later wrote. "If she had said I was handsome I wouldn't have believed her. If she had called me loathsome I wouldn't have liked it. *Passable* was what I hoped for. *Passable* is the best thing for a man to be."[23]

Angèle had been good company, but, as he later confessed, "aside from her concession that I was *passable*, which is [today] wrapped around my ego like a bulletproof vest riveted with diamonds, I retain little that Angèle said." Their affair, if it could be called that, ended without drama when Liebling ran out of money and went home. Only years later, through a passing comment from his former landlord, did

---

* The Distinguished Service Order, a high-level British military decoration commending officers for extraordinary service in combat.
† A baseball player who may not merit a starting role on the team but who can fill in dependably at any position.
‡ "You're not handsome, but you'll do."

he learn that a few months after his departure, in the winter of 1927 to 1928, Angèle had died—"not of a broken heart, but of flu."[24]

And now here he was, the war nearly over, in the restaurant where he had dined with Angèle seventeen years earlier. He was no longer young, and he no longer had a girl. His health was bad, he had debts, his wife was in a mental hospital, and his four-year, all-expense-paid gig as a war reporter was rapidly coming to an end. The future did not seem to hold much. But today he had witnessed the surrender of von Choltitz and he had liberated the Closerie des Lilas. Its owner had been so glad to see him that he had shared not only his supper, but also a treasured bottle of scotch. No reporter could have asked for a better day, and Liebling knew it.

"When we had imbibed the last of my glory," Liebling wrote years later, "I took an effusive leave and went out into the dark street. The bars that I had passed earlier were still busy, but I had no inclination to enter. Any further drinking that night would have been a letdown. I made but one brief pause—to roar at the Lion. He wouldn't roar back, and I continued to the Hôtel Néron, which I found as easily as if I had lived there all my life."[25]

TWO

The Franco-American
(Kitchen) Alliance

While Americans have been fascinated with French food and French wine since the days of Thomas Jefferson, the nation became particularly intrigued by it during the mid-1940s. For more than a decade the Great Depression had brought with it years of plain cooking on limited budgets. After that, wartime hardship brought thrift and food rationing. At the same time, though, an influx of food-savvy European war refugees were bringing their skills, talents, and awareness of food across the Atlantic with them. So even as the six writers in this study began to think and write about French food and wine in Paris, others back home had already created a nationwide appetite for it, and an interest in knowing more about it. An Englishwoman named Dione Lucas was possibly the most visible of them. Having set up her Cordon Bleu cooking school in New York in 1942, she was the leading authority on French home cooking in America by the time the war ended in 1945.

Lucas had left Great Britain for Paris in 1920 to study cello at the Paris Conservatory, but her delight with French food soon led her to drop out and enroll at the famed Cordon Bleu cooking school instead. There she proved so remarkable a student that upon graduation, she was able to persuade Henri-Paul Pellaprat, the school's distinguished chef-instructor, to allow her to open a London branch. She ran that branch, Au Petit Cordon Bleu (and its restaurant by the same name), for eight years in South Kensington, with her business partner, Rosemary Hume. By 1942, however, Lucas had decided to move with her two sons to New York, where she opened the Cordon Bleu Restaurant and Cooking School at 117 East 60th Street. (Hume, meanwhile, remained behind and continued to operate the London branch.)[1] Lucas hoped to return to London after the war, but with Britain's economy in ruins, she instead stayed on in New York permanently. Publication of her *Cordon Bleu Cook Book* in 1947 (which she dedicated to Rosemary Hume) subsequently established her American reputation nationwide. Modest, elegant, and entirely *comme il faut*, the book was an American adaptation of the one she had already published in the United Kingdom in 1936, featuring no photographs and only a few line illustrations. In 1948, she began to host her own television cooking show, *To the Queen's Taste*,* through which she became far better known to the American public.

Lucas was a formidable cooking instructor, demanding a great deal of her pupils. But most Americans watching her on television thought her disagreeably foreign and cold, for her clipped British accent and reserved manner were not well suited to the medium. ("Lucas has quite a face, doesn't she, most determined and cool," Julia Child observed to her friend Avis DeVoto. "I don't think I'd like her.")[2] Even so, Lucas's devotion to the art of French cooking was total, and she inspired a new generation of American women to cook and entertain beautifully at home. "The preparation of good food is merely another expression of art, of the joys of civilized living," Lucas wrote loftily in *The Cordon Bleu Cook Book*, encouraging her students to be women of taste and discernment, and to put more heart into the kitchen work that had until very recently been done for them by servants. "In the United States, with an abundance of good food never known in Europe, and with all the native talent and ability available, it is unfortunate that more emphasis is not placed on the importance of cooking as an art," she went on. "Preparation of good food takes time, skill, and patience, and [the] results mean the difference between mere eating to exist and the

---

* The show was renamed *The Dione Lucas Cooking Show* in 1949.

satisfaction derived from one of the major pleasures of life. Surely there is nothing more uplifting to the soul or more joyful to the spirit."[3]

Lucas was right, but her message was unfortunately phrased. Nobody likes being told they aren't doing something right, particularly by a humorless foreigner with a supercilious accent. And while Lucas was in fact a hardworking woman of few pretensions, she was also English and a perfectionist, and she couldn't hide either of those attributes from her viewers, who responded to her as "television's supreme European epicure [and] a beacon of culinary excellence,"[4] but not necessarily as a friendly or welcoming presence. Lucas's ethics, as well, seem ultimately to have limited her rise as a national celebrity: unlike her great rival of the period, James Beard, she declined to prostitute herself to the American processed food industry as a paid spokesperson, propagandist, and shill. Nor did she attempt to deceive people into thinking, as leading food journalist Poppy Cannon so readily did, that good cooking was just a carefree romp in the kitchen. Instead, she did things the French way: she ran a top-level cooking school and restaurant, and like Pellaprat, published thoughtfully and well on the type of cooking she believed in: traditional (and painstaking) French home cooking for the upper-middle-class home.

Dione Lucas was not the only food professional making a new start in the United States during World War II. Henri Soulé, New York's top restaurateur, was also a war refugee. This brilliant and ambitious Frenchman had got his start in America by managing Le Restaurant du Pavillon de France, an establishment renowned both for the quality of its food and for the brilliance of its service, at the 1939 World's Fair. When Germany invaded Poland on September 1, 1939, and Britain and France subsequently declared war on Germany, Soulé and his restaurant workers, including a young Burgundian chef named Pierre Franey, had already committed themselves to remaining in New York for the duration of the fair, which was to last well into 1940. After the German occupation of France in June of 1940, they were unable to return home, but at the same time, because they had no American working papers, they were unable to hold American jobs. Soulé resolved their predicament in the spring of 1941 by taking them up to Canada and then walking back across the U.S. border—thereby establishing all of them as war refugees. Six months later, on October 15, 1941, Soulé opened Le Pavillon, at 5 East 55th Street, and within months it was the most celebrated French restaurant in America. (Franey, however, would leave Le Pavillon to join the American army in 1942, turning down an offer to serve as General Douglas MacArthur's personal chef to become an active member of the military. He would not return to the kitchen at Le Pavillon until 1952.)

Another influential foreigner who helped popularize French food and wine in America during the 1940s and 1950s was Claudius Charles Philippe, or, as he was better known, "Philippe of the Waldorf." Born to French parents in England—his father had been chef at the Carlton Club on Pall Mall—Philippe spoke with a posh British accent even though his family came from a modest background in the Savoy. He had gone to Paris for hotel training before immigrating to New York in the early 1930s to join the staff of the newly opened Waldorf-Astoria Hotel on Park Avenue.

Philippe worked for more than a decade under the legendary chef Oscar ("of the Waldorf") Tschirky. When Tschirky retired, Philippe essentially took his place, becoming the Waldorf's vice president in charge of catering, its head of banquet department and kitchens, and also its director of sales. This enormous triple job meant that Philippe oversaw all food, beverages, service, flowers, music, and entertainment at the hotel. And since the Waldorf was then the undisputed social center of New York City (the massive new hotel featured six restaurants, eighteen public rooms, and a series of private dining rooms), Philippe was in a very strong position to promote French food and wine among the American upper classes who dined there—and, by extension, among those legions of regular folks who followed the American upper classes via newspapers, newsreels, and radio. His celebrated dinners and special events for the rich (including the extravagant "April in Paris" charity balls, held at the Waldorf from 1951 through 1959) would be organized for him mostly by Elsa Maxwell, the professional hostess, whom he had installed in a tiny apartment in the Waldorf in exchange for her brilliant services. With her assistance, Philippe redefined chic for a new generation of affluent Americans, and his emergence as the nation's leading event planner and catering manager could not have been more timely, for in the aftermath of the Great Depression many of the rich were shrinking their households, and were now entertaining instead in hotels and restaurants. Philippe's particular genius, meanwhile, lay in making the Waldorf seem indescribably glamorous through its connection to all things French. Throughout the late 1940s and 1950s he would bring in French film celebrities, recording artists, and fashion designers to make appearances and entertain at the Waldorf, often at parties and events based upon French historical, artistic, and cultural themes, such as "The Court of Versailles," "The Paris Opera," and "The Life of Rabelais."

Philippe's involvement in the shaping of upper-class American dining and drinking habits proved highly lucrative for him. He was already paid very well by the Waldorf, of course. But in addition, because the sales of his department accounted for two-thirds of the Waldorf-Astoria's yearly business and three-fourths of its profits,* and since a great deal of the business taking place there was subject to his direct approval, he could regularly demand monetary kickbacks and "gifts" from his vendors. His personal wine cellar at his Westchester estate, most of it given to him by these suppliers, contained more than five thousand bottles of best-quality French wines, including magnums of Château Mouton-Rothschild and Château Haut-Brion. But Philippe would have advocated strongly on behalf of these top French wines (and on behalf of French specialty foods and *grande cuisine* too) even if he hadn't been receiving these so-called gifts, as French food and wine were at that moment synonymous with *luxury* food and wine, and the Waldorf was the most luxurious hotel in America, and America, which had emerged from World War II as the wealthiest country in all the world, wanted only the finest.

In the coming decade, and with the help of a young wine merchant named Alexis Lichine, Philippe would find yet another way to make money: by taking a financial stake in the vineyards that produced the wines he promoted and sold through the Waldorf. Selling these wines

---

* His yearly budget for food purchases was $2.5 million; for beverages, $1 million; and for wines alone, $150,000. (In today's purchasing power, these amounts would be $22.8 million, $9.1 million, and $1.4 million, respectively.)

in the hotel also influenced their sales outside the hotel, for the simple reason that their presence at the Waldorf was a de facto confirmation of their quality. Since many of the top American wine wholesalers and dealers were regular (and favored) visitors to the Waldorf's restaurants, they kept an eye on the wines Philippe presented there, and subsequently purchased and promoted them strongly to their clients— for any wines chosen by Philippe for the Waldorf were clearly wines of unquestionable excellence.[5]

By the early 1950s, Philippe, who was by then only in his forties, had become both rich and powerful, and nowhere was his success more evident than at his country estate in Peekskill, New York, Watch Hill Farm. This grand property, where he entertained regularly, consisted not only of a manor house with a vast wine cellar but also of a greenhouse, an arboretum, and a series of formal gardens spread out over six terraces and ninety-two acres of land. The many grounds included a walled vegetable garden, an apple orchard, a grape arbor, and the estate's pièce de résistance, a formal parterre planted with twenty-five hundred boxwoods—something Philippe regally described to journalist Geoffrey Hellman of *The New Yorker* as "our Versailles project."[6]

Though he came from Savoyard peasant stock, Philippe could indeed be as grand and imperious as the Sun King. Restaurateur George Lang, who met him in the early 1950s, described him on first sight as "a hard-featured, middle-aged man with a prominent nose and alert eyes behind thick, horn-rimmed glasses," and recalled how, during their initial meeting, the narrow-shouldered Frenchman had conducted Lang's job interview while urinating in the presence of his two young female secretaries. Many others among his staff had similar memories of him as a coarse bully and petty tyrant, with an exceptional talent for controlling, intimidating, and manipulating—not just his staff, but also his clientele. Later in life, Craig Claiborne would describe him in *The New York Times* as "dominating, agile, arrogant and intense."[7] He was also an inveterate womanizer. After his first wife, Poppy Cannon, divorced him in 1949, he saw to it that his next, the French actress Mony Dalmès, spent most of her time hard at work in the Comédie-Française in Paris—thereby leaving him free to seduce any woman he liked in the *garçonnière* (or "bachelor pad") just above his office.

If Philippe was a key player in the movement to popularize French wines in America during the 1940s and 1950s, his success was based, in no small degree, on swagger: the world of luxury wine collecting is a masculine arena in which big sales are often accomplished through an adroit combination of flattery and intimidation, bullying and reassurance. From his position at the Waldorf, Philippe had the perfect platform from which to promote French wines to a nation that had up until that moment shown little interest in the stuff, preferring cocktails and hard liquor* as its intoxicants of choice, and hot coffee as its go-to mealtime beverage. More important, Philippe knew how to sell to rich Americans—and the more he sold to them, the more famous and important he became. "We sell more French wine than any other hotel in the world, including the hotels in France," Philippe informed *The New Yorker* in 1955. "Last year, we sold sixty-thousand bottles of French still wines and champagnes—mostly vintage and estate-bottled, which means the best. . . . [And] more and more Americans drink wine on account of me. They get introduced to it at the Waldorf, and then they buy it for their homes."[8] His commitment to French wines was such that, despite his busy schedule, he traveled to France yearly to select his wines in person, often doing so with his friend Alexis Lichine, who ultimately became Philippe's purchasing agent.

Philippe promoted French wines in other ways too: first through the cofounding of Les Amis d'Escoffier, the nation's foremost fraternity of dedicated gastronomes. Through regular dinner meetings at the Waldorf, this professional organization promoted French wines among its influential members, who in turn promoted them through their work. In 1950 he also founded the Lucullus Circle, a private eating club of unparalleled luxury that offered its handpicked members—a group limited to sixty rich men—a series of five wildly extravagant dinners per year, each one featuring a dazzling array of rare French wines and liquors which could subsequently be purchased for home consumption. Throughout the 1950s Philippe would also host various

---

* According to Jane and Michael Stern in *American Gourmet*, more than 60 percent of the wine consumed by Americans during the 1940s and 1950s was the sweet, dirt-cheap, alcoholically fortified "dessert wine" sold under names like Thunderbird and Night Train (p. 50).

French wine societies at the Waldorf, such as the American chapter of the Commanderie du Bontemps de Médoc. (The publisher Alfred A. Knopf, a 1956 inductee, complained bitterly to Alexis Lichine that the proceedings had been a "dreadful" waste of time.) And, as often as not, after corralling the New York metropolitan area's richest and most extravagant wine collectors into this luxury mealtime setting, Philippe also brought in its leading wine importers, advocates, wholesalers, and retailers to do their own selling—including Sam Aaron of Sherry Wines and Spirits, Robert Haas of M. Lehmann, Alexis Lichine, and Frank Schoonmaker. James Beard was often there too, because he held lucrative consultancies on both sides of the wine trade, particularly with the French Champagne and Cognac groups. When wholesalers, retailers, experts, and collectors all met and raised glasses together at New York's greatest hotel, the result was always good business—and no one profited more from that business than Claudius Charles Philippe.

⚜

The European refugees who raised American food awareness during the 1940s were not limited to cookbook authors, restaurateurs, and catering managers, however. One of the journalists who wrote best about European cuisine during the 1940s and 1950s was the New Yorker reporter Joseph Wechsberg, a Czech-born refugee who had been closely acquainted with the cuisines of Paris and Vienna in the years before the war. Like Dione Lucas and Henri Soulé, Wechsberg made a new start for himself in the United States—first in Hollywood, then, later, as a humorist, memoirist, author, and reporter. He wrote his first pieces for The New Yorker while serving as a sergeant in the U.S. Army. Gifted with a shrewd investigative mind, he also had a charming prose style that the magazine's editor, William Shawn, lovingly characterized as "light and faintly Continental." His earliest pieces included a number of slapstick reminiscences of his life as a young jazz musician in 1920s Paris; later, he wrote more deeply felt articles about the destruction of his homeland by the Nazis and the Communists. Wechsberg lost most of his relatives to the Nazi concentration camps and was horrified by the destruction of so much of Europe's cultural patrimony in the war's final years. Nonetheless, in September 1949, sensing that France was on the rebound, he traveled down from Paris to Vienne, a small town twenty-five miles south of Lyon, to write "The Finest Butter and Lots of Time," a fabulous two-part profile of France's then-greatest chef, Fernand Point of the restaurant La Pyramide.*

The article signaled the revival of French gastro-tourism, the uniquely French practice of combining automobile touring with restaurant-going. Starting at the turn of the century, and continuing intensively during the 1920s and 1930s, French food and travel writers had worked hard along with various trade groups and government agencies to classify, organize, define, rank, and rate the many fine restaurants, eating establishments, and hotel-restaurants along France's beautiful roadways as a way of facilitating this very special kind of travel experience. The same classification process was now being revived in the postwar years, for the French anticipated that as more and more American tourists began heading out of Paris by car, they would do so with a detailed gastronomic guidebook in hand.

Wechsberg knew all about gastro-tourism from his prewar years in Paris. He hadn't owned a car, but like most Frenchmen he had been a reader of *La France Gastronomique*, the twenty-eight-volume guide to restaurant dining across the country that emphasized the aesthetic integrity of provincial cuisine. (Each of its volumes was devoted to a specific geographical and cultural region.) The series had been created, written, and edited by Maurice Sailland ("Curnonsky") with the help of Marcel Rouff, author of the delightful 1924 novel *La Vie et la Passion de Dodin-Bouffant, Gourmand*. But while *La France Gastronomique* was popular, it was another guidebook, the *Guide Michelin*, that ultimately proved, in A. J. Liebling's words, "the tourist's *vade mecum*."† Founded in 1900 by André and Édouard Michelin to spur the sale of their tires, the guide was widely known and loved even before World War I. (During that war, Gertrude Stein and Alice

---

* Julia Child, James Beard, and Alice Toklas have left behind various accounts of their visits to La Pyramide. In *Charmed Circle*, James Mellow recounts how Toklas and Stein went there for a "memorable" dinner in 1937 featuring "*pâté, écrivisses* (crayfish), chicken with truffles, salad, a *bombe*, and *pétits fours*" (p. 518).

† A Latin expression for "handbook"; literally, it means "go with me."

Toklas had kept a copy of it in the glove box of the volunteer ambulance they drove, consulting it regularly for restaurant advice.) The French passion for gastro-tourism continued to expand during the economic ups and downs of the 1920s and 1930s. According to Toklas's friend the composer Virgil Thomson, the thirties in particular had been a great time for eating well all across France, with "local fare in the peasant pubs [and] *grande cuisine* in court-house towns at twenty-six francs a head—and by *grande cuisine* I mean *la grande cuisine Française*, not Swiss hotel-cooking. I mean *foie gras* and blue trout and Bresse chickens in yellow cream and *morille* mushrooms and crayfish and wild pheasant and venison with chestnut purée and ice cream of wild strawberries or of *pistache* custard and cakes made only of almond-flour and sweet butter and honey."[9] The writer Sybille Bedford would likewise point out that the development of French gastro-tourism during this time had been largely the result of France's own passion for it: French *gastronomades* could (and did) hold their restaurateurs to a very high standard. "They [the French] never stopped talking about it," Bedford wrote. "They doted on everything that went with it. The roads, the Renaults, the Peugeots, the Citroëns . . . the [*Guide*] *Michelin*, the posters ([for] apéritifs and gasolines), the maps, the road signs, the guidebooks. . . . The entire country played at it: what to eat, where to eat, what to drink with what to eat . . . what one ate last night, where to eat next Sunday, what one drank, what one paid, what was said."[10]

Now that the restaurants of the French countryside were once again opening up to postwar international tourism, Americans were curious about what awaited them, and *The New Yorker* had commissioned Wechsberg to tell them all about it. Wechsberg, however, approached the assignment in Vienne with some skepticism, for as a man of relatively simple tastes, he saw no reason "for patronizing fancy establishments when there is such an astonishing number of small restaurants all over [France] where one can get a delicious omelet, a succulent veal stew, a fine cheese, and a bottle of honest *vin du pays* for less than six hundred francs, or something under two dollars."[11] Nonetheless, he dutifully took the trip to La Pyramide (but going there by train, and booking a room for the night near the station). His subsequent profile of the amiable, six-foot-three, three-hundred-pound

Fernand Point, who greeted Wechsberg at midmorning over his daily bottle of Champagne, described a meal so brilliant (and so vast, and so breathtakingly affordable) that it must have prompted immediate phone calls to travel agents all across the postwar United States.

Advised by the genial chef on the morning of his visit that "a good meal must be as harmonious as a symphony and as well constructed as a good play," Wechsberg simply put himself into the hands of the master, who began the massive lunch with an "overture" of sensational hors d'oeuvres: a *pâté campagne en croûte*; a *foie gras naturel truffé* embedded in a ring of *crème de foie gras*; a hot sausage baked in a pastry shell served with a *sauce piquante*; a pâté of pheasant; a basket of crackling hot cheese croissants; and a plate of delicate little asparagus with *sauce hollandaise*—all accompanied by "a light, airy Montrachet." The reporter then dutifully tackled Point's *entrée*, a *truite au porte*— freshly caught trout poached in a court bouillon, then skinned, split in half, and filled with a ragout of truffles, mushrooms, and vegetables, which was then bathed in a sauce of butter, cream, and port wine. Next came the *plat*, a breast of guinea hen with morels, napped in an egg sauce. Chef Point had selected a rich, full-bodied Château Lafite-Rothschild '24* to accompany his guinea hen, and the bottle lasted Wechsberg through the cheese course, a perfectly ripened Pont l'Evêque. Dessert was a wild strawberry ice cream, made of *fraises des bois* picked just a few hours earlier, accompanied by a selection of *mignardises*, or dainty miniature desserts. After dispatching the last of them, Wechsberg concluded his meal with demitasse and a Grande Fine Champagne '04 Cognac.† And all of this had cost him, he wrote, "No more than the price of a good meal in a good restaurant in New York."

⚜

Wechsberg's *New Yorker* article (and similar accounts of postwar French fine dining in *Gourmet* and other magazines) spurred American

---

* A *premier cru* Bordeaux from Pauillac in the Médoc. A bottle of this wine, of similar age, would retail today for approximately $500.
† *"Grande Fine Champagne"* is an appellation within the Cognac region, with the word *champagne* denoting its limestone soil. (This finest of the Cognac *crus* has nothing to do with the French sparkling wine known as Champagne.)

excitement about travel abroad. And each of these accounts made clear that the French were very eager to welcome them, since despite the destruction of so much of their country by the war, they desperately needed to revive their tourist economy. They also wanted to renew their overseas trade in luxury foods, wines, and spirits—wines in particular, for France was a nation of artisan winemakers accustomed to selling their costly wares throughout Europe. But with nearly all European economies in ruin, French winemakers now needed to court the United States as a potential client for their fine products. Unfortunately for these winemakers, the majority of Americans knew very little about wine and few cared to drink it with their meals.

The French found a champion for their wines in yet another European-American, a man who, like Wechsberg, had served in the American armed forces during the war: Alexis Lichine, a Moscow-born, Paris-raised, New York–based wine salesman. His first book, *The Wines of France*, was published when he was thirty-seven. Knowing his market, Lichine wisely addressed this book to the beginner and neophyte—that is, any American interested in learning something about wine. Yet even as it served as a kindly, unassuming introduction to French wines and French wine-regions, this modest volume also instructed Americans on how to organize and stock a home wine cellar. It did so because Lichine aimed to use the book as a selling tool for his wine business, and he intended that each person who bought his book would create such a cellar, and stock it with wines bought through his firm.

Every bit as enterprising as Philippe of the Waldorf, Lichine had initially drafted his book in collaboration with another accomplished writer on wine, William E. Massee. As Lichine would later recall, "Around 1950, I conceived the idea of a book to explain estate-bottled Burgundies, which had become a specialty of mine." In this project, he was inspired by "the late André Simon, one of wine's finest writers, who contributed greatly to the reputation of wine as the highest expression of nature. . . . [But] the scope of my book quickly grew to include the wines of Bordeaux, and from there it was only a short jump to *The Wines of France*, whose publication brought me over a quarter-century of friendship with publisher and wine buff Alfred A. Knopf."[12] In order to maximize the book's effect on his business and reputation, however, Lichine decided well into his collaboration with Massee that he wanted to be credited as sole author. To do that, he had needed to renegotiate his agreement with Massee, who eventually (but only reluctantly and with a good deal of suspicion) agreed to take a higher royalty in exchange for demotion from coauthor to collaborator. Once the agreement had been reached, however, Lichine was free to publish the book under his own name with Knopf—then, as now, a highly prestigious literary publisher.

Alfred Knopf reviewed a first portion of the manuscript and liked what he saw. Both he and his wife, Blanche, had a long-standing interest in books on gastronomic subjects (and so too did their son, Alfred Jr., or "Pat," who was then working in the Knopf sales department and would in time publish well on the subject with his own publishing house, Atheneum). Wine particularly fascinated Alfred Knopf, so he decided to take a chance on Lichine and his book. Although Knopf offered only a small sum for it, Lichine had no problem with the size of the advance, since the prestige of being at Knopf meant a great deal more to him than the money involved. During the late 1930s, Lichine had worked for America's leading wine merchant turned author, Frank Schoonmaker, and Lichine had learned firsthand from Schoonmaker how important a good book from a top publisher could be to a dealer's reputation and business. Moreover, Lichine was in no way dependent on the advance money, since he made a very good living selling wine. In addition, he was already well established as a wine lecturer throughout the United States, and he knew that by selling this prestigious new book along with his wines he would be giving his audiences reason to respect his expertise, even as they became steady purchasers of his products.

Shortly after he came to an agreement with Knopf about the book's publication, Lichine shrewdly invited Knopf to come along on his spring 1950 wine-buying trip. He was determined to make Knopf his good friend. The publisher, though sorely tempted, seems to have considered this invitation for a trip to Burgundy with some reluctance, since he knew from experience that no editor can take favors from an aspiring author without implicit expectation of payback. Furthermore, there were still some issues that needed to be resolved before Lichine's book could go to press. Lichine was not the most reliable of authors, and Knopf had recently sent back the manuscript, noting with irritation, "it abounds in mis-spellings, mis-typings, and . . . repetitions."[13]

Lichine was also a difficult author to keep up with because in the past year he had been changing his address constantly and on very short notice—moving from one Manhattan address to another, then to the Caribbean, and now, most recently, to an office on the Champs-Élysées. He was also recently divorced—his ex-wife was a countess he had met on the wartime Riviera—and frequently seen out with party girls at nightclubs and restaurants. If Lichine was spending so much time traveling, restaurant-going, nightclubbing, and womanizing, Knopf wondered, when was he writing? Then again, Knopf knew from his conversations with Lichine that only by pairing good wine with good food (and preferably doing so in an atmosphere of luxury, in the seductive company of desirable women) could Lichine impress his would-be wine buyers into purchasing his rare and extravagant products.

To his credit, Lichine clearly had a very strong work ethic. He was also affable, articulate, well informed, and tremendously ambitious. Most important of all, he was eager to share his knowledge and enthusiasm. And his ability to market and sell his own book made him every publisher's dream—if only he would sit down long enough to prepare his manuscript properly for publication.

⚜

Lichine's buying trip in Burgundy with Knopf was organized and made possible by Philippe of the Waldorf: in fact, it was basically the same yearly trip Philippe and Lichine had been making since the war's end to stock the cellars of the Waldorf-Astoria. Philippe's position as a major American purchaser of highest-end French wines gave him (and any guest he brought along with him) guaranteed access to all the finest vineyards, cellars, and restaurants in France—a great eye-opening privilege and pleasure for those guests, even as it remained grueling, tightly scheduled work for Philippe and Lichine.

Lichine had first met Philippe in the 1930s, when Philippe was working under Oscar Tschirky and Lichine was working for Schoonmaker. Sharing a multicultural European background as well as vast entrepreneurial ambitions, the two quickly became friends, and later co-investors in various business projects, including French vineyards and Carribean real estate. But they had separated during the war years: shortly after its declaration, Philippe married and had a child with the journalist Poppy Cannon, a situation that spared him from the draft. Lichine, who at that point was unmarried, wisely avoided induction by speaking with some War Department contacts who just happened to be "fellow wine fanciers [he'd] sipped with at El Morocco."[14] Through them he obtained a commission as a first lieutenant, and after purchasing several smart new uniforms for himself at Saks Fifth Avenue, he shipped out for North Africa, where he immediately began his new job: sourcing fine food, fine wines, and talented cooking staff for top-level U.S. Army officers. He was so good at it that by the time the Allies invaded the South of France in August 1944, he had been made an aide to no less than the Supreme Allied Commander, General Dwight Eisenhower. The posting proved an exceptionally luxurious one, for Lichine was billeted at Eisenhower's weekend villa at Cap d'Antibes. There Lichine quickly came into close contact with some of the most powerful men in the world—including Winston Churchill, who though something of an expert on wines, quickly saw the wisdom in deferring to Lichine's expertise.[15] In fact, as the officer who arranged for all meals, wines, liquor, and entertainment, Lichine was welcome among all the top brass, who greatly appreciated his efforts on behalf of their stomachs. Tall, dark, and urbane, fluent in three languages, Lichine moved with assurance among these men of rank, power, and fortune, some of whom became his good friends.

When the war ended, Lichine returned to the wine business. Although he had a rapidly expanding clientele of upper-level wine buyers (many of whom were deeply impressed by his close working relationship with Eisenhower), Lichine now wanted to position himself before a broader group of American wine buyers and wine-store proprietors, and he knew that the best way to do so was to establish himself as a popular published author on French wines.

As an up-and-coming author, Lichine had now done something typically brilliant: he had arranged to give his distinguished publisher,

Alfred Knopf, an in-depth tour of France's best-loved wine region, Burgundy, and personal introductions to some of its most distinguished winemakers. (As Lichine knew, such "favors" were a great way of building a business relationship.) At the same time, he had provided Philippe with the distinguished company of Alfred Knopf. Ultimately, though, it was Lichine who would profit most from these introductions, for along with Philippe's gratitude and Knopf's gratitude, he would also have the gratitude of the many Burgundian winemakers the group now visited in their vineyards and cellars, who were intent on establishing their luxury products with merchants and restaurants in the United States and who were hoping for the help of influential Americans like Alfred Knopf, as well as buyers like Philippe and Lichine.

❖

The trip, which began in Paris, consisted of a busy schedule of cellar tastings and vineyard visits, punctuated by sumptuous lunches and dinners at the region's leading restaurants, including Alexandre Dumaine's Hôtel de la Côte-d'Or in Saulieu, which was quickly becoming second only to Fernand Point's La Pyramide as the finest restaurant in France. The first stop, however, was the austere little town of Chablis, high in the hills of northwestern Burgundy. Renowned for its flinty white wines, Chablis had been extensively damaged by a German bombing raid in June 1940; more recently, the vineyards had suffered from a series of extremely damaging winter freezes. But its cellars still held many treasures.

During the drive, Lichine made a fine and easygoing guide for Knopf and two other American couples who had joined the trip at the last minute, for he knew a vast amount about Burgundy, Burgundian wines, and Burgundian winemakers. Moreover, he loved to tell the story of French wine. As a teenage Russian émigré in Paris, Lichine had started his career as a public speaker by giving narrated bus tours of "Versailles by Day/Paris by Night" for the little sightseeing business his father had owned. And he began learning about French wine early in life, first by drinking it with his contemporaries and later by selling advertising space to French wine dealers for *The New York Herald*. During the late 1930s, after dropping out of Penn and working for a while in

New York, he had traveled to France again, this time to negotiate wine sales for Frank Schoonmaker. And since the end of the war, he had become even more well-connected among French wine-makers and *négociants** by forming Domaine Lichine Mugnier, a Burgundy-based bottling partnership whose list of wines included some of the region's most famous appellations and vineyards, includ-ing Musigny, Bonnes Mares, Clos de Vougeot, Chambolle-Musigny Les Amoreuses, and Nuits-St.-Georges Clos de la Maréchale. The venture was being backed by an American turned French citizen named Sey-mour Weller, who also managed Château Haut-Brion in Bordeaux for his astronomically wealthy uncle, the Wall Street financier Clarence Dillon.

The small group was traveling in two cars. Along with Knopf, Lichine, and Philippe, the later additions to the group included Stan-ley Marcus, the chief executive of the Neiman-Marcus department store in Dallas, traveling with his wife; and the American humorist J. P. McEvoy, also with his wife. Describing their adventure in his newspaper column, McEvoy played the situation for laughs. "We've just staggered off the *Île de France*," the piece began, "—now Philippe of the Waldorf wants to drag us off on an exhaustive tour of feasting and wine tasting. If my editors only realized the hardships that go with the business of writing!"

> Our first stop was Chablis . . . [where] lunch was waiting for us.
>
> We started with *pâté maison* and then a filet of sole cooked in Chablis wine. This was followed by baked ham. My notes say, "*jambon à la mode*—as tender as a baby angel." After this came a soufflé so light it took strong hands to keep it from floating out of the window.
>
> The hotel wine wasn't fancy enough for Philippe . . . so he went down the street and reappeared in a few minutes with [several more] precious bottles . . . After lunch (and three wines), which Knopf described as "sliding down a rainbow," we

---

* A wine merchant who assembles the produce of smaller growers and winemakers and then sells the resulting wines under his own name.

went into the *caves* all over town and tasted the wines. We were handed little silver wine tasters like ash trays and told what to do.

"First you look at the color," said Philippe. The cellar was dark but I did my best. "Now you take a little in the front of your mouth, swish it around, draw in some air with a kind of a slurp . . . then you spit it out."

I was outraged. "You mean after I've come 3,000 miles for this, I can't even drink it?" "Certainly not," said Philippe. "Before you finish, you'll have tasted 30 to 40 wines a day. If you swallowed this stuff, you'd go home on your elbows—as the French say."

. . . Philippe and Knopf and Lichine spit everything out. Stanley Marcus tried, but after all you can't shake off your merchandising instincts overnight. How are you going to know what you have seen if you don't take home a swatch?

As for me, how could I outrage a long line of Scotch ancestors by spitting all that good wine out on the cellar floor? I kept careful notes. . . . [Unfortunately] the next morning I couldn't read them.[16]

Press photographs show various members of the group examining glasses of wine (and perhaps trying to appear sober) while Lichine keeps a watchful eye. Knopf's notes about the trip—the first of Knopf's many Lichine-advised wine trips—include a photograph, taken in Beaune, in which Knopf watches Lichine pour out glasses for himself and a group of Frenchmen. It reads, "Luncheon hosted by Lichine and me for the Burgundy growers whose cellars we had sampled. Each guest brought a bottle for the lunch."

Knopf was sufficiently impressed with Lichine's demonstrated expertise about French winemaking that he included Lichine among his "New Authors" publicity mailing of the summer of 1950. After scheduling Lichine's book for publication in early 1951, he began to put out the good word, and that November, top American food reporter Clementine Paddleford profiled Lichine in *The New York Herald Tribune* as an up-and-coming Knopf author. She was so impressed by the fast-talking, smoky-eyed, well-tailored young man that she barely noticed that the many bottles of wine Lichine was recommending were ones that he alone was bottling and selling. In an article entitled "Estate-Bottled Burgundies Now Available Here," she simply gave his firm the best possible push:

> Alexis Lichine, a young American enjoying a reputation in Burgundy, France, as one of the greatest wine experts in the world, has started a firm in Paris specializing in estate bottled burgundies. . . . Lichine calls New York City his home, but he spends one-half of each year attending business in France. Even while [in New York] he keeps daily touch with one or another of the seventy-five Burgundy growers who supply cable reports on the crop situation. . . . Lichine's [forthcoming] book will take the reader right into the vineyards for a first-hand meeting with the man behind the bottle.[17]

But Alfred Knopf subsequently did Paddleford one better: he gave Lichine his unqualified endorsement and placed that endorsement squarely on the front cover of Lichine's *Wines of France*. There, just below Lichine's name, Knopf declared,

> This is not only the most comprehensive, but far and away the best book on its subject that has ever been written in any language. I know of no one whose over-all knowledge of French wines compares with that of Mr. Lichine, who is an expert among experts. His text is as entertaining as it is comprehensive, and his book as pleasant to read as it is useful to consult.—Alfred A. Knopf, Publisher[18]

With those three extraordinary sentences of affirmation on the cover of his new book, Lichine began his rise.

THREE

Alice Toklas Starts Over

With Gertrude Stein's unexpected death on July 27, 1946, Alice Toklas's life came apart. In losing her partner of nearly forty years, she also came very close to losing all they had shared materially: their art collection, their savings, their Paris home. The two American women had lived intimately together starting in 1907, eventually becoming so closely attuned to each other's thoughts, moods, and feelings that they routinely told the same stories, used identical figures of speech, and even finished each other's sentences. Their finances were similarly linked; for the past two decades, with Stein's money (both inherited and earned) the couple's main income. Now, with Stein gone, and with Toklas having absolutely no legal rights as a surviving spouse or domestic partner, she was short on funds, uncertain about her future, and nearly paralyzed with grief. Only with great effort had she been able to respond to the many letters and telegrams of condolence that had flooded her mailbox at 5, rue Christine, their address since 1938. "You realize surely that Gertrude's memory is all my life—just as she herself was," she confided to their good friend the Yale librarian Donald Gallup.[1] To another dear friend she wrote, "I wish to God we had gone [to our deaths] together as I always fatuously thought we would—a bomb—a shipwreck—just anything but this."[2]

The war and its aftermath had brought other losses. A number
of friends, including the poet Max Jacob, had perished. The French
university professor Bernard Faÿ, a friend who had protected Stein and
Toklas from Nazi internment and possible extermination, was given
life in prison for collaboration. And so much that Toklas had simply
taken for granted in prewar years had changed for the worse: domestic
help was hardly available, food was limited, and fuel almost impossible to obtain. Worst of all, the beautiful château Stein and Toklas had
called home every spring, summer, and fall for the thirteen years before the war—a fine rented mansion on the leafy outskirts of Belley,
fifty miles southwest of Geneva—was gone now too, and along with it
the two heavily worked vegetable gardens that Toklas had tended so
obsessively since spring of 1929. "Summers [at the château] in Bilignin
were always very busy, enjoyable, and productive," she later recalled.
"Vegetables had become a passion, flowers always had been."[3]

The vegetable garden had been particularly crucial to them during
the war years, when they had relied on its substantial produce as a main
source of sustenance. To increase production, they had expanded their
vegetable empire, turning the twenty-eight box-rimmed flower beds on
the château's glorious parterre into an elegant victory garden.[4] In summer they canned beans and tomatoes and put up soft fruits; in the fall,
they brought in winter squash, cabbages, and root vegetables for cellar-
ing. Their mania for preserving extended even to meats: at the outset of
the war, Toklas daringly purchased two enormous uncooked hams and
then pickled them, like medical specimens, in a barrel of *marc*, an eau-
de-vie similar to grappa. "It seemed madly extravagant," she later recalled, "but we lived on those two hams during the long lean winter
that followed and well into the following spring, and the *eau-de-vie de
marc* in which they were cooked, carefully bottled, and corked, toned up
winter vegetables. We threw nothing, but absolutely nothing, away."[5]

Stein and Toklas depended on foraging during those years as
well, taking crayfish from the local streams* and mushrooms from

---

* During the war, their local butcher had caught them, delivering the live crayfish to the château
in a crate. But Samuel Steward, a Chicago university professor, also recalled hunting for crayfish
with Stein (using an old umbrella to catch them) during his prewar visits in 1937 and 1939.

the forest—activities they had enjoyed, albeit far more casually, in the years before the war. (Stein "had a good nose for mushrooms [and] found quantities of them,"[6] Toklas later remembered.) When meat was no longer available, the two women relied upon fish from the nearby Rhône and the Lac de Bourget as a protein source—and the fishy odors that subsequently lingered in their kitchen created an air of "perpetual Lent" that haunted the premises throughout the Occupation. Even so, as Stein later told the reporter Eric Sevareid, those five difficult years were "the happiest years of her life" chiefly because the many hardships she experienced alongside her neighbors had brought her closer to them, and made her more aware of what was truly important.[7] Toklas heartily agreed, even going so far as to write friends shortly before her death that "though Hitler and the presence of the [Nazi] occupants was a menacing nightmare, I was happier then than today."[8]

After being evicted from their beloved château in 1942, the couple spent 1943 and 1944 bivouacked in a large, cold, gloomy house on a piney hillside just outside the nearby town of Culoz. There Toklas toiled daily in the kitchen, since the cook who came with the house was too profoundly depressed by the food-rationing situation to rise to the challenge of making meals from so little. Stein and Toklas had no vegetable garden to sustain them in Culoz either—only a couple of goats, kept for milk. The last of a ten-pound box of tea that they had been dipping into since 1939 saw them through to the liberation of 1944. So too did a jar of candied fruits that Toklas had set aside in 1939 for her "Liberation Fruitcake"—a cake she duly baked and sent to General Alexander Patch, commander of the Seventh Army, with a note of gratitude and thanks for their rescue.[9]

After peace was declared, the two women left for Paris as soon as they could. Chilly Culoz held few happy memories for them, and they were anxious to secure Stein's art collection, which had been locked up in the Paris flat since 1939. They returned to find the collection intact, and celebrated that miracle with Picasso, who dropped by within hours of their arrival to see what had become of it and of them. ("He and Gertrude embraced, and all of us rejoiced that the treasures of her youth, the pictures, the drawings, were safe," Toklas recalled.) Food being in short supply, they celebrated with a small pot of black coffee. The Germans had apparently tied up some of the pictures to take away, but those parcels had not been removed, and in the end all that were missing were a pair of Louis XV candlesticks, a footstool worked in petit point by Toklas after a design by Picasso, and a cast-iron cornstick mold given to Toklas in 1934 by Ela Hocka-day, the headmistress of the prestigious Dallas girls' school. ("What did the Germans, when they took it in 1944, expect to do with it?" Toklas would later write of the cornstick mold, "and what are they doing with it now?")[10]

The two women were glad to be back among their artworks and other possessions, but as summer began they missed their country life. The city was hot and muggy, and by now gardening (the yearly mir-acle of rebirth and renewal; the pleasure of helping things grow; the all-season harvest and ensuing delights at table) had become a joy central to daily existence. When in July 1946 Bernard Faÿ offered them the use of his country home in the Loire, they were only too happy to accept the invitation. Their journalist friend Joe Barry of-fered them a lift down in his car—but on the way down Stein took ill, and a few days later she checked into the American Hospital in Neuilly, where an exploratory surgery revealed an inoperable cancer. A few days later she died, and Toklas was alone. The devotion Toklas had brought for years to her gardening, housekeeping, and secretarial work for Stein would now be focused, instead, upon safeguarding Stein's literary legacy and maintaining Stein's art collection *in situ*. But doing so would be difficult: there were a number of complicated legal and financial issues involved, and the administrator of the Stein estate, a Baltimore lawyer, was not inclined to do much on Toklas's behalf. From his perspective, of course, Toklas was not much more than a live-in companion—not much more, in other words, than cheaply hired help.

❖

Most people who met Toklas, who was sixty-nine at the time of Stein's death, assumed she was financially comfortable because she presided over an extraordinary collection of paintings and a richly furnished apartment. Earlier in life, she had been: she had grown up in a good home in San Francisco, and her maternal grandfather, a gold miner turned rancher, had left her a quarter of his estate as an inheritance. In her teens and early twenties, she trained and performed as a classical pianist, and though not a good-looking woman—she was short and dark, with a large aquiline nose and the traces of a mustache— she had a jolie laide's taste for mildly outrageous hats and well-made clothes. She does not seem to have been overly concerned with her looks, as she had other sterling qualities, and moreover she was not focused on marriage. Shortly after she moved to Paris in 1907, at the age of thirty, she met Gertrude Stein, a plain, short, heavyset woman with a large mass of chestnut hair piled atop her head.

Toklas's first impression of Stein, whom she met at the atelier Stein shared with her brother Leo on the rue de Fleurus, had been primarily of her conversational genius. But that impression of genius had been magnified by the many fine and impressive objects among which Stein lived—not only paintings by Picasso and Matisse, but grand furniture and decorative objects, including an octagonal Tuscan table with three heavy clawed legs, a double-decked Henry IV buffet with three carved eagles on the top, and a small collection of rare antique silver. The paintings, furniture, and objets d'art at the rue de Fleurus had, in a sense, helped establish Stein's credentials in Paris as a woman of taste and brilliance many years before her writings found their way into print, and certainly before any of those writings were recognized as significant. And these beautiful things had attracted Toklas to Stein as well, for Toklas perceived Stein and her possessions as one. Stein would later recall (in Toklas's voice, in *The Autobiography of Alice B. Toklas*) that these two American women had ended their first afternoon together in the late summer of 1907, after a stroll through the Luxembourg Gardens, with a dish of praline ice, "just like [the ices in] San Francisco."[11] Beautiful home furnishings, beautiful homey foods, and beautiful places to call home would always be central to Stein and Toklas's shared life, and would attract others to them just as surely as Stein's extraordinary personality and avant-garde writings. Toklas's domestic activities were in that way a significant aspect of the Gertrude Stein salon, if not of Stein's own genius. Giving, feeding, sharing, nurturing—as well as the endless amounts of typing, filing, and other sorts of secretarial work that came with assisting a self-proclaimed genius—were just a few of the ways in which Toklas actively participated in Stein's long, slow rise to acclaim.

The two lived relatively quietly until the 1933 publication of Stein's *The Autobiography of Alice B. Toklas.* That delightful, gossipy account of Toklas's (and Stein's) life among the geniuses and near geniuses of modernism—including Picasso, Braque, Matisse, Apollinaire, Marie Laurencin, and Hemingway—had launched Stein as a popular writer and cultural icon, and in doing so made Toklas a minor celebrity in spite of herself. The two were immediately understood by the American reading public as inseparable, for the book was written by Stein in Toklas's voice and described their shared life, home, and friends in a way that established the two were one. As the painter Maurice Grosser, Stein and Toklas's friend and neighbor, later observed, "Gertrude's *Autobiography of Alice B. Toklas* is made up word for word of the stories I have heard Alice tell. In fact, the autobiography presents an exact rendition of Alice's conversation, of the rhythm of her speech and of the prose style of her acknowledged works. It is such a brilliant and accurate pastiche that I am unable to believe that Gertrude with all her genius could have composed it and I remain convinced that the book is entirely Alice's work, and published under Gertrude's name only because hers was the more famous."[12]

Coming to America together on a speaking tour in 1933 to 1934, the two women crisscrossed the country on a combination publicity campaign and sightseeing tour, enjoying the adventure even as Stein established herself as an American literary celebrity. But they were not tempted to remain—France was now their home. Likewise six years later, when World War II began, they simply relocated from Paris to their rented country home near the Swiss border, intent on remaining in France for the duration, just as they had during World War I.

When the region was liberated in 1944, CBS radio correspondent Eric Sevareid, who had met Stein in Paris in 1938, thought that a "rediscovery" of her in the little town of Culoz might make good copy. He brought along a Time-Life photographer and three other reporters on his mission, and as a result, Stein's "liberation" was widely covered not only by CBS radio, but also by *The Baltimore Sun*, the *Washington Evening Star, Collier's* magazine, *The New York Herald Tribune, The New York Times*, and, most memorably, *Life*.[13]

Stein concluded her "liberation" interview with Sevareid by presenting him with the typescript of *Wars I Have Seen*, a book she had written while holed up in Culoz. Sevareid delivered the manuscript to Random House editor in chief Bennett Cerf just a few weeks later, and Cerf rushed it into print. The timing was perfect; the book ultimately proved the greatest commercial success of Stein's lifetime. America had gone wild for the magazine and newspaper stories about these two dotty American literary ladies, elderly but resolute, who had been so miraculously liberated from the Nazis. And readers likewise snapped up Stein's book about toughing it out in France through the two world wars.

Throughout 1945 and 1946, Stein continued to put herself before the American public by lecturing at American army bases in Europe, and also by appearing whenever possible in magazines: the August 6, 1945, issue of *Life* showed a particularly memorable series of photos of Stein and Toklas visiting the ruined terrace of Hitler's Berghof at Berchtesgaden, with Stein's oddly whimsical essay "Off We All Went to See Germany" as an accompaniment. With this return to celebrity, Toklas later wrote, "our home again became a salon," with distinguished visitors from the worlds of art, politics, and culture all finding their way to the rue Christine. There were also "constant visits from American GIs,"[14] few of whom were ever turned away. Even Ernest Hemingway, who had been so enraged about Stein's treatment of him in *The Autobiography of Alice B. Toklas*, now patched things up with her, bawdily joking to a mutual friend that he had "always had an urge to fuck her."[15]

⚜

Then Stein died. After the shock of it, and the burial at Père Lachaise, and the hundreds of letters and telegrams, Toklas slowly began the process of settling the estate. And at first she felt relatively secure of her financial position because, by the terms of Stein's will, the extraordinary collection of paintings, drawings, and other artworks would remain with her for the duration of her lifetime, and she was also to receive an allowance out of Stein's capital* to continue her life at the Paris apartment. The will also stipulated that, should Toklas find herself in additional financial need, the estate might sell off works from the art collection to help pay for her "proper maintenance and support."[16] But then things became more complicated, since the art collection was ultimately to be inherited by Stein's nephew Allan—a sickly, debt-ridden businessman who lived in the Parisian suburb of Garches with his second wife. And though the will had two trustees—Allan Stein and Alice Toklas—it was probated in Baltimore, where a court-appointed administrator was to oversee all issues relating to the estate. When Toklas requested additional money to settle some debts after Stein's death, the administrator sold no artworks on her behalf, and sent her no additional money.

As a result, Toklas now found herself in some of the most difficult financial circumstances of her life.[†] Her most immediate challenge was in paying for heat, as the apartment on rue Christine, with its eighteen-foot-high-ceilings and single-glazed French doors, had never been adequately heated, not even when coal was plentiful. Now, with coal both scarce and expensive (most of the railway lines that transported it to Paris had been destroyed), Toklas had no choice but to close down most of the apartment and use a portable kerosene heater to warm one corner of the one room where she sat daily to work. But the kerosene was expensive too, and it gave off sickening fumes. "We're all possessed of more taste than shekels," Toklas observed in a letter to her dear old friend Louise Taylor in war-ravaged England; and nowhere was that statement more deeply felt than in Toklas's

---

* Linda Simon, in *The Biography of Alice B. Toklas*, states that the amount of the stipend was $400, but does not give anything more specific, nor does she give the source for this information.

† These circumstances are best understood by looking at Stein and Toklas's possessions, for they had few concrete assets apart from the art collection. They had always lived in rented apartments in Paris, and the château at Bilignin had been rented to them furnished. During World War II, cut off from American remittances, they had lived on borrowed money until Stein was able to drive over to Switzerland to sell a Cézanne. Stein had never even insured her art collection during her lifetime—and while Toklas was compelled to do so for legal reasons after Stein's death, she did so at well below the collection's actual value, because it was all she could afford to pay.

own Paris sitting room—chockablock with modernist masterpieces, yet threadbare, and as cold as an icebox.

Of course Toklas was not alone in her misery. Paris had not been bombed during the war, but Parisians suffered tremendously from hunger and cold during their four years under the Occupation. The Germans had done their best to seize and export the majority of the nation's food supplies (by some estimation, 60 percent of it) and the ration cards they had grudgingly doled out to Parisians had allowed only between 1,067 and 1,325 calories of food per day, even though an adult not engaged in heavy labor required a minimum of 2,400 calories daily.* As a result, most Frenchmen had not had enough to eat in more than four years and lived in perpetual cold from September through May. Food rationing would remain in place through 1948, with black-market foods remaining prohibitively expensive during that time. Yet Toklas, like so many other Parisians, had no choice but to pay these outrageous black-market prices or else go hungry.

Restaurants, too, remained pretty much out of reach for Toklas. Even a modest bistro meal (without anything to drink) now cost about 120 francs, or $1. Before the war, the equivalent meal would have cost a tenth that price, and would have included a generous amount of wine. A restaurant meal with a half bottle of wine now cost between 350 and 700 francs ($2.80 to $5.60), but it was still served without butter or other dairy products, which were only available on the black market. There was no getting around such prices either: all basic foods now cost at least ten times what they had in the prewar years.[17]

These shortages and hardships were just one aspect of France's devastation. France had experienced more than 600,000 French mortalities (both military and civilian) during the war, and out of France's total population of approximately 40 million, more than 1 million had been either killed, wounded, or disabled. (And these losses came on top of France's combined military and civilian casualties from

---

*Today USDA guidelines call for about 3,000 calories daily for active adult men, and 2,000 for women. During the Occupation, however, the lack of heating and increased physical labor would have made Parisians' needs higher. Moreover, many Parisians, who out of commitment to the Resistance had not registered with the Germans, did not have ration cards.

World War I, which were upward of 1.7 million.) At the end of the Second World War, 1.8 million French buildings had been destroyed; 5,000 bridges had been blown up; and 60 percent of the country's railroad stock had been ruined; meanwhile half the livestock had been killed or stolen, and three-quarters of all its agricultural equipment had been lost. The total loss to France was estimated to be half its national wealth, or the total earnings of all Frenchmen for two years; and the estimated cost of the war for France was ultimately calculated at $98 billion (in 1945 dollars; roughly $1.25 trillion today). France's economic recovery, meanwhile, was now hindered by shortages of coal, gasoline, electricity, transportation, and manpower.

Added to these very specific miseries were postwar revelations about genocide, about the massive destruction of France's cultural patrimony, about collaborationist treachery, and about the new threat of atomic annihilation—all of which contributed to the general and ongoing sense of despair. As one of Toklas's favorite younger writers, Sybille Bedford, later noted, the French in particular seemed to live with "a national sense of irreversible bereavement" because they had seen two world wars on their soil, and in each they had suffered devastating losses of family, friends, and property as well as a profound national humiliation. "If they managed to keep a glow on life," Bedford wrote, "it was because of their sensuous vitality, their readiness to enjoy what life had to offer, or what they made it offer; their cultivated and articulate capacity for taking life physically: their passion for food, their due regard for bed."[18] Toklas, taking courage and inspiration from the Frenchmen and -women around her, did her best to stay strong as well. "I have my meals on a tray in the salon to avoid the expense of heating two rooms," the seventy-four-year-old bohemian wrote five years after she had lost Gertrude Stein. "The winter queues are beyond my endurance and winter marketing is difficult and costly—to walk to the central markets and return with my baskets is out of the question. . . . [One] keep[s] one's strength for where it is most needed." Her aged feet, misshapen by arthritic swellings, could no longer fit into proper shoes, and her sandals (custom-made for her by Isadora Duncan's brother, Raymond) did little to protect them from the cold. But Toklas had always been a woman of spirit, and in the same letter (to Isabel Wilder, Thornton Wilder's sister), she noted that she had just received three old friends that afternoon who were by now equally habituated to postwar Parisian hardships: the writer Natalie Barney, the painter Romaine Brooks, and Élisabeth de Gramont, Duchess of Clermont-Tonnère—all of whom had required nothing more than a pot of tea and some cigarettes to think their chilly afternoon with her a roaring success.

⚜

Toklas had daydreamed constantly of food during the war and its immediate aftermath. She was a lifelong reader of cookbooks and a woman of hearty appetites, and she had sought out the best of French cuisine since her arrival in Paris in 1907. During her years with Stein, she also became a good (if sporadic and idiosyncratic) amateur cook. Even so, she began to think seriously of writing a cookbook only in 1947, after sending off the last of Stein's manuscripts, papers, and collected correspondence to the Beinecke Library at Yale University. The new cookbook project seems to have filled the emptiness created by the departure of the papers, over which she had labored for so many years as typist, proofreader, and archivist. But she had a more practical motive in picking up her pen, as well: she wanted access to the good, cheap, plentiful foods (and Pall Mall cigarettes) that were just then available only to qualified Americans through the embassy and military. "It came to me if I could get recipes printed in some [American] magazine I'd be as eligible [to shop at the American Embassy Commissary] as [novelist] Richard Wright," she wrote a friend, "so why not gather my recipes—make the cook book and get a job."[19]

The project was slow to evolve. Her first idea had been to write an anthology of eighteenth- and nineteenth-century French recipes—she had been collecting (and cooking) such recipes ever since arriving in France, and she hoped that by translating them into American measurements and writing intriguing headnotes, she might be able to tempt American readers into similar adventures of culinary time travel and cross-cultural exchange. But the poet and political activist Sherry Mangan warned her off the idea, saying it was far too complicated for simpleminded American readers, and adding that furthermore,

"Americans *never* read foreign recipes." Realizing that she needed more information on the American way of doing things, Toklas asked her American friend W. G. Rogers to "please send me a copy of a magazine called the *Gourmet.*"

But then, for a while, the cookbook idea was back-burnered, for the worst of her food difficulties were unexpectedly resolved by Virginia Knapik, a friend who worked at the American Embassy. Knapik simply lied on Toklas's behalf, declaring that Toklas was her aunt—thereby securing Toklas the embassy's "cellar privileges" to its good and inexpensive foods, cigarettes, and liquor. Just in time too, because Toklas's relationship with Allan Stein suddenly deteriorated, and her stipend once again seemed endangered. "He's a horror—we don't meet any more frequently than necessary—and then I don't listen to him," she wrote a friend.[20] She was at that point attempting to get Stein's many unpublished literary manuscripts into print, and from long experience she knew that doing so would probably require a financial subsidy from the Stein estate—something that, like her stipend, was contingent upon the decisions of the Baltimore executor and the assent of Allan Stein.

And she had other distractions to contend with. Each spring, along with the first fine weather, American tourists would begin to write or telephone her, asking to see the Gertrude Stein art collection. Toklas did not like to have people in without offering them a refreshment, so she would prepare tea and something to go with it: lemon shortbread was a favorite, or, for special guests, *visitandines,** little white cakes somewhat similar to *madeleines.* "A veritable invasion of compatriots and other foreigners . . . fill the flat and my time," she wrote her friend Annette Rosenshine in June 1948. "But as they come because of Gertrude there seem[s] to be nothing else to do [but entertain them]." Shopping, cooking, and hosting so many near strangers was not easy for a septuagenarian troubled by arthritis and lack of funds, but doing so helped her keep Stein's memory alive. The compli-

---

* The cakes are made primarily of beaten egg whites, ground almonds, browned butter, and sugar, and are named after the order of nuns that orginated the recipe. (Toklas's published recipe for the cakes unwittingly omits the sugar, and does not work, but has never been corrected.)

ments she received on her baking, meanwhile, bolstered her confidence in writing a cookbook.

❧

In many ways, Toklas had been preparing all her life to do just that. "Cook-books have always intrigued and seduced me," she would later admit; "when I was still a dilettante in the kitchen they held my attention, even the dull ones, from cover to cover, the way crime and murder stories did Gertrude Stein."[21] Although she had grown up in a home where servants did all the cooking, she had taken a gentlewoman's interest in knowing how to cook, what to serve, and the right way to serve it. Her acquaintance with French food, meanwhile, was long-standing, for despite the Toklas family's German-Jewish roots, their cooks in San Francisco had always cooked French food for them. Still, as she later put it, "before coming to Paris I was interested in food but not in doing any cooking."[22]

Only by living in France had she slowly become aware of the many fine (and different) cooking traditions that existed within that country—not only of *haute cuisine* and *cuisine bourgeoise*, but also the incredibly varied regional cuisines: Norman, Alsatian, Burgundian, and Provençal dishes would all would find their way into her cooking repertoire. Her exposure to the various forms of French cooking was broadened as well by her social mobility: throughout the first half of the twentieth century Toklas dined in the finest restaurants and grandest private homes, but she also ate in the most humble restaurants and artists' studios. Like A. J. Liebling, she knew and enjoyed the cooking of both the rich and the not-so-rich.

Cooking had ultimately become an important aspect of her life with Gertrude Stein: Stein, in fact, had first encouraged Toklas to express her creativity in the kitchen. Toklas's first dishes for Stein consisted of "the simple dishes I had eaten in the homes of the San Joaquin Valley in California—fricasseed chicken, corn bread, apple and lemon pie."[23] Such modest attempts—undertaken primarily to soothe homesickness—would broaden and escalate over the coming years, with Toklas collecting French recipes of historical, cultural, regional, or personal significance and then re-creating them as special treats for Stein and for their friends. She had also learned a good deal about *cuisine bourgeoise* by watching their various housekeepers, particularly their first, Hélène, who was tremendously gifted in the kitchen (but who felt very strongly that Toklas herself ought not to cook, for cooking was the job of a servant). Finally, of course, there was the cooking Toklas had done at the château they rented for so many years at Bilignin, which after all was a mere fifty miles southeast of Bourg-en-Bresse, capital of the Ain department, in a region justly famous for its chickens and for its farm produce, and "recommended by the *Guide Gastronomique* . . . [for its fine] market and provision shops."[24] Toklas's hands-on, garden-to-table cooking at the château, supplemented by these fine local ingredients, ultimately endowed her with an acute awareness of the importance of *terroir.*

Even though Toklas did not cook daily in Paris—that work fell to their various housekeepers, so long as they had one—she did enjoy cooking for special occasions, as when she decorated a cold poached sea bass, quite colorfully, for Picasso: "I covered the fish with an ordinary mayonnaise and, using a pastry tube, decorated it with a red mayonnaise . . . [and then made] a design with sieved hard-boiled eggs, the whites and the yolks apart, with truffles and with finely chopped *fines herbes.* I was proud of my *chef d'oeuvre* . . . and Picasso exclaimed at its beauty. But, said he, should it not rather have been made in honor of Matisse than of me."[25] (He was right, of course: the fish had been decorated in bright colors more characteristic of Matisse.) Toklas had also been known to step in and help friends in the kitchen, as in the comedic set piece in *The Autobiography of Alice B. Toklas,* when Picasso and his mistress Fernande are on the verge of a dinner party crisis, and Toklas saves the day by taking Fernande out shopping, then cooking up Fernande's *riz à la Valencienne* (better known by its Spanish name, *paella valenciana*) in the apartment of Max Jacob. More often, however, Toklas simply became excited about a particular ingredient—such as wild strawberries, or the beautiful baby vegetables from the Bilignin garden—and selected a radically simple preparation that showed off that exquisite item to best advantage.

As she sifted through a lifetime's worth of recipes, Toklas found herself coming back, as ever, to the realization that all of her cooking was intimately related to Stein. It was Stein, after all, who had been at the center of every meal and gathering, who had supported and encouraged all her efforts in the kitchen, and who had provided Toklas with a new cookbook to read and enjoy each Christmas. Even during the darkest winter of World War II, while the two were holed up in Culoz, Stein had somehow managed to arrange that "the 1,479 pages of Montagné's and Salles's *The Great Book of the Kitchen** passed across the [enemy] line[s] with more intelligence than is usually credited to inanimate objects." Toklas had adored that hefty and extravagant Christmas present, observing that "though there was not one ingredient obtainable it was abundantly satisfying to pore over its pages, imagination being as lively as it is."[26] During that same hungry year, Stein and Toklas discussed collaborating on a cooking-related project—for Lucien Tendret, the nephew of Brillat-Savarin and author of the brilliant and fantastical cookbook *La Table au Pays de Brillat-Savarin*, was the grandfather of their Culoz landlady. (The much-loved book had in fact been written in Culoz after Tendret had retired from his law practice in Belley.) Upon signing the lease for their Culoz house, Stein and Toklas were presented "a copy of this delectable book" by Tendret's grandson, and they immediately recognized the genius of its writing. One of the most erudite (as well as amusing) French cookbooks, *La Table au Pays* features recipes that begin with epigraphs from Plato, and a preface that can only be described as a tour de force of gastronomic historiography. (Richard Olney would write about it frequently, and adapt several of its very complicated recipes for the home cook; Julia Child, meanwhile, owned a first edition.)

La Table au Pays was all the more precious to Toklas and Stein because it described fine foods and food preparations specific to their little subregion of the Ain, known as the Bugey. The idea of translating the book into English became even more exciting when they discovered another, related text: the Tendret family recipe book—a book of everyday dishes that were entirely different from those fantastically complicated preparations Tendret had so lovingly described in

---

*Prosper Montagné and Prosper Salles's *Le Grand Livre de la Cuisine* (1929) is one of the best French cookbooks of the early twentieth century.

La Table au Pays. These were instead the simple dishes that Tendret and his family had regularly been served by their skilled family cook. In the end, however, Stein and Toklas had abandoned the project because, as Toklas later noted, "the recipes [of *La Table au Pays* were] exciting to read but are not useful even today [when the war is over]. Take for instance Lobster, Breast of Chicken and Black Truffle Salad"—a *salade composée* requiring not only lobster, capon, and truffles but also endive, ham, and turkey.

As she prepared to write her own cookbook, Toklas was grappling with another, more fundamental problem: her identity as a writer. Throughout their life together, Stein had been the writer, and Toklas had no desire now to usurp her deceased partner in that role. Moreover, there was the question of confidence: Toklas had not published anything since she was seventeen, when she had "sold a joke for five dollars to *Life*."*[27] And, in truth, since the 1933 publication of *The Autobiography of Alice B. Toklas*, Toklas's voice actually seemed to belong more to Stein than to herself, for Stein had captured it so brilliantly in that fine and amusing bestseller.

The question, then, of how she might now establish her own voice (or, looked at another way, how Toklas might now live up to Stein's earlier evocation of it) was daunting. Particularly since, as Stein had once noted (in Toklas's voice), Toklas found writing so difficult: "I am a pretty good housekeeper and a pretty good gardener and a pretty good needlewoman and a pretty good secretary and a pretty good editor and a pretty good vet for dogs and I have to do them all at once and I found it difficult to add being a pretty good author," *The Autobiography of Alice B. Toklas* had ended. "About six weeks ago Gertrude Stein said, It does not look to me as if you were ever going to write that autobiography. You know what I am going to do. I am going to write it for you . . . and she has and this is it."[28]

Given such a precedent, could Toklas come up with an equally brilliant narrative strategy, one that could respond to Stein with the same playfulness that Stein had once responded to Toklas—and with an equal (and equally tacit) testimony that, above all else, the two were one?

---

*Not *Life* the picture magazine, but an earlier, unrelated magazine by the same name.

Was it possible, in other words, for this cookbook to be more than a cookbook?

❖

As the 1940s came to an end, Toklas was once again distracted from her cookbook writing project, this time because she wanted to place Stein's entire art collection in a single museum where it would be known in perpetuity as "the Collection of Gertrude Stein." Of course, she faced total opposition in this project from Allan Stein, since Gertrude Stein had designated that the collection was to go to him when Toklas died, to do with whatever he liked. When Toklas presented Stein's cash-strapped nephew with her plan to sell the entire collection to the Yale art museum at a knockdown price, he very firmly told her no. "Allan Stein refuses not only to cooperate but will make everything as difficult as possible—he has commenced to assert himself with cold aggression," Toklas wrote a friend at about this time. "He will definitely obstruct wherever he can."[29]

When not obsessing on Allan Stein's disloyalty to his late aunt Gertrude, Toklas was doing other things to make sure that Stein's memory was honored. When the Metropolitan Museum, which had received Picasso's *Portrait of Gertrude Stein* as a direct bequest from Stein, immediately placed the painting on a several-year loan to the Museum of Modern Art—an institution Stein had always loathed, and to which she left nothing—Toklas wrote a series of outraged letters, which ultimately resulted in the early return of the painting to its Stein-designated institution.

Toklas's personal correspondence also kept her quite busy—and through it, to her delight, she received a number of cooking-related gifts. In truth, many of her friends were eager that she escape her depression, anger, and lingering grief by writing her cookbook. At one point a box of American kitchen gadgets arrived from Samuel Steward, along with replacement "twirlers" for the Mixmaster he had shipped to her from Chicago in late 1939.* Because Toklas had dropped and

---

*Steward had a lively appreciation of Toklas's cooking and was particularly touched that she catered to his many food allergies. He sent Toklas more than twenty American kitchen gadgets in the years before the war, and in 1939 thoughtfully rewired the Mixmaster to 220 volts so that Toklas could use it in France.

broken the Mixmaster's bowl in July 1940, she also requested and received two "beautiful opaline bowls"[30] from Isabel Wilder via her brother, Thornton, who brought them over to Paris in his luggage. (Toklas subsequently wrote Isabel a thank-you note including two recipes—for *gougères* and for potato quenelles—that worked beautifully using the mixer and its new bowls.) She also received a selection of American cookbooks from Stein's old friend W. G. Rogers* and his wife, Mildred. Thornton Wilder, who knew little about cooking, showed his support by bringing Toklas little delicacies whenever he visited: chocolate, tinned lobster, and, most important, cartons of Pall Mall—good American cigarettes, like strong black coffee, being an absolute necessity for the Alice B. Toklas kitchen.

Other friends encouraged her differently. Joe Barry, the American journalist who had been driving Stein and Toklas to the Loire when Stein fell ill, offered her a room as a paying summer guest at the little country place that he and his wife kept in Montmorency, a rustic village in the hills just north of Paris. Toklas was particularly taken with Naomi Barry, describing her as "one of those frightfully energetic women who are so gentle and low keyed and nonchalant that one scarcely realizes how much she is capable of accomplishing in a day's work."[31] Their house was simple and charming, its overgrown garden filled with neglected apple and pear trees. Together with Naomi Barry—a fine home cook who would ultimately become a leading food correspondent for the *Paris Herald Tribune* and a regular contributor to *Gourmet*—Toklas gathered apples good enough for the homey, American-style pies Stein had once so loved. During the same stay, Joe Barry gently encouraged Toklas not to limit herself socially to people she had known in the years before Stein's death, referring to them as "friendships in aspic."[32] He assured her that new friendships and new opportunities awaited, if only Toklas cared to experience them. Toklas seems to have realized he was right. Even Basket, the second of the two poodles she had shared with Stein, was now as "thin as a

---

*W. G. Rogers, who had met Stein and Toklas during World War I, wrote a memoir of Stein entitled *When This You See Remember Me*. Toklas, offended by his characterization of her in it, described the book to Samuel Steward as "frightfulness extreme."

hound at the feet of his master on a gothic tomb." As she wrote to Thornton Wilder in 1949, "It doesn't seem reasonable to suppose he'll be well again [and that's] not easy to accustom oneself to. He has filled the corners of the room and the minutes and me so sweetly these last years."[33]

Janet Flanner, who had recently resumed writing the popular "Letter from Paris" for *The New Yorker*, was one of the most reliable and encouraging of Toklas's friends during this troubled time. Having known each other well for decades—the world of American expatriate lesbian intellectuals in Paris being a close one—she began inviting Toklas out to openings, exhibitions, and private affairs that Toklas would not have wanted to attend on her own.[34]

Others did what they could. Toklas's childhood friend Louise Taylor visited Toklas from her home in England whenever possible. Carl Van Vechten, the New York–based novelist and photographer who was also Stein's literary executor, encouraged Toklas in her creativity; so too did Samuel Steward, who was just then getting sober, and preparing to leave academia for a new life as a tattoo artist in downtown Chicago. Toklas confided her problems and writing anxieties more freely to Steward than to most, perhaps hoping to help him place in perspective his own considerable problems (which, apart from alcohol, included rage against the academic establishment and frustration with his failure as a novelist). "It has been a bad time for me," she wrote him that September. "To have to accept [Basket's] not being well again doesn't come easy. [And] my household work seems never ending— always increasing for some mysterious [reason]—but [all the same] the long projected cookbook has yet to materialize. . . . Years ago when I spoke of it to Thornton Wilder he only said—but Alice have you ever tried to write. . . . So perhaps one has to have some experience of writing for even a cookbook. But can't one count and build upon conviction—prejudice and passion—my inadequate equipment."[35]

❖

Toklas finally made her debut as a working writer with "Food, Artists and the Baroness," a short article for *Vogue* that would later be incorporated into *The Alice B. Toklas Cook Book*. She described the piece to a friend as a "cooking thing I scrambled together." It was published in March 1950, when she was just shy of seventy-three. The article's appearance might well have been cause for a small celebration, had not Toklas received a letter of far greater importance at nearly the same time: an astounding offer to publish *all* of Gertrude Stein's many unpublished manuscripts, extended by the Beinecke Library in conjunction with Yale University Press. "The news has left me limp and overwhelmed," she wrote Samuel Steward, "bathed in the light of having beheld a vision."[36] And she was only half-joking, as this colossal project, which was expected to stretch into nine or ten volumes, assured Toklas of something she had worked nearly all her adult life to secure: her beloved partner's literary immortality.

It was only a few months later, after the excitement about Yale University Press's *Unpublished Works of Gertrude Stein* had died down, that Toklas wrote a note of thanks to Louise Taylor in London for the recent gift of Taylor's mother's cookbooks. In it, Toklas's intention for the new project finally became clear. "The [cookbook] I liked best," she told Taylor, "naturally had the most extravagant recipes—nothing one could possibly afford but that made reading it more romantic and more of an adventure. It has given me an idea for my own humble effort. A cook book to be read. What about it."[37]

FOUR

Gourmet, *Brillat-Savarin,* *and* Paris Cuisine

When Alice Toklas asked her friend W. G. Rogers to send her a copy of "the *Gourmet*" magazine as a way of learning about American tastes and interests regarding food, she was right to do so, for back in the United States, *Gourmet* was creating a whole new generation of culinary Francophiles. Founded in January 1941 by salesman-turned-epicure Earle MacAusland, *Gourmet* had quickly become the leading American food magazine of the 1940s. Its success was due partly to wartime rationing and deprivation: if one couldn't eat well, one could at least *dream* of eating well. But there was another reason the magazine flourished: it gave readers a new way of thinking about food and drink. *Gourmet* presented narratives about culinary discoveries, often made via luxury travel and adventure. Rather than delving into the mundane technicalities of food preparation,* these stories focused instead on the pleasure and enjoyment of fine dining, with evocative, image-rich articles designed to seduce. Since French cuisine was then considered the best, most sumptuous and most refined, *Gourmet* published innumerable articles on France and French cooking in its first

---

* In its later years *Gourmet* (which MacAusland edited until 1980) would shift its focus toward food preparation. (The magazine was closed down in 2009.)

decades. Some of the best were by Samuel Chamberlain and M.F.K. Fisher. While Chamberlain's coverage of France was by far the more responsible of the two, Fisher's romantic evocations would beguile American readers in a way that combined her deeply felt fiction with highly personal reportage.*

And why not? *Gourmet* was, after all, a magazine based on fantasy. Earle MacAusland was a Boston-born salesman of high style whose father had been the general manager of Reed & Barton silversmiths—a company that had long used fantasies of luxury and exclusivity to peddle its costly tablewares. Not by accident did MacAusland give his new magazine a French name. France had always offered the ultimate in luxury to the moneyed world traveler, and Americans had always equated French chefs and French restaurants with the finest food and service money could buy. Many of *Gourmet*'s early stories were set in France despite the war; and to ensure the authenticity of its French recipes, the glossy, colorful magazine bore the name of one of America's leading French chefs and cooking instructors, Louis Pullig de Gouy, on its masthead. MacAusland would continue to promote French *luxe, calme, et volupté* throughout his forty-year tenure at *Gourmet*, simultaneously enjoining his readership to think of French-style luxury dining not as gluttony, or even self-indulgence, but rather as a connoisseur's way of transcending everyday life and achieving a higher plane of being. "The word *Gourmet* signifies far more than just food perfection," he declared in the magazine's debut issue. "It is a synonym for the honest seeker of the *summum bonum* of living."

Gourmet's most delightful articles on France and its food were written by the artist and architectural historian Samuel Chamberlain, a midwesterner who had served as an ambulance driver during World War I and then settled with his wife, Narcissa, at Senlis, a beautiful market and cathedral town thirty-five miles north of Paris and just a few miles from the Château de Chantilly, where the great chef Vatel†

---

* See, for example, Fisher's fine, melancholy short story "Three Swiss Inns" in the September 1941 issue, about a group of travelers' dining experiences just as Europe shuts down for war.
† After a series of meals and entertainments created by Vatel in honor of Louis XIV at Chantilly did not succeed as planned, Vatel was mocked; then, when an expected delivery of seafood did not appear, Vatel declared, "*je ne survivrai point à cet affront-ci; j'ai de l'honneur et de la réputation à perdre*" ("I will never survive this affront; I'll lose both my honor and reputation"). Moments later he ran himself through on his épée—not once, but three times, until finally piercing his own

had met his sad end. Chamberlain worked there as a printmaker and photographer during the 1920s, then returned to the United States in the 1930s to begin a long career of writing and illustrating books on New England architecture, while simultaneously teaching printmaking at MIT. Remaining devoted to France and French culture throughout those years, at the outset of the war he published *France Will Live Again: The Portrait of a Peaceful Interlude, 1919–1939*, in which he paid tribute to the beauty of France through his drawings, prints, and photographs.

After helping MacAusland launch *Gourmet* in 1941, Chamberlain immediately began contributing a series of lighthearted short stories describing an American family's adventures with a cheerful Burgundian cook named Clémentine. These lovable tales of French cuisine (which Chamberlain wrote under the pseudonym Phineas Beck*) appeared through the October 1942 issue, and were subsequently republished as the bestselling *Clémentine in the Kitchen*. Chamberlain then returned to France to serve in Air Force Photo Intelligence during the war, and ultimately won a legion of merit, a bronze star, and the Légion d'Honneur for his efforts.

Shortly after the war's conclusion, he began an ambitious new article-and-book project (again bankrolled by MacAusland at *Gourmet*) through which he hoped to write the definitive American guidebook to the food, culture, and natural beauty of France. Ultimately published as *Bouquet de France: An Epicurean Tour of the French Provinces* (1952), the book described France's various provinces and regional specialties, and also gave restaurant listings and travel advice. A hefty *édition de luxe*, it featured Chamberlain's fine photographs, sketches, and engravings, as well as recipes adapted for American home cooks by Chamberlain's wife, Narcissa.† Although it was published and sold privately through *Gourmet* rather than through bookstores, this fine guidebook *cum* work of art soon developed a cult following, and would remain in print for the next twenty-five years. Chamberlain,

---

heart. (This famous account of his suicide is given by Madame de Sevigné in a letter to her daughter, Madame de Grignan, of April 26, 1671.)

* The name is a play on *bec fin*, French slang for "gourmet"; literally, it means "fine nose."

† In order to improve her cooking and recipe-writing skills, Narcissa Chamberlain attended a series of instructional lectures by Dione Lucas in Boston in 1947, and enrolled in the Paris Cordon Bleu in the fall of 1950. By then she already knew and liked Paul and Julia Child, to whom she and her husband had been introduced by their close friend Paul Sheeline, Paul Child's nephew.

however, ultimately felt shortchanged by MacAusland's handling of the book, for *Gourmet*'s way of doing things was not to the author's advantage. Julia Child wrote a friend that "according to the Chamberlain family . . . MacAusland wants *Bouquet de France* to be a very, very exclusive book, only for the upper classes, or something too recherché for words. . . . Sam [Chamberlain] wants to put it in every bookstore around, but not MacAusland . . . he wants it sold by private subscription to his magazine. . . . I'll bet old Sam never had a lawyer to give him any advice. That's what can happen if you deal with such people as *Gourmet*."[1]

❖

Unlike the Chamberlains, not all Americans writing about French food and wine during the 1940s and 1950s traveled there to do so. Mary Frances Kennedy Fisher (who published as M.F.K. Fisher) wrote a good deal about France from a forlorn little house in the Southern California high desert, where she lived with two young daughters, piles of debt, and a maddening, emotionally fragile, financially improvident third husband. Determined to establish herself first and foremost as a novelist and short story writer, she also tapped out essays, articles, and short books on kitchen subjects as a way of paying the bills. In *How to Cook a Wolf* (1942), for example, Fisher drew on her own experience of Depression-era hardships to address the nationwide problem of wartime food shortages. She strikes a pose of eminent practicality in that book, offering sensible advice about how to make do, even while telling mildly outrageous stories about how she herself has lived on next to nothing. But Fisher was by no means a home economist, and while many of her books would include recipes, neither was she much of a cook. She was, rather, a novelist, memoirist, and fantasist who specialized in tall tales and elaborate embroideries upon truth. Since the outbreak of the war she had lived for the most part on a rattlesnake-infested property outside San Bernardino; but having spent some time in France before the war, she returned there over and over again in her imagination, finding in the verdant memories of France, and in the story of two very complicated love affairs of her previous decades, something vastly preferable to the arid ugliness in which she was now compelled to work and live.

The daughter of a small-town newspaper publisher, Fisher had grown up in Whittier, a modest community just east of Los Angeles that would soon be swallowed up into that vast, smoggy megalopolis. After just a year at Occidental College, she left for France with her graduate-student husband, Alfred Fisher. The two spent a few days in Paris in late September 1929 before settling in Dijon, at the northern end of the Burgundian Côte-d'Or.* Al Fisher, an aspiring poet and literary intellectual, was taking an intensive course in French there before pursuing his doctorate in Strasbourg. The couple eventually extended their stay in Dijon to fifteen months before relocating to Alsace. When their money ran out (Al's scholarship was at an end), they lived cheaply for a while in a fishing village near Cannes before shipping back to California. This first visit to France was a lonely but formative time for Mary Frances Kennedy Fisher, for the country's cuisine and manners had captured her imagination even as her marriage failed to delight her—and through writing about cooking and its challenges (as well as about the heart and its sorrows), she found her voice as an author.

In 1935 Fisher began an affair with Dillwyn Parrish, an artist-author-illustrator who was a cousin of the artist Maxfield Parrish. She climbed into bed with Dillwyn, who was fourteen years her senior, despite the fact that both she and Parrish were married and neighbors. When Parrish's beautiful young wife (Gigi Parrish was four years younger than Fisher) subsequently left him, Parrish was heartbroken by her departure, despite the fact that his own infidelity had triggered the break. A man of independent means, he invited Mary Frances Fisher to join him on a trip to France that he was about to make with his mother—he was in ill health and need of rest. The relationship deepened during the course of the trip, and the two decided to stay on in Europe, in a cottage high above Lake Geneva that Parrish had bought a decade earlier with his sister.

---

* The Côte-d'Or is frequently translated as "Golden Slope," but the name actually devolves from "Côte d'Orient" ("East-facing Slope"). The name describes an enormously long southeast-facing escarpment from which many of the greatest Burgundian wine appellations originate.

The couple's time in French-speaking Switzerland was initially conceived as a rest cure, since Parrish's lungs were rapidly disintegrating from Buerger's disease, a rare and incurable arterial condition brought on by years of heavy smoking and malnutrition. They hoped the mountain air and access to Swiss medicines would help him, but they didn't. Parrish suffered blood clots, then infections, then gangrene. After having his leg amputated in 1940, Parrish decided to return to the United States. There the couple bought a property and built a house in the desert town of Hemet, where they again hoped the dry, clean mountain air would help Parrish breathe. At roughly the same time, Mary Frances divorced her first husband* and married Parrish. Only months later, however, Parrish, who was in terrible pain, chose to commit suicide with a shotgun in the couple's backyard.

M.F.K. Fisher had by then published two books—*Touch and Go*, a novel cowritten with Parrish under a pseudonym that received terrible reviews, and, before that, *Serve It Forth*, a book of essays on gastronomy, published by Harper, that had found a far warmer reception. But because neither had really established her as a writer of substance, she took a writing gig for a while at Paramount in Hollywood, and during that time became pregnant through an unnamed liaison. She kept the baby. A year later, while visiting New York, she met Donald Friede, an editor turned literary agent. Friede was just then a poor bet for a husband—having been expelled from Harvard, Yale, and Princeton as a young man, he had founded, then bankrupted a publishing firm and left numerous other places of employment under difficult circumstances. He also owed alimony to four ex-wives, and was just then facing prosecution in California for the distribution of pornography.† But Fisher was now a single mother in her late thirties, and she

---

* M.F.K. Fisher would later blame the failure of the marriage on Al Fisher's lack of a sex drive (and she would say the same about the failure of her third marriage, to Donald Friede). But Al Fisher seems from his correspondence to have been a loving and sexually attentive husband to Fisher, and his papers, now housed at Smith College (where he taught for many years, mentoring, among others, Sylvia Plath), contain several manuscripts detailing his various erotic interests and adventures.

† According to Joan Reardon's biography of Fisher, *Poet of the Appetites*, in the summer of 1946, "Donald was subpoenaed to return to California where [he was] under indictment for misusing the U.S. mail, apparently to send pornographic materials" (p. 173). Friede had also been arrested in 1927 in Boston for selling an obscene book to undercover police agents. For more on Friede's extraordinary life, see the extensive biographical note to his papers, located in the Library of Congress.

wanted to be married, and she liked Friede. Moreover, Friede's mother was rich, and he had solid expectations of inheriting her money.

When Friede's business collapsed in 1946, the couple moved back to Fisher's house in Hemet. The move made good sense, since they were now expecting a child—and moreover Friede was due back in California for his trial. Once there, however, the couple fell further into debt and Friede had a mental breakdown. Eventually they divorced, with Friede moving back to New York for psychiatric treatment, and Fisher remaining in Hemet with her two daughters.

M.F.K. Fisher was a person who knew how to attract and hold the attention of a room—in a very real sense, a performer of her own life. Drama, intrigue, manipulation, lies, and emotional turmoil were central to her fiction; they were also, not surprisingly, a persistent aspect of her quotidian reality. While in her correspondence and stories she boldly presented herself as a seductress of men, and while she would maintain a number of flirtations with men in her later years,* by the early 1950s her sexual attraction (according to her journals and letters, including correspondence with her psychiatrist) was entirely to women,† and all of her later-life sexual relationships were with women. Furthermore, her own writings (both published and unpublished) make clear that this attraction to women had existed within her from adolescence. Her first great sexual infatuation was in high school, toward a fellow student named Eda Lord, a pretty and popular rich girl who subsequently lived in Europe as a novelist and short story writer. When Fisher reconnected with Lord by mail in 1952,‡ she described the challenges she had faced since they last met:

> Dillwyn died . . . maybe you know that . . . suicide after three years of horror which were still the best in my life, perhaps.

---

*Most notably with Arnold Gingrich (1903–1976), the flashy founding editor of *Esquire* magazine. The flirtation was mostly carried on by phone and letter; Gingrich was at that point a retired and happily married grandfather living in Ridgewood, New Jersey.

†Fisher's bisexual awareness and midlife lesbianism are both painstakingly documented in Joan Reardon's comprehensive biography, which includes a detailed account of Fisher's live-in relationship with Marietta Voorhees. References to Fisher's lesbian attractions can also be found in her (published) correspondence with Gingrich.

‡In a later letter to Lord, Fisher wrote a five-page statement entitled "I Love You, Eda," in which she confessed that "all my major actions have been shaped by my abiding love for you and consciousness of you" (Reardon, *Poet of the Appetites*, p. 274).

I [then] worked in Hollywood . . . a very sterile period it would seem, and yet. . . . I was not sterile even if the studio job was, for in 1943 I had a daughter . . . [who] is [now] almost 9. . . . About two years after she was born I married Donald Friede, to our mutual damage. We had another daughter, Mary . . . a rock of a human being. . . . She is everything good in D[onald] F[riede], before he got twisted. I hope to keep her untwisted.

[My mother] Edith Kennedy died with great difficulty in 1949, and soon after that I started to get a divorce . . . I was in a very bad way . . . [suffering from] extreme emotional and physical fatigue . . . Donald could not help whipping me into bigger jobs, bigger royalties, and there I was having babies, helping people die, watching him go into a real psychic collapse.

. . . . I am very busy [here] . . . I do all the cooking, for a regular family of four and many guests . . . and work six mornings a week for the [family newspaper]. . . . [My father is now] dying of pulmonary fibrosis . . . my brother David committed suicide a year after Dillwyn's death. . . . Me, I am not at all the way I vaguely thought of myself as being. . . . I am a big woman but not ungainly, with greying hair and a smooth baby-face and tired green eyes. . . . Sexually I am in the deep-freeze . . . I hope we'll meet again.[2]

Even though the 1940s were a difficult time for Fisher, the decade was paradoxically her most productive. This was partly because she had not yet succumbed to the alcoholism of her later years, but also (and primarily) because Donald Friede, in seeking to pay off the couple's debts, agented Fisher's writing in every possible way. And writing provided Fisher with a blessed daily escape from a life she would otherwise have spent washing dishes, tending infants, and squabbling with her husband about money. While her pert little books on gastronomic subjects brought her some degree of recognition,* her second novel,

---

* Fisher's greater recognition would come later, after her short books were repackaged (by Donald Friede, again acting as her agent) as the omnibus collection *The Art of Eating* in 1954. It would be reissued many times in the following decades.

Not Now But Now (1947)—a work of commercial fiction about a beautiful, manipulative, and narcissistic sociopath—was a total failure. Of it, *The New Republic* observed, "Mrs. Fisher is an authority on cooking and eating. This is her recipe for a novel: to a generous helping of ham and corn, add artificial color and artificial flavor. Beat the whole into a light fluff. Half bake."[3] Upon consideration, Fisher seemed to agree: she disavowed the novel as a "potboiler"[4] and resigned herself, at least for the time being, to writing light, entertaining pieces on food, cooking, and travel.

In the first and most warmly received of her books, *Serve It Forth* (1937), Fisher had professed a stylish, high-minded ambivalence to the kitchen. Like many who take an interest in the literature of cooking, she was far more a reader than a cook—and was not at all ashamed to admit it, especially since she strongly resented women's traditional relegation to the stove. "Cooking . . . is, for most women, a question less of vocation than of necessity," she stated unapologetically in that first book. "They are not called to the kitchen by the divine inner voice of a Vatel or an Escoffier. Rather they are lured there, willy-nilly, by the piping of their husbands' empty stomachs. They cook doggedly, desperately . . . with a cumulative if uninspired skill." After the failure of the prewar novel *Touch and Go*, she continued on with these kitchen ruminations, at one point writing a friend, "I simply must tap out some more gastronomical nonsense to fill up a large hole in my bank book."[5] The three stylish (and short) works on food that followed were really more like anthologies, in that they appropriated recipes from other cookbooks and writings on food from other authors. There was a book on oysters, *Consider the Oyster* (1941); a book on wartime cooking, *How to Cook a Wolf* (1942); and an anthology of writings on great meals, *Here Let Us Feast: A Book of Banquets* (1946). But among these three largely derivative works was a fourth, and it was a breakthrough: *The Gastronomical Me* (1943), in which Fisher confessed some of her darkest and most significant life moments—including her doomed high school crush on Eda Lord, the messy ending of her marriage to Al Fisher, and her love affair with the moribund Dillwyn Parrish—linking these moments to specific and often transcendent food experiences, many of them taking place in prewar France and Switzerland.

These tales of thwarted eros and gastronomic fulfillment were not for everyone, though, for in prettying them up, and in presenting herself as the heroine of every story, Fisher wrote tales that verged on the incredible. Some in fact read like fairy tales. "M.F.K. Fisher's egoism is childlike and total," Alan Brien wrote in *The Spectator*, "everywhere she goes, waiters, chefs, peasants, innkeepers, little boys who sing outside cafes, chauffeurs, bus drivers, ship's captains, fall half in love with her . . . and lay their art at her knowledgeable, and appreciative feet."[6] Later critics would echo this appraisal of Fisher as someone entirely too self-serving and self-congratulatory, with Carolyn See writing in the *Los Angeles Times* that Fisher's "cutout characters" exist merely to "support [her] ferociously narcissistic vision. . . . She makes the same demands on us as a supremely irritating friend."[7] All the same, American women readers, many of them dealing with significant frustrations of their own in both kitchen and bedroom, were easily caught up in the fantasy of being a young and beautiful woman, beloved by all, romantically torn between husband and lover while living abroad in France, the land of all things rich, sinful, forbidden . . . and delicious.

At the center of *The Gastronomical Me* is Fisher's love affair with "Chexbres,"* her idealized version of Dillwyn Parrish, as he declines into a ghastly mortal illness, followed by amputations, followed by suicide. Here at last Fisher's stories could not be dismissed simply as self-serving melodrama because they were based on a series of grisly real-life experiences that had left her authentically devastated. Given the magnitude of her loss, Fisher's preoccupation with food and drink in these tales sometimes borders on the unseemly, to the point that critic Alan Brien even noted, "she is finally left alone to cook her lonely exquisite meals which neither time nor tragedy can force her to neglect."[8] But in comforting herself as best she could—often with the finest of food and drink—Fisher was doing something many readers would have loved to do themselves. Like Jean Rhys, another proto-feminist confessional novelist troubled by severe alcoholism and a profoundly messy personal life, Fisher "found" her distinctive voice

---

*Chexbres is the name of the village in Switzerland closest to the cottage Fisher shared with Parrish.

by crafting elaborate counternarratives to sort through her own indecorous life choices, failures, and tragedies. Then (again like Rhys) she made those stories ever more appealing by setting them in romantic, faraway France. Fisher actively revised and reshaped her past life to suit the needs of a compelling fantasy narrative; in doing so, she ultimately transformed its far more prosaic sorrows into something memorable and moving. No longer the faded wife and mother ("a big woman . . . with greying hair . . . sexually . . . in the deep-freeze"), she becomes instead, through the magic of fiction, the brainy young coquette, torn between lover and husband, or else bravely dining alone in the finest of restaurants.

❖

Fisher's magazine articles on kitchen life and food-oriented tales of love gone wrong were not the only way she found to write about French life and French culture during the 1940s. In 1947 Donald Friede negotiated a commission for her from George Macy, the entrepreneurial publisher of the Limited Editions Club. The project was a translation of Jean-Anthelme Brillat-Savarin's *Physiology of Taste*. Desperate to bring in some money, Friede negotiated the contract as work-for-hire—a substandard agreement for a writer that left Fisher few rights to her own work and no control over its ultimate publication. But half of the money was to be paid up front, and the couple were overwhelmed with debt. Up to that point Fisher been working on a proposal for a biography of Madame Récamier, the nineteenth-century Parisian hostess and intellectual; Fisher had long identified with Récamier as a woman of style, wit, elegance, seductiveness, and genius. However, the research for such a book required time and money that Fisher simply did not have, and "in the end," as she wrote a friend, "I am too tired to write [a book of this sort] with the nun-like ascetic self-denial and concentration it takes."[9] As a result, Récamier was out, and Brillat-Savarin—to whom Récamier was at least related by marriage—was in.

A new translation of Brillat-Savarin was not just then necessary: good English translations had been published in 1854 (by Fayette Robinson) and 1877 (by R. E. Anderson); and another in 1915 (by

Charles Monselet). In 1926 there had been yet another translation published in the United States, this one with a foreword by the legendary editor and bon vivant Frank Crowninshield. Fisher's translation would not be much different from it. But George Macy was a book packager and businessman, not a cultural arbiter; his aim was not to give the world a needed translation, or even a bestseller, but rather to create a specialty publication that suited his luxury niche market by having a contemporary author with "name recognition" attached to an *édition de luxe*. In promoting this expensive, new, finely illustrated, limited-run version of the book, Macy crassly described Fisher's as "the best-paid-for translation in modern history" and touted her as "not only the finest writer on gastronomical things since Brillat-Savarin, [but also] the best-looking."[10] A number of kitchen photographs of Fisher made up like a Hollywood starlet were sent out with the company's promotional mailings.

Brillat-Savarin's 1825 *La Physiologie du Goût, ou Méditations de Gastronomie Transcendante* has always been a book far more talked about than read, even among those who care passionately about the history of French gastronomy. Its greatest champions tend to be toastmasters, or else people who have not read it, or else people who have not read much else on the subject. Richard Olney, who read far more deeply, carefully, and passionately on French cuisine than M.F.K. Fisher ever did, observed about *La Physiologie* that it "revealed little more than the glutton that [the great chef and author] Carême had early divined in Brillat-Savarin—joined to a pompous and puzzling self-esteem. . . . My resentment [of him] and disappointment [with the book] rankle to this day." Paul and Julia Child were equally negative about the book, Julia describing Brillat-Savarin as an "insipid old brioche* whose sole use is to furnish windbags with stupid quotations," and *La Physiologie* as "pretty tough and dull going."[11]

The book was just one example of the substantial French literature of food appreciation that had developed during the nineteenth

---

*Child was unwittingly paraphrasing Baudelaire, who had famously described Brillat-Savarin as an *"espèce de brioche insipide"* in the last chapter of *Les Paradis Artificiels*. (In the same passage, Baudelaire also describes *La Physiologie* as *"un faux chef d'oeuvre"*—"a false masterpiece.")

century, a period when a number of distinguished men of letters held forth on food—most notably, Alexandre Dumas *père*, whose eminently browsable *Le Grand Dictionnaire de Cuisine* was published (posthumously) in 1873. But by far the most hands-on early-nineteenth-century French writing on the subject of French cuisine was penned by the well-born Grimod de la Reynière, who in his eight-volume *Almanach des Gourmands* (published serially between 1803 and 1812) regularly advised his Parisian readers on the purchase and preparation of the city's best-loved seasonal foods, and also offered thoughts on entertaining. The scion of a noble family and very much an enfant terrible, de la Reynière lived a life of wild parties and Rabelaisian excess, and as a result the Childs found him "infinitely more amusing [to read than Brillat-Savarin], and quite a more sophisticated type."[12] By comparison, Brillat-Savarin was merely a provincial lawyer whose oddly titled book* addressed the related arts of cooking well, hosting well, and dining well, usually doing so in the most portentous (and nonculinary) ways. Written in "meditations" rather than chapters, the text consists of a mix of dialogues, aphorisms, epigrams, and commonsense observations, along with some very weird short stories and a good deal of pseudoscientific rubbish.

Looked at critically (it never has been), Fisher's work of translation is really not much. Since translating the book had required minimal effort (thanks to the many previous translations), Fisher seems to have focused instead on writing a series of stylish and entertaining footnotes. Even here, however, she farmed out the research to librarians at UCLA and the William Andrews Clark Memorial Library in Los Angeles.[†] Then, like a hostess artfully strewing parsley over a meal prepared by caterers, she wrote up their glosses in her own witty style and, to borrow her own phrase, "served it forth." Every once in a while, nonetheless, a footnote appears that is clearly straight from her

---

*The title suggests that the book is a scientific study of how humans taste, even as the subtitle contradicts it by indicating that the book should also be understood as a poetic "meditation on transcendent gastronomy."

†The substantial work undertaken by these librarians is fully documented in the M.F.K. Fisher Papers, at Harvard. (Fisher acknowledges their "assistance" in the book's preface.) She was given particularly close help by Lawrence Clark Powell, who had been a close friend since college.

own pen—as when, in response to Brillat-Savarin's suggestion that the best way to cook spinach is slowly and gently in vast quantities of the very finest butter, Fisher instead recommends "spinach *à la mode de pressure cooker 1947,*" a recipe calling for three cellophane packages of washed or frozen spinach, boiled in a pressure cooker for two minutes, then drained, buttered, and served up piping hot.

The book was beautifully illustrated and produced, but George Macy and Fisher nonetheless came to blows about the finished product. Upon completing the manuscript, Fisher authorized a California-based literary agent to sell four excerpts of it to *Gourmet.* Unfortunately those rights belonged to the publisher, who upon learning of the sale threatened to cancel publication and sue Fisher for breach of contract. Bitter, angry threats and money demands followed, as Macy felt that the integrity and exclusivity of his *édition de luxe* had been compromised. Fisher meanwhile countered with one hysterical letter after another, also threatening her own lawsuit, until Henry Volkening, a friend who would later become her agent, gently explained to her that, according to the terms of the work-for-hire agreement Donald Friede had negotiated, it was not Macy who was at fault, but Fisher and Friede.

All the same, publication of the book ultimately proved a godsend. For an American writer intent on establishing her credentials on gastronomic topics—and yet lacking any substantial knowledge about French cooking, or training in it, or active professional work in preparing it— Fisher had done something strategically brilliant: she had linked her name for all time with that of Brillat-Savarin. It was, in a sense, the best marriage Fisher ever made, for in the coming decade the Brillat-Savarin translation would serve as Fisher's one great credential. Through her involvement with his text, she would be perceived as a leading American authority on French cuisine. Lifted to literary prominence on the basis of this gross misperception, she would return to Paris in high style in 1966, to research and write the most error-ridden book on French cooking ever brought out by a major American publisher.

❖

As American tourists began finding their way back to Paris in the early 1950s, they discovered a city that had more than eight thousand dining establishments offering the visitor a meal. Of course, not all were memorable (or even good) and for Americans passionate about experiencing good French food, a night out in Paris was far too precious to waste on a mediocre dinner. While Paris had much else to recommend it—its art, its history, and the great resurgence of style epitomized by Dior's 1947 "New Look"—its best restaurants remained a top attraction, particularly to Americans, whose strong currency also made these restaurants a fine bargain. By now French cuisine had begun to seem, in the words of one American devotee, "an edible manifestation of spiritual wisdom," and the French "a race of connoisseurs who applied patience, knowledge, and art to food, and [who] ate not just because they were hungry, but to have an aesthetic experience comparable to a great symphony or a day at the Louvre."[13] Americans also knew that the heavy prewar American interpretations of French cuisine—rich hotel fare such as Pheasant Under Glass, Vichyssoise, and Flaming Baked Alaska*—bore no comparison to the authentic French culinary delights awaiting them in Paris.

In order to find their way to the right restaurants, however, moneyed American tourists needed a dependable guide. The *Guide Michelin* (which had ceased publication when the war began in 1940, but came out in a new edition in May 1945) was one possibility, as it was undisputedly the most comprehensive and reliable guide to the restaurants of France. But it was not well suited to Americans limited by time and circumstance to a short trip to Paris. The Michelin was difficult to read and understand, containing mostly symbols and numbers. Worse, only a small portion of the guide was devoted to Paris. But even more important, Americans needed to know far more about a Parisian restaurant than simply its address and rating, since these restaurants offered a variety of cuisines and were substantially different from American restaurants in many ways: the pace

---

*Pheasant Under Glass (or *faisan sous cloche*) is a roast breast of pheasant glazed with brown sauce and chopped truffles, then placed on a seasoned crouton and presented under a showy glass dome. Vichyssoise is potato-leek soup enriched with heavy cream and served chilled. Flaming Baked Alaska consists of ice cream sandwiched between sponge cake, covered with a meringue that is briefly singed in an oven before being flamed at the table with rum. All three dishes originated in American restaurants.

of the meal, the order of the service, and the respective expectations of diner and proprietor.

James Beard, who was just then launching himself as a major American food writer, would be among the first to place his name on a book devoted to this subject. He would not, however, research or write it. His 1952 *Paris Cuisine*, which was conceived as a combination of restaurant guide and cookbook, was instead written by Alexander Watt, a Paris-based Scotsman who seems to have been convinced by Beard that the addition of Beard's name as coauthor would help set the book before the American public. In any event, this fine, short volume succeeded admirably in showing Americans just how different and wonderful dining in Paris could be.

Beard's taking more than his share of credit for *Paris Cuisine* was not unusual. In his very first cookbook, *Hors D'Oeuvre and Canapés*, Beard had taken recipes he had developed with his business partners, Bill and Irma Rhode, and published a book about them under his name only, much to the Rhodes' surprise, anger, and resentment. His first really significant cookbook, *The Fireside Cook Book: A Complete Guide to Fine Cooking for Beginner and Expert* (1949), may have featured recipes he had assembled, but he hadn't actually written the book: rather, the editorial staff of Simon and Schuster had done so, a deal Beard had engineered by agreeing to take a flat fee for the book instead of royalties.[14] Doing so was not a problem, either, because Beard considered himself more of an impresario and a businessman than a writer. When his early efforts to write for *Gourmet* proved unsuccessful, he simply began a lifelong practice of delegating the writing to others. Right around the time he put his name on Watt's *Paris Cuisine*, Beard hired his first on-call ghostwriter, a former magazine editor named Isabel Callvert, who worked for him in that capacity from 1949 through 1967. Callvert (who adored Beard) would be succeeded in time by literary editor John Ferrone, who in turn would be replaced by José Wilson, a former editor of *House and Garden*. Only with Knopf's publication of *Beard on Food* in 1974 would Beard grant a coauthorship credit to any of his in-house ghostwriters.

In any event, Beard spent the last months of 1949 in Paris, broadening his awareness of contemporary French cooking by visiting patisseries, bakeries, and confectioners even as he pursued any number of possible business ventures with French food, wine, and liquor producers and Parisian restaurateurs. During that time *Paris Cuisine*'s real author, Alexander "Sandy" Watt, a journalist who had spent more than twenty years in the city, introduced Beard to his many favorite restaurants and their chefs. Watt had come to know these restaurants from writing regularly on culinary topics for the *London Daily Telegraph*. Having spent years in pursuit of the best and most interesting culinary developments and innovations, he had a long and friendly acquaintance with many of their chefs, which was how he had been able to coax from them their most closely held secrets. "The quest for the recipes [contained herein] was not . . . just a gay and casual gastronomic holiday," he assured his readers in the book's opening pages. "It took years of becoming acquainted, of finally making firm friends of chefs, proprietors, their wives and colleagues [to obtain them] but with a few exceptions we finally won out."

Paris Cuisine (and its follow-up, *Paris Bistro Cookery*, a book focusing on more affordable Parisian restaurants that Watt published without Beard several years later) presents a remarkable time capsule of Paris's most interesting restaurants of the early to mid-1950s. It also captures a decisive moment in Parisian culinary and restaurant history, as the city emerged from postwar austerity to cater once again to international gastronomes—only this time with fresher flavors and far more streamlined service than had been common in the years before the war.

The book begins by describing for American readers the average experience of lunching in a good, quiet, midpriced Paris restaurant:

> [The] knowing tourist is in the mood for neither an establishment *de grand luxe* nor for one of the *recherché* bistros. Something in between, then. A taxi deposits him before a panel-fronted house with lace curtains in the windows on a side street. There may well be a row of orange trees on the sidewalk and behind them a few marble-topped tables and straw chairs beneath an awning. Of a surety the menu in longhand in purple ink will be posted prominently outside. So much

the better. An *apéritif* will go down well and the bill of fare can be consulted at leisure. Your knowledgeable traveler always has plenty of time at his disposal when eating in France. No self-respecting French restaurant serves food in any way save to order, so that each dish will arrive on the table at the pink perfection of succulence. Besides, there must be time to chill the wine, if rosé or white, or give it a chance to breathe, if red.

. . . You are seated, and the *maître d'hôtel* is discreetly at your elbow to guide your choice. . . . Meanwhile another discreet individual has been hovering near, attired like a waiter but carrying the wine list as his insignia. He is, of course, the wine waiter or *sommelier.* His job is to guide you through another and equally fascinating experience in selection. With your first course and your fish he will suggest, perhaps, one of the *vins de provenance directe* which, as like as not, has been chosen in the last year by the proprietor himself. . . . With the meat course and the cheese you can order a fine vintage wine, one of the treasures of the cellar. Again it is well to heed the sommelier as to a liqueur, for often the house will stock a special regional *marc*, which will provide an interesting change from a trade-name sweet liqueur or brandy.

To Watt's credit, the recipes in the book are accurately transcribed and authentically French. They would also have been, for the most part, impossible for an American home cook to prepare, since nearly all of them required ingredients (such as fresh truffles, fresh foie gras, and skylarks) that were commercially unavailable in the United States.* Moreover they were not for the faint of heart: Chez l'Ami Louis's recipe for *bécasse flambé*, for example, begins with instructions to "pick and clean the woodcocks [but] do not draw them for they are traditionally eaten with their intestines." The recipe then

---

* Only one of the two biographies written about Beard, Robert Clark's *The Solace of Food* (1993), suggests that Beard tested the recipes in *Paris Cuisine.* It does so in passing, and under the assumption that Beard did so while on vacation in New England. But given the range of required ingredients, such testing seems impossible, and Clark's notes don't offer any substantive or credible proof of it.

instructed that the robin-size birds are to be roasted in a hot oven (heads, feet, and all), after which their intestines are to be removed via the anus, chopped fine, and subsequently combined with butter, foie gras, salt, and pepper. This rich and gamey mixture is then to be spread upon a round of toasted brioche and topped with the roasted bird, the whole being flamed with Cognac at the moment of service.

Not all the recipes in the book relied upon luxury ingredients or table-side showmanship, however: Chez Marius's specialty, *pieds et paquets marseillais* ("feet and parcels, Marseille-style"), consists of sheep's trotters and rolled-up mutton tripe immersed in red wine, tomato sauce, and garlic, then topped with slices of salt pork and gently simmered for eight hours, until tender. This humble Provençal soul food, a traditional specialty of Marseille, would never appeal to the American home cook, for the simple reason that sheep's tripe and feet were not considered by most Americans to be fit for consumption. (Even twenty years later, while squiring adventurous American eaters around the South of France, Richard Olney would note that every single person on tour with him had left his or her impeccably cooked *pieds et paquets* untouched on the plate.) But in its presentation of this and other outré delicacies, *Paris Cuisine* attested to the wide variety of culinary experiences just then available in the Paris of the early 1950s. It also demonstrated how, in the words of A. J. Liebling, "*La cuisine Française* is not one cuisine but a score, regional in origin, shading off into one another at their borders and all pulled together at Paris."

James Beard would not put his name on another book on French cooking until 1971, when he published the slim but useful *How to Eat and Drink Your Way Through a French (or Italian) Menu* with his young boyfriend and protégé Gino Cofacci as coauthor. But he nonetheless remained closely attuned to the French food and wine scene throughout the 1950s. A paid consultant to a number of French wine and Cognac producers, he also consulted with French specialty food producers. (Even Louis Vaudable, owner of Maxim's, met with Beard in Paris to discuss starting an American frozen foods line under the Maxim's de Paris name.) The French, eager for American business, welcomed Beard as the biggest American food celebrity of the decade: and indeed, since closing his fashionable New York catering company,

Beard had organized entertainments at the Waldorf-Astoria, starred in his own television cooking show,* and at the same time published three cookbooks. In the coming decade he would work as a restaurant consultant in Philadelphia and New York, publish six more cookbooks, establish a cooking school, and appear on radio and television, as well as in magazines and newspapers, not only as a columnist and journalist, but also as a well-paid spokesperson for the American processed food industry.† He would also lecture on food and wine across the country, give cooking demonstrations, and judge cooking contests.[15]

His 1949 trip to France was similarly diverse in its objectives. Not only did Beard attend various food and wine tastings while visiting Paris and Bordeaux; he also met and came to terms with Alexander Watt about the coauthorship credit of *Paris Cuisine*; met with a number of restaurateurs and food trade groups; and then set off on a high-powered tour of French vineyards and restaurants organized by the San Francisco chapter of André Simon's Wine and Food Society.‡[16] Beard's good friend and neighbor Cecily Brownstone, the longtime food editor of the Associated Press, later recalled the tour (which included a series of monumental lunches and dinners, including one at La Pyramide, for the forty influential American food and wine professionals who had come together for the trip) as "the most marvelous time of my life. I was blue with food."[17]

Not surprisingly, Beard engaged in massive eating binges whenever he went to Paris. Some were so extraordinary that they threatened his health, for Parisian restaurateurs tend to go heavy on the butter, cream, cheeses, and animal fats, much to the peril of the American digestion. One not untypical day, as Beard reported to his good friend Helen Evans Brown, "I had to lunch with the Hennessy [Cognac] group, and we went to the Table du Roy§ again, and had a fabulous mussel dish as a first course . . . rich beyond belief and magnificent. But this

---

* Beard's *Elsie Presents James Beard in "I Love to Eat"* (sponsored by Borden Foods) ran only briefly in 1946 before being replaced by Dione Lucas's *To the Queen's Taste.*
† Beard's biggest clients included Bird's Eye, Green Giant, Borden, and Planters.
‡ Simon (1877–1970), a Frenchman resident in England, was a wine merchant and wine writer who founded the Wine and Food Society in 1933 with fellow gastronome A.J.A. Symons, author of the cult classic *The Quest for Corvo: An Experiment in Biography* (1934).
§ La Rotisserie de la Table du Roy, also known as Le Chef Georges, near the Opéra.

was followed by kidneys and mushrooms with a mustard sauce, which was just as rich as the first course. Then cheese and fruits. I was laid out." After lunch, the three-hundred-pound gourmand went on to cocktails and dinner. Simon Arbellot, a gastronomic journalist who would soon become director of the Kleber-Colombes Guide Touristique, had invited Beard and four other food writers that evening to sample several types of cassoulet, the celebrated bean casserole from the southwest that traditionally included various cuts of pork or pork sausage, duck or goose confit, and mutton or lamb. They did so at Le Grand Véfour, one of the great restaurants of Paris.

The first cassoulet, Beard wrote Brown, was full of "luscious tender little lamb chops cooked in the bean mixture just long enough to flavor them and still remain rare. Also mutton cooked with beans and garlic and parsley, and a delicate and wonderful dish it was. After this came the Toulouse[-style] cassoulet, made with goose, pork, mutton, country sausages . . . and slices of salt pork. . . . Then [we had] a Bordeaux with a fabulous piece of Brie. By the time I had had a coffee and a cognac I could hardly walk."

The three cassoulets shut down Beard's digestion so completely that he finally took to the sidewalks of Paris for relief, noting "three miles later I had a beer, then on to a quart of Perrier and six charcoal tablets, [and] I finally felt I could get into bed without a gas explosion rocking the hotel." Beard's nonstop gluttony on this trip (which continued on the French ocean liner home) resulted in chest pains so severe that he thought he was dying. In a panic he checked into Doctors Hospital on East End Avenue in Manhattan. A week of medical tests, dieting, and bed rest soon made him his old self again, as did daily visits from friends bearing gifts of Champagne, fine Burgundies, vintage Bordeaux, and a seemingly endless supply of snacks, savories, petits fours, and *mignardises*. "Everyone has been so wonderful to me," he wrote Brown from his hospital bed. "Philippe [of the Waldorf], Alexis [Lichine, and all] the [other] importers [have been so generous that] I could have a fully stocked bar here if I wanted it."

As the greatest and most visible food celebrity in America, Beard would continue to develop his name, face, and rotund silhouette over the coming decade. Like many present-day food and lifestyle celebrities, he saw his work as that of a multifaceted, celebrity-driven businessman, one who had far more (and far better) income-generating possibilities open to him than mere authorship. Employees did his writing for him; others solicited and negotiated prices for his public appearances; others kept his accounts. Others organized and assisted at his cooking school; still others maintained his household and his kitchen. Like Andy Warhol, whose art studio became a self-described "Factory" in which many participated in the creation of art but only one received the credit as artist, Beard developed an instantly recognizable celebrity identity as America's leading gastronome and gourmand, and was rapidly turning that composite identity into the public face of a highly successful, income-focused business. But as a result, his visits to Paris could be only brief—his many activities as a celebrity entrepreneur demanded his full-time attention back home.

FIVE

Out on the Town with Paul and Julia

Even as James Beard and Alexander Watt published *Paris Cuisine* in the United States, Paul and Julia Child were exploring the Parisian restaurant scene. The couple had been eating and drinking adventurously since first meeting in Sri Lanka during the war, but life in Paris now brought their explorations to new heights of pleasure. Paul Child had been the one with the initial interest in (and knowledge of) French cuisine, having followed Parisian restaurants (both via restaurant guides and actual visits to them) since his youthful days in Paris in the 1920s. His wife by comparison had not traveled to Europe before the war, nor did she come from a food-conscious family. Her father, whom she later described as an "Old Guard Republican of the blackest and most violently Neanderthal stripe," had made a fortune in Southern California real estate development, and her mother came to her marriage with inherited family wealth—wealth that Julia in turn inherited after her mother's early death, in 1938. Ten years later, thanks to a rich father and a maternal inheritance that began as "somewhere between $100,000 and $200,000 . . . and a lot of stock, all in IBM"[1] (and was substantially more a decade later, with an approximate relative economic status, in today's money, of more than $12,000,000, not including the IBM stock), Julia Child moved to Paris with a very large amount of discretionary income.

Paul Child, a largely self-taught artist and designer who had never attended university and had little money of his own, had taken a job in Paris with the U.S. Information Service, a federal agency charged with disseminating pro-American and anti-Communist propaganda. While based in Paris, he would oversee the agency's public exhibitions and photography projects. Unlike most public servants, the couple disembarked in Le Havre in November 1948 with a large number of possessions, ones that reflected Julia Child's extraordinary material good fortune: fourteen pieces of luggage, six steamer trunks, a gas-powered refrigerator, and a new Buick Roadmaster station wagon. Rather than take the train to the French capital, they climbed into their capacious new Buick, which they had ironically nicknamed the "Blue Flash,"* and drove there through the damp and chilly Norman countryside, stopping in bombed-out Rouen for a memorable (and now legendary) restaurant lunch.

During their first days in Paris, the couple stayed at the Hôtel du Pont Royal—a luxury hotel at the intersection of the rue du Bac and the rue Montalembert, just off the boulevard St. Germain and four blocks from the Seine. Shortly thereafter they found a long-term furnished rental just a few blocks west, in the Faubourg St. Germain: "a wonderful apartment, top floor of a big old private house, and furnished in late 19th century Versailles and authentic 1902," as she later described the place to her friend Avis DeVoto.† "Gilt, petit point and mirrors in the *Salon Louis Quelconque*;‡ real leather wall-paper in the dining room, with real sags in it. And the vast master bedroom is all covered with green material, with a marble relief of a Knight of Malta over the fireplace, and the walls peppered with hanging bibelots, and big pieces of Boule cabinetry, and moldings, and big French

---

* A "blue flash" is a phenomenon that occurs with the detonation of an atomic bomb; the irony of the nickname lay in the fact that the Childs' car was a station wagon, not a sports car. Joking references to atomic fission were common during the 1940s and 1950s, as evidenced by French designer Louis Réard's 1946 "bikini," a bathing suit introduced two months after the bomb was dropped on the Bikini Atoll and subsequently promoted as "the atom bomb of fashion."

† Avis DeVoto, wife of historian and professor Bernard DeVoto, was a book reviewer, editor, and enthusiastic home cook who later helped Child to place *Mastering the Art of French Cooking* with Knopf.

‡ *Quelconque* is French for "whatever."

windows looking over a beautiful garden. [The] kitchen [is] upstairs, big and sunny, with the steeples of Ste. Clothilde for a view, all newly painted green and white. . . . I'd happily stay right here for the rest of my life."[2]

The neighborhood was, in fact, very dull, since it was mostly taken up with government offices; just down the street stood the Palais Bourbon, housing France's main governing body, the National Assembly. Julia had quickly taken the stuffing out of their distinguished but stodgy address, 81, rue de l'Université, by dubbing it the "Roo de Loo," a nickname punningly suggestive of a toilet. Rent for their large but faded and drafty apartment in this tremendously grand neighborhood was eight dollars; by comparison, the couple's first Parisian lunch (at the restaurant Michaud,* at the intersection of the rue des Saints-Pères and rue Jacob) cost three dollars—that is, more than a third their monthly rent. But though the expense of dining out was high compared with the cost of housing, the couple had absolutely no problem paying, and they indulged themselves gastronomically from their very first moments in France. Rich meals and multiple bottles of wine were in fact a fine strategy for anyone negotiating the persistent cold and damp of dark, wintry, fuel-starved Paris—so long, of course, as one could afford it.

If Child's "memoir" of Paris is to be believed (it was written by her grandnephew, and like many ghostwritten celebrity memoirs, cannot always be trusted in its details),† the young couple stumbled upon one of France's oldest and grandest dining establishments, Le Grand Véfour, only while taking a walk through the gardens of the Palais-Royal. The lunch service had just started, and as the memoir recalls, "Though we were hardly used to such elegance, we looked at each other and said, 'Why not?'" The memoir continues on to describe a happy afternoon:

---

*Now the restaurant Le Comptoir des Saints Pères.
† *My Life in France* (2006), a pastiche of a memoir, was written by Alex Prud'homme. Julia Child died two years before its publication. While Prud'homme states that he based the book on recollections Child shared with him, much of the writing is verbatim transcription (without attribution) from her papers in the Schlesinger Library. In keeping with its as-told-to celebrity memoir format, the book features no endnotes, no bibliography, and no statement by Prud'homme about his methodology.

We were seated in a gorgeous semi-circular banquette.* The headwaiter laid menus before us, and then the sommelier, an imposing but kindly Bordeaux specialist in his fifties, arrived. He introduced himself with a nod: "Monsieur Hénocq." The restaurant began to fill up, and over the course of the next two hours we had a leisurely and near-perfect luncheon. The meal began with little shells filled with sea scallops and mushrooms robed in a classically beautiful winey cream sauce. Then we had a wonderful duck dish, and cheeses, and a rich dessert, followed by coffee. As we left in a glow of happiness, we shook hands all around and promised almost tearfully to return.

What remained with me most vividly as we strolled away was the graciousness of our reception and the deep pleasure I'd experienced from sitting in those beautiful surroundings. Here we were, two young people obviously from rather modest circumstances, and we had been treated with the utmost cordiality, as if we were honored guests. The service was deft and understated, and the food was spectacular. It was expensive but, as Paul said, "you are so hypnotized by everything there that you feel grateful as you pay the bill."

We went back to the Véfour every month or so after that, especially once we'd learned how to get invited there by wealthy and in-the-know friends. Because I was tall and outgoing and Paul was so knowledgeable about wine and food, Monsieur Hénocq and the Véfour's wait staff always gave us the royal treatment.

Although the memoir deceptively suggests that Child and her husband had little money to spare on dining out,† the date books re-

---

* Prud'homme's detail is incorrect: there were no "gorgeous semicircular banquettes" at Le Grand Véfour in 1949, nor are there any there today. (The restaurant's decoration and furnishings are neoclassical, dating to 1784.)
† In *My Life in France*, Alex Prud'homme (writing in the voice of Julia Child) notes that out of Paul Child's salary the couple had a mere fifteen dollars weekly to spare on "amusements" such as restaurant-going, and then adds, "I had a small amount of family money that produced a modest income, although we were determined to save it." But Julia Child's two biographers, Noël Riley Fitch and Bob Spitz, have documented the size of Child's inheritance (which was not small) and

cording the Childs' first months in Paris tell a very different story, and surely a more accurate one, for they are filled with notations describing substantial and costly meals in restaurants.[3] So too are the couple's many letters to Paul's accomplished twin brother (and *his* wealthy wife) back home in the United States. But faced with a grand apartment that "had no central heating and was as cold and damp as Lazarus' tomb,"[4] the Childs found that the city's better restaurants offered a toasty-warm alternative to nights in, since even the more modest restaurants had well-stoked heating stoves in their dining rooms. Newspaper columnist Art Buchwald, a good friend of the Childs and their occasional dining companion, later described these years as "the Golden Age for Americans in France . . . the dollar was the strongest currency in the world, and the franc was one of the weakest."[5] But there were other reasons the period was a golden opportunity for those Americans (or Frenchmen with sufficient income) to enjoy a restaurant meal: French meats, dairy products, and produce were once again available, and of the finest quality; and with food rationing just ended, Parisian restaurateurs were eager to resurrect classic French cuisine, so much of which had been impossible to prepare or serve to anyone, even the Germans, during the war years and their immediate aftermath.

These dining-out adventures were not only a bargain but an education. Although Paul Child was passionate about French food and wine, he had always wanted to learn and experience more. Now that he was no longer a penniless art student, he could order any food or wine he liked, at pretty much any restaurant. Julia, meanwhile, enjoyed the role of student just as much as her new husband enjoyed his role of teacher, translator, and explainer. So the experience was enjoyable for both of them, and learning about food and wine a hobby they shared. Paul would discuss various foods and wines in French with waiters and sommeliers during the course of their long, leisurely evenings out; Julia, though struggling with the language, listened and learned. Pleasure and good feeling were everywhere. Restaurant proprietors loved the couple, for the Childs knew the importance of

---

also document the Childs' restaurant dining during their Paris years (including their relative lack of concern about its expense).

making reservations, of requesting special foods or wines in advance, and of arriving on time. They drank an aperitif while consulting the menu, took their wine choices very seriously, and had a real passion not only for French food traditions but also for the particulars of food preparation. Best of all, the couple had plenty of money to spend, and they spent it freely and well—which is to say, with discernment and intelligence as well as with obvious pleasure.

Apart from Michaud, which became their local favorite, the Childs began following the Parisian custom of visiting particular restaurants for particular dishes. Having been stunned shortly after disembarking the transatlantic liner by the *sole meunière* at the restaurant La Couronne in Rouen—Child later credited the simple but extraordinary combination of finest Dover sole and finest Norman butter with forever changing her appreciation of food—she was delighted to discover that La Couronne had a sister restaurant in Paris, La Truite, run by the same family and serving the same seafood just as beautifully. She was able not only to enjoy that same dish of sole again, but also to try a more sophisticated version of it, *sole à la normande*, featuring an elegant garnish of shellfish, shrimp, and mushrooms and/or truffles. (Child liked this second version so much that she later included the recipe for it in a cookbook.) And indeed it was a dish of historic dimensions, created in 1837 by Langlais, chef of Le Rocher de Cancale, the famed restaurant on the rue Montorgueil whose customers had included Brillat-Savarin, Grimod de la Reynière, Dumas *père*, Victor Hugo, Alfred de Musset, and, most important, Balzac, who featured the restaurant repeatedly in *La Comédie Humaine*, most memorably in *La Cousine Bette*.*

The Childs also liked the *poulet gratiné*† at Au Gourmet; the tripe at Pharamond; the snails at L'Escargot d'Or; and the onion soup—*de rigueur* after a late night visit to Les Halles—at Au Pied de Cochon. For choucroute they went, of course, to Brasserie Lipp, just opposite

---

*The French critic Robert Courtine, who describes the dish as "a 'monument' of the French grande cuisine," writes about it extensively in *The Hundred Glories of French Cooking*. For more on Le Rocher de Cancale, see Anka Muhlstein's *Balzac's Omelet*.
†Richard Olney would include the recipe for this little-known dish in *Simple French Food*. Sautéed chicken parts are set in a rich custard (flavored with lemon, white wine, and Gruyère), then topped with butter-toasted bread crumbs and finished in a hot oven.

the fabled literary café Les Deux Magots, where they frequently took a cocktail, aperitif, coffee, or Cognac. On special occasions, they went to Prunier, so famous for its fish, or to Lapérouse, the ancient and celebrated restaurant on the quai des Grands Augustins. Still, it was the intimate Le Grand Véfour, with its unbelievably elegant neoclassical interiors fronting the gardens of the Palais-Royal, that quickly became their great favorite—and with good reason, for the restaurant, renowned since its founding in the eighteenth century, had recently come under the ownership of an ambitious young chef, Raymond Oliver, whose rich, no-holds-barred approach to cooking showed the influence of his Gascon roots.

At each restaurant, no matter how fancy or simple, a new social experience seemed to await. "Food is a great national sport [here], indulged in by all classes," Julia wrote home to a friend, delighted that she could participate so easily and happily in French culture simply by dining out. "One's best evenings are composed of a good dinner, and nothing else is necessary, and it takes the whole evening."[6] For a woman who could not help feeling something of an outsider— struggling with the language, she also felt herself to be "a giantess" compared with most Frenchmen*—the gracious hospitality she experienced through this early restaurant-going gave her a good deal of encouragement and reassurance. In fact, Child soon felt "I must really *be* French . . . I loved the people, the food, the lay of the land, the civilized atmosphere, and the generous pace of life."[7]

Although thirty-six, Child had never before been to Europe. But she could not have had a better guide to French culture than her husband, who spent five years in Paris† as a young man. Even though he hadn't been in France for the past eighteen years, Paul Child (who was ten years older than his wife) had been during those early days the lover of Edith Kennedy, a wealthy and cultured Boston socialite

---

* If Marcel Ophüls's documentary *The Sorrow and the Pity* is to be believed, a Frenchman of the post–World War II era was considered *"un colosse"* at five foot nine. Similarly Child's future collaborator Simone Beck, who stood just five eight, was often teased about her height—most notably by her second husband, Jean Fischbacher, who upon first seeing her emerge from her little Simca sedan observed, "what a big chassis for such a little car" (Beck, *Food and Friends*, p. 91).

† For part of this time, however, he had taught school in the Dordogne, a region in the southwest of France.

twenty years his senior who kept an apartment on the rue d'Assas. Edith "Slingsby" Kennedy had mentored Paul Child during their seventeen-year involvement, and during his years with her he had met Gertrude Stein and Alice Toklas (who lived just around the corner from Kennedy) as well as many other American writers and artists, including Gerald and Sara Murphy, Richard and Alice Lee Myers, and the poet and newspaperman Paul Mowrer. As a result, Mowrer (and his wife, Hadley Richardson, who had married Mowrer after divorcing Ernest Hemingway) became very attached to Julia and Paul Child shortly after their arrival; the Mowrers often asked the Childs out for weekends at their country home thirty miles west of Paris, near Crécy-en-Brie.

When Mowrer's stepson, Jack "Bumby" Hemingway, chose to marry in Paris in June 1949, the Mowrers asked Julia to serve as matron of honor—for their son's fiancée, Puck Whitlock, an Idaho divorcée, had no friends with her for the wedding. During the breakfast that followed at a little Norman restaurant called La Vallée d'Auge, Paul had bumped into Jack Hemingway's godmother,* Alice Toklas, and he introduced Julia to her. No substantial discussion of cooking could have taken place between the two women, as Julia had not yet begun her studies at the Cordon Bleu, and Toklas was still in the early stages of planning her cookbook. Still, in her memoir, Child (or perhaps Alex Prud'homme) described Toklas that day as "an odd little bird in a muslin dress and a big floppy hat." The Childs liked Toklas enough to include her in a Bastille Day buffet dinner for twenty at their apartment a year later, a party Samuel and Narcissa Chamberlain also attended. The evening's pièce de résistance was an impressive *ballottine* of veal that Child had worked days to prepare, stuffing it with a Cognac-and-Madeira-scented forcemeat of ground veal, finely chopped mushrooms, foie gras, and blanched chard leaves, and serving it with an unctuous Madeira-truffle sauce. The Child-Prud'homme memoir described Toklas that evening as "a fleeting, wren-like person in a tan pongee accordion-pleated skirt and wide-brimmed pongee-colored hat, [and] so small that the hat hid her face until she looked

---

*Ernest and Hadley Hemingway had named Gertrude Stein and Alice Toklas cogodmothers to Jack. Hadley Mowrer remained friendly with both women after her divorce and remarriage. Ernest Hemingway ultimately came to hate Toklas (and his hatred of her is clearly articulated in the posthumous *A Moveable Feast*). He was not present at his son's 1949 wedding.

up and you noticed that it was Alice B. Toklas. She always seemed to be popping up in Paris like that." In any event, Toklas did not linger to sample the rich, heavy *ballotine* on that sweltering evening; "she stayed only for a glass of wine."[8]

❧

As they settled into their Parisian life, Paul Child found himself taking the roles toward his young wife that Slingsby Kennedy had taken toward him more than twenty years earlier: lover and mentor, instructor and guide. Teaching and encouraging came easily to him, since as a younger man he had worked as a tutor and teacher; and he was good at sharing knowledge and encouraging creativity. He was also very good with his hands and enjoyed craft and handiwork of every sort, including bachelor-style cooking. His career as an artist had never really taken off, and he did not much like his new job, but he was intellectually and artistically *au courant*, a fine conversationalist, physically fit, and an ardent lover. Even though he was destined to be passed over for promotions—a great many people, including Julia's fellow Smith College alumna Charlotte Turgeon, simply did not like him, finding him oddly antisocial—Paul Child adored his wife, and she, him. Around this time Julia Child described him to her friend Avis DeVoto as "an able painter, [and] a most talented photographer . . . [who] can really do just about anything, including making a french type omelette. Carpenter, cabinet-builder, intellectual, wine-bibber, wrestler. A most interesting man, and a lovely husband."

Paul Child's devotion to Julia, and to the life that they were making together, is evident in the many letters he wrote and photographs he took during those years in Paris. During their few periods of separation—for instance, when Julia accompanied her father and stepmother on a sightseeing journey to Italy—the couple often wrote each other daily: "I *hate* doing anything without you," Julia wrote in one note that included her own roughly drawn image of a heart pierced by a phallus.* "I am not a whole woman without you . . . I

---

* The scribbled illustration is Julia Child's shorthand evocation of a gouache recently made for her by Paul and given to her as a gift, depicting an engorged phallus piercing a heart (both are in the Child Papers, Schlesinger Library).

want to come home to me husband."[9] Despite being in his late forties, Paul Child had a strong sex drive, and Julia was delighted by his continued attentions. In another letter to Avis DeVoto, she discreetly noted about the French habit of making love at midday that "the woman is in the home and the husband comes home for lunch . . . (I love that!)"[10] In later life, she was more open about it: "I would go to [cooking] school in the morning," Julia told a reporter, "then for lunch time, I would go home and make love to my husband."[11] Paul's delight in his wife, meanwhile, led him to write poems to her. One, a birthday sonnet, concludes,

> . . . *Accept from me, your ever-loving mate,*
> *This acclamation shaped in fourteen lines,*
> *Whose inner truth belies its outer sight;*
> *For never were there foods, nor were there wines*
> *Whose flavor equals yours for sheer delight.*
> *Oh luscious Dish! Oh gustatory pleasure!*
> *You satisfy my taste-buds beyond measure!*

Even more charming than this poem are the annual valentines Paul Child began creating and sending out to family and friends shortly after their marriage, usually including a photo or illustration of the couple.[12] In one, the two are nude in a bubble bath. In another, they sit, each wearing a red paper heart, gazing at each other and smiling. Their valentine for 1951, however, is possibly most charming of all: an elegant color illustration of a single playing card which at one end depicts Paul as Knave of Hearts (raffishly mustachioed and wielding two paintbrushes) and at the other end depicts Julia as Queen of Hearts (bosomy, wielding a cooking spoon). The two are joined at the hip. Together they are one—which is to say, different aspects of a single, and singular—being. And in fact, they often now referred to themselves as "Paul-and-Julia" or "Julia-and-Paul."

Loving couples often think of themselves as one—and Paul Child may have been predisposed to this feeling because he was similarly bonded, for better or worse, to his identical twin brother, Charlie. But in the case of the Childs, the joining of man and wife into one entity was particularly strong. Even in their correspondence they present a united front: "Paul-and-Julia" was how they corresponded (frequently and at length) with Charlie Child and his wife, Freddie* (the couple playfully wrote back as "Charlie-and-Freddie"). The twin brothers had always been competitive, with Charlie Child widely considered the family success—which perhaps accounts for the show-offy way in which Paul-and-Julia describe their many extravagant adventures in Paris in their letters to Charlie-and-Freddie. Freddie Child's fortune was larger than Julia's, but Julia Child came to Paul not only with an inheritance, but also with an enormously sunny and attractive personality—something Paul distinctly lacked. Paul's profound connection to (and dependence upon) his extroverted wife perhaps explains the great investment of time and energy he made in her education, and in the development of her vocation. He would help at first in the shaping of her mind, her skills, and her ambitions; later, he would advise, proofread, and photograph for the illustrations in her cookbooks; later still, he would conceptualize, organize, and enable her television stardom—an investment of time, energy, and creativity so profound and extraordinary that M.F.K. Fisher would later describe the Childs' union to their mutual friend Eda Lord as "their strange Trilby-Svengali relationship."[13] So while Julia Child may have married a man who was introverted, neurasthenic, depressive, and unpopular among coworkers, she had also married a man who was ardently attracted to her, talented and intelligent, and moreover profoundly dedicated to her education, happiness, and eventual professional success—which, by virtue of their shared Paul-and-Julia identity, would also be *his* success. He was that rare thing in a husband, then or now: a man utterly willing to dedicate himself to his wife's career.

❧

Although the Childs moved in an interesting world—apart from Paul's work contacts at the embassy, they knew many American artists,

---

* About Charles and Freddie Child: "he is a painter, tried making his living doing portraits after the war and found it hard to count on that alone, so does fabric designs also. She is a darling, red hair, good looks. They lived over here for about 5 years . . . love food and wine . . . and are just great fun" (Child to DeVoto, *As Always, Julia*, p. 93).

writers, and journalists*—they soon began to desire authentically "French" adventures. Paris tourists, journalists, and embassy folk were all very well, but the Childs wanted to know some "real" Parisians, and to experience the world as the French did. Julia Child now made a great effort to learn French, and in doing so began reading French literature, ultimately gravitating toward the richly textured novels of Balzac: "[I] was amazed, moved, enchanted, and said *mmm* to myself, how could he have known so much about human nature back there in 1840?" she wrote Avis DeVoto. "So I read a biography of him by [Stefan] Zweig, and then more Balzac, and [now I] find myself *une Balzacienne engloutie.*† . . . It is the stuff you can chew on and live on. I still have 85 books of him to read."[14] In another instance she noted, "What a man he was, a real giant and genius, a great and tragic figure, a fool and a romantic and a penetrating observer, and an absorbing passionate character."[15] Balzac's earthy sensualism, gargantuan appetites (for food, for drink, for public acclaim), and his shrewd awareness of the politics of everyday life, combined with his openness to all varieties of love, sexual attraction, and sexual activity, gave Child sudden access to an authentically French (if early nineteenth-century) way of thinking. Tellingly, her favorite of his novels was *Le Lys dans La Vallée* (*The Lily of the Valley*, 1835), the tale of a neglected, despised, and penniless young man who develops a passion for a woman of wealth, good family, and property. The plot was based in Balzac's own youthful experiences, but it also bore no small resemblance to Paul Child's romance with Julia.

As their acquaintance with Paris grew, the Childs found that the restaurants frequented by Americans bored them, no matter how good the food—that boredom often compounded by the know-nothing conversation of the wealthy American friends-of-family who tended to invite them out. Worse, many of them revealed themselves, during the course of a meal, to be rabid Republicans, members of the John Birch Society, and supporters of Joseph McCarthy. And few were authentically interested in French food, wine, language, or culture. "Here is a class with all the money, all the leisure, all the educational

---

*Some of their more notable writer friends included Theodore H. (and Nancy) White and Irwin (and Marian) Shaw.
†Roughly, "a fan of Balzac, engulfed by his genius."

facilities," Julia fumed in a letter. "And what does it produce but, on the whole, a lot of Old Guard Republicans with blinders on, and women who rarely develop out of the child class and create just about nothing. . . . [They are] distressing examples of conspicuous waste of good human material. They are usually the salt of the earth . . . but almost to a man anti-Semitic, anti-foreign, anti-progress, anti–Phi Beta Kappa, anti-contemporary art and music; and living in a little compartment walled about by their money."[16] After one such dinner at the Tour d'Argent, Julia noted "the restaurant was excellent in every way, but so pricey that every guest was American." Paul, meanwhile, described watching an American woman there "tasting a Clos [de] Vougeot '29, [and] say[ing], 'Well, I don't know about this, I don't believe I could drink it without stirring quite a bit of sugar into it.'"[17]

Seeking an alternative, the couple sought out restaurants with an atmosphere consistent with their sense of themselves as culturally informed, liberal, and cosmopolitan gentlefolk—or, as Julia Child liked to put it, "Upper Bohemians,"* meaning people who were bohemian in spirit but financially comfortable. The Restaurant des Artistes on the rue Lepic soon became their favorite hideaway. Modest in size and appearance, and located in the legendary artists' enclave atop the Montmartre (but worlds apart from that other artists' enclave, Montparnasse, so thoroughly overrun by boorish American tourists since the mid-1920s), the Restaurant des Artistes also appealed to Paul Child's sense of himself as an artist, for in his free time he liked to paint as well as photograph. Julia later described the Des Artistes as "a small, neat place with only ten tables [but] some fifty thousand bottles of exquisite wine." Its amiable chef, Pierre Mengelatte, had worked there since 1936. In time (and though Child never knew it) he would become a substantial French culinary figure in his own right: a president of l'Académie Culinaire de France, he also edited a revised edition of Henri-Paul Pellaprat's L'Art Culinaire Moderne, and wrote a masterful 1,200-page, heavily illustrated cookbook of grande cuisine, entitled Buffets & Réceptions.

---

* "Are you Upper Bohemians?" Child asked Avis DeVoto as they came to know each other through their correspondence. "We seem to fit into [the bohemian category]—but I don't like to eat off card tables, and I hate to sit on the floor" (Child to DeVoto, As Always, Julia, p. 74).

In November 1950, to celebrate the second anniversary of their arrival in Paris, the Childs very deliberately chose this chic little spot for their dinner, and the menu choices they made that night suggest their growing sophistication about French food and wine. They began, in the French manner, with an aperitif, followed by an *entrée* of grilled *loup de mer* accompanied by a *vin jaune* from the Jura (a specialist's wine that, like sherry, is aged under a film of yeast, which ultimately gives the wine a distinctively dry, nutty character). They moved on to a distinguished Saint-Émilion with their *plat*—venison escalopes for him, roasted larks for her—for, like her cat, Minette, Julia loved feasting on a wide variety of little birds. On another occasion at Des Artistes, she would order a roasted partridge "nesting on a toasty crouton . . . its nicely browned head, shorn of its feathers but not of neck or beak, curled around its shoulder [and] its feet, minus claws, folded up at either side of its breast."[18] And on yet another evening, Paul would write his brother, "Julie ordered a *vanneau*. . . . You wouldn't think people would eat lap-wings, would you? Must say the damn thing tasted mighty fine." The couple concluded their 1950 anniversary dinner by savoring the last of their fine Bordeaux with a perfectly ripened Brie, then lingered into the night over coffee, Cognac, and cigarettes. Only two years into their new life in France they were dining like the most knowledgeable Parisians.

Des Artistes remained their favorite little getaway all during their stay. A year later, when they entertained the glamorous actress and novelist Cornelia Otis Skinner—whose *Our Hearts Were Young and Gay*, an autobiographical comic novel about two young American women in Paris, had been published to acclaim in 1942, then made into a hit movie in 1944—Paul sensed that this fellow "Upper Bohemian" (though a working actress, playwright, and *New Yorker* contributor, Skinner was also a member of New York's ultraexclusive Colony and Cosmopolitan Clubs) would respond well to its offbeat yet entirely "correct" atmosphere.

After a matinee at the Comédie Française, the three started their evening at their "Roo de Loo" apartment with a bottle of sparkling Vouvray, which the Childs favored, as many French do, as a refreshing, amusing, and less acidic alternative to Champagne. Then they headed up to Montmartre for the special dinner Paul had ordered a day in

advance: *soufflé de turbot, sauce mousseline,** followed by *poulet éstragon*†
accompanied by a Beaune, 1928. "It was a dream-meal," Paul wrote
his brother, for Paul adored the company of beautiful, highly intelligent, well-born women, and that night he had had two of them all to
himself—as well as a fine dinner and an even finer aged Burgundy.

⚜

As time passed, however, the Childs dined out less frequently. Julia
was learning to cook, and enjoyed making meals at home. More important, all these rich restaurant foods were proving terribly difficult
to digest, particularly for a couple that had arrived in Paris with pre-
existing stomach ailments. As Julia explained to Avis DeVoto, "We
both got amoebic dysentery when we were in the Far East during the
war, and it was never discovered in the USA . . . but when we got
over here, all this good rich food brought it on with violence. . . . We
are gradually getting rid of it, but we find we can't eat with the pure
gourmandise‡ we'd like, and that *les alcöols* don't agree with us at all
(no martinis)."[19] Paul's amoebiasis was far worse than Julia's. As Julia
wrote Charlie Child, Paul "went to a French Doc who specialized in
'the American Stomach in Paris.' Doc says, 'you've got the old national complaint, m'boy . . . *coup de foie* (liver & bilious). . . . So he was
put on a diet of *no* fried foods, *no* raw foods, *no* rich sauces, *no* more
than 1 egg [per day], *no* alcohol except 1 glass of vintage wine."[20] When
even these drastic restrictions were not enough to cure him, Paul began a course of antibiotics so strong that it brought on horrific side
effects: as he described it, a "ghastly week [of] violent diarrhea, pains
in stomach, nausea, ringing ears, loss of memory, [and I] thought (for
the millionth time) 'I am probably dying.' "

"I, too, had tummy troubles," Julia later wrote. "My stomach was

---

*In this tour-de-force dish, the costly, firm-fleshed flatfish is split across the top, stuffed with a
fish soufflé, then roasted and served whole, with the risen soufflé emerging from the fish—and in
this case it is accompanied by a *sauce mousseline*, a hollandaise lightened with whipped cream.
Robert Courtine, in *The Hundred Glories of French Cooking*, describes and pictures the same dish
accompanied by a *sauce au champagne* (p. 91). Child, Beck, and Bertholle included a vastly simplified version of the dish, "*Filets de Poisson en Soufflé, Sauce Mousseline Sabayon*," in *Mastering the Art of
French Cooking*, volume 1, substituting far less costly morsels of flaked flounder for whole turbot,
and replacing the whipped cream in the sauce with a combination of cream and fish stock.
†A classic French dish of chicken in a sauce of tarragon, cream, shallots, and white wine.
‡Roughly, "a passion for eating good things in large quantities."

no longer a brass-bound, iron-lined, eat-and-drink-any amount of anything-anywhere, anytime machine that it had been. . . . 'It must be something in the water,' I'd say to myself. . . . A French doctor diagnosed my persistent nausea as nothing more than good old *crise de foie*—a liver attack. . . . Looking back on the rich gorge of food and drink we'd been enjoying, I don't find the diagnosis surprising. Lunch almost every day had consisted of something like *sole meunière, ris de veau a la crème*, and half a bottle of wine. Dinner might be *escargots, rognons flambés*, and another half bottle of wine. Then there was a regular flow of aperitifs and cocktails and Cognacs."[21]

With the flare-up of this debilitating stomach ailment, the initial "honeymoon" phase of Paul and Julia Child's experience of French cuisine began drawing to its close. Even Le Grand Véfour, they discovered, was capable of poisoning them: "having been ptomained at the Grand Véfour . . . on some lobster bisque," Paul wrote his brother, "we now say the Hell with it." That particular lobster bisque had given Paul five days of flulike symptoms, a rash all over his body, and a week of diarrhea. No wonder, then, that the couple now sought the simple pleasures available to them at home through *la cuisine de bonne femme*.

But wine—which was easier on the digestion than the strong cocktails the Childs habitually preferred[22]*—was a different matter entirely. Despite his stomach troubles, Paul was more and more fascinated with fine French wines, spending money on them accordingly. He had first become interested in wine, he later told an interviewer, "in Italy, in 1925, where I lived as a tutor of two boys, whose father and mother were musicians, Americans (and wealthy), and interested in wines and food. So was I, but my purse and my interest in owning wines had to wait another 20 years for fulfillment." Julia, when later asked about Paul's growing wine hobby, put the case even more succinctly: "as a poor artist in the 1920s he had not been able to afford the good stuff."[23] He started collecting wines in 1946, in Washington, D.C.; but nothing available through those grimly un-

---

* The Childs smoked and drank with abandon. According to Julia, a substantial portion of Paul's Paris salary went toward the purchase of American cigarettes. And as *Time* magazine later noted, "No purist, [Julia Child] thinks nothing of belting down a couple of stiff bourbons at home just before Paul serves a superb Grands Échezeaux from his 350-bottle wine cellar. She keeps tubs of Marlboros on the kitchen table, gaily dips into them for a smoke between courses."

derstocked District of Columbia liquor stores could have prepared him for the delights now available to him through the *cavistes** of Paris—where, again according to Julia, he "discovered the wine merchant Nicolas,[†] who [during the late 1940s] had access to an unusually broad and deep selection of vintages, some of which had been buried before the war [and] hidden from the hated *boches*."[‡] The perfectly aged bottles that the wine shop had apparently made available to its preferred local customers (but only discreetly and for a very limited time) were of staggering quality and value: Paul recorded purchasing a 1928 La Mission Haut-Brion for 600 francs (then, about $1.20); a 1929 bottle of Chambertin Clos de Bèze[§] for 700 francs ($1.40); and an 1899 Château La Lagune for 800 francs ($1.60). The shop delivered each bottle by hand, the precious cargo having been set upright and brought to serving temperature at the shop hours earlier, then wrapped in a cloth napkin and tucked into a basket for gentlest possible travel to the Child apartment on the "Roo de Loo."[24]

The Childs did not confine themselves to purchasing wine from Paris *cavistes*, however, for Paul enjoyed the challenge (and distinction) of stocking and managing his own wine cellar. (Their apartment, like many in Paris, came with a secure basement *cave* for the storage and aging of wine at the appropriate temperature and humidity.) As a result, the couple began visiting vineyards to taste wines, and to buy them from regional *négociants*. The capacious "Blue Flash" facilitated these shopping trips in regions famous for wine—not only the Loire, Chablis, and Burgundy (including the Mâconnais and the Beaujolais), but also, in time, the northern Rhône, the southern Rhône, and Provence. Sometimes the Childs would make their trips in the course of a day; mostly, however, they made multiday excursions.

In touring these vineyards and cellars, they found themselves acquiring an entirely new appreciation for French wines: many had

---

* A common term both for a wine shop and for its proprietor.

† Contrary to this odd statement (which is taken from the Prud'homme memoir), Nicolas is not a person but a company. Founded in 1822 by Louis Nicolas, today it is the largest chain of wine stores in Paris, with 494 shops throughout France.

‡ Pejorative French slang for Germans.

§ Chambertin, "the king of wines," has been widely recognized as one of the finest Burgundies since the days of Louis XIV; Clos de Bèze is among the finest of the *grand cru* Chambertins. Today a bottle of similar age (twenty years) would cost a wine lover approximately $2,500 retail.

been cultivated by the same families for generations, with grapes tended and picked by hand, then pressed, aged, and bottled either on the property or close by. While leery of the various trade associations— in one letter, Julia noted that "on our last day through the [Burgundy] wine territory, we stopped at the Château du Clos [de] Vougeot. . . . Inside has been pretty much crapped up . . . by the Tastevin types* . . . which I gather is really a great big rotary club"—the Childs were charmed by the hardworking Frenchmen and -women who went out of their way to assist them with on-site tastings and purchases. "We went up to Dijon and met *our* wine merchants, Noirot & Carrière," Julia noted in the same letter to her brother-in-law. "It is now run by Mme. Lancomm. . . . Her husband died just before the war from eating poisoned mussels in Marseille, and her son was killed in the war [but] she is a charming warm nice woman [with whom] we proceeded to do a bit of '*dégustation*,' in big snifter glasses. First, we had a Vosne-Romanée 1937. Delicious. Then a Pommard 1937. Superb. Then a Volnay 1925. Wooo. . . . It was a lovely friendly time."

Selecting the right wines for their dinner parties now became a deliberate, collaborative project for Paul-and-Julia. "When we're planning a meal [and] it's something special, [Julia and I will] discuss the wines to be served in relation to who's coming," Paul told an interviewer years later. "Then we check our [cellar] chart to make sure we have two bottles [and if we have two bottles] the transaction is recorded."[25] Discussing the wine beforehand was important, since the Childs subscribed to the French notion that wines chosen for a dinner should not only suit the food but match the significance and tone of the occasion, as well as the likely interests and taste preferences of the expected guests—so there was much to take into consideration, and everything was to be most carefully deliberated.

Paul's various duties of acquiring, storing, aging, selecting, and then serving good wine were all highly ritualized, and engaging in these duties pleased him no end. In going to such elaborate lengths together over securing and selecting their wines, the Childs could

---

* The Confrérie des Chevaliers du Tastevin, a group founded in 1934 to promote Burgundian food and wine.

anticipate with pleasure the evening ahead of them, then enjoy themselves at the table in a way that demonstrated both their connoisseurship
of French wines and their care and consideration for their guests.
Moreover, as Julia now presided over the presentation and serving of
the food, Paul took on the pouring, serving, and discussion of the
evening's wines as his job—thereby achieving his own brief moment
in the limelight. In a typical letter to his brother of 1950, Paul noted
with satisfaction that they had given "dinner last night for 6 [and it]
went off fine beginning with oysters. . . . We had a Chablis '37 with
the oysters, a Corton '37 with the beef & a Volnay '45 with the Brie."[26]
The possession and enjoyment of these rare and costly wines seem
almost to have carried an erotic charge for him: at one point he describes his wine collection to his brother as "a Harem full of beautiful
and eager women—waiting to be ravished." In another he smugly
describes (again to his brother) the satisfaction of "going up w/Julie
in our little elevator, smelling those fresh lilies-of-the-valley, buzzing
gently from Chambertin '28, and stroking the lovely bottom of a
lovely woman—all at the same moment—[and] I thinks to myself,
'Thaaaat's Paris, Son—that's Paris.' "[27]

❧

The kitchen is a sensual place, and few household activities are more
gratifying to the home cook than satisfying the gastronomic whims
of a lover or spouse. Julia Child's cooking for Paul Child—which meant
cooking well, for he was very particular—was not something that
came easily to her at first. She had arrived in Paris with only a basic
knowledge of cooking, and her early ventures into her kitchen in Washington, D.C. (working under the guidance of *Joy of Cooking*), had led to
some truly spectacular failures. Within nine months of their arrival,
however, Child was cooking proficiently for her husband. And because
the art and science of cooking in the French manner had become her
newfound passion, she was also attending classes at the Cordon Bleu.

Paul Child, in turn, encouraged Julia—first in her cooking education, and later in her cookbook writing, because he wanted her to
do what made her happy, and learning (and then teaching, and then
writing) made her happy. As she began her studies, he was careful to

recognize, praise, and encourage the innate creativity and playfulness that she brought to the hard work of cooking well and presiding well at table, for these were all qualities he adored in her. He also had an unflagging belief in her talents and abilities as a teacher, communicator, and performer.

Following her lead, he too threw himself wholeheartedly into this new obsession of hers, making it something they shared. This meant cohosting dinner parties (lots of them)—affairs at which he presided, to be sure, but at the same time served as butler, sommelier, dishwasher, and clean-up man. Doing so was not difficult for him because he liked hard work and he was used to it: he did not come to the dining room with the innate expectation of being waited upon. Moreover his wife's success—whatever it was to be—was also *his* success. Like the Valentine's Day cards that they sent out to their family and friends, the dinner parties they now created together were a way of sharing their happiness (and talent, knowledge, and good fortune) with all the world, while at the same time placing their love for each other (and their gift for teamwork, organization, and planning) front and center for all the world to see. In time, Julia would take this exhibitionistic game a giant step further, by presenting the idea of refined domestic happiness to all of America by way of her various cooking shows—shows in which Paul too was entirely (but now invisibly) involved. In that way Julia Child's ultimate achievement—embodying and enacting the new ideal of the hostess who cooks and serves, but at the same time is able to sit down and enjoy her own dinner party—evolved not simply out of her love of fine French food and wine as experienced in Paris, but also out of her relationship with an unusually supportive husband, a man who worked with her first as mentor, then as cohost, and ultimately as adviser and man behind the scenes.

SIX

Richard Olney Starts Out

By the time Paul and Julia Child were enjoying their third year on the rue de l'Université, increasing numbers of young Americans were arriving in Paris, attracted both by the strong dollar-to-franc exchange rate and by the booming Parisian art scene. Literature, painting, drama, dance, and jazz were all enjoying a postwar resurgence on the Left Bank, making Paris a tempting (and affordable) bohemian alternative to New York's Greenwich Village. Unlike the Childs, however, these young artists and writers did not live in the sleepy Faubourg St. Germain; instead they took cheap, rustic lodgings near the Sorbonne and the École des Beaux Arts. Among them was Richard Olney, an aspiring painter who crossed the Atlantic in November 1951. In a little more than a decade he would be the leading American publishing in France (in French and for the French) on the subject of French cuisine, but at the time of his arrival, his ambition was simply to paint in the manner of Bonnard and to live as a bohemian intellectual. "I certainly had no plan to write commercially," he later recalled. "It never occurred to me that I could write."

While his interest in good cooking dated back to his undergraduate days at the University of Iowa—where a fellow painter and friend, Jane Wilson, later recalled his introducing her to vinaigrette dressing and marinated steak—painting and the study of art history were far more important to him. The opportunity to paint in France, at one time a distant fantasy, became possible when he won a distinguished scholarship. "I had studied painting since 1944 at the University of Iowa and the Brooklyn Museum Art School . . . [and] was waiting tables nights in a Greenwich Village restaurant and painting days," he wrote a journalist friend toward the end of his life. "[Then] early in 1951 I received a letter from the Fulbright Commission saying that I had been accepted as a Fulbright scholar to study in France, a dream fulfilled (I thought). That summer my sister Margaret and I spent two months at [the] Yaddo [artists colony]. . . . [and] while there, I received another Fulbright letter reversing their decision (the only possible explanation being that they had checked with the draft [board] and discovered that I had been labeled 'psycho-neurotic')."

By "psycho-neurotic" Olney meant "homosexual," for he had been aware of his sexual identity from an early age, and when asked about it at an induction interview for the U.S. Army in 1944 he had not lied. Seven years later, the results of that interview led the State Department (which oversaw the Fulbright fellowship awards) to strip the twenty-four-year-old of his award. The decision, which could not be appealed, left Olney shattered. His parents were equally devastated. "Father was so upset," he later wrote, "that he offered to send me to Europe 'for several years' on an allowance of $100 per month." It was an amount his father could not easily afford, in part because he had seven other children still to educate. However, both Olney's parents wanted their remarkable firstborn son to have the opportunity of living and studying abroad, so they made the sacrifice. But the memory of that humiliation would linger with Olney to the end of his life—even in his later years, he could not bring himself to discuss it in his memoirs— and it was probably a contributing factor in his decision never to return full-time to the United States. Like Alice Toklas, Olney found in France a culture that would allow him to be who he was.

❧

Born in the very small farming town of Marathon, Iowa, Olney was a most unlikely expatriate bohemian. His family had no social or cultural ties to France or to French culture, nor did they have any connection to the arts or humanities. His reticent, socially conservative father worked two jobs—running the little town's small bank, and doing independent work as a notary and lawyer—while his mother cooked, cleaned, and raised their eight children. The family of ten made do in a three-bedroom home. The pared-down simplicity of their life—which featured prayers at mealtime, no alcohol, and food prepared with nourishment and economy foremost in mind—may, in retrospect, have predisposed Olney to traditional French household values, which are similarly focused on economy, simplicity, and thrift, even as it propelled him away from simple Iowa home cooking in the direction of fine French food and drink. At any rate, the bohemian lifestyle that he took up on the Left Bank of Paris, if austere to others, proved no more difficult for him than the life he had known at home in Marathon.

Olney was not the only member of his family gifted with extraordinary intelligence and intellectual curiosity, but he was by far the most motivated to see the world—and in time, he would inspire most of his siblings to do so too. James Olney, the brother with whom Richard was closest, would become a well-traveled poetry scholar, university professor, and author. John, another brother, would live in France during the 1950s before returning home to become a neuroscientist. Their youngest brother, Byron, would do his medical residency with the U.S. Air Force in Italy before becoming a cardiologist at the Mayo Clinic. Olney's sister Margaret, a painter, would come over and tour the European museums with him; so too would another sister, Elizabeth. In later years, all these siblings,* as well as their children, were grateful to Richard for the many European cultural experiences he had made possible.

Although he always wanted to be an artist, Olney had a lifelong interest in botany and zoology too, and this fascination with the natural world would continue as an adult—through gardening, foraging in the wild, and keeping birds. His kitchen was another connecting

---

* There were two other siblings: Norris, who remained in Marathon to run the family bank, and Frances, who died at age forty, and to whom Richard Olney dedicated *Simple French Food*.

point with nature. The house in Marathon at one point included a chicken run, which he helped tend: collecting fresh eggs (and occasionally helping to kill and dress chickens) had been a part of everyday life for him during the later years of the Great Depression and into World War II. After moving to the South of France in the early 1960s he would keep fowl as well, even though the aviary he constructed was primarily used to keep songbirds (as pets, not food). The illustrative drawings he would make for his cookbooks, meanwhile, demonstrate his strong awareness of plant and animal forms. An introvert, he preferred pets to friends when young: "Strong willed and obstinate . . . he spent little time with other children, preferring the company of [his] various animals—exotic fish, snakes, hamsters . . . lizards, alligators, [and] a Pomeranian dog," his brother James later remembered.

Olney was also good with his hands from a young age: along with the other Olney boys, he helped his father build things, including the playground structures in Marathon's town park. He worked part-time in a commercial greenhouse as a teenager, an experience that served him well in later years when he raised and propagated his own plants, often from cuttings or seed. His mother's habit of foraging for wild asparagus along the railroad tracks would be something he did too, years later in the South of France.[1]

⚜

Olney had his first Paris meal just a few steps from Michaud, Julia and Paul Child's preferred neighborhood restaurant. But as an art student of limited means, he ate far more humbly at "a glum little dining room for boarders" in the Hôtel de l'Académie, at the corner of the rue de l'Université and the rue des Saints-Pères:

> The plat du jour was "*gibelotte, pommes mousseline*"—rabbit and white wine fricassee with mashed potatoes. The *gibelotte* was all right, the mashed potatoes the best I'd ever eaten, pushed through a sieve, buttered and moistened with enough of their hot cooking water to bring them to a supple, not quite pourable consistency—no milk, no cream, no beating. I had never dreamt of mashing potatoes without milk and, in Iowa,

everyone believed that, the more you beat them, the better they were.

The first few weeks, my days were spent mostly in museums and, for lunch, I ate as cheaply as possible. Good food was everywhere. A dollar bought 500 francs and could pay for a meal, including wine. Small family restaurants, with husband or wife in the kitchen, the other taking orders and tending bar, while the teen-age offspring waited table, were commonplace. . . . *Petit salé* (brine-cured pork) cooked with lentils was a favorite main dish; others were *gibelotte, pot-au-feu* (called *"boeuf gros sel"* when served without its broth), *poule au pot, potée* (with sausage, cabbage and aromatic vegetables), [and] *blanquette de veau*—[all of them] slow cooking dishes based on inexpensive ingredients, which required only a talent for controlling the heat source to be perfect.[2]

Although Olney grew to love the luxury and imagination embodied in French *haute cuisine*, and even though he would be a lifelong advocate of truffles, foie gras, and the finest French wines in his writings on French home cooking, his everyday preference—like that of many food professionals—was not for fancy restaurant cooking, but for relatively simple meals made memorable through the intelligence, resourcefulness, and improvisational skills of the knowledgeable home cook. His deceptively titled *Simple French Food* would be based largely upon *daubes*, soups, braises, and *gratins*—the humble and deeply satisfying foods of everyday French family life. Likewise, he would always enjoy surprising his French guests with unassuming, down-home American foods that paired beautifully with great wines—such as the pairing of rare roast beef with a vintage Burgundy, or his mother's apple pie with a hundred-year-old Château d'Yquem.

❧

Olney quickly adapted to Paris life, both its hardships and pleasures. His early days in Paris were filled mostly with painting and museum-going, but as a young man on his own, he soon made friends. The Left Bank had long been a place welcoming to men who preferred men and women who preferred women. To live in an environment of such laissez-faire after the fear, paranoia, and persecution of McCarthy-era America was indeed a pleasure. Within a month or two he had met and become involved with Elliott Stein,* a short, boyish, bearlike Jewish-American intellectual, critic, and writer who had been living in Paris since 1948. The two counted many poets, painters, translators, scholars, filmmakers, and novelists as their friends. The poets Bill Aalto, John Ashbery, W. H. Auden, and Brian Howard; the writers Charles Henri Ford, Otto Friedrich, Eda Lord, Harriet Sohmers, and Eugene Walter; the painter Pavel Tchelitchev; and the arts philanthropist Peter Watson were just a few of the interesting people Olney considered a part of his world. He also resumed association in Paris with several acquaintances made in New York: the British-American aesthete Harold Acton, the art collector Robert Isaacson, and the poet James Merrill.

Olney took a small room at the place Elliott Stein lived, the Hôtel de Verneuil, at the corner of the rue de Verneuil and the rue de Beaune, which though just a block or so from Julia and Paul Child's favorite luxury hotel, the Pont Royal, was an establishment of a very different sort: inhabited "mostly by a down-and-out international lot of artists," it featured a ground-floor room set aside for hourly rental to prostitutes. The place, neither comfortable nor clean, had only "a single 'squat-john' or hole in the floor, furnished with torn-up newspapers and a violent flushing system, which encouraged one to stand outside the entrance before pulling the chain," and while some rooms had a cold-water sink, none had a bath or shower (instead, residents were referred to *les bains-douches municipaux*). Bed linens, likewise, were changed just once a month. The poky little rooms were really only for sleeping, reading, or making love—all other socializing took place instead at the many bars, cafés, and restaurants of the *quartier*. But at sixty cents a day, the rates could hardly be bettered.

The popular meet-up spot for Olney and his friends was La Reine Blanche, a gay bar-café just a couple of doors down from Brasserie

---

*Stein (1928–2012) edited the literary review *Janus* during 1950 to 1951 and also made screen appearances as an actor, but is today mostly remembered for his critical writings on film. He wrote for many years for *The Village Voice*.

Lipp. He would remember it years later as "a deep tunnel, lit brightly and crudely. . . . The bar [section], thickly populated by trade, was cruising territory. Beyond it were tables and booths where friends gathered." Because Olney was not looking for sex, the area's restaurants—particularly those with good wine at affordable prices— quickly became far more interesting to him. "One of the best in the *quartier* was La Chope Danton,* at the Carrefour de l'Odéon," he recalled in his memoirs. "Habitués stood at the 'zinc'[†] downstairs to drink house wines by the glass, and a spiral stairway led steeply up to the dining room. The tables were dressed with paper and the food was Burgundian or Lyonnaise in spirit. Except for a few Bordeaux and some of the grander Burgundies, the *patron*, Monsieur Moisson- nier, chose his wines at the vineyards where they were raised in casks until the month of April following the vintage, before being shipped to Paris, bottled in the restaurant's cellars and drunk within the year. I have never drunk prettier Beaujolais than his Chiroubles, Saint- Amour, Fleurie or Côte de Brouilly."[3]

For a young man raised on the simplest possible cooking, and entirely without knowledge of wine or spirits, Olney found Paris a wonderland of taste sensations. Being both curious and practical, he would chat with proprietors, waiters, and chefs about how they cooked what they cooked, where they acquired their provisions, and how they organized their kitchens. Within his first few years in Paris, he too was planning, preparing, and serving good French home- cooked meals, and in certain rare instances doing so (informally, at the request of friends) for small amounts of money.

However, wine rather than food became Olney's primary fascina- tion and delight. Even though most of his American friends preferred whiskey—and he too would enjoy it in quantity throughout his life—he was intrigued by the variety of wines available in France. The French seemed to him to have a wine to suit every possible mood, hour, and dining experience. There was nothing like it back in Iowa. In learning how and why the French drank their wine, he came to

---

* "Danton's Tankard."

[†] *Le zinc* is the counter at which drinks are served in a restaurant or bar (so named since at one time most Parisian bars had a zinc countertop). The word also describes a small café or bar.

understand it as an element of daily life—not, as Americans might have thought, as a means to inebriation, but rather as an indispensable and elemental component of every meal, like bread. Wine was relaxing, true, and even inebriating; but the French considered it nutritionally rich, a digestive aid, and generally good for one's health,* not simply a means toward intoxication. At nearly every restaurant he went to, Olney saw French diners pondering their wine lists as carefully as their menus, consulting thoughtfully with waiters or wine captains about which wine, winemaker, and vintage might suit their meal and budget best. Slowly he learned how to appreciate wine to the fullest: how to examine its color; to swirl it in the glass to release its bouquet; to sniff, sip, suck, and even chew it before swallowing as a way of obtain the full range of tastes from start to finish. The many varieties of French wine, and the many ways in which the wines were made, aged, bottled, marketed, and consumed—all these subjects interested him. So did the lore surrounding wines. He pursued this interest through reading, studying, and discussing wine at length with people who shared his enthusiasm—and such people were not hard to find in Paris. With this most pleasant form of self-education he started to taste wines extensively—both on their own and with food. Along with various outings to vineyards, he made a point of tasting yearly with the winemakers at Paris's Salon des Arts Ménagers. (Julia Child also attended every year, describing it to Avis DeVoto as "a tremendous exposition or fair of household appliances and wine tasting held in the Grand Palais . . . [with] everybody deliriously happy because [one] can always refresh [one]self with a bit of wine tasting.")[4] One winemaker Olney met at the 1953 salon, Lucien Peyraud of Domaine Tempier in Bandol, would become a lifelong friend. Teaching himself about French wines was by no means an inexpensive pastime, but thanks to living in Paris at a time when the exchange rate was very good, and also thanks to his skills in the kitchen, Olney was able to do so far more economically than most.

Olney's evenings out with friends during this first year in Paris

---

* The French have a number of rhyming proverbs on the health benefits of wine, including *"Un bon verre de vin enlève un écu au médecin"* (roughly, "A red wine a day keeps the doctor away").

were not much taken up with fine wines, though. His budget didn't allow it, and his friends were not terribly interested. Rather, his nights out tended to focus on lively conversation and the free exchange of ideas, usually over whiskey or *gros rouge*—cheap red table wine. At heart, Olney was an intellectual as well as a painter, and even in later years, when cooking and culinary writing had become his central preoccupations, he would feel quite strongly that the success of any meal depended primarily on good conversation.

One of Olney's most important friends during his first decade in France was the novelist James Baldwin, who had moved from New York three years earlier, in 1948. Baldwin's brilliant and outrageous conversational style—developed out of his early ambition to preach as a Pentecostal minister—absolutely dazzled Olney; so too did the quality of his mind and the passion of his convictions. Of their many late nights out together, Olney later remembered, "I drank more [during those first years] than wisdom should normally prescribe (which, however, did not interfere with my wine education). The usual routine was Café de Flore until closing at 1 am, La Reine Blanche, which closed at 4, and La Pergola, which closed at 6. If one wanted a last drink (which Jimmy Baldwin always did), the Royale opened at 6. [But] I rarely went to Montparnasse unless it was for midnight oysters at the Coupole."

⚜

Although Olney had little interest in the unruly, American-dominated Montparnasse bar scene (apart from that one restaurant, La Coupole, so famous for its oysters), he did not limit himself to life in the Seventh Arrondissement—or even for that matter to Paris. He was eager to see the great art collections of Europe, and also to paint *en plein air*. Traveling modestly by bus or train, he often stayed (and painted) with friends in Magagnosc, near Grasse in the Alpes-Maritimes, not far from where Alice Toklas would sometimes go on vacations, and where Julia and Paul Child would take up residence with Simone Beck Fischbacher roughly a decade later. He also toured Italy, spending a few weeks in Rome with his friend the avant-garde filmmaker Kenneth Anger. And he spent the summers of 1952 and

1953 on the island of Ischia, near Capri, where—despite the close proximity of W. H. Auden, Chester Kallman, Pavel Tchelitchev, Charles Henri Ford, and many other decidedly promiscuous gay men—he kept his distance from the nightly carousing, preferring instead to live simply with Elliott Stein. After days spent painting, reading, and swimming, the couple would make a modest meal at home or else venture out to a *caffè* for an aperitif. As an art student on a limited income, staying in made good economic sense; but living this way also suited Olney temperamentally: he was at his most relaxed when alone in the kitchen, or else in the company of just a few friends.

In the spring of 1953, Olney decided to part ways with Elliott Stein, who wanted a more varied sex life.* Because Olney was in need of studio space as well as lodging, he left the Hôtel de Verneuil for a rental in distant Clamart, a lower-middle-class Parisian suburb where he had found an atelier consisting of "three bare attic rooms, with a tiny kitchen, no bath, no toilet and no heating." Clamart was more than five miles from St. Germain and could not be reached by Métro (instead one needed to take an old suburban railroad line from the Gare Montparnasse),† but the rent there was only fifteen dollars a month, and the attic studio was large enough, and the light good enough, for Olney to be able to paint throughout the dreary Parisian winters.

In a way, Clamart was linked to the Parisian literary and artistic scene: both Matisse and Daudet had accomplished great work there. (Clamart was also linked to French gastronomy, since the word "Clamart" in a recipe traditionally indicates the presence of green peas, just as "Montmorency" indicates cherries, and "Argenteuil," asparagus.) The house at 68, rue Paul Vaillant-Couturier‡ seemed to hold great promise: Although the building was in "ill repair," it was "surrounded by an unkempt garden and courtyard, protected from

---

* In an interview for this book, Stein was open about his preference for multiple sexual partners, something Olney also cites in his memoir as a reason for their having gone separate ways.
† This line is today known as the Transilien Paris–Montparnasse. Clamart is two stops from Montparnasse, and seven minutes away.
‡ The house and its large walled garden have today been made over into an elegant residence; the window of Olney's attic atelier is clearly visible on Google's Street View feature for the address.

neighbors and the street by high stone walls," Olney recalled in his memoir. "[It] dated from 1820 and was beautiful."

Photos from the period show him comfortably installed. "The landlady, Mlle. (Suzanne) Marty . . . offered me several pieces of furniture, a coal stove, and showed me the cellar, one room of which, she said, was for my use [as a *cave*]. The toilet, on the ground floor, emptied into a septic tank and was flushed with a pitcher of water. I bought a portable, galvanized bathtub at the flea market, a replica of the narrow, elongated tub in which Bonnard stretched an immersed nude in one of his most famous paintings. . . . I [also] painted one wall of the main room with an amateurish viticultural map of France (clusters of grapes here and there), presenting [the] major vineyard regions, and began to settle in."[5] In a rare photo of the apartment, Olney sits at a table before a window, pouring a cup of coffee. The table holds some peaches in a porcelain cake basket, sliced oranges, croissants, jam, and butter. The bookcase behind him is full of his books, and beside him a large, light-filled window looks out on mansard roofs and sky.

Olney liked Clamart, for though not quite a village, it had a small-town feel—and he was, after all, a small-town boy. Mlle. Marty proved over time a delightful landlady. The daughter of a general, she had once wanted to be an actress, but her father had prohibited her from going on the stage. Now in middle age, having inherited his money and his home, she was decidedly nonconformist, and the idea of having a young American artist living in her attic pleased her no end. She soon became a regular visitor to his studio.

Others came as well, for Olney seemed to create a homey environment wherever he went. Shortly after he moved in, Olney remembered, James Baldwin asked him "if I could arrange for his old friend, Beauford Delaney, a black American painter, to rent a flat in the same house." Delaney, a spiritual mentor to Baldwin, was beginning to show signs of mental instability, and needed someone to look after him— something Baldwin himself could not do. Mlle. Marty welcomed the idea, and soon this gentle, mystical older man, a respected painter of the Harlem Renaissance, had joined their Clamart household, making over a little ground-floor apartment into a studio-home. With his arrival, the house became even more of a bohemian expatriate social center for Americans both black and white—one where creative work was the order of the day, and interesting music and good conversation (in French and English) the habits of the evening. Even the music was cross-cultural, for while black American jazz was all the rage in Paris, Olney liked French popular music too, and his record collection included older recordings by the great French *chanteuses* and *diseuses** (Damia, Fréhel, Lys Gauty, and Mistinguett) as well as contemporary singers (Germaine Montero, Marlene Dietrich, Edith Piaf, Catherine Sauvage, and Juliette Gréco). He also sought out *bal musette*, the traditional music of French dance halls—it was uncomplicated and easy to enjoy.

Paradoxically, by moving to Clamart, Olney suddenly found himself getting closer to the "real" France than most Americans ever do. Far from the tourist-dominated districts of St. Germain and Montparnasse, he found in this unfashionable suburb a fine place both to work and to live—one where the locals, because not overwhelmed by swarms of carousing foreigners, were far more open to knowing him, particularly since he lived as simply as they did. The neighborhood was bordered by a large park, the Bois de Clamart, good for walking and picnicking, and the streets were quiet and safe. Because there were not many restaurants in the area, Olney had no choice but to cook and eat as the French did. Just as his youthful experiences as a waiter in Greenwich Village had got Olney interested in how kitchens were run, so now his experience of Clamart gave him a new appreciation for the daily challenges of planning, marketing, cooking, and serving meals at home.

❧

Unlike Julia Child's beautifully organized top-floor kitchen on the rue de l'Université, so lovingly and extensively photographed by Paul Child, few images survive of Olney's garret apartment or its kitchen, which at any rate was not much to look at. Although primarily a painting studio, the apartment had a little nook for cooking that, in its romantic simplicity, might well have been part of the act 1 stage

---

* Female entertainers who perform monologues, sometimes to musical accompaniment.

set for *La Bohème*. Preserved in but a single photograph, this "kitchen" consisted of a single shelf with pots and pans hung above it. Below that, there was a tiny stove, a narrow countertop, and a small sink. But here Olney was free to experiment and learn as he pleased—and in doing so, to become ever more intimately acquainted with the habits and traditions of French small-scale domestic life. He marketed daily, because his shelf space was limited and he had no refrigeration apart from his outside windowsill. Like the French, he prepared his home cooking in small quantities, because small quantities were all his little oven and stovetop could manage. Most important, he kept an open and creative mind about *how* to create a meal. Because his pots, pans, and utensils were few, he frequently needed to improvise. Which perhaps explains why, to the end of his life, Olney would maintain that good cooking was done as much by intuition and improvisation as it was by rules and by principles: like playing jazz, it begins with a mastery of theory, technique, and organizing principles, develops through familiarity and rote practice, but ultimately comes alive through playfulness, spontaneity, and, ultimately, extemporization. "Rules in cooking are not iron-cast," he would later advise. "They are merely the expression of a well of experience formed and enriched over the centuries, re-examined, modified, or altered in terms of changing needs, habits and tastes. They are welded out of knowledge—an understanding of what happens to a material when treated in a special way. . . . One's own set of rules will form itself and become increasingly elaborate as one comes to understand the logic behind each detail, each step, to recognize the repetitions or variations of basic steps from one recipe to another; and the more elaborate the set of rules—that is to say, *the better one understands and is able to define an intricate framework of limitations*—the greater is the freedom lent one's creative imagination."[6]

In preparing these meals at home for his circle of friends, Olney naturally began to reflect upon how the commonplace and the sacred came together daily at the table. He was by no means a religious person, but he had a thoughtful and meditative nature, and he had been raised in a home where food and prayer were combined every evening. Now, living on his own as an artist and free spirit, he began to experience this sense of daily communion in a new way—not as dogma, but rather as a natural inclination to give thanks. From 1953 until Olney abandoned it in the late 1960s, the Clamart apartment would serve as a home-away-from-home for any number of people in need of a meal, a drink, or a restorative evening among friends. And since the sharing of ideas, thoughts, and feelings took place most naturally at the table, Olney began to reconsider the importance and significance of these mealtime exchanges, which were about mutual enjoyment, sharing, and inclusion. To preside, to play host, and to serve others through hospitality and friendship—all these activities brought to Olney a new sense of closeness and (as the French might say) *fraternité*—something particularly important to those living and working on the fringes of society and so very far from home. Through this daily practice of bringing people together, he began to formulate a new understanding of why eating well—not just eating good food, but sitting well at the table and enjoying the reassuring experience of a communal mealtime—was so profoundly important to a person's sense of well-being. "I have sometimes been accused of thinking of nothing but food and wine—of being bound irreparably to the bestial pole," he would later write. "I do, in fact, think a great deal about food and wine and I would like my readers to share with me the belief that food and wine—that the formalization of gastro-sensory pleasure— must be an essential aspect of the whole life, in which the sensuous-sensual-spiritual elements are so intimately interwoven that the incomplete exploitation of any one can only result in the imperfect opening of the great flower, symbol of the ultimate perfection which is understanding, when all things fall into place."[7] Cooking, serving, and eating together was, he felt, a holistic practice—nourishment not only for the body but for the mind, the heart, the soul.

He suggests something similar in a headnote, never published, on the nature and purpose of soup:

In the beginning soup was basic sustenance—a daily pot of soothing nourishment that ritually gathered the family to-gether in communion around the hearth in which it was made. Soup was the meal and, in concurrence with more evolved sophisticated concepts of dining, it continues to represent the body of the meal for many people. . . . "Soup" derives from "sop." It is the bread over which a pottage, a broth, hot milk or another liquid is poured; in certain regions of France, *la soupe* still means the crust of bread and not the liquid that is poured over it. . . .

". . . *Et trempez votre soupe.*"* These words wind up many a soup recipe in French cookery books, old and recent. The phrase is a magical incantation, stamped out of ancestral memory; it entreats one never to forget the sacred role of bread—the bread that, in Christian tradition, was always slashed with the sign of the cross before being put in to bake; it reminds one of the criminality of waste, of the rare luxury of being able to take pleasure in simple things—and it embodies ritual, which magnifies meaning in all things.[8]

Olney's convivial nature—he was not always as mystical, solemn, or otherworldly as this passage suggests—soon led him to hold weekend-long parties in Clamart. Dubbed the "Saturday Night Function" after the old Duke Ellington tune, such a gathering usually began on Saturday afternoon and extended well into Sunday, with people arriving and departing as they liked, and various meals being prepared and consumed throughout, and various *vins et alcools* on offer for the duration. Along with the core participants Beauford Delaney, James Baldwin and Mlle. Marty, Olney could usually count on the company of Baldwin's good friend Mary Painter—a beautiful, hard-drinking, Minnesota-born army statistician and Marshall Plan economist who had been living in Paris since 1947. Intelligent, fun, and more than a little wild in her taste for men, Painter was also quite generous in her contributions to the weekend's festivities, for her connection to the army PX gave her access to good American whiskey at rock-bottom, duty-free prices. There was also Bernard Hassell, a penniless, good-looking African-American whom Olney had recently met at La Reine Blanche. Since arriving from New York, Hassell had

---

* Trans.: Pour your soup over slices of bread. (The verb *tremper* means "to soak.")

found work for himself as a seminude dancer in the Folies Bergère—a job he loved because he had a fine body and he liked showing it off. While Olney sensed Hassell was not right for him as a partner— needy, illiterate, and dishonest, he could also turn violent—the attraction between them was too powerful to deny. "When we touched, there was something like an electrical explosion," Olney remembered of their first night at the bar, "so we hopped a taxi to Clamart to touch again."

Friends of friends were also welcome at these weekend-long parties, and occasionally someone truly surprising would turn up, such as John Ashbery or the novelist Henry Miller. (An old friend of Beauford Delaney, Miller had lived many years in Paris on next to nothing, and so had a greater than average appreciation for Olney's good cooking.) Every once in a while, an Olney brother or sister would visit, prompting much feasting and celebration. John Olney had a job with the U.S. Army in nearby Orléans, and James Olney was completing his dissertation in Britain; both brothers liked good wine, and Olney helped them to find it and consume it. In time, Margaret Olney came over to see Paris, and so did their youngest brother, Byron. But it was really James, a poetry scholar of rare intelligence and charm, who was Richard Olney's closest ally during his Paris years. The brothers corresponded frequently, and their surviving letters detail their wide-ranging intellectual curiosity—for Richard's was hardly limited to the study of painting, cooking, and wine. In time, James would (rightly) point out that Richard's cookbook prose carried echoes of Baudelaire, Colette, Proust, and even Virginia Woolf. "There is a spirit in [his writing] that one almost never finds in cookery writing," James would observe, "and [also] a serene, unaffected assurance . . . that can only come from being thoroughly at home and, as it were, inside the subject. . . . Great care is taken [by Richard] to appeal [to the reader] through language—for what else has a writer to work with?—to [describe] an experience that is essentially preverbal or postverbal or not verbal at all."

Olney's extraordinary ability as a writer on food and wine was reinforced, throughout his life, by James Olney's keen appreciation for his writing (as well as for his cooking, wine knowledge, and menu planning). No wonder then, that French readers were, in time, so taken with Olney's articles for *Cuisine et Vins de France*: he wrote more thoughtfully on the subject of French food than practically anyone else of his generation, and certainly more thoughtfully than anyone else then writing for that magazine (with the possible exception of Robert Courtine of *Le Monde*, who wrote for them only occasionally). Of course to do so as a foreigner and non-native speaker of French was no small thing, particularly since the French consider their cuisine a leading manifestation of their social and cultural identity, one that is perhaps second only to the French language itself. Marcel Rouff had probably described the relationship of French cuisine to French national identity best when he had written, in 1924, that "a quiche Lorraine . . . or a Marseille bouillabaisse . . . or a potato gratin from the Savoy has all the refined richness of France, all its spirit and wit, its gaiety . . . the seriousness hidden beneath its charm . . . its mischief and its gravity . . . the full soul of its fertile, cultivated rich earth."[9]

Given that this was the case, Olney's ability to write sensitively about French food and wine for the French (and *in French*), and yet to do so from the American perspective, and with a clearly American identity—well, such a thing was, on the face of it, almost impossible even to conceive. But Olney would live, study, and cook in France for the better part of a decade before making his name and reputation as a writer at *Cuisine et Vins de France*. For now, he was simply at the beginning of a very long and laborious apprenticeship, as thinker-writer-cook.

❖

With so much coming and going from the studio in Clamart, and so much eating and drinking, Olney found himself pouring an awful lot of wine for friends. Since he needed to do so economically, he began buying wine both by the case and then by the keg, in many instances *en primeur* ("in advance of the harvest") to get the best deal. Luckily his cellar in Clamart was cool and humid year-round, making it ideal for storing wine, and he had plenty of space down there too, meaning he could take delivery of any number of kegs. "I remember buying several cases of Château Ducru-Beaucaillou 1947* [in 1953] for 700 fr[ancs] ($1.40) a bottle. [And] each year, in April, I [was able to buy] a keg each of Pouilly-Fumé, Beaujolais-Villages, and one of the Beaujolais first growths, Côte de Brouilly, Morgon, or Chiroubles, which after a few weeks' rest in the cellar, I put into [my own] bottles," he later noted.[10] Unlike the Ducru-Beaucaillou, these latter appellations were simple "quaffing" wines—agreeable, far from costly, and meant to be gulped down while young. They were therefore perfect for an artist running weekend house parties on a maximum budget of a hundred dollars a month.

Nonetheless, Olney remained intensely curious about fine wines, so he sought them out by the bottle when dining out. One of his favorite restaurant companions was Mary Painter. Together Olney and Painter made regular yearly visits to Chez l'Ami Louis, a hole-in-the-wall bistro famed not only for the quality and simplicity of its dishes but also for their expense.

"Situated in a narrow dark street in an out-of-the-way quarter (3ème), to the ordinary passer-by it must be hard to believe that this insignificant façade with its tiny entrance should hide a restaurant where such fine food is to be found," Alexander Watt wrote about the joint in *Paris Cuisine*, adding that "the little dining room is very simply decorated with mirrors on the plainly painted walls. There is sawdust on the tiled floors. The marble-topped tables are covered with gay striped cloths. At the far end of the room there is an open hatchway through which Monsieur Antoine, chef and proprietor, can be seen in the kitchen at work. The atmosphere [of] Chez l'Ami Louis is quiet and unpretentious. There are only four persons in the entire establishment: Monsieur Antoine, his wife, one waiter, and one dishwasher in the kitchen. . . . There is no written menu; Madame Antoine tells you verbally what there is to be had."[11]

Olney was more critical of the place than Watt, but during ortolan season a visit was *de rigueur*. A European songbird about the size of a sparrow, the ortolan has long been considered one of France's

---

* A second-growth wine from the Saint-Julien appellation in Bordeaux. Today a bottle of this wine with a similar bottle age would retail for $85 to $150, depending on the year.

ultimate gastronomic delicacies. It is a regional specialty of the Landes department in Southwest France.* "Mary had a passion for the table and she adored ortolans," Olney later recalled. "[The songbirds] were fattened in cages for a couple of weeks before being force-fed a few drops of Armagnac for the sacrifice, plumed and packed in cases to be shipped to Paris . . . [and] in the ortolan season, spring or fall, we went to Chez l'Ami Louis . . . a simple, even rather slummy, bistrot† in appearance, which may have been the most expensive restaurant in Paris. The floors were spread with sawdust, the tables with news-sheet, the dining room was heated by a coal stove and stove-pipes, the walls were dusky from their emanations and there was no wine list beyond the half-dozen wines scribbled to the side of the menu. A large proportion of the clientèle was American." What Olney found most disturbing about the place, however, was the personality of the owner. "Monsieur Antoine, the Swiss chef-proprietor . . . was a mad-man; he hated all sauces—in fact, he hated most French food and was contemptuous of all his colleagues. At Easter-time, he served legs of milk-lamb, roast to order, and, in late autumn, rare-roast woodcock (*bécasse*). We began [our meal of ortolans] with his duck foie gras, firm and pink, accompanied by a slice of raw country ham, cured on the bone; the ortolans were merely sautéed in butter for a few minutes."[12]

Olney would come to regret the French tradition of eating of little birds once he settled in the South of France: the bird traps his neighbors set on his property robbed his house and garden of their pleasant company and song. (He ultimately made up for this loss by breeding Fischers' lovebirds and Australian cockatiels, constructing an aviary in which he kept more than thirty pairs.) As a young man curious about French culinary traditions, however, he enjoyed this meal of foie gras, country ham, and ortolans—despite the bellowings of Monsieur Antoine and the exorbitant price of his wares.

Alice Toklas's good friend Janet Flanner reported on ortolans in

---

* Although the ortolan has been a protected species since 1979, a number of Frenchmen continue to eat them—most notably, President François Mitterrand, who famously consumed them as part of his last meal, on New Year's Eve of 1995.

† This is Larousse's preferred French spelling of *bistro*.

The New Yorker at roughly the same time Olney and Painter were eating them, for suddenly all of Paris seemed to want to eat them too:

> To catch them at this time of year, nets are set upright in the grainfield stubble, and live ortolan decoys are tied to them, to flutter invitingly. The hunters blow on little whistles devised to imitate the ortolan song, which is pretty. The birds, flying in dense coveys, must be entangled in the nets by the hundreds to make the hunt worthwhile. The hundreds are then packed into cages, and placed by the peasants in dark rooms, to keep them drowsy and inert, and are stuffed in the gloom for a fortnight with millet seed. . . . This season, they cost two hundred fifty francs each, and two—or at most three—make a serving, for they are the richest bird in the gourmet's aviary. They are not supposed to be touched by knife or fork (though honestly they taste fine on a fork); the eater is supposed to seize them by the beak with the fingers of one hand and consume them, bones and all, beginning with the feet. The diner's free hand should be used like a cover over the ortolan to capture its fragrance, which is enticing; the bird's role is to please both the olfactory and the gustatory sense of man. It is ritually chewed slowly, to give it a chance to melt in the eater's mouth. Old engravings show ortolan-eaters with napkins hoisted like tents over their heads to enclose the perfume, and maybe also to hide their shame.[13]

Chez l'Ami Louis was just one of the many Parisian restaurants Olney and Painter visited together during the early 1950s. And just like Paul and Julia Child, Olney soon realized the city's most picturesque and celebrated restaurants were not necessarily its best. Lapérouse, a grand old restaurant famed for its private dining rooms (just down the street from Alice Toklas's apartment, on the quai des Grands Augustins), proved an expensive case in point. After completing a fine portrait of James Baldwin, Olney wanted to commemorate the achievement by organizing "a luncheon with Mary, Jimmy, Beauford and Bernard at Lapérouse, one of the hallowed gastronomic temples of the day, in a private 'salon,' . . . [so I] went around in advance to discuss the menu with the *maître d'hôtel* and the wines with the *sommelier*. The *maître d'hôtel* recommended *petits pois* with the duck—'but,' I said, 'it's not the season.' He assured me that tinned peas were superior to fresh peas, so I figured we had nothing to discuss." Olney found the wine captain's recommendations equally dubious. "The *sommelier* was of the old-fashioned breed—he pocketed a commission from négociants on the wines he sold and pushed them hard. We drank a négociant's Corton-Charlemagne and I don't remember the reds." In the end, the meal was not much more than "restaurant cuisine, marked by the taste of basic sauces . . . [but] we had a good time [all the same], partly because of the nineteenth century aura of the private room, the opposite walls of which were mirrors on which had been scratched with diamonds the names of hundreds of *cocottes** and their gentlemen."[14]

Olney had a better time at Maxim's de Paris, that ultraluxurious remnant of La Belle Époque that had experienced a revival after the war thanks to its ambitious owner, Louis Vaudable. "The art nouveau décor and the schmaltzy violins were other-worldly. . . . Alex Humbert was chef. I treasure the memory of very fresh scallops with coral tongues of roe in creamy saffron sauce, accompanied by a 1937 Meursault," Olney wrote. "The food was very good, the service attentive and the wine list was spectacular, with '28 and '29 first growth Bordeaux at affordable prices. The *sommelier* was genuinely excited to have clients who drank wine; the beautiful people drank mostly champagne, [he said] and the tourists drank rosé de Provence." Like A. J. Liebling (who had also lived on remittances, and was equally alert to value for money), Olney scrutinized the menus and wine lists of the restaurants he visited with consummate interest, often well in advance of his meal there, and while dining he frequently asked the restaurant professionals to guide him. Being just as unassuming as Liebling, Olney was able to enter into the dialogue about the food and wine easily and without pretense, and since he did so from a respectful and well-informed standpoint—in fluent if accented

---

* An old-fashioned term of endearment for a young woman or girl, the word *cocotte* (which roughly translates to "chick"or "chickie") can also mean (as it is used here) a kept woman or demimondaine. Oddly enough, the word is also used to describe a small casserole dish or ramekin, as in *oeufs en cocotte*, "eggs (baked) in a pot."

French—he made some remarkable discoveries as well as lasting friendships this way. Restaurant owners and cooks seemed to recognize him as that rare bird: an American who was entirely *au courant* with contemporary French food and wine.

✤

In taking up French cooking, Olney looked to Escoffier for his core knowledge. But older French writings on cuisine delighted and intrigued him too, and he soon began collecting French nineteenth- and twentieth-century cookbooks both for reference and for pleasure, gradually creating a substantial library of mostly secondhand cookbooks and works of gastronomy. While he never thought of cooking professionally—introverted and highly strung, he knew himself temperamentally incapable of working in a restaurant kitchen—he nonetheless wanted to learn all he could about French cuisine. Rather than attend a cooking school, though, he simply practiced on his own, and also forged close friendships with a number of brilliant chefs and restaurant proprietors who were happy enough to share their wisdom with him.

Putting tasting experiences into words was another activity that fascinated Olney, for he shared the French passion for *le mot juste*. Describing the experience of drinking wine—with its many fleeting and elusive flavor suggestions—ultimately became one of his greatest pleasures. His knowledge of wine slowly became encyclopedic, thanks to his gifted palate, fine memory, strong work ethic, and remarkable staying power. He went about tasting not as an amateur would—that is, not simply for the pleasure of drinking and knowing wine—but rather as a young sommelier might, which is to say, as an expert-in-training. Whenever possible, he engaged in diligent, consistent, and systematic tastings of French wines and read extensively on the subject. To supplement this tasting and reading experience, he traveled to France's many wine regions whenever he could, either alone or in the company of his brothers and friends, there engaging in vertical tastings* in order to know each type of wine at its various stages,

---

*Tastings of a single wine over the course of several years (e.g., Clos des Mouches 1952, '53, '54 and '55).

from first pressing through maturation through final years of drinkability. Tastings of this sort could be tedious and were certainly uncomfortable (they usually involved a lot of standing around in cold cellars and spitting), but to truly know wine, one needed to travel, to observe, to compare, to remember, and, above all, to taste and discuss. Through doing so, Olney became ever more respectful of French winemaking as an ages-old tradition, one bound to French soil, to French culture, and to French regional (and national) identity as well as to family and regional histories. He also became more aware of French manners, expectations, and modes of expression—for these tastings were complex and nuanced social interactions, never just a basic discussion of products and prices.

Olney's writing on wine—particularly in his later books about Yquem and Romanée-Conti—is very fine. For those who care about it (and surprisingly, many people who collect and drink fine wines do not care about wine writing, seeing it as something else entirely), his descriptions are often a revelation. But even in a casual note to a friend, his observations on wine can astonish. Here, for example, he writes a note to a fellow wine lover about what he means by the term "finesse":

> To me, a wine with finesse is a wine of a certain age. Depending on the wine, it may be ten years old or a century old. To age gracefully, it must have a solid structure, in such serene balance that one is not conscious of its separate components. Finesse is delicacy, elegance, and complexity; it is ethereal. A fine wine is sometimes likened to lace. Of course, it is not like lace—a mouthful of lace would be disgusting. When a Burgundian discovers finesse in a wine, he may compare it to the Christ Child's velvet britches. Words are useless. Finesse is not a fruit, a smell, or a taste, it is an aura. No tasting note can touch it.[15]

Olney began hatching a plan in the fall of 1953 for a weekend road trip down to Burgundy. His intended destination was the Hôtel de la Côte-d'Or in Saulieu, owned and run by Alexandre Dumaine, now heir apparent to Fernand Point as France's greatest chef.* Dumaine's cuisine was said to be lighter and fresher than Point's, yet similarly imaginative, and similarly focused on locally sourced meats, fish, produce, and wines. So the trip was to be, in its way, a gastronomic pilgrimage.

Since Olney was starting out from Clamart, on the southern outskirts of Paris, he was not far at all from the Route Nationale 7, "La Route des Vacances," the main road from Paris to Burgundy (and from there continuing down through the upper Rhone, Provence, and the French Riviera, thus explaining its nickname). When Olney booked two simple rooms at the famed Saulieu hotel-restaurant by telephone, he conferred with Madame Jeanne Dumaine about their meal, because he particularly wanted to try a dish that required ordering several days in advance.

The drive took three hours heading south and west from Paris, and Painter did all the driving, for none of the others—Olney, Baldwin, and Delaney—knew how to operate an auto. As they made their way past the Forest of Fontainebleau in her heavily laden minicar, the foursome were in high spirits; an overnight trip to the French countryside was a rare thing for all of them, and they were looking forward to an extraordinary meal. The ride was further enlivened by yowls from Caesar, Mary's semiwild cat. Painter had insisted on bringing him, packing him into a wicker basket for the trip.

They arrived in Saulieu in late morning, with just enough time to settle into their modest rooms—one for Mary and Caesar, the other for the three men—before Olney and Painter met personally with Dumaine to discuss the evening's menu. As Olney would later recall in his memoirs, their specially ordered main course had been inspired by a recipe in Lucien Tendret's "chatty, anecdotal, sometimes cranky" 1892 *La Table au Pays de Brillat-Savarin*—the same recipe book that

---

*Stein and Toklas had visited the restaurant approximately fifteen years earlier, during the late 1930s, shortly after Dumaine had taken over as chef and earned the restaurant its three-star rating. As Toklas noted in her *Alice B. Toklas Cook Book*, "The Côte-d'Or then had as its proprietor and chef a quite fabulous person. First of all he looked like a great Clouet portrait, a museum piece. He had great experience and knowledge of the history of French cooking from the time of Clouet to the present. From him I learned a great deal. At dinner that evening we realised that he was one of the great French chefs. Each dish had a simplicity and a perfection."

Alice Toklas and Gertrude Stein had considered translating into English during the last years of the war. Among that book's many extraordinary dishes were a number of sumptuous pâtés and terrines Olney would re-create in years to come, "intricate mosaics, in cross-section, of pistachio-speckled light and dark forcemeats, alternating with striped layers of dark game and white meats, punctuated with fingers of red tongue, white back fat and black truffle." Tonight, however, he had advance-ordered something for which Dumaine was famous: *poularde à la vapeur de Lucien Tendret*.

The dish was a highly refined variation on the classic Lyonnaise preparation *poularde demi-deuil* ("chicken in half-mourning"), a dish both enormously simple and fantastically complicated. Julia Child would go into ecstasies about it; Toklas, for her part, had first tasted it shortly after World War I in Lyon, where it had been personally carved for her by no one less than la Mère Fillioux.* In Dumaine's updated version of the recipe, thickly sliced black truffles were inserted beneath the bright yellow skin of a *poularde de Bresse*—the finest and most flavorful chicken in all of France—thus making it seem to be "dressed in half-mourning."† The *poularde* (a hen that had been spayed in order to fatten it for the table, just as a rooster is castrated to become a capon) was then chilled overnight so that the rich taste and odor of the truffle could infuse the bird's dense flesh. The following day, after being brought to room temperature, the plated bird was set upon a tripod, and the tripod was positioned over a quantity of double consommé in a *marmite*, an earthenware cooking container. The *marmite* was sealed airtight with a cloth ribbon, and the truffled *poularde* was gently pressure-cooked by the fragrant steam of the rich double consommé.‡

---

*La Mère Fillioux was the professional name of Françoise Fayolle (1865–1925), one of the great woman chef-restaurateurs (or *mères*) of Lyon and the mentor of Eugénie Brazier ("La Mère Brazier"), the first female chef ever to achieve a Michelin three-star rating. Fillioux made a practice of carving each *poularde* personally at the customers' table, and did it so brilliantly that her famed chicken-carving knife is now permanently enshrined in the Musée Escoffier de l'Art Culinaire in Villeneuve-Loubet, near Antibes.

†During the nineteenth century, families who had experienced a death responded by dressing in black clothing that reflected their state of mourning. As time passed, they would transition to a state of half-mourning, during which their wardrobe was only partially black.

‡The brilliance of the dish, as many have noted, relies as much upon the painstakingly composed,

To begin the meal, Dumaine recommended an *entrée* both light and rich, featuring a complicated sauce: *filets de sole éminence*. He helped Painter and Olney choose the wines that would accompany the two dishes, for there were many fine Burgundies on his list. Olney was touched by Dumaine's unassuming thoughtfulness and courtesy in their discussion of meal, wine, and budget. In fact, toward the end of his life, Olney wrote about the evening in a way that suggests Dumaine and his beautifully run restaurant brought him to a new awareness of French haute cuisine.

But the central significance of the evening was, first and foremost, that of a fine meal shared among friends, the memory of which would stay with Olney long after Delaney, Painter, and Baldwin had all passed away:

> The "Filets de Sole Éminence" consisted of an assemblage of folded, poached sole filets, slices of lobster tail and pike quenelles, with a creamed lobster "à l'Américaine" sauce.*
> The quenelles, composed of pounded and sieved pike flesh, egg-white and cream, were firm, but light as a soufflé. The first wine, a Montrachet[†] 1934, was a golden, vaporous dream.
>
> The chicken arrived in its *marmite*, the cover sealed by a dampened ribbon of cloth wound round and round the rim, which, when unwound, released a flood of truffle fragrance. The chicken was served with its juices, which had collected in the plate, and accompanied by creamed morels. The wine, a Beaune Dames Hospitalières[‡] 1947, was good, but not memorable. With the cheeses, we wanted to be astounded, so

---

reduced, and clarified consommé as it does upon the quality of the *poularde* and the substantial presence of black truffles.

* A traditional sauce composed of concentrated lobster stock, white wine, Cognac, tomato, and tarragon.

[†] Considered by many to be the greatest dry white wine in the world, Montrachet is an *appellation d'origine contrôlée* and a *grand cru* vineyard of Burgundian chardonnay. Today a Montrachet of similar age (twenty years) would cost more than $500 retail.

[‡] A *cuvée* (or blend of wines) composed entirely of wines of *premier cru* vineyards. The *cuvée* is auctioned off yearly at the Beaune wine auction held by the Domaine des Hospices de Beaune on behalf of the charity hospice, founded in 1443 during a period of misery, famine, and plague. (Today a bottle of this well-known wine, similarly aged, would cost around $60.)

we asked Madame Dumaine to consult with the master (who never left the kitchen during the service); he sent to the table a cool bottle of La Tâche* (Domaine de la Romanée-Conti) 1951, a despised vintage with no more than a year of bottle age; it was transcendent—I had never tasted anything like it.

. . . After the service, Dumaine would leave his kitchens and settle into the bar to smoke a Gauloise and converse; his conversation never strayed from the technical aspects of cuisine and how he had adapted classical techniques to his own sensibilities. . . . We drank 1904 cognac with him, and liked it so much that we carried some to our rooms. Beauford dozed off, Jimmy's glass was empty and he reached stealthily for Beauford's when, suddenly, Beauford opened his eyes. The scene was re-enacted several times before, finally, Beauford's eyes failed to open and Jimmy emptied his glass. Like so many things remembered, the incident is meaningless, yet when I think of Dumaine, of the steamed chicken or La Tâche 1951, I see Jimmy's hand moving towards Beauford's glass, and I hear Beauford saying, ". . . Just resting my eyes."[16]

---

*La Tâche, which roughly translates as "the task," is the name of the small *grand cru* vineyard, roughly 12.5 acres, that is part of the Domaine de la Romanée-Conti, a Burgundian estate producing some of the world's greatest wines. Today a bottle of La Tâche, similarly aged, would retail for approximately $3,500.

SEVEN

Becoming Julia Child

Even before beginning her culinary training in Paris in the autumn of 1949, Julia Child was reading French cookbooks with real pleasure. She found they gave her a new way of appreciating French culture and increasing her acquaintance with the language, even while instructing her about French cooking practices. American cookbooks interested her much less; while she owned and had brought to Paris a copy of *Joy of Cooking* (a cookbook with a distinct personality, as evidenced by its original subtitle, *A Compilation of Reliable Recipes with Casual Culinary Chat*), Child often referred to the book as "Old Mrs. Joy," as if to suggest the author was a careworn drudge. And while she owned Fannie Farmer's plainspoken 1896 *Boston Cooking School Cook Book*, she hadn't even thought to bring it to France.

French cookbooks were different, however. The first to seduce her was *Gastronomie Pratique: Études Culinaires Suivies du Traitement de l'Obésité des Gourmands** (1907), written by Henri Babinski under the pseudonym Ali-Bab. This genial, slightly mad thousand-page cook-

---

*Trans.: *Practical Gastronomy: Culinary Studies Followed by Treatments for Gourmand Obesity*. An edited-down and relatively humorless English-language version was published by McGraw-Hill in 1974, but at only 471 pages, it is no substitute for the original.

book presented more than three thousand dishes from all over the world, described cooking practices from the time of the caveman until the present day, and finished by offering its readers dieting advice. It also gave tongue-in-cheek insights about the relation of eating to key moments in French history—noting, for example, that Louis XVI's "abnormal and constant craving for food" had made him unable to resist "the charms of a copious luncheon" during the royal family's ill-fated flight to Varennes: "Although he had effectively calmed his hunger pangs," Babinski concluded, "he and his family paid for it with their heads." Babinski/Ali-Bab could be equally outrageous in his opinions of foreign cooking, noting at one point that "Spain is a lovely country, but, as for its cuisine, the less said the better," and elsewhere dismissing Russian food by reminding his readers that "in 1815 the Cossacks camping on the Champs-Elysées ate candles."[1] During her first winter in Paris, Julia Child stayed up night after night to read the book in bed—doing so, according to her husband, Paul, "with the passionate devotion of a fourteen-year-old-boy to *True Detective* stories." Even at this very early moment in her culinary education, Julia Child seems to have appreciated the playfulness and humor inherent in culinary exploration, and to have considered cooking not so much a daily obligation as a form of entertainment.

As Child became more serious about cooking, however, she turned her attention to the undisputed genius of the French kitchen, Auguste Escoffier. His *cuisine classique*, the practice of restaurant and hotel cooking that he had codified in the early years of the century, did not focus on economy, simplicity, nutrition, or speed of preparation; rather, it emphasized luxury, sophistication, and greatest possible pleasure for the diner. His *Guide Culinaire* (first published in 1903, continually revised through 1921) was the bible of *cuisine classique*: it laid out a specific set of organizing principles for restaurant cooks to aid in their re-creation of his recipes. Escoffier's aim in doing so had been to demystify (and streamline) the extremely complicated (and time-consuming) practices developed in the previous century under France's leading chef, Carême, so that food could now be prepared rapidly, efficiently, and, most important, *to order* in a restaurant setting. Escoffier subsequently published *Ma Cuisine* in 1934, just before his death a year later. This fine and hefty book was a much simplified version of the *Guide Culinaire* specifically addressed to "the ordinary housewife [who] will find [here] delicious recipes within the limits of her purse."[2] Escoffier's vision of French restaurant cuisine (and, later, its homemade equivalent) was so very influential in postwar France that most of the Americans excited about French food from the 1940s through the 1970s were (at least initially) tasting and responding to dishes in his repertoire. At the Cordon Bleu, Child would receive her practical training from Max Bugnard, who had worked under Escoffier as a young man, and who remained a disciple of Escoffier even as he modified and streamlined a number of Escoffier recipes (both at Le Cordon Bleu and in the pages of *Cuisine et Vins de France* magazine) for home preparation.

But Child read other French authors as well, most notably Prosper Montagné: Paul Child had bought her Montagné's encyclopedic *Larousse Gastronomique* during their first years in Paris, and it sat on a shelf in her kitchen along with *Joy of Cooking*. She also had his *Le Grand Livre de la Cuisine*, the same book Stein had given Toklas for Christmas of 1943. Other, more recherché nineteenth-century titles also interested Child, notably Lucien Tendret's 1892 *La Table au Pays de Brillat-Savarin* and Grimod de la Reynière's highly entertaining, eight-volume, Paris-centric *Almanach des Gourmands*. Among the more practical, twentieth-century cookbooks she learned from, one stood out in particular: Evelyn Ébrard's *Le Livre de Cuisine de Madame E. Saint-Ange*.* This 1927 masterwork had been based on Ébrard's thirty-year involvement with her husband's monthly magazine, *Le Pot-au-Feu* (founded in 1893). But Ébrard's immersion in cooking predated that magazine, as she had been a home cook long before becoming a cooking instructor, cooking columnist, and finally (pseudonymous[†]) cookbook author.[3] Perhaps as a result, her fine and exhaus-

---

* The pseudonym Saint-Ange was derived from Ébrard's maiden name. The cookbook has been translated into English by Paul Aratow as *La Bonne Cuisine de Madame E. Saint-Ange*.

† The French passion for privacy and discretion has led many of that nation's culinary authors and writers on gastronomy to publish under pseudonyms. Simone Beck, for example, is the pseudonym of Simone Fischbacher (née Beck). Perhaps the first Frenchwoman to fully embrace cookbook celebrity was socialite Marie Pierre Adélaïde Lévêque de Vilmorin. "Mapie" (her family nickname turned *nom de plume*) married a nephew of artist Henri de Toulouse-Lautrec in 1933, becoming Countess de Toulouse-Lautrec. After studying cooking with Édouard de Pomiane, she

tive cookbook explained not only how to cook classic French dishes, but also *why* the techniques and practices called for in each recipe were necessary. Containing more than 1,300 recipes, it was the first great twentieth-century French cookbook to be published by a woman. Child adored it for its clarity and precision, and depended heavily upon it in her cowriting and rewriting of *Mastering the Art of French Cooking*. In 1953, as she began formulating her own exceptionally clear, direct, and highly detailed recipes out of a first draft composed by Simone Beck Fischbacher and Louisette Bertholle, Child noted in her correspondence that she was relying most heavily on four books for master recipes and information: Escoffier (either *Le Guide Culinaire* or *Ma Cuisine*), Montagné's *Le Grand Livre de Cuisine*, Babinski/Ali-Bab's *Gastronomie Pratique*, and Ébrard's *Le Livre de Cuisine de Madame E. Saint-Ange*. And she later described Ébrard as "my mentor in my early days in France."

But even as she immersed herself in such reading, Child realized her need for professional instruction. She was encouraged in that direction by a Smith College acquaintance, Charlotte Snyder Turgeon.[4] Turgeon had been a year below Child at school (graduating in 1934), and had first traveled to Paris in 1936 with her new husband, Frederick King Turgeon, a professor of French at Amherst College, who was just then taking a research sabbatical in France. After Charlotte complained to her husband of being "bored to death" by the lectures at the Sorbonne, "King" Turgeon (himself a keen amateur cook) suggested she enroll at the Cordon Bleu. Under its esteemed chef-instructor Henri-Paul Pellaprat* she ultimately received the school's much coveted (but at that time rarely awarded) diploma. Several years later, through a connection in the Harvard University French Department, she was asked to translate the classic French cookbook *Tante Marie*[†]

gradually evolved from society columnist into magazine cooking editor, and from there into best-selling cookbook author. Mapie de Toulouse-Lautrec was also the inventor of *Elle's* wildly popular detachable recipe cards, which Roland Barthes wrote about at length in his *Mythologies* (1957).

* Pellaprat's influence on home cooks was enormous, thanks to his *L'Art Culinaire Moderne* (1936), which quickly became the standard French reference work on "correct" cooking and entertaining in the home.

† *Tante Marie* ("Aunt Mary"), originally published as *La Veritable Cuisine de Famille par Tante Marie*, was an anthology assembled by the Taride publishing house. Since it had no actual author, the publisher used the name of his sister, Alice Marie Taride, for copyright and bibliographical purposes.

for Oxford University Press (both because Turgeon had just served that editor an exemplary French meal, and also because Dione Lucas had just abandoned the project to publish her *Cordon Bleu Cook Book*). By 1948, with her children no longer needing as much of her time, Turgeon was eager to prove herself as a professional writer—and since she considered the *Tante Marie* to be "the *Fannie Farmer* of France," she proved a fine and enthusiastic translator. By the time she bumped into Julia Child in Paris in the spring of 1949 (she was attending some brushup classes at the Cordon Bleu while her husband took another sabbatical), *Tante Marie's French Kitchen* was receiving very fine reviews in the United States. Shortly after discussing that new book with Turgeon while the two shared a Paris taxi, Child enrolled at the Cordon Bleu.

Turgeon's 1949 contribution to the American understanding of French cooking was a substantial one, for her translation of *Tante Marie* renders this authentically French cookbook into perfect, minimalist English. A plain little volume about the size and shape of a hymnal, *Tante Marie* takes a very pared-down approach to cooking instruction; the recipe for *boeuf bourguignon*, for example, is a mere five sentences. Even so, the original French version, published in 1903, had sold five million copies by the time Turgeon was asked to translate it. And while most of its recipes were simple* to the point of dullness, the book was highly specific about presentation: for example, a puree of tuna fish, hard-boiled eggs, and butter commonly served as an hors d'oeuvre in France was always to be "shape[d] into a pyramid, place[d] on a small serving dish, and decorate[d] with sprigs of parsley and a little mayonnaise." As such, the dishes were distinguished by their straightforwardness, purity, and rigid adherence to formula.† "The fact

---

*Not all, however. For instance, *tête de veau à la vinaigrette* calls for splitting a calf's head, removing the tongue and brains and cooking them apart, soaking the head overnight in cold water, boiling it for two hours, cutting the remaining flesh from the skull, and then arranging it on a platter (along with the sliced brains and tongue) accompanied by a garnish of parsley, with a vinaigrette passed separately.

†Like many cooks before and after, Alice Toklas both admired and abhorred the inflexibility of French culinary traditions. "We foreigners deplore the strict observance of a tradition which will not admit the slightest deviation in a seasoning or the suppression of a single ingredient," she later wrote. "For example, a dish as simple as a potato salad must be served surrounded by chicory. To serve it with any other green is inconceivable. Still this strict conservative attitude over the years has resulted in a number of essential principles that have made the renown of the French kitchen" (*The Alice B. Toklas Cook Book*, p. 3).

that few changes have been made in the many editions [of the book] bears witness to the fundamental secrets of French cooking—timelessness and simplicity," Turgeon noted in its preface. "French cuisine, despite its reputation for quality and artistry, is basically simple. . . . [Moreover] this cookbook is written for modest homes where one is obliged to consider time and money." As a faculty wife interested in helping women on modest incomes feed their families with minimal fuss, Turgeon felt strongly enough about these opening words of the original *Tante Marie* that she would repeat them, italicized and in French, at the end of her translator's preface.

But *Tante Marie*'s call for simplicity and thrift was not destined to capture the American imagination of 1949. Nor was the book's modest format—as Jane Nickerson of *The New York Times* observed, "[It] isn't explicit and extensive enough for the June bride who hardly knows a double boiler from a fry pan."[5] Furthermore, Americans were tired of the austerity mandated by the Great Depression and World War II. They wanted a return to abundance and pleasure, and they now had the money and leisure to pursue both. The book's modest commercial success would not deter Turgeon, however; this upright New England bluestocking would remain passionately engaged with French culture and cuisine over the next two decades. Even while running her own economy-minded cooking school in Amherst, she would undertake the five-year project of translating the *Larousse Gastronomique* into English. And she would also translate many other leading French books on cooking and entertaining, including one by her mentor Pellaprat and two by Mapie de Toulouse-Lautrec.

❧

Julia Child began her studies at the Cordon Bleu in the fall of 1949. Morning sessions featured lecture demonstrations, and afternoon sessions consisted of hands-on cooking practice. A number of other American women, including culinary writers and journalists, were studying there at the same time: apart from Charlotte Turgeon, there was Freda de Knight,* the food editor of *Ebony*, and Narcissa Chamberlain, who

* De Knight, of Salem, South Dakota, had published her *A Date with a Dish Cookbook* in 1948, basing it upon recipes from her two much loved columns for *Ebony*: "A Date with a Dish" and

was then composing the recipes for her husband's *Bouquet de France*. And a *Life* magazine article* published in 1951, written by the American woman journalist Frances Levison, describes the school as a place in which the majority of students are women. Study at the Cordon Bleu would become even more popular among American women after the success of the 1954 Billy Wilder comedy *Sabrina*, in which the impossibly glamorous Audrey Hepburn plays an ugly-duckling chauffeur's daughter who transforms into a great beauty while taking a year of vocational training at a Paris cooking school.

Like most of the other American women who attended the Cordon Bleu during this period, Child found the school on the fashionable rue St.-Honoré physically dirty, poorly stocked, and chronically disorganized. She also felt that the tuition was unduly expensive, although it would hardly be thought so by contemporary American cooking-school standards.[†] Even so, the school enabled her to work side by side with two hands-on instructor-chefs with whom she eventually became friends: Pierre Mengelatte, who ran the kitchen at the Restaurant des Artistes in Montmartre, and, more important, Max Bugnard, a former restaurant owner who was just then semiretired and working occasionally as a private chef as well as cooking instructor. Since Bugnard was the senior of the two, and the teacher to whom Child reported, and since Child occasionally hired him to work in her home, the two soon developed a warm and mutually beneficial friendship.

Guest lecturers came to the school regularly to give talks about French cuisine. One of the most distinguished author-journalists to speak during Child's time there was the great French food authority Maurice Edmond Sailland, better known by the pseudonym Curnonsky.[‡][6] Born in 1872, Sailland had come to Paris from Angers as a young

---

"The Little Brown Chef." The book predates her time at the Cordon Bleu, however, and shows no discernible French influence in its later editions. (Some of those later editions were published as *The Ebony Cookbook*.)

* Levison's article is "First, Peel an Eel" (*Life* magazine, December 1951).

[†] The tuition was then $150: adjusting for inflation, the cost today would be about $1,500. Current tuition for a year at the Culinary Institute of America (admittedly a very different sort of institution) is in the range of $27,000.

[‡] Sailland thought Curnonsky a "ridiculous nickname," even though he had coined it himself, in 1895. It was based on the Latin *cur non?* ("Why not?") to which he added *"une syllabe russe ou polonaise: SKY"* (Sailland, *À Travers Mon Binocle*, p. 15).

man to attend the École Normale Supérieure. From there he had subsequently launched himself as a humorist, novelist, and journalist before taking up gastronomic writing. From the turn of the century until his death in the mid-1950s, he was a central figure of the French culinary world.

Like the French-born, London-based cookbook author and restaurateur Marcel Boulestin (who was only a few years his junior, and a friend), Curnonsky began his literary career by working as one of the many ghostwriters of the entrepreneurial author-critic-businessman Henry Gauthier-Villars (or Willy), who was also the first husband (and mentor-turned-exploiter) of the novelist Colette. During his early years as an author, Curnonsky cowrote three racy popular novels* with his roommate, the poet and novelist Jean-Paul Toulet, and a number of humor books with the translator J-Wladimir Bienstock. At the same time, through work in advertising, Curnonsky coined the term *"gastronomade"* ("gastro-nomad") and also invented Bibendum,† the Michelin tire company's roly-poly gastronomic cartoon character. (Curnonsky and Bibendum do in fact look very much alike; and according to his biographer, Simon Arbellot, Curnonsky had signed his weekly newspaper column as "Bibendum" starting in March 1908.) Curnonsky's passion for good cooking, good wine, and fine dining made his move from humor, journalism, and fiction into full-time gastronomic writing a natural progression.

By 1921, working with the novelist, poet, and critic Marcel Rouff, Curnonsky began publishing *La France Gastronomique*, a twenty-eight-part guide to French provincial cooking and restaurants. As that great project neared completion in 1927, he was elected *"Prince Élu des Gastronomes"*‡ in a nationwide poll of French restaurateurs, cooks, and food journalists. In 1928 the French government took his honors one step further, naming him a chevalier of the Légion d'Honneur (and

---

* The two men published two of their three novels (*Bréviaire de Courtesan* and *Le Métier d'Amant*) under the pseudonym Perdiccas; the third, *Demi-Veuve*, was published under Curnonsky's name alone.

† Bibendum is a shortening of Michelin's Latin slogan for its tires, *Nunc est Bibendum* ("Now we must drink"), purportedly a reference to the tire's ability to "drink up" all road obstacles.

‡ *"Prince Élu"* indicates that Curnonsky was an elective monarch—that is, a prince elected by the people.

greater governmental honors would follow later). Unwilling to rest on his laurels, however, he founded l'Académie des Gastronomes, modeling this yearly assembly of literary food enthusiasts (including Édouard de Pomiane) after similar assemblies held by the Académie Française. Three years later, in 1933, Curnonsky cofounded l'Académie du Vin de France, which remains today an important trade group for the French wine industry.

With the shutting down of the French hospitality industry after the German invasion of 1940, Curnonsky withdrew to farthest Brittany, to Riec-sur-Bélon, where he boarded at the restaurant-hotel of a legendary cook, Mélanie Rouat, about whom he later wrote with fondness and good humor. He returned to Paris after the war to resume his career as a journalist, and in doing so became the titular head* of the newly founded *Cuisine et Vins de France* magazine. In 1953 he published his massive *Cuisine et Vins de France* cookbook.

By the time Child heard him speak at the Cordon Bleu in 1950, Curnonsky was recognized as a national treasure and beloved throughout France. Now nearing eighty, he had published nearly fifty books on French cuisine, and was essentially the public face of French gastronomy: a powerhouse of a writer-intellectual, gifted with both style and wit as well as a profound knowledge of French cuisine in all its many forms. But it was easy enough to dismiss this genial, big-bellied man—as Paul Child did—as nothing more than a gastronomic freeloader. "He's written + eaten + drunk off [his] reputation [for sixty years]," Paul wrote to his brother. "Now 80, he gets up at 4 pm, and starts his day with a soft boiled egg. Shortly afterward he goes out for a tea or a cocktail—it's a question of choosing which invitation to accept, there being always more than he can use. Back to bed again at 4 am, following a theater, or music, or a night club at someone else's expense; and after writing a bit. Not a life like yours or mine."[7]

Curnonsky's talks at the Cordon Bleu were both erudite and droll. In them, however, he repeatedly advocated on behalf of the integration of regional cuisine—including its most humble dishes—into the repertoire of *haute cuisine*, insisting that the finest of food preparations

---

*The real acting director of the magazine was Madeleine Decure.

might well be based on humble ingredients, provided that they were handled with great sensitivity and skill.

✣

While she enjoyed attending these lectures, Julia Child preferred learning practical skills in the Cordon Bleu's basement kitchens. Honing her knife skills in particular became an obsession: as she wrote a friend, "If you can't do fast knife-work, no chef will take you seriously." Max Bugnard had been chopping, boning, turning, slicing, mincing, and dicing for years—and Child adored him for it, as well as for his appearance, which was basically that of an aged and bespectacled bunny rabbit. "He is 74, [a] former associate of Escoffier, former chef and owner of the *Petit Vatel* [restaurant] in Bruxelles," she later wrote a friend. "[He] lost all during the war, and is now semi-retired, and looking for a bit of private lessonry and private dinner-partying. Just a darling man, *archi-bavarde** about life in '*la belle époque*' and fun to hear him talk of what 'they did.' . . . [He's] a wonderful teacher and cook . . . and friend." Not content with the group lessons she was receiving from him at the Cordon Bleu, Child sometimes hired Bugnard to give her private lessons, either one-on-one or with friends. "Had a lovely afternoon today with my old chef Bugnard," she wrote at one point. "The two of us spen[t] a happy 3 hours cutting up veg, cleaning chickens, precooking things . . . working with a professional, you pick up a new trick or two every session. I am so glad I spent the hours I did learning [from him how] to use the knife professionally."[8]

Bugnard helped her in other ways as well. Child did not get along with the owner-director of the school, Elisabeth Brassart, because both women had strong, even domineering personalities. After being challenged by Child, Brassart seems to have responded by stonewalling Child's efforts to schedule the exam for her diploma. (Exams for the advanced diploma were traditionally offered only at the discretion of the instructor, and in recognition of exceptional talent.) "I hate only a very few people [in this world], one being Mme. Brassart, head

---

* Trans.: Ultratalkative.

of the Cordon Bleu, who is a nasty, mean woman," Child later wrote, likening the school's administrator to Senator Joseph McCarthy for her sheer perversity and evil.[9] Bugnard gently interceded with Brassart on Child's behalf, persuading Brassart to schedule Child's test for April 1951. Unfortunately Child failed that test, and then needed to negotiate yet again with Brassart, this time for a second attempt at the coveted diploma. "My disgruntlement is supreme, my *amour propre* enraged, my bile boiling, my impotence inexhaustible," she wrote Charlie and Freddie Child, going on in the same letter to damn Brassart for being so money-focused. She then imagined a different sort of cooking school, one "run on different lines; and the main idea of the school is . . . to make cooks out of people, and not to make money . . . an establishment dedicated to learning and the enjoyment of cooking through friendliness and encouragement and professionalism. . . . [Unlike here, where in] an atmosphere of hate and distrust one is filled with the feculence of cancer, the uneasiness of swallowed anger [and] everything becomes bilious."

If Child was unusually eloquent in that letter, perhaps it was because she was envisioning her own future teaching career even as she wrote it. But while Child's dislike of Brassart was deeply felt, her judgment of Brassart was a little unfair. At the time, Brassart was the owner of a struggling and undercapitalized cooking school. The school's founder, Marthe Distel, had died in the late 1930s, leaving it to a Catholic orphanage even as Henri-Paul Pellaprat, her brilliant partner of many years, retired at age eighty. When Brassart purchased what remained of the Cordon Bleu in 1945, she became director of an institution that was essentially a ghost of its former self. Brassart's strategy in building it back up was to enroll as many new students as possible. To do so, she created two types of classes: one for privileged housewives, newlyweds, debutantes, and others with money to spend. The second, with its less convenient classes (which met from 7:30 to 9:30 in the morning), was designed for American men taking advantage of the tuition benefits available to them through the GI Bill. Child, with her zeal for order and organization, had no patience for the dirt, worn crockery, faulty electric ovens, and overall mismanagement she encountered there. Moreover, she thought the two-tiered system patently unfair to women, relegating them to classes for housewife-dilettantes (though others, including *Life* magazine, reported that the GI's taking classes there were just as casual about their cooking instruction, spending a good deal of their "school" time playing pinball in the café next door).

Child describes Brassart repeatedly as a peevish, vindictive, money-grubbing game-player. "From my perspective," Child later wrote, "Madame Brassart lacked professional experience, was a terrible administrator, and tangled herself up in picayune details and petty politics. . . . The lack of a qualified and competent head was hurting the school—and could damage the reputation of French cooking, or even France herself, in the eyes of the world."[10] According to the Child-Prud'homme memoir, Chef Mengelatte (who is routinely misidentified as "Mangelatte" throughout that account, as well as throughout Julia Child's correspondence) had confided to Child that "the school was doing a great disservice to the *métier*, as the administration was focused on a mad scramble for money rather than on the excellent training of their pupils . . . It was sad that even such an energetic chef [as Mengelatte], with such a deep-seated sense of artistry, had to fight so hard to protect a civilized piece of French culture from barbarism."[11]

Child's assertion that someone needed to save French food culture from the barbarians running the Cordon Bleu is an odd one. (It is worth noting that, contrary to Child's assertions of her incompetence, Brassart would remain the successful owner-director of the Cordon Bleu for the next forty-five years.) What is clear, however, is that in enrolling at the Cordon Bleu, Child had needed to do things Brassart's way—which is to say, the French way—and she was not one to be bossed around. Paul Child had been dealing for some time now with similarly autocratic (and idiosyncratic) French management styles through his work at the U.S. Information Service, where, according to Julia "he had to be a combination diplomat-hustler-bully, in order to navigate the wildly different styles of the French and American bureaucracies."[12] "Paul and I were temperamentally more sympathetic to the French [way of doing things]," Child noted many years later, "but we were also its victims." Too intelligent, self-assured, and privileged to be flunked on her exam like a common French housewife, Child pushed hard for her do-over*—and, with it, her permanent, successful exit from the Cordon Bleu with diploma in hand.

Scheduling that second exam took a while, in part because Child herself had a complicated travel schedule. After returning from a two-month vacation in the United States, she found she had still not received a firm date for the retest, and once again she asked Bugnard to intervene. (Little as she may have thought of either Brassart or the Cordon Bleu, she really did want that diploma.) In August 1951, four months after failing the first exam, Child was allowed to take the exam again. This time, however, she took the test in her own well-organized kitchen on the rue de l'Université. After completing what she described as "a very simple written section," she cooked a basic meal for her friend Helen Kirkpatrick and for her examiner, Max Bugnard.[13] Bugnard passed her without comment or commendation. She received her diploma by mail a month later.

❧

But something much more significant to Child's future took place during 1951: she joined Le Cercle des Gourmettes, an upper-class women's club for food and wine enthusiasts, and through it began to form an understanding of how culinary culture related to French home life. More important, she came to know Simone Fischbacher (née Beck), a rich and stylish Parisian whose money, like Child's, came to her through inherited wealth rather than through marriage—a situation that gave her a good deal of independence in her marriage. Beck's roots were Norman; her maternal grandfather, Alexandre Le Grand, a former wine *négociant*, had struck it rich through the invention, proprietary ownership, and sole manufacture of the wildly popular Bénédictine liqueur, which he distilled in the small Norman town of Fécamp. (And his impressive art collection is still housed there, in his massive Palais Bénédictine, on a street that bears his name.) Beck's father,

---

*The French are not big on makeover exams, as evidenced by the standards of their *baccalauréat* degree, which even today allows only those students who have scored very near misses to take the "*épreuve de rattrapage*"—and then only a full year after failing the first examination. (Child's first exam, by her own account, was a total failure.)

Maurice-Jules Joseph Beck, was an art and furniture collector and "a man of impeccable taste" who owned a profitable silicates business. As a result of all this good fortune, Beck had grown up in a Norman-Edwardian château located in Rainfreville, just outside of Dieppe, with a household staff of six (including, of course, a cook). As a strong-willed young woman from a highly traditional family (she had been sent to convent school and was a devout Catholic), she was also something of a tomboy, perhaps because her preferred hobbies of hunting, fishing, and horseback riding kept her at a distance from her perfectionist mother. For a while, impressed by the exploits of Charles Lindbergh, she had wanted to become a woman aviator. After her first marriage she had settled instead into the life of a fashionable Parisian matron: impeccably dressed, with an apartment off the avenue Foch decorated by Paul Poiret, she entertained a good deal, even as her favorite pastime consisted of driving her very stylish English sports car (a Talbot 10-CV sports coupé) down the broad boulevards of Paris at very high speeds.

When she and her first husband ultimately proved sexually and emotionally incompatible, she had, with the blessing of her dying father, divorced him—something highly unusual for a woman of her background, religion, and class. Then, in late 1936, she met Jean Fischbacher, a good-looking young businessman from an Alsatian Protestant family. They found they had a good deal in common: as a boy, he'd spent his summers in Normandy less than a mile from her childhood home. He nicknamed her "Simca" after watching her emerge from the tiny little Simca 5 (a French version of the Fiat Topolino) that she was driving when they first met.[14] Despite their different religions the two became lovers and married within the year.

Julia Child first met Simone Beck Fischbacher at a party in late 1949* and had had several lunches with her since—they truly enjoyed each other's personalities regardless of their very different backgrounds and upbringings. Moreover, Child realized from Beck that she had much yet to learn about French cuisine: "my schooling had given me the

---

* It was a cocktail party for one hundred held in the Saint-Germain-en-Laye home of George Artamanoff, a Russian-born American businessman and the first president of Sears International Inc., who was then working with the Marshall Plan.

basics, but [Beck] gave me the finesse, enlarged my culinary vocabulary, and imbued me with the French attitude about food."[15] Beck had studied at the Cordon Bleu during the 1930s, between her first and second marriages, working with Pellaprat at roughly the same time as Dione Lucas and Charlotte Turgeon, and often having Pellaprat over to her home to give her private cooking instruction. This had the added benefit, as she later wrote, of facilitating "small dinner parties prepared by him, my cook, and me. . . . We all cooked together . . . everything was presented stylishly, as *haute cuisine*."

During the war Jean Fischbacher, who had enlisted as an officer, was captured by the Nazis, and Beck left off her practice of *haute cuisine* to concentrate instead on raising and providing basic foodstuffs for her family (primarily by tending chickens, goats, and rabbits at the family's château, even as it was partially occupied by Nazi officers). She also traded black-market bottles of Bénédictine for foods she could then pack up and send off to her husband at his prisoner-of-war camp. Strongly opposed to the Nazis and the Pétain government, she quietly allowed her elegant new apartment in Neuilly to be used as a drop-off point for forged identity papers, thus discreetly aiding in the Resistance.

Since the war's end she had again returned to cooking, both as a would-be cookbook author (working in collaboration with her friend Louisette Bertholle) and also as an officer of Le Cercle des Gourmettes, which she had joined at her husband's suggestion. Jean Fischbacher had urged her to do so when his own entry into France's most prestigious (and socially exclusive) all-male gastronomic society, Le Club des Cent, proved more difficult than expected.*

Le Cercle des Gourmettes had in fact been formed after a gala dinner in 1927 held by Le Club des Cent, one to which the club members' wives had also been invited. During the evening a toast had been offered to the great male chefs who had shaped France's cuisine. The wives, led by an American named Pauline Ettlinger, had

---

* In her memoir, *Food and Friends*, Beck explained Jean's difficulty in gaining admission to Le Club des Cent ("The Club of the One Hundred"): "As with the Académie Française, a member of the Club des Cent had to die (even if from overindulgence!) before a new candidate could be admitted."

objected to the toast and in short order banded together to form Le Cercle des Gourmettes. The men of Le Club des Cent had not thought Le Cercle would last, but twenty-four years later it was still going strong. Unlike Le Club des Cent, which was primarily a dining club, Le Cercle des Gourmettes expected its members to oversee the cooking of a lunch (utilizing the member's cook and scullery help, and sometimes adding a professional chef). The *brigadière* ("hostess of the day") was charged with devising the complete menu—not only the food but also the small wines* that were to accompany it—and also with decorating the table, and choosing the china, linens, and silver that best suited the meal. (The *brigadière* was welcome to participate in the cooking if she liked, but few did.) After the lunch was served, the merits of the food, wines, and table setting were evaluated and discussed by the members, making the luncheon not only a pleasurable experience but also, it was felt, an educational one.

Le Cercle des Gourmettes also organized restaurant outings and wine tastings (or *"goûters de Bacchus"*†), with the husbands invited to both. "The idea behind [the Gourmettes] is to exchange recipes and build awareness of food and its presentation, but it [is] largely a social lunch overseen by a professional chef," Child wrote some ten years after her first club meeting. She would maintain in a letter to a magazine editor in 1963 that "it is not at all an exclusive club—the only requirement is an enthusiasm for food and for cooking";[16] however, during her time there in the early 1950s, club member Marie-Thérèse Carrier, writing in the club's minutes, noted very much to the contrary that "among the many gastronomic clubs that exist in France, the Cercle des Gourmettes is the only one for women [and it is] not open to anyone who wants to join; indeed the severity of its admission process is equalled only by that of the Jockey Club."‡ Simone Beck

---

* A "small wine" is a wine of lesser reputation. France has many such wines, which often provide good value for the money.

† Roughly translated, "snack-time for Bacchus."

‡ Le Jockey-Club de Paris was the city's most prestigious men's club. (I have translated from Mme. Carrier's minutes, written of course in French.) Alex Prud'homme's account of the Gourmettes included in *My Life in France* is misleading largely because it is drawn from an unnamed American magazine article written in the mid-1960s. Prud'homme states that Child attended luncheons at the test kitchens of the Gaz de France headquarters—but that is impossible, since the building was not

likewise noted in her memoirs that it was highly exclusive: "it was what we would call a *mondain* assemblage of women from a certain social class, to the manner born. They had to know the finer points of food, but more important, they had to come from the right family background. The family tree mattered more than table manners. Everybody got dressed up for the lunches. . . . I had no complexes about my breeding and manners, and I knew more about cuisine than many of the members, [all of] whose names I [made sure I] knew by the time I went to the [first] lunch. The elegant meal was held at one of the members' houses, a huge place fit for a grand reception."[17] Even the name of the organization is a telling one, for in French a *gourmette* is not a female gourmet (*gourmet* is a masculine noun), but rather a "chain bracelet." Thus the name suggests, through subtle wordplay, a circle of well-dressed women, even while it punningly (and discreetly) hints at women who love good food and wine.

Though she was initially delighted to be part of the group, Child soon decided it was an anachronism: as she wrote Avis DeVoto, "[the] poor old club is pretty sad. All the original members are now so old, in the[ir] 70s, and were of the generation who never really did any cooking anyway, just eating. So here were 20 of these old dames, chattering away, drifting in and out, and nobody doing any cooking except Simca and me [and Max Bugnard]."[18] In February 1951, after attending two meetings, Child invited seven of the Gourmettes to her home for a lunch prepared by Bugnard: *"Je désirais vous présenter le chef, Max Bugnard, ancien confrère d'Escoffier, ancien chef et propriétaire du Petit Vatel à Bruxelles, actuellement fixé a Paris, dont j'aimerais à vous faire apprécier les qualités,"** she wrote in her very correct note of invitation. (She was hoping to find some new work for him even as she was lobbying to become a club member.) Beck may have suggested the idea of hiring Bugnard to Child, since in doing something similar with

---

constructed until the early 1960s, and Child was attending the luncheons only from 1951 through early 1953. By contrast, Mme. Carrier's minutes note that the lunches during those years were prepared in various kitchens; most receptions were in the home of the vice president of Le Cercle des Gourmettes, Mme. Charpentier, whose reception rooms were distinguished by *"un caractère d'élégance du meilleur ton."*

* Trans.: I would like to introduce you to chef Max Bugnard, an old colleague of Escoffier, formerly the chef-owner of Le Petit Vatel restaurant in Brussels, now living in Paris, whose qualities and abilities I should like to help you appreciate.

Pellaprat, she had learned a great deal. ("Before I met Pellaprat I had no intention of making food my métier," Beck later stated in a book on the French dinner party. "All I wanted [then] was to be able to receive* my friends better. [But] he's still the one I put above everybody else. Pellaprat was the clearest, the simplest, and most direct. I'm still making the hollandaise he taught me in 1934.")

Beck was just then the *brigadière-en-chef* of Le Cercle des Gourmettes—in essence, its driving force. One of the youngest and liveliest women in the group, she was a person of extraordinary good looks, style, and vigor. She was also a self-described "fanatic perfectionist," having inherited this trait from her mother. As a girl she had enjoyed helping her family's cook in their Norman kitchen, occasionally preparing desserts or entire meals; now, in her early forties, she was a highly experienced Parisian hostess who entertained regularly both in town and in country, and had strong thoughts on how to do so, many of which came from her father, an Anglophilic Frenchman† of starchy late Victorian manners and ideas. Her Norman manor-house background, her Parisian studies with Pellaprat, and her married life (first in the Sixteenth Arrondissement, and subsequently in posh suburban Neuilly) had all taught Beck that there were very specific and "correct" ways of extending invitations, organizing menus, setting tables, and receiving guests.

In addition, Beck had been working for some time now with another club member, Louisette Bertholle, on developing a French home-cooking cookbook for Americans, basing it, she later recalled, on "my mother's black recipe notebooks, [and our cook] Zulma's cuisine, [and] tips from chefs in restaurants, and [from catering chefs who worked with us at the] *Gourmettes*."[19] Bertholle, who Paul Child thought "a perfect Frenchwoman,"[20] knew America and Americans far better than Beck, because her husband worked for an American chemical company, and she had recently spent several years living in the United States. The two women had already produced two small prototypes of the book in booklet form. Their manuscript in progress, meanwhile, featured more than one hundred detailed recipes.

---

* "Receive" is Beck's translation of *recevoir*, meaning "to entertain at home."
† He was, in fact, half-British, the son of an English mother.

Of these two women, Julia Child was most drawn to Beck, perhaps seeing in this tall, handsome woman a French version of herself: both were strong-minded and energetic, and cooking was their shared passion. Both were also childless, and so (unlike Bertholle, who was often distracted by child-rearing) could give their full and undivided attention to their work in French cuisine. According to Child's biographer, "Each called the other *une force de la nature* [and] Julia also called Simca *la Super-Française.*"[21] But there were differences too: Beck was an immensely proper and formal person for whom correct manners and polite interactions were always of greatest importance. Child's American habit of clowning, teasing, and poking fun at people was not something in which Beck easily took part. Rather, she believed in good manners always.

Similarly, when Beck had guests to dinner in her home, everything needed to be absolutely appropriate to the occasion: not merely the menu, but the wines, the table settings, the seating arrangements, and even the guests. "For a *dîner très fin*, a private dinner, the point is to bring together people who are intellectually compatible, on the same social rung, and who share the same way of life and religion," she once explained. "The same social rung I must insist on. In France it's most important of all. Money doesn't count. It's breeding that does. Intellect, too." The people who came together at Beck's table needed not only to share the same basic social background and way of life, but also the same core beliefs: "You'll never find a communist in my house," she told the same reporter. "You can mix people from the same milieu, but putting a gardener in with an artist, a *paysan* with a minister—*ça va pas du tout.** The barbecue, where everyone joins together and has a good time, that has nothing to do with France. The melting pot works in the United States but not in this country."[22]

Ideas about keeping to one's own class were not unknown to Julia Child (she had grown up in Pasadena, in a restrictive country-club setting, with a father who was a member of the John Birch Society), but as an adult she had rebelled against such close-mindedness and prided herself on being able to mix with just about anyone. And as

---

* Trans.: That simply won't work.

the wife of a low-level government employee, doing so had become, to some extent, her job. But it was also something she felt simply to be right and just, and something she even enjoyed, for she disliked social pretense. (She would later recall that as a young woman "I was always careful to tell [my] Aunt Theodora when she was boasting about her socially illustrious antecedents that John Alden and Priscilla [Mullins] were indentured *servants!*") Through her marriage to Paul Child— who, though he too came from a "society" background, had grown up without money, and had chosen the path of the self-styled artist-intellectual—Julia had become even more liberal. In that way, she was clearly the opposite of Beck and the other Gourmettes. Even though Child's background was unmistakably wealthy, socially exclusive, and privileged, and even though her own manners, bearing, and accent were undeniably patrician, her newfound ambition was really just the opposite: to create a cooking school, a cookbook, and (in time) a television cooking program that would enable anyone from any background to have easy access to knowledge (and, through that knowledge and a bit of hard work, access to fine French food).

In attending Le Cordon Bleu, Child had focused on restaurant-style cooking techniques. But now, through the Gourmettes (and specifically through Simone Beck), she was coming into direct contact with something altogether different: upper-class French customs, preferences, and prejudices regarding the table. As a result she was compelled to face a central paradox regarding her own interest in fine French cooking and fine French dining: namely, that the kind of French cuisine she had been enjoying, with its emphasis on luxury ingredients and labor-intensive preparations, was undeniably classist and exclusionary. While Child loved *haute cuisine*, she felt that preparing and eating delicious food ought to be within every person's grasp, not simply a privilege of the very wealthy. And so as she slowly got to know Beck and Bertholle, she began to realize that what she really wanted to do was democratize and demystify French cuisine for Americans— something neither of the other two women had ever foreseen as part of their project, and that neither could quite comprehend (not least because both relied daily on their cooks to run their kitchens).

While Charlotte Turgeon had already presented a radically simple version of modest French home cooking for Americans through her translation of *Tante Marie*, that book had been too plainspoken and limited in its ambition to have much of an effect on American home cooks. In addition, the flavors and cooking ideas presented within that book had been relatively modest and artless. Child, through her experience of French restaurant-going, through her studies at the Cordon Bleu, and now, through her connection to fine, upper-class French *cuisine bourgeoise* via Bertholle, Beck, and Le Cercle des Gourmettes, was imagining something different and far more ambitious. In the coming years, she would work with Beck and Bertholle to put together a collection of household recipes that drew upon Escoffier's (far more elaborate) *cuisine classique* to capture the tastebuds (and imagination) of the American reader-cook.

In later years Avis DeVoto would describe Fischbacher and Child's joint work on this project, which grew into *Mastering the Art of French Cooking*, as "one of the great collaborations of history. The [two women] are absolutely necessary to each other [and] it is the combination [of the two] which makes their work together so revolutionary." But this collaboration was not simply one of a gifted French cook and an equally gifted (and far more analytic and precise) American cook and recipe writer.* It was also to be, although no one yet realized it, the collaboration of a privileged Parisian gentlewoman with an American self-described "Upper Bohemian" whose secret, Promethean ambition was to demystify grand French upper-class cuisine, and thereby deliver it, like the gift of fire, to the middle-class American home.

In April 1951 Beck and Bertholle (and their husbands) came to lunch at the Child apartment, where Chef Bugnard helped Child prepare them all a fine meal. Two weeks later, the Childs went to the Bertholles for a dinner prepared by their cook. More lunches and dinners—at the Childs', the Fischbachers', and the Bertholles'—were to follow in the fall; so too would lunches for just the women, ending with a long lunch at the Des Artistes in early December, during which the three resolved to open a modest French cooking school for

---

* "Simca is a creative [and technical] genius," DeVoto once noted. By contrast, she felt, "Julia is deeply logical, orderly, accurate, painstaking, patient, determined to get all this knowledge clearly on paper" ("Some Scattered Notes," Avis DeVoto Papers, Schlesinger Library, Harvard University).

Americans. Paul Child, who described the stylishly coiffed and dressed Beck, with her pale white skin and bright pink cheeks, as "a flashy and charming *Française* of about 42,"[23] wrote his brother with the happy news that "Julie + Simca + Bertholle are planning to start a little cooking-school, classes to be limited to 4 students."[24] All three women seemed to think that jointly teaching "a few classes to Americans in Paris" might eventually help them in the writing of a book.*

⚜

By late 1951 Paul Child had overcome the worst of his amoebiasis, and was able once again to eat and drink what he liked. Julia held a number of fine and imaginative dinner parties at their home that fall, through which the couple solidified older friendships and forged some new ones. The couple's more distinguished guests included, among many others, the expatriate American hostess Alice Lee Myers and her husband, Dicky; Samuel Chamberlain's wife, Narcissa; Robert Penn Warren; Theodore H. White; Pierre Mengelatte of the Restaurant des Artistes and the Cordon Bleu; and Max Bugnard (but this time, happily enough, as the guest, not the cook). It was a busy autumn, also featuring picnics in the countryside, many dinners in restaurants, and various luncheons, receptions, and teas at the American Embassy related to Paul Child's work. But as fall came to a close, the Childs braced themselves, since Parisian winters are grim, featuring short, damp days, leaden skies, and bone-chilling cold. Faced with the prospect of another dreary January far from home, Julia decided to do something truly spectacular for Paul's birthday.

It was to be a wildly luxurious affair, and at the same time something rather kooky: a mock state dinner, featuring homemade decorations and costumes. Having endured a serious gastric illness for the past year, Paul, who tended toward depression, needed some bucking

---

*In her memoir, Simone Beck Fischbacher writes that she had sought out Julia Child from the very earliest moment of their acquaintance as a potential third partner in their book project, having been told by the social activist and bestselling author Dorothy Canfield Fisher, an early reader of the Beck-Bertholle manuscript who sat on the board of the Book-of-the-Month Club, that they needed to "get an American who is crazy about French cooking to collaborate with you . . . That is the angle you will need" (*Food and Friends*, p. 161). (Dorothy Canfield Fisher had been a friend of the Fischbacher family since meeting them while doing relief work in France during World War I.)

up as he faced the landmark birthday of fifty. Julia, meanwhile, loved to amuse her guests as well as dazzle them with her good cooking, and she was always dreaming up new ways of having a good time.

But there was a little more to it than that. For one thing, both Paul and Julia Child were sensing that their time in Paris was drawing to a close. The U.S. government was now less interested than previously in creating propagandistic exhibitions selling the American Way of Life to the French. So Paul Child had begun making inquiries about a new job, one that would probably take them elsewhere. And their friends were slipping away too: Paul and Hadley Mowrer, who had taken such pains to make the Childs feel welcome in Paris, had already moved back to their farmhouse in New Hampshire. Alice and Dicky Myers were fed up with the French and would soon be heading home as well. And the sweet couple who ran La Vallée d'Auge restaurant, where Bumby Hemingway's wedding breakfast had been held, had also disappeared. As Paul explained to his brother, "the husband [is] the chef—and a good one—and the wife the caissière.* Yesterday . . . Mme. La Caissière was standing near the restaurant and we stopped to chat. She was crying. Her husband is dying of cancer of the throat. The Vallée d'Auge is sold. She's moved to a 3-room apartment, their life savings are going to doctors. There's no hope of his recovery." No wonder, then, that the Childs felt the need to lighten the mood by throwing a party.

All that month the couple planned the menu and the wines, devised a guest list, sent out invitations, and then set about creating the evening's party favors and costumes. Photographs of the big night show their apartment hung with ornamentation, and host, hostess, and guests all wearing silly sashes, tiaras, and other decorations. "We made spiffy 'medals' of colored silk ribbon, enamel pins, and nonsense inscriptions for each guest," Child recalled in her memoir. "Mine was labeled 'Marquise de la Mousse Manquée.' "[25] The many (archaic) formalities being lampooned were to some extent ones that the Childs had thought so absurd in the American diplomatic circles in which they were compelled to move because of Paul's job; but they were also

---

* The cashier of the restaurant, traditionally the wife of the chef-owner.

a way of poking fun at the starchy ways of the French upper classes, so proud of their aristocratic backgrounds and distinguished family names. The place settings and dining protocols for the evening were nonetheless entirely "correct," since Julia Child had recently learned the importance of such things through Le Cercle des Gourmettes, as well as through her friendship with Simone Beck.

Paul and Julia Child were the hosts that evening; Max Bugnard was the chef, and for scullery help, they had their mildly demented housekeeper, Jeanne, long since dubbed Jeanne la Folle.* "I had once pictured French maids as chic creatures in starched aprons—shades of *Vogue* magazine," Julia wrote in her memoirs. "Coo-Coo [Coquette, their second cleaning woman] had changed that perception, and now our latest, Jeanne, shattered it forever. She was a tiny, slightly wall-eyed, frazzle-haired woman with a childish mind that often wandered astray."[26] Paul hired in several other workers as well: a *maître d'hôtel* to help at the table, and a steward to pour the wines. "With 12 at table I figgered [*sic*] we'd need that many for ease & efficiency," he wrote his brother, then proudly laying out the evening's planned menu:

Amuse-Gueules au fromage, with Krug 1943
Boal rétour des Indes, 1826 (After long discussion w[ith] various
    authorities, we decided to open the meal with it alone.)
Rissolettes of Foie Gras Carisse† served with Château Chauvin
    1929
Filet de Boeuf Matignon‡ (w[ith] same wine)

---

*Another of Paul and Julia Child's inside jokes: they had nicknamed their hapless maid after Joanna of Castile (Joanna the Mad; Jeanne la Folle in French), one of the great mad queens of history.

†Chef Bugnard seems to have followed Escoffier's example in creating an elaborate preparation of cooked foie gras, chopped truffles, and other ingredients shaped into a little patty or croquette. Similar dishes (none named "Carisse") can be found in Escoffier's *Guide Culinaire*, along with *soufflés de foie gras, quenelles de foie gras*, and *timbales de foie gras*.

‡Child would include a version of this recipe in *Mastering the Art of French Cooking* as *filet de boeuf braisé Prince Albert*. In the version served at the party, a filet of beef was partially sliced and stuffed between the slices with a *matignon* filling of cooked diced carrots, onions, celery, ham, tongue, and Madeira. The whole filet was then wrapped in cheesecloth, browned, and then briefly casserole-roasted before being unwrapped and served. Child's simplified version in *Mastering the Art* (pp. 303–5) specifies a horizontal stuffing of *foie gras* and truffles, and calls for a slow braising rather than final roasting, with the *matignon* mixture incorporated into the final sauce rather than stuffed between the slices of meat.

Les Fromages (Camembert, Brie de Melun,* Époisses, Roque-
fort, chèvre) served with Chambertin 1923
Fruits refraîchis†
Gateau du demi-siècle‡ (birthday cake) served with Moët &
Chandon Brut Imperial 1943.
Café, cognac, liqueurs (we have a 100 year old cognac, *parmi
les autres*§)
Havana cigars, Turkish cigs, etc.

Food and wine played a starring role that evening. Paul had been
collecting rare wines since arriving in Paris, and the ones he had
selected for his birthday dinner would surely give their guests something to talk about: two different vintage Champagnes bottled during the height of the Occupation; a 29-year-old Chambertin, the
Burgundy prized above all other wines by Louis XIV and Napoleon;
a 23-year-old, near-perfect Saint-Émilion;¶ a 100-year-old Cognac;
but, most amazing of all, a 125-year-old Madeira, Boal Rétour des
Indes, 1826,** a fortified wine dating from the days of Charles X—a
wine so remarkably old, rare, and well traveled that the Childs planned
to serve it unaccompanied at the beginning of the meal. These were
good choices for a man just turning fifty: all suggested that maturity
can endow both grace and finesse. The food, meanwhile, was pure
Escoffier: the finest and most costly of ingredients, given the most
loving and elaborate of preparations. The *foie gras rissolettes* and decon-
structed filet of beef courses reflected the Childs' prosperity, to be

---

*A distinctive variety of Brie (with a drier, darker, stronger-flavored rind) made in the town of
Melun, just south of Paris.
†Another Escoffier favorite: diced fresh fruits tossed with a liqueur or eau-de-vie to "refresh" them.
‡Trans.: Cake of half a century.
§Trans.: Among others.
¶Château Chauvin would be classified a *grand cru classé* three years later, in 1955. (Before that,
despite the high quality of the wine, no classification scheme existed for the Saint-Émilion
AOC.)
** "Rétour de l'Inde" or "Rétour des Indes" signifies that the wine had been shipped to India and back
again (or sent on a similarly long ocean voyage), a process thought during the nineteenth century to
improve the taste and quality of the wine by artificially hastening its maturation, through the distress
caused to the wine by the ship's movement. (This treatment was given not only to Madeira, but also
to sherry and Bordeaux wines, and also, in some rare instances, wines from Burgundy.)

sure, but also their love of French *haute cuisine* at its most outrageously complicated. The cheese offerings, meanwhile, were simply an embarrassment of riches—and while most wine-loving Frenchmen would be shocked at the idea of presenting a Chambertin with a Roquefort, a chèvre, or an Époisses,* the sheer luxury of so many fine cheeses surely spoke for itself. The *gâteau du demi-siècle* meanwhile suggested that a sense of humor is always helpful when facing the landmark year of fifty.

During the evening there would be a recital of light verse and occasional poetry, something Paul had excelled in since his days with Edith "Slingsby" Kennedy. Julia accordingly contacted their guests in advance to suggest they write something in his honor. "Many of the guests brought charming, skillful and witty poems to read between the courses," Paul wrote his brother in the days that followed. While none of these verses has survived, several of Paul's do, including his hymn in praise of *pâté de foie gras*, "Paean to Pâté," which might easily have been recited over Max Bugnard's elegant *rissolettes de foie gras Carisse*:

> *We welcome you with roundelay*[†]
> *Oh baveuse,*[‡] *glistening pâté!*
> *We welcome you with unctuous lip*
> *With eye aflash and tongue adrip.*
> *And we salute the genius Frog—*
> *The chef, or monk, or pedagogue—*
> *Whose concept bold to utilize*
> *A goose's liver in this wise*
> *First brought to Man this wondrous food:*
> *Creating tongue's beatitude.*

---

* Fine wines, delicate and nuanced in flavor, generally taste better against milder cheeses. Roquefort, unusually salty as well as strong and sharp, can be paired with a sweet wine—most famously, sauternes—but it is not a good foil for a fine wine. Similarly Époisses de Bourgogne, with its violent odor, is a difficult cheese to pair with any fine wine. Chèvre meanwhile has an astringent quality that pairs well with the dry white wines of the Loire, but does little for a noble Chambertin.
[†] A circle dance.
[‡] French for "dribbly," from the french noun *bave*, "saliva."

Unfortunately Paul had come down with a sudden, massive dental abscess three days before the party. An "advanced case of pyorrhea* . . . suddenly [made] the jaw bone decide to reject a tooth," he wrote his brother, "form[ing] a pocket of pus and gas which beg[an] to push the tooth out of its socket. Every time you bite it is like poking a boil . . . eventually 3 [of my] teeth will have to be pulled." For the purpose of getting through the evening, his dentist ground down the surfaces of two of the affected teeth so that Paul could close his mouth. But shortly after leaving the dentist, Paul bit down hard on his heavily numbed tongue, and by the evening of the dinner party he was running a high fever and was barely able to chew or swallow, much less taste or enjoy. Nauseated, dizzy, and sweating, his tongue so swollen he could barely speak, he endured the pain as best he could, and as his long awaited fiftieth-birthday celebration unfolded so grandly around him, he dutifully sipped treasured wines whose flavors escaped him entirely. Julia, garlanded with roses and wearing a golden crown as well as her sash and medals, presided over their exquisite table with unflappable good humor. While in her later recollection Paul "was hardly the Birthday Boy of our dreams,"[27] she nonetheless considered the evening a triumph.

And of course it was, for the dinner was a public celebration of the Childs' happy marriage, of their material well-being, and of their recent mastery of home entertaining in the best and most up-to-date French style. In the space of just three years Julia, with Paul's support, had gone from being a woman who could barely cook or speak French to a poised wife and hostess who could serve just about anything and entertain just about anyone. Together the couple had mastered the art of the dinner party. Picnics, *fêtes*, *soirées*, and *dîners intimes* were all now part of their repertoire. In this playful showing-off (really a performance) of what they most cherished—their love for each other, their love for Paris, their love for French culture, their love for the good food and wine of France—they turned what had once been a private adventure into a larger act of generosity and inclusion. The party gave pleasure to all, and opened up new worlds and experiences

---

* Also known as periodontitis (an acute inflammation of the gums).

to others even as it magnified the Childs' own delight in all they had, all they had learned. No wonder, then, that in the weeks that followed, both Julia and Paul began to think of how best to continue on with these semipublic explorations and demonstrations of the good life.

Paul's fiftieth-birthday party seems, in retrospect, to have established a dividing line between all that had happened to the couple, and all that was yet to happen. Moving away from the mere enjoyment of food and wine in Paris, and away from their private enjoyment of each other through good food and wine, they were now moving toward something that ultimately became more meaningful and sustaining: the sharing of knowledge. But at the same time, the party also marked a reversal in the couple's relationship. It was as if the Knave-Queen valentine of 1951 had now been turned upside down: Julia, on top, crowned queen of the kitchen and dining room; Paul, the artist-recluse, beneath her and supporting her, the dearly loved jack-of-all-trades.

⚜

Eight days after Paul's birthday party, Julia taught her first cooking class. She had only just finalized the plans for the school,* so was hardly ready to start teaching, but when a small group of would-be students made inquiries, all three women leapt into action. "Lessons started chez nous Jan. 23 amid vast twittering from the University St.† chicken-run," Paul wrote his brother, "what with three teachers and three [female] students plus Jeanne-la-Folle to do the washing up." Julia, meanwhile, wrote her sister-in-law Freddie Child that "the atmosphere is . . . homey and fun and informal, [with] passionate pleasure from both pupils and professors."[28] Initially, each class cost 600 francs (just two dollars). "The school runs at a very modest profit— Paul's words are 'you are in business so you won't lose money,'" Julia explained. Because students prepared more food than they could eat at the lunch concluding each class, Child decided to invite other

---

*The Childs, the Fischbachers, and the Bertholles came to their final agreement about how to operate the school over dinner at the Restaurant George Sand just a few days after Paul's birthday party.

†University Street was another of the Childs' tongue-in-cheek nicknames for the rue de l'Université.

women in to join them for the meal. "The cooking school now takes guests for lunch @ 500 francs a shot," Paul wrote Charlie. "The girls . . . want to pull their friends in to see their wonders. We usually seat 8 or 9 women. . . . V[ery] merry, self-congratulatory, and fun."[29] In the end it would be the most informal of schools, open only when Child, Beck, and Bertholle were in town, and free of other obligations, and in the mood to teach. And profit was not anyone's first concern. After sitting in on a couple of the classes, Paul began to participate too, by selecting wines for the meals being prepared, and by explaining the importance of pairing of wines properly with foods—and since he too liked to take a glass while doing so, he thought nothing of decanting a twenty-year-old Bordeaux for these demonstrations.[30]

Despite the lack of profit, the school proved enormously valuable to Child. Through it she quickly discovered the challenges inherent in teaching French cooking to Americans who knew absolutely nothing about it, and in many cases required a good deal of hand-holding and reassurance. Luckily, Child's earlier experiences in the OSS and at the U.S. Information Service had led her to recognize her own facility for explaining things clearly and precisely, primarily through her development of filing systems. (At USIS, she had devised a foolproof filing system for its enormous photo archive.) During these years of glorified secretarial work, Child had come to realize that she had "the kind of orderly mind that was good at categorizing things,"[31] and that she took real pleasure in "trying to design an idiot-proof system" through which any ordinary person could easily gain access to information.

In uniting with Beck and Bertholle, Child was now moving away from the restaurant-style cooking she had been taught at the Cordon Bleu in favor of *la cuisine bourgeoise*. ("My ideal pupils would be just like the kind of person I had been," Child later wrote, "those who aspired to be accomplished home cooks, capable of making the basic themes and variations of *la cuisine bourgeoise*, but didn't know where to begin.") While much of *Mastering the Art* (which in its first drafts had been entitled *French Home Cooking*) was adapted from the modified restaurant-style cooking taught by Max Bugnard at the Cordon Bleu (and from a similar style of cooking that Pellaprat had taught Beck a decade earlier), Bertholle and Beck had initially focused in their manuscript on dishes commonly enjoyed by upper-class and upper-middle-class French families. As a result, the new cooking school became a laboratory through which this better sort of French home cooking might be presented, in a more streamlined form, to Americans. In a nod to Le Cercle des Gourmettes, the three initially called their school L'École des Gourmettes,[32] but upon reflection they subsequently modified the name to L'École des Trois Gourmandes ("The School of the Three Hearty Eaters"),* with Paul Child designing the school's insignia as a "3" that bore a sly resemblance to a pig's tail.

At the back of it all, however, lay the incomplete Beck-Bertholle cookbook manuscript. As Child recalled the situation, Beck and Bertholle "faced the daunting job of finishing their work without a real understanding of how to write for the American market. They almost shyly asked if I might, perhaps, be willing to help them finish their book. . . . I first read their nearly six hundred page manuscript in early September 1952. Its problems and its potential immediately jumped out at me." Having only just learned about French cooking, and being authentically American, Child realized that she was their missing link to an American readership. "I had come to cooking late in life," she wrote in the memoir, "and [I] knew from firsthand experience how frustrating it could be to try to learn from badly written recipes. [As a result] I was determined that our cookbook would be clear and informative and accurate, just as our teaching strove to be. . . . I'd turn this from a rewrite job into an entirely new book."[33] In the end, Child's vision for the cookbook would be of an exceptionally clear, step-by-step cooking course. "It ain't an encyclopedia," she wrote Avis DeVoto. "[It's] a how to cook book."[34]

❧

A few months after Paul's birthday dinner and the "opening" of L'École des Trois Gourmandes, another significant birthday meal took place. The hundreds of guests at this dinner were nearly all French,

---

* The Child-Prud'homme memoir states that the three women changed the name "for diplomatic and psychological reasons," but there were surely also some legal concerns, since the school had no formal ties to Le Cercle des Gourmettes.

for the honoree was France's most distinguished food critic, celebrity, and gastronomist. *"Hommage à Curnonsky à l'occasion de son 80e anniversaire,"* a gala birthday dinner for the eighty-year-old grand gourmand, was held in late October 1952 at the Relais Gastronomique Paris-Est, the newly renovated restaurant at the historic Gare de l'Est whose chef, René Viaux, had won the coveted title of Premier Cuisinier de France in a 1949 open competition. Alexander Watt, singing its praises in *Paris Cuisine*, described the place as "surely the finest station restaurant in the world."

Unlike French cuisine, which enjoys a global reputation, French food writing is not much known or appreciated outside of France, which perhaps explains why Curnonsky's droll yet perceptive writings on French cuisine have never been translated successfully into English. And in truth the best of his writings would be difficult to translate, for they draw on an insider's knowledge of French ingredients, regional identities, and culinary traditions; they also involve wordplay, witticisms, and jokes that are quite specific to the French language, history, and popular culture. Within France, however, Curnonsky is remembered as the twentieth century's great spokesman, critic, and advocate on behalf of French cuisine, as well as its great good-natured promoter of food enjoyment—especially because, along with his work as a discerning and good-humored writer on gastronomy, this great walrus of a man was the founder of many organizations within France that lovingly promoted French food and wine. Neither a businessman nor an entrepreneur, he was instead a journalist-observer-humorist turned organizer, promoter, and public figure.

While Beck and Bertholle already knew Curnonsky—they had in fact cajoled him into writing an introduction to their little forty-eight-page booklet, *What's Cuisine in France*—Julia Child had yet to make his acquaintance. Attending his birthday celebration seemed like a good first step toward getting to know him and winning him over to their newly reimagined cookbook project. The Childs' invitation to the dinner came to them by way of the two gastronomic clubs to which they belonged—Le Cercle des Gourmettes and the Club Gastronomique Prosper Montagné—both of which were participating in this gala evening of feasting, speeches, and merriment.

Paul had only recently joined the Club Montagné. He had done so after attending one of the stag restaurant dinners arranged by Le Cercle des Gourmettes on behalf of the members' husbands—a group of men known, when out on their own, as *"les Princes Consorts Abandonés."** This eclectic group of late-middle-aged French businessmen brought together by their wives' dining club turned out to be one Paul really enjoyed, and which he later described as "the group of civilized, witty, intelligent gourmets I have been looking for all these years." He learned a great deal from them too—for while he had previously organized wine tastings with the American Club of Paris (once inviting the London-based wine expert Pierre Andrieu to speak to the group), the *Princes Consorts Abandonés* were Frenchmen who needed no such education. They already held fully formed ideas, prejudices, and opinions about French foods and wines, since after all they been enjoying them all their lives. But because that group met only occasionally, Paul decided to try out the Club Montagné, which also organized dinners in fine Paris restaurants. The club had only just been founded by restaurateur René Morand, a friend of the recently deceased Prosper Montagné, so joining it was relatively easy. Its stated goal was nominally to defend, preserve, and teach the coming generations *"les secrets de la grande cuisine française,"* but it was open to just about anyone—and many of its members were in fact in the food and wine business, utilizing the club for informal networking opportunities.

Four hundred such food enthusiasts from clubs all over France came together to attend the great *"Hommage à Curnonsky."* The participating organizations included Le Club des Cent, L'Académie des Gastronomes (of which Curnonsky had been both founder and president), L'Académie des Gais Gentilshommes Gastronomes, L'Académie des Psychologues du Goût (which Curnonsky had founded in 1922), La Société de l'Admiration Mutuelle, Les Amis de la Table, L'Association des Gastronomes Régionalistes, L'Association de le Presse Gastronomique et des Écrivains Gastronomes (a club specifically for

---

* That is, "the abandoned prince consorts"—playfully suggesting that the women of Le Cercle considered themselves "ruling queens" who had abandoned their husbands to have a good time at their club.

food journalists and food authors), La Chaîne des Rotisseurs (another gastronomic "brotherhood," which Curnonsky had only just cofounded in 1950), Le Comité du Tourisme Gastronomique du Touring Club de France, Les Compagnons de la Belle Table, La Confrérie des Chevaliers de la Poularde, Les Purs-Cent, La Section d'Art Gastronomique du Salon des Arts Ménagers, and La Société "Les Disciples de Brillat-Savarin." Just as at Paul's birthday dinner, all guests attending Curnonsky's *grande fête* were advised to wear their decorations (tiaras, medals and the like) even as they loosened their belts for *la grande bouffe*.

The eleven-course menu celebrating Curnonsky's eightieth birthday featured many of the regional foods and wines he had championed as a writer. Each place setting came with nine wineglasses, but even before guests were seated they were offered a tenth: a *vieux* Pineau des Charentes, the fortified sweet white wine so popular among the French as an aperitif. The first course consisted of oysters farmed in Marennes—a *commune* in the Charente-Maritime—accompanied, in an unusual pairing, by a dry Alsatian Riesling. The second course was turbot braised in Riesling with crayfish, which was also served with a Riesling. After these two luxurious seafood courses came a roast: a dish created especially for the evening, tournedos "Curnonsky," accompanied by a Château Monbousquet 1947 Saint-Émilion. The *entremet* was a sorbet with Armagnac, followed by roast partridges accompanied by a Burgundy (Geisweiler Réserve 1943 *en magnum*). Then a salad; then an assortment of chèvres from the Loire, served with a Vouvray demi-sec 1948. Two dessert courses followed: a *bisquit glacé marquise* served with a sweet white Anjou (Côteau de Layon, Cru de Bonnezeaux 1949), followed by a birthday cake, "*Le Gâteau du Prince*" (recalling Curnonsky's moniker, "*Prince Élu des Gastronomes*"). These desserts were served with three Champagnes: Bollinger, Krug, and Perrier-Jouet. The meal concluded with coffee, three kinds of Armagnac (including a Lafontan 1872 *en jéroboam*), as well as Cointreau and kümmel.

The jolly evening was taken up, in the French manner, with many long-winded speeches. There was also a great deal of official congratulation on Curnonsky's lifetime accomplishment. But the evening was clearly much more than a birthday party: it was a celebration by and among the French of the resurgence of French cuisine, gastronomy, pride, and national identity. Despite massive losses to France's agricultural sector, infrastructure, and workforce in the war, France's food and wine had once again established itself as the greatest, most celebrated, most sought after in all the world. So whatever else the party may have been—feast, birthday, celebrity roast, and food lover's convention—it was first and foremost an evening for France and the French. Although the Childs were glad enough to witness the moment, they must also have recognized that they were present more as observers than participants—for much as they loved France and French culture and cuisine, they were not and never would be French. So long as the couple remained in France, their place in the French food establishment would never be more than that of the enthusiastic (and foreign) consumers. In that sense, like Paul's fiftieth birthday party, the *"Hommage à Curnonsky"* marked a turning point for the Childs, reminding them, as never before, of their American identity.

⚜

Ten days after the party, on November 7, 1952, Julia Child joined Bertholle and Beck for a visit to Curnonsky at his apartment at 14, place Henri Bergson, a leafy square just behind the Gare Saint-Lazare. There, at four in the afternoon, the confirmed bachelor received the three married ladies in his bathrobe and pajamas. Child gave him a carton of embassy-purchased Chesterfield cigarettes, in what she later described as "a gesture of admiration and friendliness." Beck did most of the talking because as a Parisian who had followed Curnonsky's writings for years, she knew just how to flatter and amuse him—and, of course, she adored him as well: "His piquant writing intrigued le tout Paris of gastronomy," she later wrote in her memoirs. "He was . . . the ultimate critic of gastronomic quality, a poet for the food world." Child, for her part, later remembered him as "rotund, with twinkling blue eyes, triple chins, and an eagle beak. His ego was enormous, but so were his charm and the breadth of his knowledge."[35] The meeting ended on a good note, with Curnonsky agreeing to come to dinner chez Bertholle shortly thereafter.

When that evening arrived, the three women hovered attentively around him throughout, and Paul Child discreetly captured the scene in a series of photographs for possible later use in L'École des Trois Gourmandes' publicity efforts. In this sly cozying up to Curnonsky, Child later admitted to Avis DeVoto that the three *Gourmandes* had their cookbook foremost in mind: "I was thinking it might be useful to have [our cook]book reviewed by a really knowledgeable French gastronome." But by the end of the evening, she realized Curnonsky would take little interest in a French cookbook for Americans, however good it might be, adding in her note to DeVoto, "I am [now] rather sure it would be shrugged off [by him] as being OK but not really French."[36] As it turned out, Child need not have worried about Curnonsky's opinion, for he was virtually unknown in the United States, and his opinion would have meant little to the book's reputation or sales.

Beck and Bertholle, of course, were in heaven to have this grand old man to dinner. "Urbane, mustachioed, and well dressed, Curnonsky regaled us with his charm and skill as a raconteur," Beck later remembered. "We were a little nervous about cooking for this great expert, but he was always good-humored and tactful."[37] Beck was so pleased with the success of the dinner that she later published it as "Un Dîner de Fête pour Curnonsky" in her memoir-cookbook, *Food and Friends*. The meal began with a Champagne aperitif accompanied by *"les diablotins"* ("little devil" bite-size tidbits with cheese). The main course was *poulet aux écrivissses* (a classic chicken fricassee with crayfish) accompanied by a Meursault, followed by a *salade verte et fromages variés* served with Beck's favourite wine, Château Margaux. For dessert, they made *Chantilly glacé aux fruits frais*, a raspberry-strawberry flavored iced mousse served in little baskets carved from oranges, accompanying it with even more Champagne.

During the course of the dinner, Julia Child became increasingly irritated at the realization that, once again, the French dialogue about French cooking was one in which apparently the French were always right, and the foreigner always wrong. "At the party was a dogmatic meatball who considers himself a gourmet but is just a big bag of wind," Child wrote DeVoto. "They were talking about Beurre Blanc, and how it was a mystery, and only a few people could do it, and how it could only be made with white shallots from [the] Lorraine* and over a *wood fire*. Phoo. But that is so damned typical, making a mystery out of perfectly simple things just to puff themselves up. I didn't say anything as, being a foreigner, I don't know anything anyway. This dogmatism in France is enraging. . . . Usually, because I have had to study up on everything to inform myself, I know more [about French cuisine] than they do . . . [and I find] dogmatism founded on ignorance or hot air is hard to take. . . . Most of the writers [on food here] aren't actually cooks, and far too many of them [are] concerned with pure chi-chi."[38] Child's memoir similarly noted, "My problem as a practical American was the deeply ingrained chauvinism in France, where cooking was considered a major art: if Montagné said such-and-such, then it was considered gospel, especially by the men's gastronomical societies, which were made up of amateurs and, my, how they loved to talk!"[†39]

But Child's growing frustration with the French (and particularly with sexist French *men*) only strengthened her resolve to cowrite an instructional cookbook stripping French cuisine of its chauvinistic "chi-chi" even while making its delicious results available to all who took an interest in good food. She was an American, after all; and this was the American way.

---

*Child surely meant to write "from the Loire" (not "from the Lorraine") for that is where *beurre blanc* (or *beurre blanc nantais*) originated, as a sauce for fish taken from the Loire River, and made from butter, local dry white wine, and shallots grown in the sandy soil of the Loire Valley. (The Loire and the Lorraine are on opposite ends of France.)

†Child may have disliked the French habit of discussing one's food at the table (and in many Anglo-Saxon cultures, it is considered improper, because it is potentially embarrassing) but the French do so without inhibition, often with zeal. As Robert J. Courtine, food critic for *Le Monde*, wrote *in The Hundred Glories of French Cooking*, "Cooking is much more than cooking. In the first place, it is a tradition, and like all traditions it has its origin in the infancy of a country's soil, or a certain ingredient, or a nation's customs. Geography, history, religion, manners, all have rocked its cradle to some extent. . . . And that is why one should talk about good food as one eats it. What better subject for mealtime conversation than the meal?" (pp. 10–11).

EIGHT

"As If a Cook Book Had Anything to Do with Writing"

As Alice Toklas began thinking about writing her cookbook in the early 1950s, economic and social changes had taken place back in America that created a new kind of cookbook reader. With servants in short supply after the war, wives and mothers faced a new daily challenge of cleaning, managing, and cooking for their families on their own. As a result, educated upper-middle-class women who in previous years would not have spent much time thinking about kitchen matters were now compelled to do otherwise, and in doing so, to reconsider cooking. Although Toklas's newly reduced circumstances had made her day-to-day existence in Paris far more difficult, they were also leading her toward a new, hands-on way of writing her cookbook, one that would prove enormously attractive to cultured American readers.

Of course, Toklas had been adapting to this new way of life for some time. The outbreak of war had changed everything in France, and "we, like everyone else, adapted ourselves as best we could to the new conditions. The old life with servants* was finished and over."[1] The most drastic change had come when she and Gertrude Stein had

---

* Stein and Toklas had had a hard time keeping servants even in the prewar years, particularly at

been evicted from their Bilignin château and were compelled to move to the "large, rather pretentious home on a hill near Culoz, farther up the Rhone."[2] This new rental came with two servants, but neither was satisfactory. The cook, Clothilde Baul, was "old, tired, pessimistic," and when faced with the meager rations allowed their household through food coupons, she simply refused to cook. "So it fell upon me to do most of the cooking," Toklas later wrote, "while a great cook sat by indifferent, inert."[3] Even worse, their housekeeper, Olympe Baul, hated Stein and Toklas so much that Stein actually feared she would denounce them to the Nazis.[4] Once safely back in Paris, Stein and Toklas engaged a new *bonne à tout faire* ("a maid who does everything") named Gabrielle, but Toklas did not get on with her, and later told a friend that Gabrielle had tried to blackmail her.* After Gabrielle left, she took on a *femme de ménage* named Madeleine Charrière, but Madeleine—who would stay on with Toklas to the bitter end—came to her just once a week, and then only to do the heaviest housework.

✤

Toklas was an exacting cook and housekeeper who always demanded as much of her servants as she did of herself, which may explain why so many servants left her. She never doubted her own impossibly high standards, however, instead simply observing, "unfortunately there have been too many unsatisfactory [servants in my employ], and too many of the satisfactory ones did not stay long. . . . During forty-five years many servants come and go for many different reasons." Which is not to say she was indifferent to the hardships of a servant's life: Stein and Toklas had always been sympathetic to the lives of working women, and grateful for their help. Stein's *Three Lives* told the stories of three working-class women in Baltimore, two of them household servants; and her *The Autobiography of Alice B. Toklas* had contained many anecdotes about their domestics. The first housekeeper Stein and Toklas had shared was Hélène, "one of those admirable *bonnes* in

---

their relatively isolated country home. By the time war was declared, they had help of a local widow, Eugénie Roux, only one day a week.

* The blackmail attempt was based, Toklas said, upon Gabrielle's knowledge of Toklas's funding of Bernard Faÿ's escape to Switzerland.

other words excellent maids of all work, good cooks thoroughly occupied with the welfare of their employers and of themselves," Stein noted in *The Autobiography of Alice B. Toklas* (then adding, almost as an afterthought, "she made a very good soufflé").[5] Hélène left in 1913 but came back in 1916 because "her husband had fallen on hard times and her boy had died."[6] Toklas had rarely been allowed to do anything in Hélène's kitchen but watch. "From Hélène I learned nothing about cooking," Toklas herself later admitted. "She would have thought such an idea was misplaced. A lady did not cook."

Before Hélène's return, however, Stein and Toklas had been unable to afford a proper housekeeper, and instead, as Toklas wrote, "our history with *femmes de ménage** commenced. It was a long and not always a happy one." During that time, they were compelled to do their own marketing and cooking, since *femmes de ménage* do not cook. "I used to say Gertrude Stein was the chauffeur and I was the cook. We used to go over early in the morning to the public markets and get in our provisions. It was a confused world."[7]

During the 1920s other servants came and went. First Jeanne, then Léonie, then a beautiful young Bretonne named Jeanne Poule,[8] a fine cook who was eventually discovered to have a second life as a prostitute. ("*La cuisine c'est la femme*,"[†] Toklas observed wistfully of her. "Her sauces had unknown, delicate, and still exotic flavors.") Starting in 1929, Stein and Toklas struggled mightily to find a housekeeper who would not mind relocating to Bilignin for half the year—and apart from the inconvenience of relocating to the country from Paris, any housekeeper arriving in Bilignin found a house both large and old-fashioned, with a steady stream of houseguests adding to her long list of chores. Moreover, Toklas could be fanatical about her housekeeping there: Cecil Beaton recalled that at Bilignin "the cakes of soap in the bathroom [were] placed in rigid, edge-sharp precision," and the meals were always the "best food" because Alice watched over the cook with "a rapier eye."[9] During the summer of

---

*Unlike a live-in, do-everything housekeeper (a *bonne* or *bonne à tout faire*), a *femme de ménage* simply does housecleaning (and perhaps laundry) and lives out.
†Trans.: The character of the woman is reflected in her cooking.

1933, the servant shortage at Bilignin became so acute that Stein even discussed it in her odd quasi-novel *Blood on the Dining Room Floor.*

❧

In the years following Stein's death, by comparison, Toklas did much of her own cooking, even when single-handedly entertaining friends like Samuel Steward, Thornton and Isabel Wilder, and the poets James Merrill and Claude Fredericks.* (When Toklas learned that Fredericks planned on working for three months at his mother's restaurant in Houston in order to finance his upcoming nine-month stay in Rome, she wrote Louise Taylor in great excitement, "We should all go over to the US and make a fortune!")[10] Toklas also entertained a struggling surrealist artist she had known in the years before the war, Brion Gysin. English born, Canadian raised, and a naturalized American citizen of Swiss descent, Gysin was thirty-four when he met up with Toklas again in the early 1950s—having left off his work as a Paris-based surrealist to serve in the American army. After being named a Fulbright fellow in 1949, he seemed to be headed for a university career, but academic life bored him, so he returned to making art. Shortly after visiting with Toklas in Paris he left for North Africa with the writers Paul and Jane Bowles. There he would remain for nearly a decade, corresponding with Toklas sporadically until his return. Upon receiving a letter from Algiers in which he complained bitterly about the great financial insecurity of his life, Toklas sweetly wrote back,

> Security—what a fearfully limiting experience that would
> be. As for capital, I've not had any—when I was young I ran
> up debts—which was pleasant. Then I came over here and
> never knew where money was to come from—mostly it didn't.
> G[ertrude] S[tein] bought pictures and spent no money on
> anything else to be able to do so. Except during the two wars
> when we didn't know or care what we spent we lived like

---

* Fredericks published two posthumous works by Stein at his Banyan Press. When Merrill and Fredericks, who were a couple at the time, were spending a year in Europe, they visited Toklas several times, once bringing along Merrill's parents.

church mice and it amused us to go about like gypsies. Now *mes petites économies* are not so diverting and put one in the banal majority. So you see our situations have points of resemblance. Your particular gifts and my lack of any certainly flourish best in a not too great luxuriance.[11]

Money was nearly always on Toklas's mind these days. Chronically short of funds, but wanting to help Bernard Faÿ, she had sold two small works on paper from the Stein collection without asking for the approval of the Stein executor in Baltimore. Upon learning of the sale, Allan Stein insisted that Toklas submit complete inventories of every single object in the rue Christine apartment, thereby formally separating all of Gertrude Stein's possessions from those of Toklas even as they remained *in situ*. Then, however, as Toklas informed her friend Louise Taylor, "Allan Stein suddenly but not unexpectedly died,"[12] leaving his widow, Roubina, with even greater money problems. "He seems to have left . . . a colossal amount of debts,"[13] Toklas explained to Taylor.

As a result, Toklas's own money problems increased, since both the Baltimore executor and the Allan Stein family were no longer so kindly disposed toward her, no longer so trustful of her caretaking, and certainly much more stingy about sending along her stipend. Despite all this, Toklas continued to think of Stein's collection of paintings as something over which she would ultimately have final say, writing Carl Van Vechten, "As soon as I hear that [Roubina Stein] has come to terms with [her stepson] Danny Stein . . . I will open the subject with my lawyer [and hopefully I will] put through my long cherished little dream of selling [the Gertrude Stein art collection] *en bloc* to a museum so that Baby's* collection will not be dispersed over the landscape. This is the only thing that Allan's death will have facilitated."

Although now seventy-five, Toklas clearly had no lack of gumption. Hoping to earn some money by publishing articles in American magazines, she asked Joe Barry, who had just been hired to work in New York as an editor at *House Beautiful*, to provide her with an introduction to its editor in chief. Elizabeth Gordon Norcross, the editor,

---

*One of Toklas's pet names for Stein.

in turn invited her to send in a writing sample. "I got off my article to Mrs. Norcross* of *House Beautiful*," Toklas wrote Van Vechten shortly afterward. "[I am] a pessimist about what she will think about it and an optimist about receiving a check for it."[14] Meanwhile she pushed Van Vechten to set her name and face before the American public again, this time as a Paris-based food writer. "Which photo of me did you show at the NY Public Library," Toklas wrote him about a Gertrude Stein exhibition he had just curated there. "Did you label it author of recipes? Did you say more recipes in progress?"[15]

Toklas now approached Jenny Bradley, the widow of William Bradley (who had been the literary agent for *The Autobiography of Alice B. Toklas*) about her cookbook idea. The Bradley Agency, located on the Île St.-Louis, had counted Toklas's friends Ford Madox Ford and James Joyce among its early clients. Since her husband's death in 1939, the Belgian-born Jenny Bradley had continued to cultivate French and American authors at her agency *cum* salon. Blaise Cendrars, Mina Curtiss, James Baldwin, Patricia Highsmith, Jean-Paul Sartre, and Richard Wright were just a few of her many clients.

Apparently, Mrs. Bradley proposed the Toklas cookbook idea to two American editors. In May 1952, Toklas informed Van Vechten that "Mrs. Bradley sent word through Mina Curtiss† that she had an offer for a cook book from someone for me and as I wanted to see her about Bernard [Faÿ]'s manuscripts‡ it was easy [for me] to combine the two things in one visit [to her office] before she left for N[ew] York. [One offer] was from Harper. It will be necessary to find out from the [other] man at Rinehart [publishers] if they are ready to give an advance. Mrs. B[radley] thought she could get 2 or 3 thousand from one of them. That would suit—to have something to ease the present situation and something ahead."[16] But in the end neither Harper nor Rinehart would offer Toklas a contract up front. Rather, Harper simply advised Bradley that the house would consider offering

---

* Using the professional name Elizabeth Gordon, Elizabeth Gordon Norcross was editor in chief of *House Beautiful* for twenty-three years, from 1941 through 1964.

† The sister of Lincoln Kirstein, the founder of New York City Ballet, Mina Curtiss was an accomplished author, editor, and translator. Bradley often gave her translation work.

‡ Toklas had sponsored Faÿ's 1951 escape to Switzerland from a French prison hospital, where he had been serving a life sentence for collaboration. A historian, Faÿ published in both French and English; Toklas was apparently hoping to help him find an American publisher.

a contract to Toklas after seeing half the manuscript. As it turned out, Toklas received a contract only five months after delivering the completed manuscript, and did not receive her "advance" payment until three months after that contract was signed and returned.

❖

In the meantime, despite her limited finances, Toklas continued to receive guests at 5, rue Christine. In early June 1952 she threw a party for the cast of the Gertrude Stein–Virgil Thomson opera *Four Saints in Three Acts*, which was just then having an international revival.* Since the black American cast had come all the way to Paris to perform Stein's work, Toklas wanted to have them up to the flat and show them some hospitality. With considerable effort she assembled "four very large cakes and [several platters of] *petits pains (au pâté)*† along with a punch and tea," so that all might refresh themselves while enjoying the legendary paintings collection. Virgil Thomson came too—despite some very serious ups and downs with Stein, he had managed to hold on to his friendship with Toklas. So too had his lover of many years, Maurice Grosser (whom Toklas, with characteristic astringency, described as "a poor painter but a charming person—intelligent, witty and sensitive"[17]). The two men, both good cooks, had long shared a little studio on the quai Voltaire, where they "prepared simple and delicious dinners" to which they had regularly invited Stein and Toklas.[18] Both were great supporters of her cookbook project, and both would ultimately contribute recipes to it.‡

The journalist Naomi Barry described her lunches with Alice Toklas in those days:

The most memorable table I have known in Paris was in an apartment over a printing plant at 5, rue Christine. The en-

---

*The opera had been written and composed in 1927–1928 and had its debut in Hartford, Connecticut, in 1934.

†A *petit pain* is a small, soft, glossy, oblong bun, with a taste and texture resembling that of a brioche. Toklas apparently used them to make small sandwiches filled with pâté.

‡Thomson's contributions included a shad-roe mousse, *gnocchi alla Piemontese*, and a Calabrian pork *"alla pizzaiola"*; Grosser's were for shrimp in butter and baked fish with stuffing.

trance was little better than a slum, but in the old quarter of Paris the entrance tells little. Once you were inside, the rooms were spacious and the furniture, the *objets d'art*, the bold individuality of taste, the reflection of strong personalities made you feel as though you had gone straight through the looking glass. . . . Toklas was the first true gourmet I ever met. She knew how to grow, to buy, to prepare, to cook, to savor, to serve—and how to put food in its proper place. She understood flavors so that you were deliciously tormented trying to grasp them. A lunch at the rue Christine lasted three hours if you broke away brusquely, but it was more likely to be a leisurely four hours, for the meal was meant to be a trampoline for conversation and pithy criticism. . . . In Miss Toklas' apartment the food always fitted the surroundings and the company. In its preparation, she was always finicky about every detail.[19]

After an early summer of nonstop (if light) entertaining, Toklas took several retreats to the country: first to La Régie, a rambling manor house on a large country estate near Bourges, where an attractive acquaintance, Madame Debar, maintained *chambres d'hôtes* and a walled garden for Parisians (and their dogs) in need of fresh air and quiet. In August she went to visit Virginia Knapik, her friend at the American Embassy, and her husband, Harold,* in the South of France, near Grasse. And in September she toured Spain with Joe and Naomi Barry, becoming fascinated there by a number of local foods, including gazpacho, that would ultimately find their way into her cookbook. Finally, as the days grew shorter and colder, Toklas once again began to think about the project, writing Isabel Wilder in a note of thanks (for whiskey and Pall Malls) that "winter is on the way—only a couple of days into autumn and woolens are being worn and the heater is going. . . . The cook book is started and very soon bending over an imaginary stove will keep the temperature a-mounting and a-mounting."[20]

---

* Harold Knapik had come to Paris to study music. Both he and Virginia were later revealed to have been CIA operatives. (See Janet Malcolm, "Gertrude Stein's War," *The New Yorker*, June 25, 2013.)

A few weeks later, Basket wandered through the salon's French doors, out onto the rooftop and, losing his way in the dark, fell twenty feet into the courtyard below. "With the misadventure he lost the little confidence he had been slowly achieving," Toklas wrote Samuel Steward. "Isn't it too sad that this is the way he is to end his days."[21] Within the month he was gone. "Basket is no more—he died quite suddenly at the vets today," she told another friend. "His going has stunned me—for some time I have realized how much I have depended upon him and so it is the beginning of living for the rest of my days without anyone who is dependent upon me for anything."[22]

Shortly thereafter, Toklas began experiencing fatigue, nausea, vomiting, abdominal pain, joint pain, fever, itching, and, most surprising, a sudden dramatic yellowing of her skin and her eyes. She had somehow come down with hepatitis. The illness exhausted her completely, and left her entirely dependent upon her *femme de ménage*, Madeleine, for more than four months. "I haven't been well—exhausted," she wrote Louise Taylor. "Pernicious jaundice—a most beautiful but entirely misplaced Chinese yellow! Neither grave nor painful—at first [I was] sleeping and dozing—now just sleeping—a nice highly unalarmist doctor tells me all is well it only requires patience—quiet—a rigid but agreeable diet—all and every kind of food except no fats. . . . [He] wants me to continue the rest cure for some time yet. I see no one—do not telephone—and am feeling better. Now don't think of me as miserable. . . . *Dieu soit loué**—on the contrary the enforced rest is a luxury."[23]

During this long period of isolation Toklas finally got to work on the book. As she later wrote, "[The *Cook Book*] was written as an escape from the narrow diet of monotony and illness, and I daresay nostalgia for the old days and old ways, and for remembered health and enjoyment [all of which] lent special lustre to dishes and menus barred from an invalid table, but hovering dream-like in invalid memory. Illness sets the mind free sometimes."[24] The book was drafted and typed in the fourteen weeks of 1953 between her recovery (approximately

---

* Trans.: Praise God.

mid-March) and the end of June, when she explained to Samuel Steward, "My shameful silence was due to a long boresome attack of pernicious jaundice and to the equally boresome writing (?) of a 75,000 word cook book in half the time—the latter to earn the pennies to pay for the former. The incompatible combination has exhausted me and tomorrow I go to the hospital for a checkup. One doesn't get over easily one's first illness in fifty-nine years!"[25]

✣

However difficult the circumstances of its creation, the *Cook Book* is a seemingly effortless combination of memoir and culinary exposition. "Though born in America, I have lived so long in France that both countries seem to be mine, and knowing, loving both, I took to pondering on the differences in eating habits and general attitude to food and the kitchen in the United States and here," Toklas writes in her introduction. "I fell to considering how every nation . . . has its idiosyncrasies in food and drink conditioned by climate, soil and temperament. . . . Such speculations led me to rout about among my huge collection of recipes and compile this cook-book."

Toklas begins the book by presenting some thoughts on French cooking and dining traditions. "The French approach to food is characteristic; they bring to their consideration of the table the same appreciation, respect, intelligence, and lively interest that they have for other arts, for painting, for literature and for theater,"[26] she notes. She then goes on to discuss the various ways food is cooked, served, and enjoyed in French homes, from luxurious feasts to simple suppers. In the next chapter she recalls various dishes she has had the pleasure of sharing with famous artists, and then moves on to a chapter entitled "Murder in the Kitchen," in which she playfully describes her various experiences of transforming living creatures into succulent meals— her anecdote about smothering a basket of pigeons being particularly ghastly. Next comes a chapter on gazpacho and its variants, with cold vegetable soup explorations extending as far as *chlodnik*, or borscht. A longer chapter, "Food to Which Aunt Pauline and Lady Godiva Led Us," then describes Stein and Toklas's adventures in gastronomic tourism during World War I (while driving their slow-moving ambulance-van, nicknamed "Aunt Pauline"*) and afterward, during the 1920s (while exploring France in a Ford two-seater so stripped of ornament that they dubbed it "Godiva").

The following chapter, entitled "Treasures," includes recipes collected over the years from various treasured sources: from Norah (the Toklas family cook in San Francisco) to Josephine Baker, to Alexandre Dumas *fils*, to Stéphane Mallarmé—with the latter's recipe† in his own memorable words. Toklas, ever sensitive to language, considered recipes something like poems: "When treasures are recipes they are less clearly, less distinctly remembered than when they are tangible objects," she notes halfway through the chapter. "They evoke however quite as vivid a feeling—that is, to some of us who, considering cooking an art, feel that a way of cooking can produce something that approaches an aesthetic emotion." And that, in brief, seems to be the *Cook Book*'s central and quietly astonishing assertion: that good cooking, and good cookbook writing, can be comparable to art and literature, in that both are capable of provoking a strong, often complex, set of combined emotional, intellectual, and physical responses—not only because of the taste of the food (real or imagined), but also because of the wealth of personal, social, and cultural memories and associations that these foods (and their preparation, and their recipes) make manifest—to the palate, to the mind, to the body, and to the heart.

"Food in the United States in 1934 and 1935," the next chapter, combines Toklas's anecdotes of her and Stein's publicity tour for *The Autobiography of Alice B. Toklas* with various American recipes Toklas collected on the trip. After that comes "Little-Known French Dishes Suitable for American and British Kitchens," a chapter featuring a collection of good, practical preparations. The next, "Food in the Bugey During the Occupation," returns to the hardships Toklas and Stein had endured in Bilignin and Culoz during the period 1939 to

---

*"Auntie" or "Aunt Pauline," the Ford Model T adapted for ambulance work, had been named after Stein's aunt by marriage, who, Stein reported in *The Autobiography of Alice B. Toklas*, "always behaved well in emergencies and behaved fairly well most times if properly flattered" (p. 172).
†The recipe is for something he calls coconut marmalade: grated coconut cooked in a sugar syrup, then enriched with egg yolks, chilled, and served cool.

The Lion of Belfort, Place Denfert-Rochereau (Courtesy of the author)

A. J. Liebling during World War II (Courtesy of Cornell Rare Book and Manuscript Collections)

A. J. Liebling, 1944
(Photograph by David
Scherman, LIFE Picture
Collection; courtesy of Getty
Images)

Dione Lucas standing before
her Cordon Bleu Restaurant
and Cooking School, New
York City (Courtesy of the
Schlesinger Library, Radcliffe Institute,
Harvard University)

Claudius Philippe,
"Philippe of the Waldorf"
(AP Images)

The publisher Alfred Knopf pours a 1904 Richebourg for its producer, Louis Gros, while Henri Gouges, president of the Burgundy Producers Association, looks on. Alexis Lichine is seated at center. Other winemakers attending this Beaune 1950 lunch included Baron Thénard, Pierre Damoy, Charles Noëllat, René Engel, and Claude Ramonet. (Courtesy of the Harry Ransom Center, the University of Texas at Austin)

Gertrude Stein and Alice B. Toklas picking flowers at Bilignin, 1937 (Photograph by Cecil Beaton; © the Cecil Beaton Studio Archive at Sotheby's)

Stein and Toklas in the garden at Bilignin, 1937 (Photograph by Bobsy Goodspeed; courtesy of the Gertrude Stein and Alice B. Toklas Papers, American Literature Collection, Beinecke Rare Books and Manuscripts Library, Yale University)

Toklas and Basket in Bilignin, 1937 (Photograph by Cecil Beaton; © the Cecil Beaton Studio Archive at Sotheby's)

Toklas, Stein, and Basket "liberated." Culoz, spring 1944 (Photograph by Carl Mydans; courtesy of Getty Images)

Stein, Basket, and Toklas at 5, rue Christine, Paris, 1938 (Photograph by Cecil Beaton; © the Cecil Beaton Studio Archive at Sotheby's)

Samuel Steward, Basket, and Toklas on the roof outside the rue Christine apartment, 1952 (Courtesy of the Estate of Samuel Steward)

Mary Frances Kennedy Fisher (M.F.K. Fisher) with her third husband, Donald Friede (Courtesy of the Schlesinger Library, Radcliffe Institute, Harvard University)

The neoclassical interior of Le Grand Véfour, Paul and Julia Child's favorite restaurant during their early years in Paris (Photograph by Michel Langot; courtesy of Le Grand Véfour)

Montmartre (Photograph by Samuel Chamberlain)

The Church of Saint-Germain-des-Prés and the Café des Deux Magots (Photograph by Samuel Chamberlain)

Paul and Julia Child; France, August 1949 (Photograph by Paul Child; courtesy of the Schlesinger
Library, Radcliffe Institute, Harvard University)

Chef Fernand Point (left) and Joseph Wechsberg (Courtesy of the Estate of Joseph Wechsberg)

Julia Child's kitchen at 81, rue de l'Université. Irma Rombauer's *Joy of Cooking*, Ali-Bab's *Gastronomie Pratique*, and Prosper Montagné's *Larousse Gastronomique* can all be seen on the bookshelf behind Bernard DeVoto's *The Course of Empire*. (Photograph by Julia Child; courtesy of the Schlesinger Library, Radcliffe Institute, Harvard University)

Richard Olney painting in his garden in Clamart, 1961

(Photograph by Byron Olney; courtesy of Byron Olney)

Olney's photo of his modest Clamart kitchen (Photograph by Richard Olney; courtesy of Byron Olney)

Richard Olney (right) with his brother John; Paris, mid-1950s (Courtesy of Byron Olney)

Olney breakfasting in the Clamart Studio, 1961 (Photograph by Byron Olney; courtesy of Byron Olney)

Olney's *Portrait of James Baldwin*
(Photograph by Richard Olney; courtesy of Byron Olney)

Olney and his lover, Bernard Hassell (Courtesy of Byron Olney)

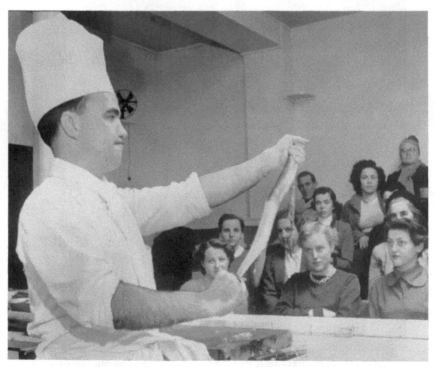

An instructor peels an eel during a lecture-demonstration at the Cordon Bleu, 1951.

(Photograph by Nat Farbman; courtesy of Getty Images)

Julia Child and her teacher Max Bugnard at work together at the Cordon Bleu (Photograph by Paul Child; courtesy of the Schlesinger Library, Radcliffe Institute, Harvard University)

Madame Elisabeth Brassart, director and owner of the Cordon Bleu, hands out diplomas at a graduation party featuring madeleines and sparkling Vouvray, 1951. (Photograph by Mark Kaufman; courtesy of Getty Images)

1945, often with a grim sense of humor: "In the beginning [of the war], like camels, we lived on our past," she jokes, before delving into the dreary specifics of their deprivation. After that comes the penultimate chapter, the one that would launch the book's *succès de scandale*: "Recipes from Friends."

The chapter evolved out of Toklas's very strong desire to be done with the manuscript. As she wrote Louise Taylor in March 1953:

> About the cook book. You won't think too badly if I throw myself upon you with a thud will you. This is the situation— Harper is willing to give me an advance and a contract when 30,000 words are in their hands (12,000 more to go) and they want the rest—40,000 more—for the First of May. You will see the grind this is. So one chapter (how pretentious of me to write that) will be devoted to recipes of friends—undoubtedly the only thing of merit in the deadly dull offering. The two Van Vechtens—Virgil [Thomson]—Pierre Balmain—Marie Laurencin—Francis [Rose]—Dora Maar—Isabel Wilder— Virginia and Harold Knapik have consented and the Low-Beers* and Brion Gysin will undoubtedly. Now may I add Red's† Circassian chicken [recipe] from your inexhaustible supply and use your names.[27]

In the end, thirty-two friends (comprising an idiosyncratic Who's Who of international celebrities, socialites, and intellectuals, many of them gay, lesbian, or bisexual) would contribute a total of eighty-one recipes. They included Dora Maar, the photographer-artist and former mistress of Picasso; the stage actress Fania Marinoff, in private life Mrs. Carl Van Vechten; the couturiers Pierre Balmain and Princess Dilkusha de Rohan; the aesthete Lord Gerald Berners; the artist Sir Francis Rose and his writer wife, Frederica (who published as Dorothy Carrington); the translator, writer, and journalist Fernanda Pivano,

---

* Toklas is referring to the daughter of her old friend Clare Moore de Gruchy, Anne, and Anne's husband, Dr. Bela Low-Beer.

† The nickname of Louise Taylor's husband, Lieutenant Colonel R. H. Redvers Taylor.

who had recently married the architect and designer Ettore Sottsass; the art dealer and businessman Georges Maratier; the Chicago social-ite and arts patron Elizabeth Fuller Chapman; the painter and cos-tume designer Marie Laurencin; the Turkish-born painter Nejad Melih Devrim; the socialite Mercedes de Acosta; the writer Natalie Clifford Barney; the Texas school headmistress Ela Hockaday; Mary Crouch Oliver, whom Paul Bowles had introduced to Toklas; Gerald and Sara Murphy's sister-in-law, Noel Haskins Murphy; the painter who had kept watch on the rue Christine apartment during the war, Katherine Dudley; her sister, Madame Joseph Delteil (née Caroline Dudley), who had brought La Revue Nègre (including its stars, Jo-sephine Baker and Sidney Bechet) to Paris in 1925; Joseph Delteil, the French writer and poet; the fashion photographer Cecil Beaton; and finally, the artist Brion Gysin. There was also a scattering of French friends, including Madame Debar, who ran the rural retreat La Régie; Madame Berthey Cleysereque, an acquaintance; and Madame Chaboux, a doctor's wife who had lived near Stein and Toklas in the country.

Of all the contributions to the "Recipes from Friends" chapters, one stands out as being entirely unlike the others: Aspic Salad, con-tributed by the wife of the arts journalist Carlton Lake.* Years later, Lake described how Toklas had insisted upon having this American convenience-food recipe after coming to dinner at their apartment on the quai de Bourbon:

> The dinner [prepared by my wife] was delicious . . . a widely
> varied fresh fruit cup; a plump *poulet de Bresse*, crisply golden
> on the outside, tender and moist inside; roast potatoes; long,
> slender, very young haricots verts; an aspic salad; and a straw-
> berry tartlet: fluffy *crème anglaise* topped by tiny, perfumed
> fraises des bois, in a pastry boat so light and flaky that it
> melted almost on contact. Alice ate every bit of her dinner

---

*Lake had his doubts about Toklas's cooking, describing one of her lunches as "consist[ing] of one-inch strips of a pinkish, stringy, fibrous flesh of some kind, bathed in a pink-to-beige thick sauce with a rather acrid aftertaste." He refrained from asking what he was eating, "afraid that when she told me, the truth would far outdistance my most morbid imaginings."

and . . . it was then that [she] told us about the cookbook she was working on. She was using recipes of her own but including a number from friends. "And I want the recipe for that aspic salad in it," she added. "It's absolutely perfect. I've never had one that good."

No pins were dropped but I could see my wife trying to fade quietly into the background.

She had inherited that recipe from my mother, who undoubtedly had clipped it from the pages of *The Ladies' Home Journal*. Beneath the aspic's suave pastel surface lurked a number of embarrassingly low-brow ingredients: Campbell's condensed tomato soup, Philadelphia cream cheese, Miracle Whip salad dressing. How do you tell that to Alice Toklas? My wife talked all around the question. Alice kept coming back to the recipe. In the end my wife agreed to send it to her in the morning.[28]

It was a very different recipe, however, that ultimately brought massive press and popular attention to the book: Brion Gysin's Haschich Fudge. Toklas, relying on Gysin for a recipe, assumed that its last ingredient, "canibus [*sic*] sativa" was an obscure North African herb. The recipe featured an uncharacteristically arch, non-Toklas-y headnote:

This is the food of Paradise—of Baudelaire's Artificial Paradises: It might provide entertaining refreshment for a Ladies Bridge Club or a chapter meeting of the D.A.R.* In Morocco it is thought to be good for warding off the common cold in damp winter weather and is, indeed, more effective if taken with large quantities of hot mint tea. Euphoria and brilliant storms of laughter; ecstatic reveries and extensions of one's personality on several simultaneous planes are to be complacently expected. Almost anything Saint Theresa did, you can

---

*The Daughters of the American Revolution, a conservative and socially exclusive American women's club.

do better if you can bear to be ravished by *"un évanouissment reveillé."**

The recipe also suggests that Toklas was acquainted not only with "haschich" but also the plant from which it was derived:

Take 1 teaspoon black peppercorns, 1 whole nutmeg, 4 average sticks of cinnamon, 1 teaspoon coriander. These should all be pulverized in a mortar. About a handful each of destoned dates, dried figs, shelled almonds and peanuts: chop these and mix them together. A bunch of *canibus* [*sic*] *sativa* can be pulverized. This along with the spices should be dusted over the mixed fruit and nuts, kneaded together. About a cup of sugar dissolved in a big pat of butter. Rolled into a cake and cut into pieces or made into balls about the size of a walnut, it should be eaten with care. Two pieces are quite sufficient.

The after-note, too, strongly suggested Toklas was familiar with the cultivation of "canibus":

Obtaining the canibus may present certain difficulties, but the variety known as *canibus sativa* grows as a common weed, often unrecognized, everywhere in Europe, Asia and parts of Africa; besides being cultivated as a crop for the manufacture of rope. In the Americas, while often discouraged, its cousin, called *canubis indica* [*sic*], has been observed even in city window boxes. It should be picked and dried as soon as it has gone to seed and while the plant is still green.

But these words were not Toklas's.[†] In her rush to complete the manuscript, Toklas had merely incorporated the text of Gysin's letter

---

*Trans.: A feeling of having fainted while yet awake.
[†] Samuel Steward, who was in close contact with Toklas throughout the entire affair, later noted in his *Dear Sammy*, "Alice included the recipe without being actually aware of what it was; even the

to her into the manuscript, doing so without proper attribution. So began a misunderstanding that would snowball in the months to come.

✣

If the penultimate chapter of the *Cook Book* was its most provocative (due to its apparent openness to drug use for pleasure), the final chapter is by far its most moving. Yet for those unacquainted with the circumstances of Toklas's life, this deeply felt ending is quite easily overlooked, for it is presented in such extreme understatement as to remain, as Toklas herself remained most of her life, hidden in plain sight. Entitled "The Vegetable Gardens at Bilignin," the chapter briefly discusses Toklas's life during the period 1929 to 1943, when "for fourteen successive summers the vegetable gardens at Bilignin were my joy, working in them during the summers and planning and dreaming of them during the winters." The planting season began shortly after Toklas and Stein's arrival from Paris in early April, and ended in late October, when the last vegetables were harvested and the garden was closed down for the winter. Only then, Toklas wrote, would they move back to Paris to resume their urban existence.[29]

While most of Toklas's working life had been devoted to supporting and nurturing Stein, the two vegetable gardens in Bilignin were her own vast creative endeavor:* a multiyear enterprise in which Stein would often lend a hand, but over which Toklas had complete authority, and into which she poured her heart and soul. The project began with the complete restoration of the château's two fruit-and-vegetable gardens in 1929. Since they were in a sorry state of neglect, a team of men were hired to do the clearing of the beds, the turning of the soil, and, most horrifying, the eradicating of a vast, seething nest of snakes. After that, Toklas did as much planting and tending as she could, employing a young man from the little hamlet just outside the château's front gate "to do the heavy work."[30] Both vegetable gardens

---

introductory comments were Gysin's." (Steward knew this firsthand, having discussed it with Toklas in person.)

*During the 1920s Toklas relied on an expatriate American novelist neighbor, Louis Bromfield, for gardening advice. Bromfield devoted his later life (which he spent mostly in Ohio) to practicing and writing about organic, self-sustaining, and pesticide-free gardening and farming.

needed daily tending, for they were rife with accumulated weed-seeds. Moreover the chalky soil needed constant enrichment and watering. "The work in the vegetables . . . was a full-time job and more," Toklas wrote. "Later it became a joke, Gertrude Stein asking me what I saw when I closed my eyes, and I answered, Weeds."

But when the vegetables started to produce, all that hard work resulted in miracles. "The first gathering of the garden in May of salads, radishes and herbs made me feel like a mother about her baby—how could anything so beautiful be mine," Toklas wrote. "And this emotion of wonder filled me for each vegetable as it was gathered every year. There is nothing that is comparable to it, as satisfactory or as thrilling, as gathering the vegetables one has grown."[31] This sense of the miraculous had extended, naturally enough, into the château's vast, old-fashioned kitchen, and ultimately to the Stein-Toklas dinner table, which was distinguished by its elegant simplicity. "When [the] vegetables were ready to be picked it never occurred to us to question what way to cook them," she wrote. "Naturally the simplest, just to steam or boil them and serve them with the excellent country butter or cream that we had from a farmer almost within calling distance. Later still, when we had guests and the vegetables had lost the aura of a new-born miracle, sauces added variety."

The chapter continues with a number of favorite vegetable recipes and concludes with the observation that, after the sharing of all this home-grown produce with friends and guests, the greatest pleasure Toklas took in her garden was at the final gathering-in of vegetables at the very end of the season:

> When autumn came, the last harvest was so occupying that one forgot that it meant leaving the garden for the return to Paris. . . . The day the huge baskets were packed was my proudest in all the year. The cold sun would shine on the orange-coloured carrots, the green, yellow and white pumpkins and squash, the purple egg plants and a few last red tomatoes. They made for me more poignant colour than any post-Impressionist picture. Merely to look at them made all the rest of the year's pleasure insignificant. Gertrude Stein took a more practical attitude. She came out into the denuded wet

cold garden and, looking at the number of baskets and crates, asked if they were all being sent to Paris, that if they were, the *expressage** would ruin us. She thought that there were enough vegetables for an institution and reminded me that our household consisted of three people. There was no question that, looking at that harvest as an economic question, it was disastrous, but from the point of view of the satisfaction which work and aesthetic confer, it was sublime.

Toklas, writing all this in 1953, concludes the book with a vision of that long-lost garden on the final day of their tenancy, when in the middle of the war they were compelled to pack up, say goodbye forever to the château of Bilignin, and remove to the gloomy house above Culoz:

Our final, definite leaving of the gardens came one cold winter day, all too appropriate to our feelings and the state of the world. A sudden moment of sunshine peopled the gardens with all the friends and others who had passed through them. Ah, there would be another garden, the same friends, possibly, or no, probably new ones, and there would be other stories to tell and to hear. And so we left Bilignin, never to return.[32]

Toklas strikes a note of optimism in these understated lines, but contrary to her assertion, there would never be another garden for her. Still, the dream of having and maintaining a garden in the country remained with her to the end of her life. In one of her last letters, two months before her death, she wrote a friend, "I shall never have a garden again. I think and dream of one."[33]

❧

By early summer of 1953 the *Cook Book* manuscript had been sent off to Harper, and Toklas struggled with the sense of aimlessness and depression that every author feels after the completion of a substantial piece of writing. In a note to Janet Flanner, she described "the disorder

---

*The fee for shipping cargo (such as the vegetables) via train.

in which my life proceeds,"[34] and to her old friend Lawrence Strauss, who had been a neighbor in Paris from 1906 to 1911, she wrote, "the cook book is finished and sent off and I'm coming to terms with my age—so that's that."[35] But as it happened there was more work to be done: the *Cook Book* needed illustrations. Toklas turned to Sir Francis Rose for help.

Stein and Toklas had first met Rose in the early 1930s, through the well-born Anglo-Irish painter Meraud Guevara (née Guinness). At that time he had been, in the words of Maurice Grosser, "a well-to-do and vastly irresponsible young Englishman, quite pleasant looking but with a rather childish speech defect of spitting. . . . [But] nobody took his painting seriously then and no one takes it seriously now." And indeed, though Rose had been a protégé of Christian "Bébé" Bérard and Jean Cocteau, the only person ever really to believe in him as a fine artist was Gertrude Stein, who collected a good deal of his work during the decade they knew each other as friends. "To explain Gertrude's faith in him," Grosser went on, "I must suppose that she was less interested in his painting than in his personality. . . . the tumultuous excesses of Sir Francis's life and his undisciplined facility convinced her [of his significance.]"

Unrestricted access to a large, inherited fortune, combined with a youthful immersion in opium smoking and cruising for rough trade, had left Rose, a British baronet domiciled in France, vulnerable to blackmail and physical abuse. If his memoirs are to be believed, in 1934, when Rose was twenty-five, his lover, Ernst Röhm, was the most prominent of three hundred Nazis arrested and then murdered in a purge known as the Night of the Long Knives.

Shortly thereafter, Rose left Europe for a new life in Peking. A few years later, he continued his world travels in the United States, there losing much of his fortune in a stock market swindle. He finally came back to France in the late 1930s, accompanied by a thuggish American boyfriend who then stole much of what remained of his money and property. He moved to London at the outbreak of World War II, and during the war got married.

By the early 1950s Rose had returned to Paris, there resuming his masochistic escapades with rough trade. Carlton Lake, who knew him as a neighbor on the quai de Bourbon,* avoided him whenever possible, since "he could be entertaining in small doses but he was not the ideal dinner guest: he was a nonstop talker, a shameless name-dropper (the Duke of Alba, Madame Chiang Kai-shek, Guy de Rothschild and on and on). . . . [My wife] always complained that he was a wet hand-kisser, in addition to which he dipped snuff."

While Toklas had been exasperated by Rose throughout their long acquaintance, she also had a soft spot for him. And because Rose had already illustrated several small children's books, Toklas felt confident in asking him to illustrate her *Cook Book*, hoping that in doing so she might help him through a particularly troubling period of sexual self-degradation involving a young man he subsequently adopted as his son.† *"Entre nous* I have engaged to keep him fairly respectable," Toklas wrote Samuel Steward. "He has cost his wife too much—probably in both tears and *dinero*."[36] When Rose delivered the illustrations, Toklas was delighted, for Rose's long acquaintance with Toklas had enabled him to create rough but accurate drawings of Bilignin for her—of its front gate, its vegetable gardens, and its kitchen—as well as to render a passably handsome portrait of Toklas herself, one that ultimately graced the cover of the book's first British edition. "Francis has done some really beautiful line drawings for [the cookbook] and a dust cover," she wrote Steward sometime later.[37] Maurice Grosser, who thought Rose's artwork deplorable, would only concede that they "well exhibit[ed] his amateurish and untrained vigor."

❧

After the manuscript arrived at Harper and Bros., Toklas was finally given her contract by Simon Michael Bessie, a Harvard-educated editor who later wrote (with a touch of false modesty) that his "sole qualification for having anything to do with a book about food and cooking was a prodigious appetite for food (and wine) and a fascination for anything Alice did or said." His editorial obliviousness to the

---

* Although Rose was no longer able to afford his home on the quai de Bourbon, he retained its *chambre de bonne*, or top-floor maid's room, as a pied-à-terre.
† For further details, see Spring, *Secret Historian*, pp. 143–68.

errors in the book's text and recipes does suggest however that he was not cut out to edit cookbooks. He seems to have spoken with Toklas about the book only once before she sent in the completed manuscript, and very briefly and casually at that.* Michael Joseph publishers was contracted to bring the book out at roughly the same time in the United Kingdom.

In the early 1950s, top book publishers were not as zealously focused, as they are today, upon the vetting and copyediting of recipes. But even for a book of the period, *The Alice B. Toklas Cook Book* is riddled with an outstanding number of mistakes, misspellings, incorrect ingredient quantities, and cooking instructions that simply do not work. Toklas had assembled the manuscript at great speed, and like most home cooks, she had not had the time, interest, or temperament for testing (and retesting) her own recipes. Nor did she think to test (or question) the recipes of her friends. But there were other copyediting problems as well: the finished book carried misspellings of proper names and ingredients (including "Brian Gysen" for Brion Gysin—one of the few that was subsequently corrected). And no one involved with the book seems to have noticed that Gysin's "fudge" recipe contained a controlled substance until British reviewers began to discuss it in the press.

In the United Kingdom, no action was taken by publishers to remove the book from bookshelves or to excise the fudge recipe. But in New York things were different, for American paranoia about marijuana was at an all-time high. Vilification of the substance had been on the rise since the naming of Harry J. Anslinger in 1930 as commissioner of the Federal Bureau of Narcotics, and it had intensified through the efforts of conservative news magnate William Randolph

---

* Bessie's "Happy Publisher's Note to the 1984 Edition," written thirty years after the book's publication, includes the suggestion, evoked through an (imagined) dialogue, that Bessie and Toklas were old friends, that he begged her in person to write her memoirs, and that in declining to do so she had graciously allowed that she would instead write him a cookbook "full of memories." But correspondence shows that they did not meet to discuss the idea for the book (or the quality of the subsequent manuscript) before the book went to press. Bessie's note also states that the lunch Toklas gave Bessie in October of 1954 (that is, after the book had gone to press) was for the purpose of "testing recipes." But that too is nonsense, because recipes are tested before a manuscript is sent to press, not after. Bessie came out with his "Happy Publisher's Note to the 1984 Edition" seventeen years after Toklas died, though—so she could hardly correct his account.

Hearst. By 1935 federal authorities were describing marijuana use as an act of "civic corruption." Passage of the Boggs Act in 1951 made possession of cannabis a federal crime requiring a mandatory sentencing of two to ten years, with fines of up to twenty thousand dollars.

Time magazine got the scoop on the Toklas "drug" story with a short piece about the *Cook Book* in its "People" section of October 4, 1954:

> The late Poetess Gertrude (*Tender Buttons*) Stein and her constant companion and autobiographee Alice B. Toklas, used to have gay old times together in the kitchen. Some of the unique delicacies that were whipped up will soon be catalogued by the US publisher, Harper & Bros., in a wildly epicurean tome called *The Alice B. Toklas Cook Book*, which is already causing excited talk on both sides of the Atlantic. Perhaps Alice's most gone concoction (and also a possible clue to some of Gertrude's less earthly lines) was her hashish fudge ("which anyone could whip up on a rainy day").[38]

The piece then published the entire hashish fudge recipe in a footnote, a decision that subverts the article's tone of moral outrage— and makes the piece seem, on second reading, far more antihomosexual than antidrug in its cheap-shot animosity.

Harper contacted the U.S. Attorney General to make sure that the federal government would not interfere with the book's American publication. In due course the publishing house was advised that merely writing about marijuana was not itself illegal. But in order to be sure the book would have no problems, Bessie excised the hashish fudge recipe, even as it was included in the UK edition. This whiff of scandal, made even more scandalous by Stein and Toklas's hidden-in-plain-sight lesbianism, came together with the current American fascination with Paris, with French food and wine, and with Left Bank avant-gardism to create an immediate demand for the *Cook Book* nationwide: it sold seven thousand copies in its first month in the United States, and within three weeks of its publication, it had gone into its fourth printing.[39]

A week after the notice appeared in *Time*, Bessie came over to Paris for a visit. Toklas invited him to lunch, and also invited Thornton and Isabel Wilder,* both of whom knew and liked the editor. She did so despite having major financial difficulties: she had long since spent the small advance she had been given for the book on heating her apartment, and no additional royalties would come to her until mid-1955. In fact she had only recently fended off an old friend's suggestion that a charity subscription be taken up on her behalf, writing Dilkusha de Rohan:

> It's a complete misunderstanding of my financial situation under which you are laboring. Perhaps it's belated symptoms of jaundice on my part that's made me sound [so] to your vivid imagination—if it has ears—that could allow you to suppose me in want. . . . Not at all—at all—at all. I have the right to sell a picture or pictures for my maintenance. That does not happen to be something I would care to do. So please put [away] your idea of coming to my rescue by having a subscription taken for my benefit or turning the flat into a tourist center or any other equally absurd project. Frankly—my dear Dilkusha I would be very angry indeed with you if it wasn't certain that you had allowed your too lively imagination and sympathy to run away with you. You'll be forgiven only—but freely—if you will tell me you have completely misunderstood the situation— that if you have spoken to anyone about it you will at once correct it—and that you forget the whole episode.[40]

Bessie recalled their afternoon in the decrepit apartment in this way:

> For some reason, probably money, which she then had very little of despite the immensely valuable things on the walls, Alice decided to do without a maid, which meant the tiny

---

* Wilder and his sister, both unmarried, kept house together just outside New Haven, and often traveled together.

and aging figure spent most of the lunch running back and forth between kitchen and dining room. Wilder, one of the world's politest men, stood up every time Alice did. When she had put a huge platter of fried chicken on the table and Thornton was still at half-mast, she tried to help him to some chicken, saying curtly: "Thornie, for God's sake, sit down and I'll give you some chicken. Which do you prefer; light or dark?" The great man turned to his sister Isabel and asked: "Which is it I prefer?" "Oh, God," said Alice, "Help yourself, dear Thornie." And back to the kitchen.[41]

For her part, Toklas described the lunch to Yale librarian Donald Gallup as a fiasco: "Bessie—Harper's present editor—was here, and the lunch [I] cooked was a triumph of ineptitude—*petit malheur** and an immobilised right hand." But the get-together had served a dual purpose: it let author and publisher get to know each other a little, and it soothed Toklas's hurt feelings about the unpleasant piece in *Time*. Thornton Wilder was particularly helpful in putting the latter into perspective. As Toklas noted to Gallup, "I hope you weren't as shocked as I by the notice in *Time* of the hashish fudge! I was also furious until I realized it was really in the cook book! . . . Thornton said no one would believe in my innocence as I had pulled the best publicity stunt of the year."[42] In a similar note to Samuel Steward, she wrote, "The story of Haschich Fudge is a scream. It was contributed by a friend who lives in Africa. . . . It is my ignorance not to have suspected what the few leaves were—of course I didn't know their Latin name. So when *Time* did that vulgar malicious paragraph I was furious." She then added, "You will love Francis [Rose's] lovely illustrations. . . . [He] has become a good boy for the moment at least."[43]

A day after she wrote to Steward, the first major American review of the book was published, in *The New York Times*, by detective novelist Rex Stout.† His "To Cook Is to Cook"[44] described the book as

---

* Trans.: A bit of bad luck.

† Stout (1886–1975) took a great interest in food and often reviewed food-related titles; his fictional alter ego, sleuth Nero Wolfe, was an epicurean and gourmand.

fascinating, and added that "at least a third of the 350 [recipes] are well worth a sampling." But he also pointed out that one recipe (for roast turkey) called for four cups of whole truffles, and so might not be suitable for the American kitchen. *New York Times* food editor Jane Nickerson followed up with a second review the next day, noting that Toklas's recipes were "interesting, inspirational and often, from the American viewpoint, impractical and time-taking. Miss Toklas makes no concessions to the quick meal; she would not know how. But she has written the directions for her dishes from her heart, and despite the fact that they may call for truffles and hare's blood, we must respect her for it."[45]

The *Cook Book* immediately established itself as *sui generis*—neither cookbook nor memoir, but a brilliant, deftly comic hybrid. As a result, and despite its harsh early words, *Time* magazine came back shortly after the book's American publication with a long and entirely laudatory review that gave readers a better sense of the delights that lay within, even as it mocked Toklas for her homeliness and "prattle":

> It is reasonably certain that no man ever said to Alice B. Toklas: "If you could only cook!" Small, wiry and quite bereft of feminine charm, she was once cattily described as "the lady with the melancholy nose." But cook she could—or at least she went into the kitchen armed with glorious recipes.
>
> For close to 40 years Alice was companion, housekeeper and quite often chief cook and bottle washer for Fellow U.S. Expatriate Gertrude Stein, who made her name a literary household word with *The Autobiography of Alice B. Toklas* (which was, of course, the autobiography of Gertrude Stein). One thing the two spinsters and their arty friends loved was good food. . . . Now 78, Alice has written a book herself, and, since it is a cook book, it is probably more usable and readable than Author Stein's own volumes.
>
> . . . What gives the *Cook Book* its special charm is the stream of Alice's prattle, in which the recipes appear like floating islands, in no particular order. . . . In Palma de Mallorca, a French cook almost started a riot in the market place

by showing Alice how to smother pigeons (the cook said it made them fuller and tastier). The information came in handy when Alice fixed some braised pigeons on croutons for Gertrude, using six "sweet young corpses" choked by her own hands. . . . This is richer cooking than most U.S. diners are used to, but it will be the fiercest Francophobe who can read Alice's recipes and not hanker for a taste, the dullest cook who will not want to get to the kitchen and try them out. *The Alice B. Toklas Cook Book* is, after all, the work of a lady who can ask (and leave unanswered) the painful question: "If one had the choice of again hearing Pachmann* play the two Chopin sonatas or dining once more at the Café Anglais, which would one choose?"[46]

The New Yorker was equally laudatory:

It is plain, even on short acquaintance, that this is a valuable book. The fundamental soundness of Miss Toklas' approach will almost certainly commend the volume to perceptive amateurs, whether or not they consider their great-aunt's formula for this or that superior to hers. She offers many dependable recipes for delicious and exciting dishes, as well as for a few surprising ones (a recipe for jellied salad that includes canned tomato soup, cream cheese, and commercial salad dressing might well have come straight from Topeka) but it is the author's salty comments and her contagious feeling for good cooking that give the book its zest.[47]

Toklas's timing was better than she knew. By 1954 Americans were living well (and cooking well) at home, and though magazines such as *House Beautiful* were advocating strongly on behalf of convenience foods, many would-be gourmets were opting to experiment with the preparation of fine food. As they gave their cocktail parties

---

* Vladimir de Pachmann (1848–1933) was a concert pianist famed for his brilliant renderings of Chopin.

and dinners, these up-and-coming suburbanites sought to do so in the sophisticated ways of the French. In women's magazines, culinary terms such as *en croûte, au vin, au gratin, à l'orange, au poivre,* or *cordon bleu* were becoming more and more common; so too were ambitious French desserts like the soufflé. To learn about such things from Alice Toklas was both thrilling and informative.[48]

The book was distinctive for another reason. Although the French themselves would always remain foreign and inscrutable to readers back home, Toklas was American—and after nearly fifty years of living in France, much of it spent among the great literary and artistic geniuses of the century, she made a perfectly congenial guide, translator, and go-between. After all, she was a study in contrasts: at once a homebody and a sophisticate; a behind-the-scenes cook and a well-connected hostess; a dedicated homemaker and an artsy bohemian. Her simple revelations about French cuisine were presented with elegance and wit. A new generation of status-conscious Americans, with their ultramodern kitchens and newly packaged foodstuffs, were delighted to salute the old-fashioned and time-honored ways of her cooking, and of French cooking generally. Her casually written recipes for classic French and Continental cuisine may not have proven fail-safe in the kitchen, but her writing was nonetheless considered the Real Thing—and in that way, an inspiration. "Gourmets everywhere came out of the underbrush and gourmet cooking came into the public domain," Carlton Lake later wrote about the book's effect on the American public. "[Toklas] was the democratization of *haute cuisine.*"

Young intellectuals such as Janet Malcolm, then just a teenager, also found the book irresistible, but for a different reason. As Malcolm (who would later write perceptively about Stein's and Toklas's war years) described the experience,

> The book . . . was given to me by a fellow member of a group of pretentious young persons I ran around with, who had nothing but amused contempt for middlebrow American culture, and whose revolt against the conformity of the time largely took the form of . . . writing mannered letters to each

other modeled on the mannered letters of certain famous literary homosexuals, not then known as such. *The Alice B. Toklas Cook Book* fit right in with our program of callow preciousness; we loved its waspishly magisterial tone, its hauteur and malice. "The French never add Tabasco, ketchup or Worcestershire sauce, nor do they eat any of the innumerable kinds of pickles, nor do they accompany a meat course with radishes, olives or salted nuts," Toklas wrote, as if preparing a manifesto for us. Her *de haut en bas* footnote pointing out that "a marinade is a bath of wine, herbs, oil, vegetables, vinegars and so on, in which fish or meat destined for particular dishes repose for specified periods and acquire virtue" filled us with ecstasy. . . . [As I leaf] through my copy of the *Cook Book* . . . [my] underlinings and marginal comments also highlight the passages—such as those quoted above—whose tart snottiness gave me special delight.[49]

Toklas surely hadn't intended to be tartly snotty. But she did have deeply felt opinions about how to cook, and her language reflected those opinions. She had now lived more than half her life in France; naturally she had absorbed and incorporated various everyday French locutions into her thinking and writing.* As a result, many Americans, including Malcolm, were puzzled by her rather grandiose turns of phrase. But Toklas felt quite sincerely that elegant phrasing had its place in the discussion of cooking—for that was the French way, from the most modest of French cookbooks (such as those by her beloved Édouard de Pomiane) to the most ambitious and encyclopedic.

Toklas's *Cook Book* (which was "as much a cook book as *Moby Dick* is the story of a whale hunt," according to *The New Republic*)[50] was in fact both discreet and monumental. Through a form of writing

---

* The sentences Malcolm quotes are a case in point. "Repose" is borrowed from the French verb *reposer* ("to leave," "to rest," or "to let settle," used much more commonly in French than in English). "Bath" is similarly drawn from the commonly used noun *bain*, which describes any liquid in which something is submerged—as, for example, the *bain marie*, the simmering hot water "bath" used in ovens to promote even cooking, or a *bain de friture*, a pot of frying oil. Toklas's use of "acquire virtue," meanwhile, is her adaptation of the French expression *mettre en valeur*, more commonly translated as "to show off to advantage" or "to enhance."

that most Americans considered little more than a manual of house-hold instruction, she had crafted a gentle, unassuming memoir of her life with Gertrude Stein. In doing so, she created a work that would, in time, equal *The Autobiography of Alice B. Toklas* in popularity, book sales, and critical acclaim. Moreover, at the height of the McCarthy era Toklas had told the story of two women who had lived together openly as partners, loved each other deeply, and made no apologies for that love or that life. And she had also made clear that her cooking, gardening, and housekeeping had been undertaken with the same mindfulness as any artistic endeavor. Despite her own ambivalence to the cookbook as a literary form, she had suggested through her *Cook Book* that the art and literature of cooking deserved a place, however humble, within the greater world of ideas. Through this modest, charming, deeply personal cookbook-memoir, Toklas had adroitly positioned herself (although, again, surely without intending to do so) as the first truly significant (if unlikely) celebrity homemaker-cook of the American postwar era.

NINE

"I Am a Merchant of Pleasure"

Like Alice Toklas, and later Julia Child, Alexis Lichine was both a popularizer of French culture and a demystifier of it; but unlike both of these writers, he was first and foremost a merchant. When he began his career in the United States, wine drinking and wine collecting, particularly of French wines, was mostly a specialty pastime of the rich and privileged. By the end of his career, the French wines he imported were being enjoyed at all levels of the American socio-economic spectrum. And while many different individuals (and market forces) played a role in the democratization of French wine during these years, Lichine's contribution was unique, as was the trajectory of his career: he began as a purveyor of highest-end luxury French wines but became an importer best known for good, sturdy, dependable, and correctly made French wines priced for everyday consumption. He popularized these sturdy wines alongside the fancier ones, doing so through lectures, demonstrations, and books pitched as much to the common man as the millionaire.

Lichine came to his work primarily as a salesman, not as an educator—he was in the wine business to make a profit, and his profit came from bringing good French wines to America and selling them hard. While in interviews and in his own writings, he might describe himself as a gentleman evangelist of wine and discuss his product as a great, civilizing force, he was, in the main, a self-proclaimed "merchant of pleasure." Like any merchant, his first goal was the accumulation of wealth through judicious buying and selling.

With *Wines of France* (1951) Lichine established himself in print as a leading American connoisseur of French wines. But by the time it was published he had already built up what was arguably the best French wine list (with the best prices) in the United States, specializing for the most part in good, honest, domaine- and château-bottled wines. The book, however, confirmed his brilliance as a friendly and approachable wine connoisseur and set him before the public not merely as a salesman, but rather as a genial educator and authority who also just happened to be a wine merchant.

Lichine was not the first American wine salesman to develop such a business strategy. His model in doing so was his former mentor and boss, Frank Schoonmaker. Ten years Lichine's senior, Schoonmaker had dropped out of Princeton as a young man to write about travel, and his first books were addressed to young adventurers on a budget. But by the time Lichine met him, just after the Eighteenth Amendment was repealed, Schoonmaker had opened his doors to the public as a New York wine dealer. Simultaneously, Schoonmaker began covering wine for *The New Yorker* in "Notes from the Wine Country"—a series of delightful, informative, and often comic sketches about life in the wine world, both abroad and at home. He also published elegant and erudite catalogues of his wine offerings, inspired by similar catalogues published by Nicolas in France. These catalogues were essentially glorified mail-order brochures, full of lush and evocative descriptions of wines that were designed to both entertain and educate the consumer, even while inducing a thirst that could be satisfied only through purchase.

⚜

Lichine began his career in the wine trade by traveling through the vineyards of France during the mid-1930s for the *Paris Herald Tribune*, which had hired him to drum up advertising from French and Algerian winemakers interested in tapping into the post-Prohibition American wine market. The work made Lichine conversant, as few Americans then were, with France's various wine regions, and also with the many types and varieties of wine produced in France. Through this work Lichine also became aware of the relatively common practice among *négociants* of *"coupage"*—that is, "cutting" good, expensive wines with cheap, relatively coarse wines, often from Algeria or the Midi,* as a way of maximizing their profits. *Coupage* was forbidden in all wines created under the AOC (*"Appellation d'Origine Contrôlée"*) system, which had been introduced for French wines starting in 1919. But nominal government enforcement of this "controlled designation of origin" began only with the formation of the Comité National des Appellations d'Origine in France in 1935—and strict enforcement of it would not begin until many years later.

While blending wines from various producers within a region was—and remains—legal for a certain grade of French *Appellation d'Origine Contrôlée* wines, the practice of blending an AOC region's fine wines with cheap, low-quality wines from elsewhere was (and is) not. As Lichine later explained:

> Until the 1930s, a great deal of wine outside of the château-bottled wines of Bordeaux was fraudulently labeled. Now virtually every variable that goes into the making of wine is strictly regulated by the rigorous and enlightened laws known as the *Appellation d'Origine Contrôlée,* or A.O.C, . . . The A.O.C. Laws apply to about 33 percent of France's wines. Less stringent laws govern the lesser wines, about 5 percent of total production . . . [and] the remaining 62 percent of French wine production is officially lumped together as *vins ordinaires* . . . meaning generally cheap, common wines with little claim to distinction.[1]

Frank Schoonmaker had been aware of this practice of *coupage*, and he had written about it a lot. He knew that guaranteeing his

---

* A colloquial expression for all of southern France, from the Atlantic Coast to the Italian border.

American buyers French wines that were unadulterated by *coupage* was a great way of building his client list. To ensure the integrity of his wines, he traveled to France personally during the 1930s to inspect, discuss, taste, and order. While there he got to know Raymond Baudoin, who in 1927 founded *La Revue du Vin de France*, a publication that worked hard to expose such crooked practices.* With Baudoin's assistance, Schoonmaker began developing a plan to go straight to the wine producer for his product, bypassing all (possibly unscrupulous) *négociants*.

When the twenty-four-year-old Alexis Lichine joined Schoonmaker's business in early 1938, he arrived with a substantial client list of his own, including the Waldorf-Astoria Hotel.[2] In short order, Schoonmaker put Lichine to work with Baudoin to secure these château- and estate-bottled wines from trustworthy French winemakers. During the summer of 1939, just weeks before the war broke out, Lichine and Baudoin went on a wine-buying expedition in France, and the two set up bottling lines for a number of Burgundian domaines so that their wines could bypass all French *négociants* and instead be shipped directly to Schoonmaker in New York.

Lichine and Schoonmaker suspended their importing work with the declaration of war, with both men entering military service. Once the war ended, Lichine tried to persuade Schoonmaker to give him a full partnership in the firm,† but Schoonmaker declined, and so Lichine set out on his own. Within a few months he was in France again, where he met and joined forces with the Paris-based Wisconsin native Seymour Weller.

Weller had lived in Europe most of his life: he went to school in Switzerland, fought in France in World War I, married a Frenchwoman, and became a French citizen. When Clarence Dillon decided to pur-

---

* After World War II, the Institut National des Appellations d'Origine (INAO) took over from the Comité National des Appellations d'Origine, and the new agency was much more rigorous about inspection and enforcement in AOC regions.

† The two men remained barely cordial after the split, each feeling wronged by the other. "Alexis heard that I was going to Germany with Frank [Schoonmaker] and was worried," James Beard wrote Helen Evans Brown in 1958. "Jesus there are just as many prima donnas in the wine business as there are in any other. I like both of them and don't want to fight. I still think Frank taught Alexis all he knows" (Beard to Brown, May 6, 1958, *Love and Kisses and a Halo of Truffles*, p. 210).

chase Château Haut-Brion in 1935,* he appointed Weller president of the company that oversaw the château's operation. Weller used his uncle's vast financial resources to restore the park at Haut-Brion, modernize the manor house, renovate and bring electricity to its *chais* (or storage sheds), and install all-new vinification equipment. He then remained to watch over the domaine and its wines, creating an enormous pile of refuse at the entrance to the Haut-Brion wine cellars as a way of protecting them from pillage throughout the war.

Once the war was over, Weller resumed work at Clarence Dillon's offices in Paris on the Place Vendôme. It was there that he met Lichine, who was just then setting up his own little export office on the Champs-Élysées. In 1948, when Lichine was given the plum job of rewriting the entire Waldorf-Astoria wine list and restocking its wine cellars, he invited Weller along on the buying trip—seemingly just for the fun of it, but surely also as a way of impressing upon Weller the depth of his knowledge, experience, and negotiating skills. The two started their new business shortly thereafter, and when Lichine began bottling and shipping his direct-from-the-domaine Burgundies to the United States, Weller was not only bankrolling the operation but was also an active partner in the business. And when the two men subsequently visited Bordeaux together, Lichine had the best possible introduction and credentials, because Weller was well-known in the Médoc as the president of Haut-Brion.

While spending time there with Weller, Lichine learned that the nearby Château Prieuré-Cantenac was for sale. This former Benedictine priory dating from the sixteenth century had essentially fallen to ruin (and so had its vineyards), but Lichine nonetheless saw in it a remarkable business opportunity. "There were no bathrooms, and the only running water was rain leaking through the roof," he later recalled, "but I thought it had possibilities. There was an air of enchantment about it."[3] Enchanted or not, the modest little château and its vineyards had two important attributes for an ambitious winemaker-businessman: first, it had been rated a fourth-growth

---

*The 1935 purchase price was 2.3 million francs—$148,387 in 1935 dollars, roughly equivalent to $2.6 million today.

château in the Classification of Bordeaux Châteaux, and was therefore a known, recognized producer of a wine that could easily find purchasers simply on the basis of the prestige accorded by that classification.* Second, the château's location—in the village of Cantenac, in the Haut-Médoc, about fifteen miles north of the city of Bordeaux—placed it squarely within a *commune* bearing a highly admired AOC recognized the world over: Margaux.† And while French regulations limited the amount of wine Lichine would be able to bottle and sell under Prieuré-Cantenac's proprietary label, Lichine knew he would be allowed to produce any amount of a second wine‡ at the château—and all of that second wine was wine he could sell, by rights, as Margaux.

Lichine had many other ambitions for his vineyard. Once he had got his bottling line up and running, he intended to buy open-market Cabernet Sauvignon, merlot, Cabernet Franc, petit verdot, and malbec juice from various wineries in the Bordeaux region, and then vinify, blend, and bottle them under his own name—calling these wines, for example, Alexis Lichine Bordeaux red wine, Alexis Lichine Pauillac, or Alexis Lichine Saint-Émilion, depending on the proportions and varietals being used in the blend. In doing so, he would be following a business model established in the 1930s by the maverick winemaker Baron Philippe de Rothschild§ (of nearby Château Mouton-Rothschild in Pauillac) whose innovative, low-cost Mouton Cadet label was similarly blended from juice purchased on the open market and blended into a generic red Bordeaux—an inexpensive wine that carried the

---

*The Bordeaux growth classifications—or *crus classés*—are part of a five-tier ranking system developed in 1855. First growth, or *premier cru classé*, is the most highly valued of the five. Although today largely considered outdated and inaccurate, the classification system remains a potent selling tool—not least because *all* the *crus*, from first to fifth, are permitted to carry the important phrase *"grand cru classé"* on their labels.

†Along with its *premier cru* Château Margaux, the *commune* of Margaux contains twenty other *cru classé* châteaux—more than any other commune in Bordeaux.

‡This second wine was sold, during Lichine's years there, under the name Château Clairefort.

§De Rothschild (1902–1988) had been evacuated to Pauillac at the outbreak of World War I. Unlike his father and grandfather, who had owned the estate but taken little interest in the making and selling of its wines, the young playboy returned there to manage the family's château, and he did so brilliantly. (Château Mouton-Rothschild is not to be confused with Château Lafite-Rothschild, also in Pauillac, which was run by his distant relative, Baron Élie de Rothschild, from 1946 to 1974.)

glamorous (and therefore sales-generating) Mouton and Rothschild names on its label.[4] Lichine's practice of buying in grapes, then vinifying, blending, bottling, and selling regional wines in this way would be where he ultimately made his greatest profit in the Médoc: these low-cost wines, their quality vouchsafed for American buyers by the Lichine name, would create steady, high-volume sales. Today the creation and marketing of such open-market wines is a standard business practice among top winemakers (just as, in the fashion world, prêt-a-porter lines are now routinely spun off by couturiers); but in the 1950s the practice was seen as an unusual and highly irregular one for a prestige winemaker or wine merchant. It was also considered vulgar (and wrong) by the stolid, old-fashioned, highly class-conscious wine families of Bordeaux.[5]

Even as he foresaw the potential of his château to produce and bottle all these wines, Lichine realized that the picturesque estate and its *chais* might easily serve yet another purpose, as a publicity center and headquarters for his worldwide business empire. The main building, the old priory, would certainly make an elegant venue for business entertaining. At the same time, the outbuildings could serve as the home of a bottling and storage facility, something that Lichine would need to create as he gathered wines from all over France for their consolidated export to the United States.

By creating this centralized new business model—in which extensive storage and shipping capabilities were combined with business offices and entertaining space—and also by cutting out all the French middlemen who had previously been involved with the sale (and possible adulteration) of regional wines being shipped to the United States, Lichine planned to streamline the highly complicated, multistep business of judging, ordering, receiving, bottling, resting, storing, and then repackaging wines for export. Until that moment, wines that had been blended, bottled, and rested at their place of origin were usually shipped to the exporter at an inflated cost, not only because of the middlemen involved, but also because of the weight of the bottles themselves, which being both heavy and fragile, entailed high freight costs. Lichine wanted to change all that by bringing in the wines via tanker trucks and bottling them on-site. The château may have looked to others like a crumbling Benedictine monastery, but Lichine envisioned it as the future home of an innovative, international wine-trading corporation, bottling operation, and shipping center, the likes of which no Frenchman had ever dreamt.

✤

What is probably most amazing about Lichine's career during the early 1950s—in fact, his entire career, right until its catastrophic denouement—was that he was so tremendously undercapitalized. Unlike his fellow château owners Clarence Dillon or Philippe de Rothschild, Lichine was not one of the megarich. Indeed, he was not rich at all. He had not bought a château as a prestige-enhancing hobby, as many rich men do. On the contrary, he came from a family that had only just barely escaped the Russian Revolution, he had started out with next to nothing, and he had been absolutely determined to make a fortune from his very earliest days. Thirty-eight when he purchased Château Prieuré-Cantenac, he had been working hard in the wine business since his early twenties—and if he had very little to show for that hard work in the way of capital, it was only because the Great Depression and World War II had conspired to get in his way.

His expenses were high too. Like most salesmen of luxury goods, Lichine was compelled to keep up appearances: selling to the rich required one to look and act rich oneself. All his adult life, no matter what his financial situation, Lichine made a point of living and dressing like a movie star (even his military uniforms were ordered from Saks Fifth Avenue). He would always have a beautiful, well-dressed woman on his arm, and the most fashionable home address. The wine writer Anthony Dias Blue later recalled, "Everything with him was either imperial or grand. He acted like a character out of a European movie of the 1930s. He also played and lived that role. He was very tall and imposing, so he dominated any room upon entering. [He was] always very well dressed . . . a dandy."[6] When traveling to sell wine, Lichine booked the best tables at the finest restaurants and nightclubs. Here of course there was method to his madness: in many instances, the proprietors and headwaiters at these establishments were providing him with quid-pro-quo introductions to their best and biggest-spending customers in exchange for his generous tips.[7]

The wine dealer Sam Aaron and his wife, Florence, Lichine's good friends since the 1930s, worried about Lichine living so far beyond his income, and they hoped this habit would change when he married. But Lichine's first wife, Renée de Villeneuve, a French-speaking countess turned fashion designer, had been a celebrated clotheshorse even before she met Lichine on the Riviera, and (according to Florence Aaron) she had changed her clothes three times a day during the course of their very brief marriage. At any rate by 1947 it was over—their union lasted less than a year—and Lichine was once again out with a succession of beautiful models, actresses, and would be Hollywood starlets, including (briefly) Grace Kelly. But as any salesman knows, the company of a beautiful woman is a great way to beguile and win over a client, so this sort of "dating" was actually an aspect of his business.

Whatever income Lichine did not spend on himself, his business, or his women was often spent, amazingly enough, on other various risky but potentially high-yield investments. The man was by nature a gambler. One of his earliest such investments was an enormous parcel of beachfront acreage on St. Croix, purchased in partnership with Philippe of the Waldorf, that the two men hoped one day to turn into a vast and glamorous Caribbean resort. (They never did.) As a result, Lichine needed to put together a series of loans from friends in order to finance the restoration of Château Le Prieuré-Cantenac. He purchased it for approximately $16,000 (the equivalent of $150,000 today) using loans from three close friends: the investment banker Gilbert W. Kahn of Kuhn, Loeb; Armagnac *négociant* Duc Pierre de Montesquiou-Fezensac; and Jean Béliard, then the consul general of France in Chicago.[8]

Lichine was a dreamer, visionary, and optimist. Though advised, he later wrote, that "the ruinous state of the house [and vineyards] would take decades and a fortune to restore. . . . I disregarded [all] warnings, and took a plunge I have never for a minute regretted."[9] Even as he began that work, he petitioned to have the château renamed after himself—thus further advancing his visibility, both in the Médoc* and in the United States. Although such a name change was unprecedented, and not at all likely to occur, Lichine persisted: "I applied to the Marquis de Lur-Saluces, then the president of the Committee of Classified Growths, [and] in 1953 [he] officially authorized the change of the name to Château Prieuré-Lichine."[10] By forever joining his name to that of a noble Margaux *appellation*, as well as to the picturesque priory and its celebrated vines, Lichine was now no longer merely a Russian-born American wine salesman with big dreams. Rather, he was placing himself before the public as the owner of an ancient fourth-growth château in Margaux that carried his name—thereby tacitly implying that the family of Lichine had long tilled its noble soil.

❦

Shortly after Lichine purchased the Prieuré, Seymour Weller offered him the job of export manager for Château Haut-Brion, a position that carried both prestige and a substantial salary. It was not a difficult job: Haut-Brion, a Bordeaux *premier cru classé*, is one of the most celebrated wines in the world, and so most of Lichine's work consisted of deciding which purchasers might have those bottles of wine released yearly by the château. In granting such favors to would-be purchasers, Lichine continued to forge business contacts with top American buyers of the most luxurious French wines. Between this remunerative new appointment and his other plum job (of selecting wines for Philippe at the Waldorf, also not terribly difficult, and also good for networking), Lichine had clearly arrived. No wonder, then, that in that very same year of 1951 he dedicated *Wines of France* not to a loved one, but rather to the two men who had established him in those top jobs, and done so much else to help him in his career: Seymour Weller and Claudius Philippe.

Lichine was particularly grateful to Weller because opportunities to make money in the Médoc were then few, and many of its winemakers were facing financial ruin. Lichine initially assumed that given

---

*Within the Médoc, a sub-region of Bordeaux, lie the celebrated *appellations* of Saint-Estèphe, Pauillac, Saint-Julien, and Margaux (as well as the less known *appellations* of Listrac-Médoc and Moulis-en-Médoc).

the financial desperation of these winemakers, he would be able to build up his export portfolio to include some great wines from the Médoc, Graves, and the Libournais.* To his surprise, however, the region's *négociants* and *vignerons*† proved surprisingly resistant to his proposals. They were set in their ways and they did not like outsiders:

> The history of the Bordeaux wine community since the Second World War is essentially that of the Bordeaux shipping families. . . . They carry on business today much as they did in the past—in the low-keyed, dignified manner that has come to be part of the Bordelais spirit . . . [But] after the Second World War, the shippers . . . [discovered that their] reliable pre-war markets had shrunk, and some [of those markets], like Argentina and Germany, had disappeared completely. Blinded by their respect for past practices, the established shipping families neglected their responsibilities to increase the existing markets and explore the new ones, such as the United States and even France itself, which, until this last decade, has been as ignorant of its great wines as any country.
>
> This shortsightedness and obstinacy is the result of generations of inbred values and inbred blood. Intermarriage has long been the rule in the snobbish, closed world of the Bordeaux shipping firms. Matchmaking between the de Luzes, Cruses, Johnstons, and Calvets, to mention a few, was the standard operating procedure. These families, as well as a few others, were the important ones [and their snobbery was] passed [down] from generation to generation . . . [To make matters worse] these shippers . . . kept a stranglehold on the wine growers of Bordeaux, from the largest château to the smallest peasant, . . . [and] this pattern of local family control

---

* Graves, a Bordeaux wine region southeast of the city of Bordeaux, is home to the Graves, Pessac-Léognan, Sauternes, and Barsac AOCs, along with several others. The Libournais is a Bordeaux wine region located on the right bank of the Dordogne; its most celebrated AOC wines are Pomerol and Saint-Émilion.
† A *vigneron* is a person who cultivates grapes for winemaking. In the United States the term used is winegrower.

endure[d] until the late fifties and early sixties, when I
[showed them through my own success that] new markets,
particularly the United States, had great potential for growth.[11]

At first only a few château owners would speak to Lichine—most
notably, Baron Philippe de Rothschild, who had nothing to lose by
knowing him because, despite having grown up in Bordeaux, he was
himself something of an outsider and maverick, not least since he
was Jewish. Lichine also had an amicable relationship with Pierre
Ginestet of nearby Château Margaux, primarily because he purchased
so many of Ginestet's top-priced wines for the Waldorf-Astoria. However, the majority of the Bordeaux wine-trading and winegrowing
establishment saw Lichine as a sharp, aggressive, fast-talking foreigner intent on stealing their business. Thus even as he settled into
the Prieuré, Lichine discovered he was widely disliked by a close-knit
group of xenophobic locals—a "wine oligarchy, run by a firmly en-
trenched group consisting of influential brokers, wealthy shippers,
and proprietors of the great châteaux . . . *l'aristocratie du bouchon.*"*[12]
Even though he was helping them to modernize their vineyards† and
was hoping to work with them to expand their overseas markets, the
members of the "cork aristocracy" would not willingly have anything
to do with him.

One thing that truly baffled Lichine about *l'aristocratie* was its
complete indifference to selling its wines directly to the public. When
he first arrived in the Médoc, hardly any of the growers (apart from de
Rothschild) would receive visitors for on-site tastings or sales. The
châteaux were shuttered most of the year, opened to invited guests
only, and only on the rarest of occasions. Tourists hoping to taste these
famed Bordeaux wines, visit the pretty manor houses, and load up
their cars (as Paul and Julia Child had done so happily on their trips
to Burgundy, which had a far more tourist-friendly culture) were

---

*The cork aristocracy.
†Lichine brought a special model of tractor designed specifically for vineyards; prior to its arrival,
all such work had been done by mules. In his 1974 *New Encyclopedia of Wine and Spirits*, Lichine
boasted, "The Loiseau vineyard model, which I introduced . . . has now been sold throughout
Bordeaux for over thirty years" (p. xxiii).

given no access to on-site tasting rooms or *caves*. Instead, they encountered locked gates and surly custodians. Lichine immediately realized that he had a magical opportunity to sell his wines at full retail price without any competition, and without incurring any of the expenses of shipping, sales commissions, or even of renting a storefront. And so, in brazen defiance of local custom, he opened the Prieuré to tourists and began offering both *dégustation* ("wine tasting") and *vente directe* (direct sale). To encourage visitors, he constructed a series of Louis Quinze–style billboards along the Médoc roadsides, guiding would-be customers to his gates. "It was widely denounced as a desecration," a friend and observer later noted, "but [Lichine] refused to give up ground, and, instead, put up more signs, meanwhile insistently preaching the gospel of advertising and public relations."[13]

⚜

A year after Lichine bought the Prieuré, Château Lascombes came up for sale. Just two miles from the Prieuré, Lascombes came with forty-three acres of the best *terroir* in the Médoc.[14] With an asking price of approximately $70,000, Lichine figured he would need at least $150,000 to capitalize the purchase and renovation. So he began rounding up potential investors. This time, however, he decided to tap well-known public figures as his investors, with the secondary aim of using their names to raise the profile of the château among American wine collectors. After years of lecturing across the United States, Lichine shrewdly recognized the power of celebrity to add grandeur and desirability to any product.

Upon presenting Château Lascombes—whose wines were a *deuxième cru classé*—to a handpicked group of celebrity acquaintances (selling the investment idea to them both as an opportunity for profit and an adventure in prestige winemaking), he quickly signed up a stunning list of investor-shareholders, including some of the richest and most powerful people in America: David Rockefeller, soon to become the chairman of the Chase Manhattan Corporation; John Ringling North, president of the Ringling Brothers and Barnum & Bailey Circus; Admiral Lewis Strauss, chairman of the Atomic Energy Commission; Maxwell A. Kriendler, vice president of "21" Brands and the famed '21' Club in New York; Jan Mitchell, proprietor of the equally famous Manhattan restaurant Lüchow's; Gilbert W. Kahn, who apart from his work at Kuhn, Loeb was the son of the fabulously wealthy Jewish-American financier Otto Hermann Kahn;* Jerome K. Ohrbach, president of Ohrbach's Department Stores; Mrs. Muriel R. Pershing, daughter-in-law of the late general John J. Pershing; Max Burns, former president of Shell Oil; George F. Baker, Jr., a director of the First National City Bank of New York; and the French actress Mony Dalmès, Philippe of the Waldorf's second wife.[15]

By the terms of the offering, none of these investors (there were ultimately thirty-five) would ever be allowed to own more than a 10 percent share in Lascombes, and all would remain silent partners. Lichine retained approximately 25 percent[†] of the shares and control of the winery's day-to-day operations.[16] Yearly dividends were to be paid in wine. Each of the celebrities would serve as a goodwill ambassador of the wine produced at the château; and their names meanwhile gave Lichine his own very distinctive bragging rights as he crisscrossed the United States selling all of his French wines to everyday Americans.

Lichine also began reaching out to the American food establishment to get them excited about Bordeaux. James Beard, with whom he had once worked at Sherry's wine shop, was transfixed by the feasts Lichine laid on for him there, writing Helen Evans Brown about "an interesting dinner at Lichine's . . . [featuring] an excellent cheese soufflé for the first course. Then a thick rump steak of beef roasted rare, with cèpes[‡] . . . and quantities of braised endive—a perfect combination of flavors, along with red wine. Cheese for the end of the meal. The beef was what many French consider the best. They take oxen which have worked in the fields for years and retire them for one year to pasturage, where they relax and eat like fools. They are then slaughtered and

---

*Kahn is best remembered for his grand Long Island home, Oheka Castle (built in 1919), the second largest private residence in the United States.

†Accounts vary concerning Lichine's share: he told reporter Arnold Wechsberg in 1957 that his share was 30 percent, but other, later accounts place Lichine's share at 20 percent (Hennessy, *The Pope of Wine*, p. 120).

‡Better known in America as porcini mushrooms, cèpes are a specialty of Bordeaux, where they are traditionally sautéed in olive oil with garlic and shallots (a dish known as *cèpes à la bordelaise*).

aged and have plenty of fat and flavor. It is completely different from the beef to which we are accustomed."[17]

The following year, on another trip, Beard marveled at the French ability to serve world-class meals on the Paris-to-Bordeaux train. "The four of us had a Pullman compartment, and they served our lunch there—hors d'oeuvre, with five different vegetables in sauce Grècque, stuffed eggs, sardines and sausage. Then trout amandine, an excellent tournedos Rossini with chip potatoes and haricots verts, a salad of endives, cheese, and a fruit ice cream with wafers and coffee. And [of course] a large choice of wines."[18] In short order, Lichine saw to it that Beard (who had consultancies with the Cognac and Champagne trade groups, as well as wine dealers Sam Aaron and Julius Wile) was ritually enthroned during the Feast of Saint Vincent as a Commandeur du Bontemps de Médoc.*

The enthronement was cause for yet another *grande bouffe*. After a morning spent touring and tasting with Lichine, Beard was lionized at a gloriously rich, wine-soaked Saturday afternoon luncheon for sixty. "We started with a soup of vegetables in cream to heat us up after that really cold period in the cellars," he wrote Helen Evans Brown. "Then *foie gras* of duck—fresh, with Madeira sauce and raisins—[followed by] guinea hen with a truffle sauce, potatoes and tiny green beans, [then] cheese, [then] a wonderful cake with ices, and then fruit. The wines were impeccable, being the choice wines from seven different vineyards in the district. Afterwards we had cognac and coffee and such things until late in the afternoon. . . . Then [we went] back to Lichine's after some vineyard visiting. . . . [and] we had a big dinner party at the Prieuré that evening and [then] went off to . . . [another] party . . . [at a] small château [owned by Lichine's business manager]."[19] Many of Lichine's investors and clients would follow in Beard's footsteps in the years to come, learning through such feasting how well fine Bordeaux wines complemented French *haute cuisine*. And of course, in doing so they also forged a lasting emotional connection to the Médoc, and to Lichine.

---

* This honorary title is bestowed upon many dozens of people each year—essentially anyone considered by the Bordeaux wine establishment to be a "great lover of our wines to which they [will] swear their faithfulness."

When not receiving his many guests at the Prieuré, Lichine continued to maintain a grueling American travel schedule, one through which he sold wines to his current clients, sought out new clients, and lectured to the public on French wines as a way of attracting even more people to sample his wares. *Wines of France* was, of course, his calling card at each of these whistle-stop affairs. "My activities [in America are] as an importer, distributor, and all-round crusader on behalf of wines," he would declare at these talks, emphasizing again and again that he was quite the opposite of a traveling salesman. Yet for many years Lichine was just that, taking three or four six-week trips per year across the United States by propeller plane, train, and even bus, going as deep into the American heartland as possible, and selling to all and sundry.

One reason Lichine needed to travel so much was that each of the states he visited had its own complicated way of regulating wine sales. With the repeal of Prohibition, each state had been allowed to adopt its own particular ways of regulating and controlling the alcohol industry—and of course collecting state taxes. The supply chain was broken up by state regulators into three tiers: producers, distributors, and retailers. Since ownership of all three tiers by one person or company was prohibited, and since most retailers at that time preferred to sell spirits rather than wine, the average wine salesman had a nearly impossible challenge in getting his wines into the hands of the American consumer. "The American market for wine after the Second World War was hard to crack," Lichine later wrote. "Many states [barred] an outside importer from having any contact with the client, whether as a wholesaler or retailer. [And] many of the wholesale liquor distributors in the late 1940s were onetime bootleggers, reluctant to take on a product for which they foresaw no market, [while many liquor] retailers . . . felt the same way. My only recourse was to take the crusade for wine directly to the consumer."[20]

Across the United States, Lichine made sure that each potential client had a great first experience with his products. In his lectures and tastings, he presented himself as an advocate on behalf of a noble and civilizing beverage rooted in antiquity. He was exceptionally generous with his knowledge of wine history and lore, and through his many lectures and tastings and dinners, he offered clients the benefit of his vast expertise, even as he poured interesting and delicious new wines into their wineglasses.

Lichine also helped neophyte American fanciers of French wines in ways that were not necessarily motivated by self-interest—as when, after a dinner at the London Chop House in Detroit, he listened to Lester Gruber, the restaurant's owner, describing the European wine-buying trip he intended to take. "I tore up his proposed itinerary and gave him a revised version, based on [the] trip I had made two years earlier with Alfred A. Knopf," Lichine later recalled (with typical name-dropping aplomb). Lichine earned no commission on the wines Gruber subsequently bought on that trip—but simply by putting the restaurateur in contact with the right people, he made sure that Gruber had the best possible experience of the regions and their wines.

The resultant goodwill that Gruber felt toward Lichine—combined, of course, with the highly competitive prices Lichine could offer him and a streamlined delivery process that guaranteed his wines arrived in pristine condition—ultimately resulted in the two men settling into a long, loving, and mutually rewarding business relationship. "My high-handed methods produced a lasting friendship [with Gruber] and eventually helped to establish wine as an indispensable feature of the Detroit restaurant scene," Lichine recalled more than a decade later. "It was not long before bottles [of fine French wines] began to appear on the tables of [Detroit's] private homes as well. This scenario, recast and rescripted as necessary, repeated itself from city to city across the country."[21] In his later years, Lichine liked to tell a similar story about walking into Antoine's restaurant in New Orleans, ordering six wines, then immediately pronouncing three of them "disgraceful and undrinkable." The proprietor came to his table, and the two men ended up talking late into the night. By the next morning, Lichine had an order from Antoine's for more than a hundred different wines. This brash, in-your-face selling technique, a Lichine specialty, would later be described by a popular journalist as "a formidable combination of savoir-faire and chutzpah."[22]

Lichine scored similar successes all across the American heartland, where locals truly appreciated his guidance in finding, ordering, and aging wines properly. Akron, Atlanta, Chicago, Cleveland, Dallas, Milwaukee, Minneapolis, and New Orleans were ultimately his best markets after New York, San Francisco, and Los Angeles. "In the early days," he told one interviewer, "I took six-week trips and covered the country in depth. In each town I'd speak to women's clubs, radio and TV talk shows, anywhere. I would take three very social people and install wine cellars for them. They'd introduce me to their friends and eventually the local retailers. After that I'd go to the wholesalers and turn them around, and then go out on calls with their salesmen."[23] His travel through these cities and towns was so frequent that even late in life he could recite the schedules of buses running between Toledo and Akron, and the trains between Chicago and Springfield.[24] And when this wide-eyed new American clientele asked Lichine how best to develop a connoisseur's palate such as his own, Lichine lost no time in giving them the merriest of answers: "Simple," he told them. "Buy a corkscrew and use it."[25]

Through giving three wine seminars a day in each city he visited—all of them open to the public—Lichine drummed up more and more "converts." And much to his own surprise he also became a sought-after public speaker.[26] City by city and town by town, he was slowly convincing American consumers, American liquor salesmen, and American liquor wholesalers that French wines deserved a place at the American table. "The legal bottlenecks that impeded the wholesaler, the retailer, and the restaurateur [were all based on] interstate and intrastate licensing systems [that were] so complicated that businessmen felt they could hardly spare the time to unravel the red tape that accompanied a shipment," Lichine later explained. "Fear of wine—the great unknown—had been at the root of the problem."[27]

✦

By 1953, Lichine was on his way to riches. He owned the Prieuré-Lichine and enough of a controlling interest in Château Lascombes to comfortably refer to the place as "his." He also owned (or, to be more exact, co-owned*) a total of 3.4 acres in three Burgundian *grand cru* vineyards: Bonnes-Mares, Latricières-Chambertin, and Mazy-Chambertin. These three vineyards in Burgundy, however tiny, were, like his holdings in Bordeaux, enough to give him bragging rights as a Burgundian *vigneron* among American wine dealers and wine collectors.

His next step in growing his company and his brand was to found a shipping company in Margaux, Alexis Lichine et Cie. By this point he was both undercapitalized and leveraged, so he raised the funds through a small group of investors from Minneapolis. Through this new shipping company, all Lichine's wines—not only his château-bottled Bordeaux and estate-bottled Burgundies, but also the wines he was trucking in from the Beaujolais, the Mâconnais, the Loire, and several other regions of France—were brought together at his bottling and storage facility. There the majority were bottled, rested, then placed into shipping containers for delivery to American distributors or large-scale individual buyers (usually restaurants), stopping only briefly with an agreed-upon importer to satisfy the legal requirements mandated by the U.S. three-tier system. And because overseas shipping rates were determined by the container (rather than by weight), Lichine made a practice of filling the leftover space within each container with his inexpensive regional "estate" wines (that is, inexpensive regional wines that nonetheless came from named producers). These wines carried a lower unit cost (and profit), but still had a bit of cachet since they carried the name of their winemaker. These moderately priced bottles would eventually provide Lichine with a far more dependable revenue stream than his more expensive wines, since fine wines vary greatly in quality (and value) depending on weather and harvest, and moreover are attractive only to a smaller group of deep-pocketed, specialist buyers. By assembling all of his various wines under one roof in Margaux, not only was Lichine cutting down on shipping costs, he was also increasing his quality control: the bottling, labeling, storage, and shipping were now all his own work. He was

---

*Lichine shared the small strips of vineyard in Mazy-Chambertin and Bonnes-Mares with a New Orleans investment banker, Robert J. Newman.

saving money on shipping, eliminating middlemen, expanding his brand name, and safeguarding the quality and dependability of his product, all at the same time.[28] In short, he was bringing American business practices to the Médoc.

"The export company which bore my name soon grew to be one of the largest dealing in fine wines in France," Lichine later wrote. Indeed, within just a few years his operation had expanded to the point that he had to leave his offices in Margaux for a new and far grander seat of operations on the quai des Chartrons, the legendary Bordeaux *négociants'* address on the banks of the Garonne. By then Lichine had finally made inroads among local wine producers, and was helping them to bottle and sell each of their *cuvées** under their own labels. He did so by granting them the use of his bottling lines, his labels, and his warehouses—and, most important, by connecting them to his interested American clients. Slowly but surely, Lichine was persuading the close-knit Frenchmen of Bordeaux to work with his organization. "It was no discountable feat for a Russian-born Jew to [be] so persuasive," *People* magazine would later observe, "but the French have a special fondness for anyone who can make money for them."[29]

---

* A *cuvée* may be loosely translated as a type, blend, batch, or "vatful" of wine. (The word is derived from *cuve*, meaning "cask.")

TEN

Aromas and Flavors
of Past and Present

One of the most extraordinary aspects of Alice Toklas's second, nearly forgotten cookbook concerns its writing, for the majority of the text is written in words not her own. Food journalist Poppy Cannon, the ex-wife of Philippe of the Waldorf, put the book into its final form, and in the process turned it into a collaboration. Because the two women disagreed on just about every aspect of food preparation, *Aromas and Flavors of Past and Present* is not only an inconsistent book but also a wildly self-contradictory one—in short, a publishing fiasco.

Toklas knew very little about American processed foods before meeting Cannon, but in the spring of 1954 Elizabeth Gordon, the editor of *House Beautiful*, invited her down to Venice for a trip through northern Italy. Gordon wanted Toklas to write an article on turn-of-the-century American architecture and furniture and had promised her, in Toklas's words, a "fat fee." But upon learning that Toklas had a cookbook coming out, Gordon changed her mind, and instead introduced her to *House Beautiful*'s food editor, Poppy Cannon, who was also on the trip. As Cannon later recalled,

> [Elizabeth Gordon] had [already] given [me] a glowingly savory account of miraculous luncheons that Miss Toklas had

cooked for her in the apartment on the Left Bank. . . .
Almost immediately [at that] first meeting in Venice there
began between Alice Toklas and me a conversation about
food and cooking that has continued by word and letter for
years. She began it by telling me that while she enjoyed reading my articles in *House Beautiful* on the subject of the modern epicure she disagreed with me about almost everything,
and particularly with my basic belief that it is possible to be
an epicure, even an epicure-cook, in a hurry.

Between speed and ease and excellence there could be,
she felt, no possible connection. All processed or prepared
foods, canned, packaged or (horror of horrors!) frozen, were to
be regarded not only with suspicion but disdain. In gondolas
and galleries, in churches, in palaces, in markets, antique
shops, cafés and automobiles, our colloquy continued.[1]

Sipping aperitifs at the Danieli as the sun set on the Grand Canal,
Cannon and Toklas surely made an odd-looking pair. Toklas was
scarcely five foot tall and conservatively dressed in a sturdy, long-
waisted gray traveling suit that had been made for her more than a
decade earlier by Stein's protégé Pierre Balmain. "Her gloves were
Paris perfection," Cannon later wrote, "but her small feet were
unexpected—in flat leather sandals like those Isadora Duncan used
to wear." Cannon, by comparison, stood six foot tall, and favored
colorful turbans that made her look taller. And while the seventy-
seven-year-old Toklas spoke slowly in low tones—"like a viola at dusk,"
according to the poet James Merrill—Cannon, not yet fifty, was raucous
as a cockatoo. "We talked about France, talked about books, talked
about vineyards and people and wine," Cannon remembered. "Then,
inevitably, we talked about food, in which both of us took a breathless
interest."

Toklas responded warmly to this large, domineering, slightly outlandish woman—for, like Gertrude Stein, Cannon loved being the
center of attention and exuded a heavy sexual charisma. The warmth
between them was apparently mutual; as Cannon wrote her husband,
"Alice Toklas is a sweet, gentle little darling with a black mustache

and short-cut hair with bangs which also look like a mustache, but in ten minutes you have forgotten all that and hear only the kind, warm, wise things she says."[2] Another connection drew them together as well: Walter White, the head of the NAACP. Toklas (and Stein) had met and adored Walter White in Harlem in the early 1930s, with Toklas later describing him as "the blue-eyed blond Negro who had chosen to remain black."[3] Cannon, meanwhile, had conducted an on-again, off-again love affair with White since the late 1920s, and in July 1949 she had married him, making him her fourth husband. White had needed to leave his (black) wife and children in order to be with Cannon, and their divorce caused a scandal so great that it nearly ended his career; in fact, only Eleanor Roosevelt's threat of leaving the NAACP kept him from summary dismissal.

Even then, feeling against the two newlyweds ran high. Shortly after their marriage White and Cannon had been featured together on the cover of *Ebony* under the headline "Famous Negroes Who Married Whites," with an accompanying article and photo spread that briefly made Cannon the most reviled woman in black America, for it characterized her as a privileged white sexual predator and home wrecker. A substantial segment of white America presumably despised her for her marriage to Walter White as well, for at the time of their wedding, interracial marriages were still illegal in twenty states, and lynchings of black men who had involvements with white women, while fewer than in the prewar years, still occurred with some regularity. Cannon responded to this widespread animosity with blithe insouciance, however. The world was changing, and she loved White, and he loved her—and to her mind, that was all that would ever matter. "In more than one city," she would later write in her memoirs, people often "jumped to the conclusion that I, being many shades more brunette than Walter, must be the colored partner."[4]

A tough and ambitious career woman, Cannon had been working full-time since dropping out of college her freshman year.[5] Nevertheless, in all her writings she embraced the traditional feminine roles of wife, lover, and helpmate, repeatedly declaring that husband and family were far more important to her than any job or salary. But like much of what Cannon wrote or said, these words cannot be taken at face value. Consider, for example, her second cookbook, *The Bride's Cookbook*, a hyperromantic celebration of married love. The book features a series of love poems, some of them erotic, in praise of married bliss; but they are love poems that Cannon had written to her lover, Walter White, a married man, while Cannon was herself married to her three previous husbands. The book featured a good deal of culinary hypocrisy as well, for even as Cannon counseled young brides that the best way to a man's heart was through his stomach, she was advocating unequivocally on behalf of highly processed, factory-prepared convenience foods.*

This apparent contradiction—the insistence that factory-prepared food can make the best and most loving home cooking—was just one of the many paradoxes that made Cannon's rise in the New York food world so breathtaking. But American women of the 1950s were eager to escape kitchen chores and the tedium of daily meal preparation, and the processed food industry was eager to support the fantasy that doing so was not only possible, but good for all concerned. And Cannon happily took money directly from these manufacturers (doing so as an advertising consultant) even as she wrote up their products in articles for magazines (as a food editor and food journalist), oblivious to all questions of ethics.

Just as Cannon constantly mixed fact and fiction in her recipes, so too did she fictionalize much of her life story. Her name (with its playful evocation of a child's toy) suggested a privileged WASP background, and many assumed she came from one: the 1949 article in *Ebony*, for example, described her as a Vassar graduate who not only presided over a grand Connecticut estate but was also a fixture of "the Park Avenue Set." Not so: she was born Lillian Gruskin to middle-class Lithuanian Jews who had emigrated from South Africa to Kittanning, Pennsylvania, a little town forty miles northeast of Pittsburgh. There her father had spent his days running a modest five-and-dime while his wife succumbed to depression and mental illness. Their marriage, dominated by arguments and debt, had ended in divorce

---

* "Convenience cooking" is a style of cooking that relies on semiprepared or prepared foods as a starting point for the home cook.

during Cannon's adolescence. "When I was very young," she noted in a rare moment of candor, "bills and money problems . . . were much more regular in our household than good meals."[6] As the eldest child of four, she had been called upon to cook, clean, and look after her siblings. After working for a while in advertising, she married a Yale librarian, and though the marriage ended shortly after the birth of their only child, she kept her husband's name, Cannon, professionally. Her second marriage, to an engineer, ended in widowhood, but left her with a second child, some money and an old house near Danbury, Connecticut. Cannon's third marriage, to the notoriously difficult, autocratic, and womanizing Philippe of the Waldorf, gave her yet another child—and, thanks to her own shameless audacity and talent for self-promotion, instant credentials as a culinary journalist. (Philippe, meanwhile, was able to avoid the draft through his new status as a married man and father.)

Cannon landed her first full-time magazine job in 1940, when she became a food columnist at *Mademoiselle*, the newly founded "magazine for smart young women."[7] She got the job just a year after the death of her second husband and right around the time of her marriage to Philippe, and signed her articles with a pseudonym, Fillip, based on his name. Unlike Philippe, however, Cannon was not one to insist upon classical French cooking. Rather, she preferred the fast and amusing approach to entertaining at home. Whether whipping up "a smooth cocktail party, a buffet supper, an evening snack, [or] intimate little dinners for two," Cannon advised her readers that "it's all out of tins—but with verve, my Dear, with dash."[8] In 1953 she moved from *Mademoiselle* to *House Beautiful*, where her preference for convenience foods posed no problem at all to the Hearst Corporation: she was now writing for an upwardly mobile readership of wives and mothers with a passion for ease and convenience. Her articles accordingly evoked a world of beautiful, spacious suburban kitchens filled with all the latest and finest labor-saving appliances, even as her recipes called for minimal cooking and lots of packaged convenience foods.

Cannon's breezy, lighthearted style perfectly suited corporate advertisers, many of whom were just then developing and launching highly profitable processed food lines. Readers, meanwhile, responded with delight to her playfulness, creativity, and escapes into gastro-nomic fantasy. Her preference for flambéing foods before guests, using newfangled electric gadgets at table, and giving her slung-together recipes the fanciest and noblest of French names was very much in the spirit of the times.

In 1952 Cannon published *The Can-Opener Cookbook*, which main-tained that all convenience foods—whether in boxes, packets, or cans—were just as delicious as anything prepared fresh. "At one time a badge of shame, hallmark of the lazy lady and the careless wife, today the can opener is fast becoming a magic wand, especially in the hands of those brave young women . . . who are engaged in frying as well as bringing home the bacon," she wrote. She also declared that meals made from cans required the utmost in creativity, sensitivity, and good taste from the clever, time-pressed hostess, mother, or spouse. "When I ply my busy little can opener," she wrote, "I move onto the scene the way a chef comes in after a corps of kitchen helpers has done the scullery chores—the drudgery of cooking. Armed with a can opener, I become the artist-cook, the master, the creative chef."

Cannon felt that with a good sense of showmanship, the "artist-cook" could blithely put a gourmet meal on the table in just minutes. "A chef does not serve a dish, he presents it; and his presentation is every bit as important as his preparation," she declared. "Much of the difference between just cooking and epicurean cooking is the differ-ence in the way the food is served."[9] While this statement is basically untrue—the preparation of a fine meal is not predicated on flair with a can opener or a good hand with chopped parsley—it helped make the case for something all America wanted: a quick, easy dinner re-quiring minimal prep time or mess, one that could nonetheless be served up with love.

Like James Beard, Poppy Cannon considered her unrelenting ad-vocacy of processed foods to be a service to the American homemaker and her family. Unlike Beard (whose massive belly and many fine cook-books attested to his real love of tasty, well-prepared food), Cannon seemed to lack any sincere interest in the taste, texture, or integrity of her creations, and as a result her recipes often read like parodies. Her Roast Canned Chicken Flambé with Black Cherries, for example, involved rubbing a whole canned chicken with salad oil, rum, and Kitchen Bouquet (a seasoning featuring dark brown caramel coloring, intended to make foods look as if "roasted"), briefly baking it, surrounding it with a garnish of canned Bing cherries, and then dousing everything with rum and setting it alight at the dinner table.

French restaurant food was, of course, the inspiration for this lunacy; and Cannon knew all about French restaurants through her marriage to Philippe, who presided over one of the finest (and largest, most expensive, and best publicized) French kitchens in America. Moreover, she knew from Philippe that "French" was an unassailable byword for "classy"—and in that way, a great handle for selling a recipe. "Although [canned] stews are notoriously under seasoned," she would write at one point, "they can be transformed with a rinse of red wine, a clove of garlic, parsley, half a bay leaf, and a flicker of mixed herbs to make something akin to *Le Boeuf en Daube* as served in France."

Throughout her writing, Cannon routinely cited France, French restaurants, and French cooking as the ne plus ultra of culinary perfection, even as her own "French" recipes were not much more than combinations of prepared and semiprepared convenience foods slopped together in the most primitive ways. Her Lobster à l'Armoricaine, for example, called for a can of tomato soup, whipping cream, dry sherry, a chopped onion, and three cups of canned cooked lobster. "Heat slowly all together over hot water," she instructed, "but don't boil!" The mixture was then to be spooned out over triangles of white toast, and preferably served by candlelight.[10] Likewise, her *escargots à la bourguignonne* called for two cans of snails boiled in a can of Campbell's consommé and a cup of white wine. Lots of chopped garlic was then to be added at the end of cooking (for flavor), after which the dish was to be presented in an earthenware crock, "blazing hot with plenty of French bread and a robust wine." Even something as simple as a béchamel sauce (which is nothing more than butter, flour and milk, and takes three minutes to prepare) could be simplified, Cannon insisted, by the use of a canned product: her Easy Béchamel recipe consisted of a can of cream of mushroom soup thinned with water.

To those like Toklas who cared about real French cooking made with fresh, wholesome ingredients, "French" recipes of this sort were revolting. But to Cannon—and to the American women who eagerly bought her books—the recent advances in American food-packaging technology meant freedom, and if the price of that freedom was vastly diminished flavor, texture, or nutritional value, well . . . so be it. "Prepared stews, soups, sauces, and quick-frozen specialties have been made with the same ingredients that you would use, and [are prepared] with time, art and skill," Cannon breathily insisted. "All that remains for you [to do] is to translate them into your own idiom, to serve them in your own inimitable fashion, and with your sweetest smile."[11] It was a woman's love for her family, she insisted, that made the home-cooked meal special, not those thankless hours spent chopping onions or stirring soup. "Z is for the *Zest* which can be added only by your loving hands," Cannon reassured the new bride in the last sentences of *The Bride's Cookbook*, "an unnameable, evanescent, mysterious, and enchanting something which makes a dish served up by a bride to her love wonderfully and unbelievably enticing. [Through it] you too will find a thousand culinary ways to say: 'I love you.' "[12]

❖

Not surprisingly, Cannon's professional credentials were just as bogus and "Frenchified" as her recipes. Promotional materials for her *Can-Opener Cookbook* describe her as "a commandeur of the Chevaliers des Tastevins [who] last summer was received into the *Commanderie des Cordons Bleus de France*, an award . . . given only to those who have made important innovative contributions to gastronomy." But in reality the Confrérie des Chevaliers du Tastevin was merely a trade organization that gave its membership to any dedicated consumer of its high-end wines, and the Commanderie des Cordons Bleus de France (which despite its grand name had only been founded in 1949) offered membership to literally *anyone* interested in eating well. Neither of these so-called awards was an award, and neither was in any way indicative of achievement or expertise. But apparently no American ever thought to question these French credentials—or perhaps none knew how, since France was so very far away. Only Cannon's embittered third husband, Philippe of the Waldorf, would ever actually denounce Cannon publicly, doing so after their divorce by describing her to a gathering of food experts as "a robot to a can opener."[13]

Those who worked closely with Cannon, however, could only marvel at her rise, which was based on a uniquely American combination of narcissism, cynicism, and opportunism. One of her assistants, Joan Gage, recalled years after Cannon's death:

> After I graduated from Columbia's Graduate School of Journalism . . . Poppy Cannon was my first boss. She was then the food editor for the *Ladies' Home Journal*. . . . Being one of her worker bees was not easy, for she considered that my job description included cleaning her home, writing her by-lined column, preparing her meals and generally taking care of her. It was interesting that, in all the time she was working as food editor for *Ladies' Home Journal* and turning out recipes daily, the stove in her apartment was never hooked up and working, and she sent me out daily to get her take-out food. I have dozens of Poppy Cannon stories . . . They don't make magazine editors like that any more.[14]

One of the reasons for Cannon's success (not just as a food editor, but as a well-paid advertising consultant) was her ability to cloak her no-holds-barred sellout to the processed foods industry in a chirpy rhetoric of freedom, patriotism, wifely devotion, and progressive American values. Describing herself repeatedly as the "First Lady of American Cooking," she gave editorial credibility to a type of noncooking that was both an unhealthy expedient for the harried American homemaker and a vastly profitable enterprise for U.S. processed food manufacturers. "Our cooking ideas and ideals {in America} have their roots in many lands and cultures," Cannon declared in her first cookbook, "but our new way of achieving gourmet food can only happen here—in the land of the mix, the jar, the frozen-food package, and the ubiquitous can opener." The American melting pot was to Cannon the best possible vessel in which to cook up these miracle foods, for only Americans were bold enough to embrace the new—not being bound, as Europeans were, to the tiresome, time-consuming, meaningless cooking traditions of yesteryear. "Escoffier demands over and over again slowly simmered, painstakingly clarified white or brown stock," Cannon noted dismissively (and wrongly*). "Now, canned consommé or chicken broth provides an admirable answer, [as do] bouillon cubes or meat extracts, plus hot water." America seemed to agree with her: "Cannon's can opener might well provide a shortcut to a reputation for being a new candidate for the Cordon Bleu," an early, enthusiastic reviewer noted of *The Can-Opener Cookbook*. Her "gourmet approach to canned and packaged goods [features] imagination and zest and originality . . . [as well as] heartening advice on how to serve the succulent dishes."[15]

With the runaway success of *The Can-Opener Cookbook* and the equally popular *The Bride's Cookbook* two years later, in 1954—it was published just as she was meeting Toklas in Venice—Cannon assumed her place as one of the most influential women in the American food world. Having clawed her way up from nothing, she was now a prosperous, happily married cookbook author, journalist, magazine editor, advertising consultant, and processed food spokesperson, and she was appearing regularly to give cooking advice on radio and television.

⚜

Because Alice Toklas lived far across the Atlantic in Paris, all she really knew about Cannon was gleaned from Cannon's work in *House Beautiful*. Toklas's robust dislike of those articles was tempered, however, by the good time Elizabeth Gordon showed her on their lavish, no-holds-barred, expense-account trip through northern Italy—and also by Cannon herself, all bosomy vivacity and throaty laughter. "It was lovely," Toklas subsequently wrote her childhood friend Louise Taylor about the adventure. "In Venice I loved the light the food and food shops and the Venetians. . . . Five days there and then by automobile . . . to Padua (ah the Giottos bowled me over)—and to six lovely days in Florence—so much more wonderful than I

---

* Escoffier's *Guide Culinaire* indicates that stock (whether white or brown) is merely to be strained, not clarified; clarification is reserved for *bouillon*, a soup delicacy.

remembered. . . . And oh such food!"[16] Moreover, Toklas was no fool: *House Beautiful* promised to pay her a relative fortune at a moment when she could barely afford kerosene for her space heater. Thus, even as she disdained the idea of writing on food for women's magazines— later describing it as "a kind of feminine journalism that [is] not to my taste"—she was drawn back by the promise of a paycheck.

Toklas eventually contributed five pieces to *House Beautiful*. The first two were simply extracts from *The Alice B. Toklas Cook Book*, but the third came out of Cannon's idea of giving Toklas an electric blender and seeing what she could do with it. (Cannon had recently written an article in which she herself was pictured seated, using a blender in front of her dinner guests. "Poppy makes Salmon Mousse in a blender," the caption read. "This dish can easily [and very dramatically] be made at the table.") Although Toklas had little room for the machine in her primitive Paris kitchen (a space that was, according to her friend Otto Friedrich, "small, ill-equipped, and hardly an inspiration for her culinary marvels"), she soon found that she loved it, and had no problem devising some very good recipes utilizing it. One, for quenelles, was simply a variation of the recipe she had developed for her 1939 Mixmaster, but the others—a salmon soufflé with a shrimp sauce; a slow-roasted leg of mutton slathered with a liver-and-onion purée; a close-grained "meatloaf" in the style of a pâté; and a chocolate mousse featuring blender-whizzed egg whites—were written specifically for the new appliance. Several others were simple and delicate: Toklas found that a perfectly ripened tomato, for example, could be whizzed into a pink froth that was then spooned over baby lettuces; and that fruits at the peak of their flavor could be pureed, either singly or in combination, to create a simple dessert that needed only a tablespoon of kirsch or homemade ratafia (and perhaps a bit of sugar and/or lemon juice) to delight and refresh.

Toklas's last two articles for *House Beautiful* were on cooking with Champagne and cooking with Cognac. They seem to have been commissioned through the influence of the Champagne and Cognac industries, working through the American public relations firm of Edward Gottlieb and Associates. To help her in her research, Toklas was sent on back-to-back press junkets to the Champagne and Cognac regions. "I was taken to Reims . . . by car," Toklas wrote her friend Princess Dilkusha de Rohan. "It was a scream—we were lunched and dined royally—drank champagne from 11 o'clock on all day—saw the cellars—and much, much better the incredible abbey* . . . and met endless hospitable and amusing people. No sooner had we returned [to Paris than] we were off to Cognac and Jarnac. The thought of two times Cognac was a nightmare—unswallowable firewater that it is to me. . . . But you appreciate Cognac by its odor not by its taste so all was well. Once more [we were] wined and dined and I returned a wreck."[17]

Toklas's subsequent recipes for cooking with Champagne—she described them as "royal dishes"—were imaginative even by French standards. She had been making one of these recipes for years, a capon braised in Champagne then served with artichoke hearts and asparagus tips. But others were developed out of historic recipes: a young hare simmered in Champagne and finished with a sauce of truffles, Cognac, and heavy cream; sautéed kidneys in a Champagne sauce; and a *salade composée* featuring Champagne-braised sweetbreads, stewed mushrooms, and baby melons, all set atop delicate lettuces, with a glass of the finest chilled Champagne to be poured over the platter at the moment of service. For those interested in alternative ways of drinking Champagne, she devised an old-fashioned punch recipe calling for Champagne to be combined with finely diced fruits, fresh fruit juices, Tokay,† green tea, and Cointreau.

Toklas's suggestions for cooking with Cognac were equally inventive, with some of them reflecting the everyday use of Cognac (or any kind of brandy) in the French kitchen: a simple buttery sweet potato and orange casserole, for example, and an authentic French onion soup—both were enlivened by a touch of that spirit, which lent its characteristic richness and aroma to the finished dish. However, Toklas also presented some impossibly complicated recipes in the same piece: spring chicken parts, for example, coated in bread crumbs, fried in clarified butter, flambéed with Cognac, then served with a sauce of

---

* The former Abbey of Saint-Rémi is better known as Reims Cathedral.
† A celebrated sweet, aromatic late-harvest wine from Hungary.

fresh oysters, fresh truffles, and more Cognac. Even more recherché was a dish she had resurrected from an eighteenth-century cookbook, calling for turkey legs, first roasted, then gently braised in a rich bouillon flavored with Cognac, onion, garlic, and cloves, then served with a sauce of sweetbreads and mushrooms that had been stewed together with butter, Cognac, lemon juice, and parsley.

❦

Even as she composed these recipes for *House Beautiful*, however, Toklas was balking at the idea of writing a sequel to *The Alice B. Toklas Cook Book*. Simon Michael Bessie of Harper and Bros. wanted it, but she did not think of herself as a cookbook writer, at one point even insisting to a friend that *The Alice B. Toklas Cook Book* had been "undertaken solely to earn some pennies."[18] More to the point, an ambitious young editor, Robert Lescher, had recently started encouraging her to leave off such dull endeavors (and, with them, her relationship with Harper) to write instead a literary memoir for him, at Holt. Lescher contacted her through James Beard's literary agent, John Schaffner, whom Beard had recommended to Toklas after Toklas parted ways with Jenny Bradley. Beard had adored *The Alice B. Toklas Cook Book*, and since that first meeting with Toklas he had been inviting her out to costly restaurants whenever visiting Paris. So, paradoxically, even as Toklas found herself being courted by a major American food celebrity and pursued by his influential agent of culinary authors, she was ever more eager to escape cookbook writing and return to the world of literature that she had known so well with Stein. "No one sends me novels any more—they send me cook books," she wrote bemusedly to her old friend Bernard Faÿ. "Frankly those by Americans on American food are deplorable."[19]

Bessie still wanted whatever Toklas might write, however—and since he held an option on her next book, she needed to come to an understanding with him. Toklas didn't care much for Bessie,* but at

---

* Toklas's one surviving letter to Bessie (dated July 6, 1957) is an angry one concerning the author photo he had chosen for Janet Flanner's *Men and Monuments* (1957). But her real dislike of him from 1957 onward was rooted in his decision to publish Elizabeth Sprigge's *Gertrude Stein: Her Life and Work* (1957), a book Toklas deemed "abominable."

the same time she lacked a clear sense of her legal obligation to Harper, and she wanted to be free to work with Lescher. So after some thought, and oddly enough without consulting Schaffner, she simply decided to write two books, giving a cookbook to Bessie and a memoir to Lescher. To that end, she began developing a cookbook idea about the proper use of herbs and spices, asking Carl Van Vechten to send her a book on the subject, Milo Miloradovich's *The Art of Cooking with Herbs and Spices: A Handbook of Flavors and Savors,*[20] and at the same time querying her friend Samuel Steward about any old-fashioned uses for herbs and spices he might remember from his Ohio childhood. When Schaffner pressed for news about the cookbook project, Toklas merely responded "there is nothing [here] but a large cardboard box of recipes."[21] A while later, however, she sent off a batch of those recipes directly to Bessie. In short order Bessie contacted her with an offer that she accepted, signing a contract with him on May 22, 1956.[22] In it she agreed to supply him with a manuscript of fifty thousand words—a third less text than *The Alice B. Toklas Cook Book* but still a substantial piece of writing, and one that Bessie hoped might contain more of the fine, memoiristic material that had made *The Alice B. Toklas Cook Book* such a tour de force. Toklas began assembling the new book in a desultory way while visiting her friends the Knapiks that fall in Magagnosc, in the hills above Cannes. "Here it is restful and quite sunny," Toklas wrote Samuel Steward, "and I spend my days trying to achieve fifty thousand words from the box of recipes—to be delivered to Harper's at the end of November! Not likely. Half that has become my goal."[23]

Upon reading her first draft, Bessie sent it back with word that it needed more work. In her effort to be done with the project (and receive the payment due on the publisher's acceptance), Toklas then came up with a new idea: getting Poppy Cannon to whip the manuscript into shape. Toklas introduced Cannon to Bessie, after which the two women signed a letter of agreement, specifying that Cannon would work with the recipes just as she had at *House Beautiful* (that is, leaving all of Toklas's original writing intact, but adding additional commentary) and also providing an introduction to make the book more accessible to an American readership.[24]

Why Toklas—who had defended the integrity of Gertrude Stein's writing for years—would simply hand Cannon so much control over her own book is not easy to say. It may have been due to her ambivalence to culinary writing as a literary form (as she had declared in the last line of the *Cook Book* "[it is not] as if a cook book had anything to do with writing.*") But her choice also seems based, at least in part, upon her trusting relationship with Cannon—since in each of the articles for *House Beautiful,* Cannon had published the recipes exactly as Toklas wrote them, with all the ingredients and procedures Toklas specified.[25] Finally, however, the decision was one of expedience, because at this point Toklas desperately wanted to move on: her memoir for Robert Lescher at Holt and her own mortality were now very much on her mind. In fact, with her health failing, she had recently begun her conversion to Catholicism.†

There was also, of course, the question of money. Having little of it, and being very much in need of it, Toklas rightly hesitated to abandon a project for which she had a final payment pending. Three years earlier, in 1954, when the building at 5, rue Christine had been sold to new owners, all the sitting tenants (including Toklas) had been given the option of purchasing their apartments, and all except Toklas had bought in. But Toklas didn't have the funds, and was under the impression that "the French law protects aged ladies so I can stay on for the rest of my days."[26] Unfortunately, this was no more than magical thinking. The new owners of the building immediately began working to evict her. They did so by gathering evidence that her apartment was not properly occupied—for Parisian renters were protected from eviction only if they inhabited their apartments a full eight months of the year. Toklas's many absences (for health-mandated escapes to warmer climates) were from that moment on carefully documented by paid informants, soon becoming a matter of public record in the housing courts—a state of affairs that would ultimately

---

* Thornton Wilder had once questioned Toklas's ability to write, prompting this response, which then reappeared on p. 280 of the *Cook Book.*
† Her conversion began in Easter of 1956 and was complete in December 1957, when she took her first communion.

have disastrous consequences for not only her tenancy but also her control over the Gertrude Stein art collection.[27]

So Toklas needed someone she could trust to help her finish the new cookbook and get paid. She had recently come to a similar collaborative agreement with the novelist Max White, a former Stein protégé, in which she appointed him the cowriter of her new memoir* for Lescher. As with Cannon, Toklas retained "full authority and final determination as to the content and style of the book" in her agreement with White. But after only six weeks of working together,† White realized that the collaboration was not going to work. He discarded all his notes and moved to Spain without leaving a forwarding address. As he later explained to his lawyer, Toklas had simply been "too feeble minded to work on the book she's proposed. Miss Toklas couldn't remember her memories . . . there was no basis [there] for a book."[28]

Toklas relinquished control of the new cookbook just when she ought to have paid closest attention to it. After a brief visit with Toklas in November, Cannon returned to New York, typed up her own lively version of the manuscript, and then, without showing it to Toklas, sent it directly to Bessie for publication.[29] Bessie seems not to have taken too great an interest in it—understandably so, as it was hardly the book he had hoped Toklas would write. When Toklas herself finally saw Cannon's version of the manuscript, she threw up her hands and refused to involve herself further. To her friend Samuel Steward, she expressed amazement at Cannon's benighted understanding of the Stein-Toklas salon, a place in which, according to Cannon, "Cézanne Hemingway Picasso and Matisse were all contemporaries."‡ Nonetheless, she was resigned: "the tone [of the introduction is so] over laudatory [of me as to be] embarrassingly untrue," she wrote Steward, "but [the book] will bring in enough pennies to pay for the plumbing repairs and a trip this summer for the [arthritis] cure

---

* The letter of agreement with Max White notes "we shall jointly write [a book] concerning my life, my memories and experiences." (Max was a *nom de plume*; his real name was Charles William White. Stein described him in 1940 as "the most promising American writer that has come [my] way.")

† The letter of collaboration was written in May 1958; White broke it off (and left Paris) on June 14, 1958.

‡ Hemingway was born sixty years after Cézanne.

at Acqui."*[30] The only additional work Toklas did on the manuscript (at Bessie's "enraged" insistence, as she later described it) was to revise nine recipes that had been so carelessly written as to be incomprehensible.

❧

Cannon's introduction to *Aromas and Flavors of Past and Present* begins with an obsequious homage to Toklas as a thoroughly modern cook-intellectual—that new sort of woman, educated and sensual, now to be found in up-to-date kitchens across America. "In history there have been many scholarly epicures and many epicurean scholars," Cannon begins, but "rarely have the two been combined as [Toklas] has combined them":

> At this moment of history this is a matter of considerable significance, since millions of well-educated persons, men and women, are faced . . . with the need to do [kitchen] chores that [are] dull and depressing or tremendously stimulating—depending upon the point of view. Perhaps the way of Alice B. Toklas is the way out—the liberation— . . . [for] although she is steeped in the traditions of classic French cuisine and imbued with a great respect for and understanding of seventeenth-century gastronomy, Miss Toklas represents an extraordinary innovation . . . [she is] an intellectual, an epicure and a practical cook [who] can cook at the same high level of perfection as she talks and writes about food. This is a new development in the gastronomic world.[31]

This gassy praise quickly gives way to the story of Cannon's *own* involvement with the cookbook: a story in which a sensible, level-headed, and thoroughly modern food editor travels to Paris to work with an aged celebrity on her troubled manuscript. Together the two women learn a lot from each other, forge a lasting friendship, and create "aromas and flavors of past and present"—with Toklas stubbornly

---

* Acqui Terme, an Italian spa town fifty miles north of Genoa.

insisting upon the aromas and flavors of the past, and Cannon brightly proposing the aromas and flavors of the present.

The two women began their work together, Cannon reveals, in the spirit of rapprochement: "[In] the autumn of 1957, when it was decided that I should help with the editing of Alice Toklas' second cook book, almost unconsciously I had [already] adopted many of [Toklas's] ideas. And she, instead of disagreeing [with me] as she had before, had decided that what I wrote was 'not only interesting but woman-of-the-worldly.' "[32] Cannon then digresses to discuss their working conditions: "on several occasions [during my trip] we worked in my rooms at the Plaza-Athénée . . . [which had] been remodeled to look like quarters on a yacht—a yacht moored among the rooftops of Paris with a breath-taking view of constantly changing clouds around the Eiffel Tower! Basil, the courtly Russian floor waiter, brought our lunches. On the day we finished we celebrated with lobster soufflé. And a Corton Charlemagne 1952!"

But Cannon then admits that "mostly we worked at [Toklas's] apartment on the Left Bank," initially describing it (in a subheading) as "NO LAVENDER OR OLD LACE" and subsequently pronouncing it:

A romantic if not too comfortable setting for work on a cook book. The gaze of Picasso's harlequins was upon us—priceless examples of his rose and blue periods. . . . It was [a] cold and gray . . . November [and] we sat beside a seventeenth-century mantel of polished white marble. But the fireplace has been boarded up for a hundred years [and] the house [was] much too old, the chimneys much too crumbly to permit a fire. Heat comes stingily from a kerosene-burning stove shaped like an old-fashioned wash boiler. It gives out headachy fumes. Nevertheless it is a lovely room full of treasures and remembering. . . . We spread our notes and papers over the sofa upholstered in horsehair, the natural color of a shining bay mare, and on the two small slipper chairs which Gertrude Stein embroidered in *petit-point** over designs drawn

---

* The embroidery was done by Toklas, not Stein.

by one of their more frequent dinner guests—one Pablo Picasso. . . . Nothing in their apartment has changed since Gertrude Stein died in 1946. The past is immanent there—indwelling, inherent.

Cannon soon finds that Toklas is not to be trifled with: "it would be a great mistake to assume any sentimentality in the atmosphere or the attitudes of Alice B. Toklas. The sweetness-and-light school of thought and expression are completely alien [to her]. She bristles, sparkles, crackles, lashes out—especially when the subject is food and the object[s] of her ire [are my] penciled editorial corrections, suggestions and questions in the margin of her manuscript."[33] But Cannon then goes on to praise Toklas, noting that "the essential characteristic of [Toklas'] cooking . . . is a meticulous regard for detail and nuance. . . . Each morsel must, in the Toklas tradition, be perfect of its kind, chosen and prepared with love, understanding and erudition."[34] She subsequently suggests that by emulating Toklas, the average American housewife can achieve transcendence: "exquisite and thoughtful cooking in the Alice B. Toklas tradition will not only exercise but also appeal to the mind. . . . It [will] lift the heart and stimulate the spirit."

But Cannon was not that sort of cook, and her headnotes to Toklas's recipes clearly demonstrate her basic indifference to Toklas's "exquisite and thoughtful cooking." In fact the two writers remain in complete and utter disagreement about how to cook from the first recipe to the last, with Cannon consistently undercutting Toklas's authority and contradicting her recipe instructions even as she praises her wisdom and brilliance. The tussle begins with the very first recipe, a delicate White Soup of Artichokes, with Cannon immediately noting that "a package of frozen artichoke hearts and a can of Swanson's chicken broth make an admirable version of this soup [and] if you use a blender you needn't bother about sieving or straining."

But how could it be otherwise? Toklas preferred quality, subtlety, and thoroughness, whereas Cannon was all about fast fixes and last-minute special effects. Toklas was obsessively detail-oriented at the market and in the kitchen; Cannon felt that to cook from scratch was to ignore all that was best on supermarket shelves. Toklas saw cooking as an art; Cannon saw it as a "dull and depressing" series of daily chores made less onerous through shortcuts and smart shopping. Toklas believed in the wisdom of past cooks; Cannon believed in the modern, industrialized future—a world in which all but the most basic cooking chores would no longer be required, thanks to the miracle of ready-to-eat supermarket fare.

In *The Alice B. Toklas Cook Book*, Toklas had described the profound effect the open-air food market in New Orleans had had upon her in 1934: "how with such perfection, variety and abundance of [fruits and vegetables] could one not be inspired to creative cooking?" she asked. "We certainly do overdo not only the use of the word ["inspired"] but the belief in its widespread existence. Can one be inspired by rows of prepared canned meals? Never. One must get nearer to creation to be able to create, even in the kitchen."[35] Now, similarly, at the beginning of *Aromas and Flavors*, she briefly urged her readers to "use only the best the market offers. If the budget is restricted, restrict the menu to what the budget affords. Cook with the very best butter, draw on your best wines to flavor a common piece of meat or of fish. This will exalt your effort, stimulate, intensify, indeed magnify the flavor. Your appreciation and appetite will increase. You will add to the pleasure of your guests." She likewise recommended a French sense of restraint in the planning of the meal: "consider the menu carefully, that there is a harmony and a suitable progression, as you do for the arrangement of a bouquet or of the planting of a bed of flowers. . . . In the menu there should be a climax and a culmination. Come to it gently. One will suffice."

But Cannon undercut such advice in one recipe headnote after another, adjusting Toklas's recipes for canned, boxed, or deep-frozen American grocery-store ingredients, doing so through the use of italics. Her interference was such that, in the end, half the book would be written in Cannon's italics. To make the question of attribution even more confusing, all Toklas's recipe titles were also in italics, and Cannon's introduction to the book, meanwhile was printed in regular roman type. And Cannon habitually used so many exclamations and italicized words in her writing that, typographically speaking, *whole passages of the book seem both* manic!—*and* schizophrenic.

Cannon's headnotes, meanwhile, abound in misinformation (red mullet "is difficult to find in markets except those of Harlem"*), and also in odd, childlike serving suggestions ("julienne potato sticks seem particularly appropriate as an accompaniment [for beefsteak] and you can get very good ones in tins"). She also regularly calls for unnecessary high-tech appliances (temperature-controlled electric skillets, deep-fryers, tabletop rotisseries, and blenders), perhaps because she knew them to be loved by gadget-happy Americans. Above all, however, Cannon pushes substitute ingredients: Knox gelatin for beef knuckle; Swanson chicken broth for stock; frozen chicken for fresh squab; packaged frosting mix for chocolate-rum icing. In one particularly astounding headnote she even suggests abandoning Toklas's recipe (for onion soup) entirely: *"Consider that this is said in a whisper: you can use Miss Toklas' ideas {for homemade onion soup} even though you resort to canned or dehydrated onion soup . . . {Just} use her croutons . . . {and} add half a cup of cognac."*

But, hard as Cannon tried, Toklas's recipes did not adapt well to convenience cooking. Apart from a handful of relatively simple ones (such as Slip-And-Go Easy, a dessert made of beaten cream cheese, jelly, and sugar), the collection consisted mostly of complicated novelties (Parmesan Bavarois and Frozen Aiolli[†]) or else showy, labor intensive restaurant-type dishes (such as Truites en Chemise, in which boned trout are sautéed in butter, topped with a thickened mushroom sauce, then gently folded into crêpes and served at the table from a buttered chafing dish—a specialty, at the time, of the Relais Gastronomique Paris-Est). Without a memoir to contextualize them, such time-consuming preparations were far too complicated for the average American home cook of 1958—and certainly no fan of Cannon's would have wanted to attempt them. Yet Toklas was adamantly opposed to

---

* Red mullet (*Mullus surmeletus*), known in France as *rouget* or *rouget de roche*, is a fish of the Mediterranean and eastern Atlantic, with a delicate white flesh similar to that of perch or red snapper. It is altogether different from gray mullet (*Mugil cephalus*) commonly found in brackish waters in the United States, which has a muddy, unpleasant flavor, something like that of wild catfish.
[†] That is, *aioli*, the Provençal garlic mayonnaise made with olive oil.

shortcut cooking of any sort, as she had recently told Naomi Barry in the *Paris Herald Tribune*:

> Everybody [in America] is trying to become a short-order epi-
> curean cook. When everybody cooks there is no cooking.
> Cooking, like any art, is not for the millions. . . . [American]
> women . . . feel they must try everything, and . . . they cheat.
> I call using ready-made tins cheating. They substitute corn-
> starch and flour instead of thickening with eggs and butter.
> They put gelatin in their puddings. . . . American women won't
> buy butter, but they will buy expensive tins. [I dislike] the
> whole school of economizing time while advertising quick
> ways to glamorous food.[36]

Toklas's brilliance as a recipe writer lay, if anything, in her idiosyncrasy—she enjoyed flavor combinations as outrageous as her hats, and such flavor combinations were comparatively rare in Ameri-can cookbooks of the period. In fact, many of her favorite flavor com-binations dated back—as Toklas herself did—to the days of Belle Époque *grande cuisine*. The book's second recipe is a good example: in Soup à la Cardinale, a rich beef bouillon is flavored with parsley, cinnamon, and nutmeg, thickened with powdered hazelnuts, then poured over toasted crusts that have been spread with a rich paste of grated parmesan and freshly sautéed, finely chopped calf's liver. So is Eggs à l'Hypocras,* hard-boiled eggs peeled and cut in half, then coated in a fritter batter and deep-fried in olive oil, then served with a sauce composed of rosé wine, honey, vinegar, cinnamon, cloves, cay-enne, Cognac, and clarified butter. ("The sweet-and-sour flavor," Tok-las notes, "is quite enticing when one becomes accustomed to it.") Pike in Half-Mourning is a similarly complex, old-fashioned recipe featuring both black truffles and a green mayonnaise as flavorings for this delicate poached freshwater fish, while Quo Vadis Cake, named

---

*Hypocras is a French fortified wine, dating from the Middle Ages, strongly sweetened with honey and flavored with ginger and cinnamon. It is named after Hippocrates, the famed physician of ancient Greece.

after the bestselling novel, contains hefty amounts of candied angelica, candied pineapple, candied orange peel, and candied cherries baked in a sponge cake batter that has been poured into a buttered tin lined with slivered almonds. (And that recipe wasn't even French; Toklas had first prepared it in San Francisco in 1896, at the age of nineteen, having clipped it out of a local newspaper.)

❖

When *Aromas and Flavors of Past and Present: A Book of Exquisite Cooking* was published in November 1958—a year after Cannon visited Paris to work with Toklas on the revision—none of Toklas's friends quite knew what to say. For one thing, the volume did not even look like a cookbook: printed in small format, its nondescript beige cover featured a slight line drawing of a squinting old woman's face, presumably (but not recognizably) Toklas's.* There were no interior photos or illustrations. Authorship of the book was ascribed to Toklas on the cover, with a smaller credit for "Introduction and Comments" going to Poppy Cannon. A color photograph of Cannon (in a boldly patterned wrap of fuchsia and purple, standing over a tureen of beige soup) was distributed by the publisher for publicity purposes. (So too was a small black-and-white photo of Toklas and Basket, taken by Carl Van Vechten nearly a decade earlier.)[37] Readers and reviewers were understandably confused. "Harper's sent me the galleys of Alice's cookbook," James Beard wrote his friend Helen Evans Brown. "It is the Gospel according to Alice B. Toklas edited by Poppy Cannon, who uses Swanson chicken broth and frozen artichokes. There is about as much Alice in it as there is Elizabeth Barrett Browning."[38] Janet Flanner, meanwhile, wrote an aptly sardonic review for *The New Republic*:

> *Aromas and Flavors of Past and Present* is a remarkable new cook book with a split personality, containing two hundred precisely detailed and delicious recipes by the famous Miss Alice Toklas of Paris, accompanied by useful annotations by

---

* The British edition, published by Michael Joseph, featured a far more conventional illustration: a drawing of a platter of roast fowl, elaborately garnished with crayfish.

Mrs. Poppy Cannon of *House Beautiful*, which will often help the American Kitchenette Gourmet to avoid the bother of cooking anything like as well as Miss Toklas. . . . In Miss Toklas' recipe for "Fresh Artichokes à la Catherine de Medici" which calls for "three cups ground raw pigeon breasts" [Mrs. Cannon] suggests *sotto voce*, in italics, that you may substitute quick-frozen chicken breasts and even quick frozen artichoke hearts. . . . From this cook book two utterly different vistas of food preparation emerge. There is the first picture of Miss Toklas . . . pursuing her treasured procedures for metamorphosis, masterly from fifty years of practice, by which she patiently creatively changes what is edible into a borrowed French gustatory art. [Then] there is the other picture, the efficient color photograph of the American food processes, canned or frozen for eternity as matters of hasty convenience, presided over by Mrs. Cannon with her eye on the clock, as the epicure-cook in a successful hurry.[39]

Charlotte Turgeon might very easily have panned the book, for she had by now translated several great French cookbooks and was several years along in her translation of Montagné's thousand-page *Larousse Gastronomique*. But while Turgeon knew *Aromas and Flavors* was nothing compared with *The Alice B. Toklas Cook Book* (which she had loved), she saw no point in trashing the new offering—particularly since, as a busy writer, cooking instructor, faculty wife, and mother, she was sympathetic to the daily need for rapid food preparation in the middle-class American home. As she wrote in *The New York Times Book Review*:

For years, at least to the public eye, Miss Toklas seemed to dwell in the shadow of her famous companion, Gertrude Stein, but more recently through publication of two cookbooks she has revealed herself to be an energetic and independent person in her own right. She is convinced, for instance, that there is no equal to the classic French cuisine, which is based on the proper appreciation and preparation of each and every food, and she holds no brief for modern short-cut methods and gad-gets. In this the present book she is aided by the keen and efficient Poppy Cannon, who believes that good cooking . . . should not require too much time or even too much effort.

What makes the book fun is seeing these two ladies get together. Miss Cannon shows her approval of Miss Toklas' the-ories in her admiration of the recipes offered here. On the other hand, Miss Toklas succumbs to a few packaged mixes and dis-covers the wonders of an electric blender for which she writes inspired recipes. This book would not be by Miss Toklas if there were not some very unusual recipes, but Miss Cannon keeps the busy housewife in mind, and the result is a book that is refreshing to read and a promise of exciting eating.[40]

Toklas had received an advance of $1,250 for the book, a good deal of which she had subsequently paid out to Cannon. What she got back in return—apart from a few kind notices—was a very public humili-ation. As feminist food historian Laura Shapiro later noted, "Nobody had ever written about [Toklas] in such a blatantly commercial manner—nobody would have dared. [Until this moment Toklas's] public per-sona [had always been] unrelentingly formal and dignified. Toklas had always refused to be pulled into the empty spotlight after Stein's death. . . . Now, for the first time, she had forfeited control. . . . [and] this was not how Toklas wanted to go public."[41]

Cannon, for her part, was oblivious to the pain and humiliation she had inflicted on Toklas. She would continue to pay lip service to French cuisine until about 1969, doing so through various conve-nience cookbooks, most notably *Eating European Abroad and at Home* (1961). But then, like most of America, she would just as abruptly reverse her opinion, telling Nora Ephron in an interview that "there is an awe about Frenchiness in food which is terribly precious and has kept American food from being as good as it could be. . . . French cooking is gooking it up. All this kowtowing to so-called French cook-ing has really been a hindrance rather than a help."[42]

ELEVEN

"A Dreamer of Wine"

Alexis Lichine's business empire expanded rapidly during the mid-1950s, but by 1957, signs of strain were beginning to show everywhere, and his decades-long correspondence with Alfred Knopf demonstrates it. Impressed by the success of *Wines of France*, Knopf had immediately contracted with Lichine for a far more ambitious project, to be called *Alexis Lichine's Encyclopedia of Wines and Spirits*. But six years later the book was still far from finished, and Lichine, rather than meeting his contractual obligation, was instead hustling Knopf to help him publish a wine book in French. Lichine had already enlisted the help of Paris-based Jenny Bradley—the same literary agent who had brokered Toklas's deal for *The Alice B. Toklas Cook Book*—to find a French publisher for *Wines of France*. But Bradley was unable to do so, most likely because French privacy and libel laws are exceptionally strict, and as a result, writers such as Lichine who attempt to expose corrupt individuals or businesses face significant legal challenges. In January 1957, Lichine wrote Knopf proposing a new strategy: he wanted to take some of the text of *Wines of France* and combine it with some of the text of his half-done *Encyclopedia*, and translate the whole thing into French for immediate publication.[1] When Knopf wrote back with a very firm no, Lichine responded:

After six years, no publisher in France has ever been found for *Wines of France*. After several conversations with Mrs. Bradley, the same might very well be true of the *Encyclopedia*. . . . I am not writing these books as an author primarily looking for royalties. If such were the case . . . the *Encyclopedia* . . . is a losing proposition and a luxury that no author or individual could afford, even by writing off the losses to personal satisfaction.

I undertook the *Encyclopedia* at a great cost in both time and money, both of which I could ill afford . . . for purely and simply business reasons. . . . I figured that I would recoup my losses by writing them off to prestige which I would acquire through the publication of this book in various parts of the world.

At the present time in France, I am fighting a battle for my very existence. . . . This battle has already started in France and my entire future is at stake. As I have increased in stature, a large segment of the wine industry in France has started an organized cabal against me. In Burgundy, billboards bearing my name have been smeared [with excrement]. Once repainted, these billboards were sawed off at the base and [my assistant, Pierre] De Wilde had to make a special trip to Burgundy to put the case in the hands of the *gendarmerie*. The crooked shippers of Burgundy realizing that I was the first and practically the only one to denounce their methods and procedures, have tried to stifle every effort I have made in order to keep the French public ignorant of their malpractices.

In Bordeaux last summer, the Cruses* formed a purchasing monopoly group mainly directed at me to prevent me from buying from the great châteaux. Half of my time in France was spent in building up enough strength around me to break up this monopolistic group. . . . Although the Cruses, Calvets, Kressmanns and other [top *négociants* in Bordeaux]

* The Cruse family, one of the leading *négociant* families in Bordeaux.

are outwardly very friendly, behind my back they are trying
to prevent me from reaching the French people. Their aim is
to sell regional wines at exorbitant prices. They want to preserve
the status quo. . . . My books when published in English in
France are of little use to me as a much needed weapon. . . . I
have dedicated my life to the cause of wines, and at the present time I am engaged in a battle. Therefore, I must be very
insistent. . . . As I am not prepared to capitulate to those who
are trying to obliterate me, I need this particular weapon
with which to defend myself.[2]

The anger, hostility, and (perhaps justifiable) paranoia expressed
in the letter evoke Lichine far better than the mellifluous and gentle-
manly narrative voice of his first wine book, or of the two other books
that were yet to come. Other documents in the Knopf archive show
equally unsavory aspects of Lichine's personality—most notably, his
indifference to contractual obligations, even before *Wines of France* was
published.[3] His rough treatment of coworkers and employees is also
manifest in Knopf's records; throughout their twenty-year professional association, Knopf would receive letters of complaint and/or
threats of legal action from various writer-researchers Lichine hired
and then discarded.

Alexis Lichine's Encyclopedia of Wines and Spirits was a large reference book, and so had required the work of not just one coauthor, but
rather a succession of them—people known variously as coauthors,
researchers, and contributors. The journalist and biographer William
Fifield initially agreed to cowrite the book with Lichine, and the project started out well enough, with Lichine giving Fifield, his wife, and
his two children rooms at Château Lascombes so that Fifield might
work long hours writing the book while Lichine tended to his export
business. After two years, however, Lichine proved so abusive that Fifield simply quit. "It will always be a matter of regret with me that
collaboration with Alexis proved difficult, and finally impossible," Fifield wrote Knopf in 1958, even while expressing regret that the sections subsequently penned by others had been so abysmally researched
and written. Fifield, like William Massee before him, would later
write to Knopf publishers—in this case to its president, William

Koshland—to double-check that his "with the collaboration of" was still going to appear, as contractually agreed, on the title page.

There were also a series of bitter, angry letters from Edgar Kanarik,* whom Lichine had apparently hired after Fifield's departure. According to Kanarik, Lichine promised him a title-page credit, then avoided putting the deal into writing.[4] Kanarik ultimately received no credit at all for his contributions to the *Encyclopedia*[†] (and he got no satisfaction from Alfred Knopf either). But thanks to Kanarik, Knopf now knew that Lichine had enlisted a series of hacks to write his big book. "[Alexis] wrote with a pen and a 4-by-5-inch leather-bound Tiffany booklet," his third wife, the actress Arlene Dahl, later recalled. "He had enormous help with [the] young men. . . . They would do [the] research, then [Alexis] would have his lines typed up. . . . He was a fabulous executive."[5]

Alfred Knopf disagreed. "This is really atrocious," he wrote Lichine about the first draft in 1957. "If, as I suspect, this text is being written by several hands, then before it ever goes to the publisher, it should be reviewed, revised, and put into final form by one person—not your publisher."[6] The next installment pleased Knopf no more,[7] but by then Lichine had far more important things to worry about.

In the spring of 1957 Bordeaux was beginning the second of two terrible growing seasons. During the winter of 1955 to 1956 the vineyards had been heavily damaged by the worst cold wave in ninety-eight years. In April 1957, a late frost devastated the vines just as they came into flower, drastically reducing their pollination—and with it, the expected tonnage of grapes. Lichine had been counting on a large, good harvest to help out his finances, for he had just moved into a luxurious new apartment at 2 Sutton Place South, in one of New York's most expensive neighborhoods, and his new wife, a former fur model named Gisèle Edenbourgh,[‡] was expecting a baby. For a man whose life had previously consisted of adrenaline-soaked, chain-smoking, fifteen-hour

---

* Kanarik's only known book is *Poems and Reflections* (1960), a sixty-two-page volume written in English and French.

[†] Two other writer-researchers would, however: Jonathan Bartlett and Jane Stockwood.

[‡] She was born Gisèle Straus in Frankfurt in 1925, but her half-Jewish family left Germany before the war. (She kept her first husband's surname after their divorce.)

workdays, and continual late nights out with a Rolodex full of women, the adjustment to domestication brought with it a growing sense of personal accountability and financial obligation.

Money remained, as always, a major issue. On paper, Lichine was now the owner of a luxury apartment in New York, two châteaux, and two businesses (one in New York, one in Margaux) with a total of thirty employees. His export company had just reached $1.7 million in gross sales. But bringing in payment on those sales took time, and he had a great deal of overhead. Now the second of two back-to-back disastrous growing seasons had brought him close to bankruptcy.[8]

Just a couple of months after that disastrous spring frost, Lichine received a phone call from Joseph Wechsberg, the *New Yorker* reporter known as much for his financial acumen and investigative reporting as for his good-natured writing on gastronomy. A streetwise Czech émigré who had initially trained as a lawyer, Wechsberg had recently become fascinated by Lichine's self-proclaimed success on two continents and wanted to explore it in depth for *The New Yorker*—much to Lichine's alarm. "Seemingly [Wechsberg] is only going to cover the Bordeaux section of all my nefarious activities," Lichine wrote Knopf that summer, in a note warning that Wechsberg might soon be asking Knopf some tricky questions.[9] But in fact the majority of Wechsberg's on-site research took place in France in late August or early September 1957,* just as Lichine was at the height of his anxiety about the coming *vendange*. As it happened, those of the grapes that had survived the spring frost had done exceptionally well over the summer—and, were they to make it to harvest, Lichine was going to be all right financially. But between the present and the moment of harvest lay the possibility of devastating hailstorms, heavy rains, and rot.

Lichine and his wife—Wechsberg described her as "a strikingly good-looking brunette of Belgian and German extraction"—picked Wechsberg up at the Lyon train station. The couple were on their way home from a nine-day business trip to the Côte d'Azur, and while Mrs. Lichine was particularly eager to get home to her infant (who

---

* Although the specific dates of the visit are not given in the article, Wechsberg notes that the Lichines are traveling without their four-month-old daughter, Alexandra, who was born in May 1957.

though only four months old had been left in the hands of a nurse), Lichine chose instead to drive north, into Burgundy, to conduct a frantic round of wine tasting and buying in the torrid late-summer heat and humidity, doing so in part so that Wechsberg could have a chance to see him on the job. Wechsberg kept detailed notes of the adventure, the first long, sweaty day of which ended with a late dinner at Alexandre Dumaine's Hôtel de la Côte-d'Or in Saulieu.

Wechsberg did a remarkably good job of researching and explaining Lichine's multifaceted enterprise:

[Lichine] operates almost simultaneously in the roles of vintner, buyer, exporter, importer, and salesman, meanwhile keeping up a drumfire on both sides of the Atlantic aimed at changing the ways both of Frenchmen, who produce good wine but who are not, in his view, very clever when it comes to selling it, and of Americans, [who were mostly] brought up in the tradition of beer, cocktails, and highballs. . . . As a buyer, he roams the vineyards . . . selecting the choicest [wines] with such discernment that the Waldorf-Astoria, '21,' the Pump Room in Chicago, and Antoine's in New Orleans, among other clients, rely heavily on his judgment in stocking their cellars; as an exporter, seated at his desk in Margaux, he ships nearly half a million bottles of wine a year to this country, each with the legend "Selected by Alexis Lichine" printed on its label; as an importer, seated at his desk in Long Island City—a lone wolf now, working independently of the firm that bears his name— he buys great quantities of wine, including a good deal of the wine he has exported; and as a salesman, he persuades New York State wholesalers to buy the wine he has imported, and although rigid licensing restrictions elsewhere deny him the right to exercise to the full his distinctively suave version of the hard sell, he manages, by dealing with licensed importers in other states, to have his wares sold through much of the country. . . . [When not actually buying or selling wine,] he ranges all over the United States extolling, in educational pep talks before any likely gathering that will listen to him, the virtues of wine as a household beverage . . . [like] a viticultural Billy Graham.[10]

Elsewhere in the article Wechsberg noted that:

[His] responsibilities [as an importer and exporter] would be enough to consume the full energies of most men, but Lichine, to top it all off, has made himself an unofficial spokesman, propagandist, and watchdog for the entire wine business, equally vocal in the United States, where he repeatedly hustles from coast to coast urging the populace to forsake coffee with meals in favor of wine . . . and in France, where, covering less territory but pleading no less eloquently, he regularly tours the wine country in an effort to persuade vineyard owners to raise their ethical standards and modernize their way of doing business. . . . [Last year] the [French] Ministry of Agriculture [asked him] to submit a report on the steps that should be taken to increase the sale of French wines in the United States. . . . His proposal . . . is known in France as *Le Plan Lichine*.[11]

While delighted by Lichine's ascent as a wine merchant, wine promoter, and small-scale *vigneron*, Wechsberg was not unaware of certain ethical gray areas in Lichine's advocacy of his own product line. Nor was he oblivious to certain half-truths perpetuated by Lichine about the French wine trade, which Wechsberg ultimately ascribed to "a potent [blend] of altruism and self-interest." Lichine's edginess about his grapes was palpable as they sped the four hundred miles from Saulieu to the Prieuré in Lichine's enormous new Oldsmobile, for, as Wechsberg could not help observing, he was chain-smoking and popping tranquilizers the whole way. "After dealing in wine for twenty-five years, he suffers from the perhaps occupational disorders of insomnia and gout," Wechsberg later noted, "and when he is traveling, as he almost incessantly is, he takes along enough pills to stock a corner drugstore." Blazing his way across the Massif Central with wife and journalist in tow, "Lichine grew more and more nervous [about the possibility of a hailstorm] and swallowed more and more pills, until his wife advised him to stop at the next town and telephone the Priory."[12] The phone call settled Lichine's nerves somewhat, but not before Wechsberg realized how much was at stake.

Wechsberg was duly impressed by Lichine's steely certainty in tasting and selecting wines during their time in Burgundy. "In a strongly competitive field in which a man is only as good as his taste buds, [Lichine] knows that he has to be right nearly all the time if he is to remain solvent," Wechsberg wrote. "He has been known, under pressure of circumstances, to put in a fifteen-hour day at the task, during which he might taste as many as two hundred wines. [And] when he is finished at last, he is able not only to recall and compare the characteristics of all of them but—even more astonishing, perhaps—to enjoy a glass of wine with his dinner."[13] Whether such a statement was actually true (to taste two hundred wines in a day and "recall and compare the characteristics of all of them" is simply not possible), one thing was certain: Lichine, a great salesman, had completely sold Wechsberg on his genius.

The car arrived back at the Prieuré to find a house party in full swing: Lichine now kept a year-round open house at the estate for his wine clients, whether or not he was in residence. ("So many people avail themselves of [their] hospitality that Mrs. Lichine can't recall ever having dinner alone at the Priory with her husband," Wechsberg observed.) After excusing herself to check on the baby, Mrs. Lichine returned to oversee the making and serving of dinner—an intentionally down-home meal of *omelette au jambon*, *blanquette de veau*, and strawberry soufflé, each simple course paired with a fine wine.

Since a group of stockholders and their families were staying at Château Lascombes and had been waiting some time to see Lichine, Wechsberg accompanied him there the next day, with the intention of touring the vineyards. Lichine had recently erected eighteen grand flagpoles in the courtyard of the Renaissance-style château, each one flying the flag of a different country; as he quickly informed Wechsberg, they had been a gift to Lascombes from David Rockefeller, a stockholder, who had acquired them from their previous site, the plaza in front of the United Nations. Wechsberg was duly impressed, both by the grandiose spectacle and its Rockefeller backstory.

Wechsberg's week in the Médoc gave the journalist a good sense of Lichine's character and vision. But it gave him an even stronger awareness of just how much the French wine establishment now so clearly despised him—particularly since Lichine had just announced his embarkation upon an exceptionally controversial new project, a revision of the Bordeaux Wine Official Classification of 1855. This ranking system, which had been used to classify the region's wines for more than a hundred years, was generally agreed upon in private to be both inaccurate and obsolete, yet at the same time it remained vital to the world's perception of Bordeaux as the greatest (and most regulated, quality controlled, and hierarchically organized) wine region in the world—and thus was utterly necessary to the area's main industry and lifeblood. In pressing loudly for its reclassification, Lichine seemed on the verge of exposing the region's corruption, and thereby undermining its credibility and marketability. The majority of the Bordeaux wine establishment not only wanted the system kept in place; it wanted all discussion of its flaws kept to an absolute minimum. "He was [already] beyond doubt the most discussed and least liked man in the whole of Bordeaux," Wechsberg wrote after canvassing the neighborhood. "[Since] he began to attack the holy Classification . . . even men whom Lichine had come to think of as friends began making it plain that they would rather not be seen with him."[14]

When it appeared in 1958, Wechsberg's two-part New Yorker article was much more a celebrity profile than an investigative report—and a public relations coup for Lichine, since it reinforced the growing American perception of him as America's greatest connoisseur and importer of French wines. Its title, "A Dreamer of Wine" (which Wechsberg had taken from Lichine's admission that he sometimes counted wine bottles the way other insomniacs counted sheep), reflects the bemused approach Wechsberg ultimately took in describing Lichine's ascent to wealth, power, and acclaim. Nevertheless, even a casual reader caught a whiff of humbug in the piece, for while fine wine was, just as Lichine said, a miracle of nature and a source of unparalleled enjoyment and pleasure throughout history, it was also quite obviously a commodity—and Lichine, apart from being an evangelist of its beauty, its rarity, and its soulfulness, was also its biggest hustler.

In the months that followed, Lichine continued his effort to re-classify the great wines of Bordeaux. Working with a committee of Bordeaux-based growers, shippers, and brokers, he spearheaded the effort that would either revise the Bordeaux Wine Official Classification of 1855 or else scrap it entirely in favor of a new system. Lichine and his group came up with a tentative new set of rankings in 1959, entitling it "Classification des Grands Crus Rouges de Bordeaux." This new classification, while clearly more sensible and up-to-date than the Classification of 1855, nonetheless provoked immediate hostility from the Bordeaux wine establishment (many of whom characterized it as "malicious, incompetent, and unjust").[15] As a result, the Institut National des Appellations d'Origine, the government body regulating French AOC wine production, considered but then ultimately rejected the draft of the document—and, worse yet, returned it not to Lichine's group for a revision, but to two different local governing bodies for review: the Bordeaux Chamber of Commerce and the Académie des Vins de Bordeaux. When neither recommended its adoption or proposed an alternative to it, the project was dead. Lichine would publish a version of his proposed reclassification in 1967 in *Alexis Lichine's Encyclopedia of Wines and Spirits*, but even within his own book he would bury it in the encyclopedia's entry on Bordeaux rather than give it prominence in the book's appendices (where the Bordeaux Wine Official Classification of 1855 instead retained pride of place). "When one considers the outcry, disputes and lawsuits brought about by a new classification," Lichine later wrote, "one must reluctantly conclude that no such new classification—however much needed—is likely to win adoption. . . . It was [merely] to encourage and reward those who work hard for the best quality that I undertook [it]."[16]

❖

Just a few months after the Lichine profile appeared, Philippe of the Waldorf, Lichine's former boss, was arrested. Federal authorities had been conducting a two-year investigation of high-salaried major-domos in New York's top hotels, and in doing so discovered that Philippe's enormous annual purchasing for the hotel (roughly $2.5 million in food and $1 million in drink) had enabled him to extort large amounts of cash and material goods from his suppliers for the better part of a decade. They also concluded Philippe had been stealing large sums from the Waldorf employees' tip fund.[17]* Officials also established that Philippe had covered up these ill-gotten gains by bribing his accountant with free dinners and other hotel "services." They ultimately established that he had evaded $88,706 in income taxes in the years 1952 through 1955, based on undeclared gratuities and kickbacks in the range of $300,000,[†] and as a result, a federal grand jury handed down a five-count indictment for tax evasion. After two years of court battles, Philippe and his lawyers would arrange that he plead guilty to just one of the five counts, but Federal Judge Simon H. Rifkind, upon imposing the maximum fine of $10,000, would note in total disgust that "no sum was too small for this man to clip." A civil action followed immediately after, as the IRS sought unpaid taxes and penalties. Newspapers across the country covered the story closely, since Philippe had been a leading figure in café society for more than twenty years, and his philandering ways had also made him a regular presence in the gossip columns.

With his name and reputation sullied by the court case, Claude Philippe was forced to conclude his twenty-eight-year run as "Philippe of the Waldorf." Still, he was far from ruined: he remained rich, still owned his grand estate in Peekskill, and still presided over its five-thousand-bottle wine cellar. Even as the newspapers reported on his dismissal, he spun the story to his advantage by announcing that he had chosen to leave the Waldorf to work for an old friend, the real estate magnate William Zeckendorf.[18] But few were fooled; in the end, Zeckendorf would employ Philippe for only a year, and on releasing him from his contract would tell reporters, "we are very glad to have been able to help him when he needed friends."[19] Moving from consultancy to consultancy in the years to come, Philippe would remain active in the hotel trade, but never in the position of power and influence he had once known. Late in life he would lose a good

---

*The tips under Philippe's jurisdiction at the Waldorf were reported to be worth more than $1,000,000 a year ("Tax Fraud Is Charged to Philippe," Associated Press, The [Spokane] Spokesman-Review, Oct. 3, 1958, p. 28).

†In today's dollars, approximately $780,000 and $2.6 million, respectively.

deal of his money when an ambitious real estate project of his, a luxury Carribean resort known as La Belle Creole, went bankrupt while still under construction in Saint Martin.

⚜

Lichine, too, was facing some rough years. Alhough he and his wife had a second child, a son, in 1960, Gisèle abruptly left him for another man in 1963.[20] Lichine then faced more disastrous Bordeaux vintages in 1963, 1964, and 1965, a situation that further complicated his finances. But while visiting Los Angeles in 1964, he met film star Arlene Dahl, who had recently divorced for the third time and was now resuming her career as an actress. (The tip about her availability to date came to him through their mutual friend Hernando Courtright, a wine enthusiast who owned the Beverly Wilshire Hotel.)[21] A former Miss Rheingold Beer, Dahl had started her career by modeling lingerie at the age of sixteen, and in the years following, her romantic exploits had made her a sensation in the tabloid press: after briefly dating then-congressman John F. Kennedy, she married the actor Lex ("Tarzan") Barker in 1951, then divorced him for Latin heartthrob Fernando Lamas, having a son with him before that marriage ended in 1960. She then married a millionaire, Christian R. Holmes III, and had a daughter with him before separating, ultimately divorcing him on grounds of mental cruelty.

Lichine had a lifelong appreciation of beautiful women, but Dahl was more than a stunningly sexy redhead—she was a force of nature. Since 1951 she had headed Arlene Dahl Enterprises, marketing her own proprietary brands of lingerie, cosmetics, and perfume, even as she published a syndicated beauty column entitled "Let's Be Beautiful." When she met Lichine she was writing her first beauty book, *Always Ask a Man*, which ultimately sold more than a million copies— which was, to be sure, far more than Lichine would ever sell of *Wines of France*. As a man who had been delighting audiences for years with his anecdotes about Grace Kelly,* Lichine knew the power of a

---

* Grace Kelly helped Lichine write the index to *Wines of France*, a story he recounts in his *Encyclopedia of Wines and Spirits* (see also Hennessy, *The Pope of Wine*, p. 164). Lichine had met Kelly through Philippe of the Waldorf, who is said to have had an affair with her.

beautiful starlet to clinch a sale. So he decided not just to date Dahl, but to make her his wife.

"He followed me for nine months while I was filming in Spain and London," Dahl later recalled.[22] Married in Bridgetown, Barbados, in December 1964 (just two months after Dahl's divorce from Holmes was made final), the couple subsequently honeymooned in Hawaii, with both wedding and honeymoon covered extensively in the newspapers.[23] But their new life together quickly proved far more complicated and frustrating than Dahl expected, particularly during the six months that the family (which included her two children as well as his) spent yearly in Bordeaux. "It was like running the Lichine Hilton," she later told an interviewer. "From May to October we had the four kids and two châteaux full of guests. . . . There were twenty-five bedrooms at Château Lascombes and seven bedrooms at the Prieuré. . . . Of course, I had all sorts of chefs, nannies, and maids, but it really was a full-time job."[24] And Lichine himself soon proved an even greater challenge, for, as she subsequently noted, he had "a terrific temper, even worse than Fernando's."[25]

In truth, Lichine was struggling professionally, with his business facing new and entirely unexpected obstacles. Large international corporations, realizing the power of luxury brands to drive sales, had recently started buying up the legendary Bordeaux-based *négociant* businesses as well as the region's most prized châteaux. The châteaux and their vineyards were particularly vulnerable because new French inheritance taxes were forcing many French families to sell them simply to pay death duties. Likewise the bad harvests of 1963, 1964, and 1965 had left many *vignerons* and *négociants* overwhelmed by debt. As Lichine later described it:

> By settling the shippers' bank debts, [a] foreign [corporate] investor could convert the interest paid on loans into increased profits . . . [and] once freed from debt, many shipping companies could, in fact, be profitable. Many offers [that came in from foreign corporations] were too good to refuse: Barton and Guestier became a property of Seagrams [of the USA and Canada]; Delor was bought by Allied Brewers of the United

Kingdom. . . . Cruse was bought by Société des Vins de France; Eschenauer was taken over by Holt . . . [and] de Luze was acquired by Bowater . . . [before being] resold to Rémy Martin Cognac.[26]

The *négociants* who had up to now been Lichine's greatest enemies were suddenly being swept away by vast, faceless corporations intent on doing just what Lichine had been doing for the past ten years—modernizing the marketing, sale, and transport of French wines for a growing global market. But these big corporations had far more capital than Lichine did and threatened to muscle him out of the business.

Charrington United Breweries was one such outfit taking aim at his operation. They first approached Lichine in 1964 about buying his company. These conversations continued until 1966, a year Lichine found himself particularly worried about his future, and Charrington, for its part, was particularly eager to buy him out. Charrington's head, Edward Plunkett Taylor, one of Canada's wealthiest men, was just then in the process of merging the firm with Bass Breweries to create Bass Charrington, Britain's largest brewing group. Once that merger reached completion, Taylor wanted to move the company into the French wine industry.

Although Lichine had been working all his life to build his name and brand, he was tempted by the vast sums being discussed by Bass Charrington. Moreover, Taylor's office presented him with a highly seductive deal specifying that Lichine would remain closely involved in the business—for they considered Lichine indispensable both as its resident connoisseur and figurehead.

This appeal to Lichine's vanity had the desired effect. After a protracted negotiation, Lichine struck a deal, at the age of fifty-three, for an undisclosed sum* in which he sold to Bass Charrington nearly everything he held: the exporting company based in Bordeaux, the

---

* Leslie Hennessy, in *The Pope of Wine*, gives an estimated purchase amount of $2 million (roughly $15 million today). But given that Lichine became independently wealthy from the deal even as he bought an apartment currently valued at $16 million, that amount seems underreported.

complete bottling line in Bordeaux, the import side of the business
in New York, and all of the inventory Lichine then held in both Bordeaux and New York. (He did not part, however, with his winemaking operations at Château Lascombes, Château Prieuré-Lichine, nor
with the contents of their respective wine cellars.) Lichine then used
some of his new wealth to purchase a fourteen-room duplex apartment (with its own two-thousand-bottle wine cellar) at 998 Fifth
Avenue, a luxury building that had housed some of America's wealthiest families (including Astors, Vanderbilts, and Guggenheims) since
its construction in 1912.[27]

Only months after the ink was dry did Lichine begin to realize
that his lawyers had made a few mistakes. The first was one he and
his lawyers could hardly have foreseen, because Lichine had always
considered the quality of his product of paramount importance to the
success of his business. But as it turned out Bass Charrington was not
particularly interested in maintaining that high level of quality. Partly
the problem was a cultural one: Bass Charrington was a brewing business, and brewing produces a stable, uniform product. Winemaking,
by comparison, creates a highly variable product,* with results based
not only on *terroir*, but also on the vagaries of nature, on the choices
made by the individual winemaker throughout the vinification, blending, and bottling processes, and ultimately on the choices made by the
wine merchant about storing and shipping the product.

Throughout his career, Lichine had provided his clients with
French wines that were well made and correct to type, and he had
treated those wines with care in delivering them to the consumer. He
had fully expected to continue with this quality-control aspect of the
work after he sold his company to Bass Charrington. But as he now
discovered, he was no longer in charge of such decisions. Rather, the
executives at Bass Charrington were—and to his amazement they
uniformly chose to purchase average (or below-average) French wines,
trusting that the strength of Lichine's name and reputation ("An

---

* Today's mass-produced wines are much less fragile and much less variable, in part due to fining
and filtration, in part due to the widespread use of additives (both natural and chemical), and in part
due to the replacement of damage-prone wooden corks with plastic stoppers or secure screw-top caps.

Alexis Lichine Selection") would clinch their sales. When Lichine insisted they stop, they did not; and when he persisted, they fired him. Much to Lichine's astonishment, the new corporate owners of the company that bore his name—the same corporate owners that had insisted so much on his importance to the company's ongoing operation and success—had abruptly given him the sack.[28]

Faced with the fact that his name was now being used to sell low-quality wine, Lichine realized how his deal had gone terribly wrong in yet another way: through it, his name and reputation were being permanently and irrevocably damaged. The sullying of that name became even worse once Bass Charrington began a nationwide advertising campaign to persuade Americans to quaff Alexis Lichine wines just as they might chug down a beer or knock back a shot of whiskey. One such television ad depicted a bottle of Alexis Lichine rosé being dumped into a large beer mug, followed by a Lichine white wine being slopped into a martini glass, and then Lichine red wine being splashed into a shot glass, while an unctuous voice-over suggested, "Drink an Alexis Lichine wine with *any* kind of food . . . or *any* time you feel like *relaxing* with a *drink*!"

But what could Lichine do? In selling the wine selections company that bore his name, he had also unwittingly sold the right to his name. Worse, he could not possibly contest Bass Charrington's rightful ownership of his name, since in 1964, just two years before selling the company, Lichine himself had seen to it that Alexis Lichine et Cie had registered the name "Alexis Lichine" with the United States Patent and Trademark Office—thus confirming Bass Charrington's rights to ownership. And, to add insult to injury, Lichine now also discovered that the noncompete clause written into his deal with Bass Charrington meant that he could never start a new business that might in any way rival the one he had just sold.

For a man who was born to sell, and whose entire ability to sell was based on a good name that had taken him years to develop into a name-brand, the intentional sullying of that name, combined with permanent loss of his own legal right to use it, and on top of that the complete prohibition about engaging in *any* sort of wine dealing, was nothing short of a triple catastrophe. Lichine had got his big payout, to be sure; but he was now no longer a player in the only game he had ever wanted to play.

❧

"In 1966, I sold my shipping firm—Alexis Lichine and Company—to . . . Bass Charrington . . . [and] two years later, I was completely out of the wine export business," Lichine wrote in what would be his final book, *Alexis Lichine's Guide to the Wines and Vineyards of France*. "I was thirsting to get back into the trade, but repurchase of the Alexis Lichine name was beyond my resources." Bass Charrington then bought Château Lascombes out from under him as well—for, much as he might have wanted to hold on to it, Lichine had not been able to stand up to his thirty-five shareholders, all of whom found Bass Charrington's $3 million offer* irresistible. These celebrity investors had done very well for themselves by Lichine over the years—along with yearly case allotments of Château Lascombes Margaux,[29] each had been able to vacation with Lichine as often as he or she liked—and each now did equally well in cashing out, realizing a profit from cost, adjusted for inflation, of 1,218 percent. Although Lichine also profited from the sale (making roughly $750,000 for his shares), he had not wanted to sell.† Doing so against his will to the corporation that had just bought and ruined his name and reputation made the whole transaction even more bitter.

Lichine was now the rich man he had always wanted to be, but at the same time, he was devastated. At one point the degraded quality of the new Alexis Lichine wines upset him so deeply that, working through Somerset Importers, he sold his consulting services back to Bass Charrington in an effort to boost the wine's quality, hoping even as he did so that Somerset would exercise its option to purchase the Alexis Lichine Wines unit from Bass Charrington. But Somerset shut down before that could happen, and Lichine never regained control of the wines unit, nor of his name. (In fact, even many years after

---

* About $22 million today.

† When Lascombes was sold again, in 2011, it went for $260 million. Had they not sold when they did, the original investors would have seen a profit, even with the initial cost adjusted for inflation, of more than 22,000 percent. (See Jane Anson, "Château Lascombes Sold for € 200m," *Decanter*, July 10, 2011.)

Lichine's death his son, Sacha, would be prohibited from using the name Lichine in his own, entirely new, wine exporting company.*)[30] Meanwhile another firm, Seagram Château and Estate Wine Company, took up Lichine's business model, and by working directly with Bordeaux winemakers it became the leading importer of quality Bordeaux wines to the United States. Through the indifference and mismanagement of Bass Charrington, the model Lichine had developed and perfected out of Schoonmaker's brilliant original idea was simply abandoned by his company's new owners—and another unaffiliated organization scooped it up, and made millions.[31]

Lichine's marriage to Arlene Dahl barely outlasted the sale of his business. The two divorced in 1969, with Dahl (who was already planning her next marriage) asking Lichine for nothing apart from a carpet. But his rage at her departure was such that she ultimately needed a lawyer to get it.[32] Similarly the barrels of wine that Lichine had given to both of Dahl's children as yearly birthday gifts during the years of their marriage—barrels that Lichine had then kept safe in his cellars at the Prieuré—suddenly turned up one day in Dahl's Los Angeles driveway—ten barrels in all, summarily unloaded without advance warning or explanation. Dahl took this expression of anger in stride: two of her three previous husbands, Lex Barker and Fernando Lamas, had been equally temperamental.[33]

Unfortunately, Lichine's run of bad luck was not yet finished. In 1967, after many years in the making, *Alexis Lichine's Encyclopedia of Wines and Spirits* was published in New York and London. Alfred Knopf had originally hoped to publish this *magnum opus* in 1958, but the ups and downs of Lichine's business ventures had thrown the book off schedule, and so had its required rewrites.† And although in 1958 the *Encyclopedia* might have been heralded as the defining work of its generation, by Christmas of 1967, it faced serious competition from two equally significant books: *Wines of the World* by André Simon, which at 719 pages was an even longer book than Lichine's, and *Wine*

---

* As late as 1995, Sacha Lichine was denied the use of the Lichine name in the court case *ALC v. Sacha A. Lichine Estate Selections, Ltd.* By then, Bass Charrington had sold Alexis Lichine & Cie to Pernod Ricard, which managed it under their subsidiary Crus et Domaines de France.

† The book had been extensively edited at Cassell, its British publisher. (See the *Encyclopedia*'s acknowledgments for details.)

by Hugh Johnson, a hefty book by a twenty-eight-year-old British wine prodigy. When all three arrived at the busiest book-selling time of the year, *The New York Times Book Review* could do little more than cover all three in a single review of less than half a page. "This is a big year for wine books or, it might be more correct to say, a year for big wine books," the critic noted of the "three whopping volumes." Much to Lichine's regret, the one singled out for praise was by "the dean and grand old man of wine" (André Simon was then ninety-one). "If you were allowed but one book on wine, this would have to be it," the *Times* declared conclusively. Hugh Johnson, meanwhile, was singled out as "a young and highly articulate Englishman." Lichine, by comparison, was merely an "extremely well-informed American wine pundit and merchant."[34]

There was nothing particularly malicious in that characterization, nor in the placement of Lichine behind Simon and Johnson. Simon was just reaching the end of a glorious career. Having written 104 books on or related to wine, he was without a doubt the world's most highly respected wine writer in English. And the up-and-coming Hugh Johnson also needed to be given his due. Lichine's *Encyclopedia* therefore came in third, as a solid reference work that demonstrated "a vast knowledge, prodigious research, exemplary condensation, [and] admirable completeness. . . . [and while it] is hardly for the beginner, or the summer hammock reader, it is still a must for the oenologist, and belongs on the shelf of everyone seriously interested in this vast and fascinating subject." What went unsaid by the reviewer was that the book lacked the charisma of Lichine's first, perhaps because the new volume had been composed with a crew of hired help. Moreover, unlike *Wines of France* (which had been sprightly, amusing, and full of youthful brilliance), the *Encyclopedia*, like its middle-aged author, was bulky, slow-moving, and best enjoyed in small doses.

Even so, Alfred Knopf was apoplectic at the scant attention paid to Lichine, since he considered the book a major achievement and had been banking on its financial and critical success. In a strongly worded telegram to the *Times* publisher Arthur Ochs Sulzberger he came straight to the point: TIMES BOOK REVIEW AND ITS EDITOR MAKE A NEW LOW IN MY ESTEEM AND A NEW HIGH IN MY RESENT-

MENT AT THE OUTRAGEOUSLY SHABBY TREATMENT GIVEN NEXT SUNDAY TO ALEXIS LICHINE'S ENCYCLOPEDIA. DETAILED BILL OF COMPLAINT TO FOLLOW. He subsequently wrote Sulzberger that he was "moved as much by heartbreak as by indignation to writing this letter, for I know what went into the making of this encyclopedia and would feel exactly as I do were I not its publisher at all. . . . Considering the all but universal esteem in which wine is held as a civilizing influence on man, one would expect even the *Book Review* to reflect upon an awareness of the steady growth of the understanding and the consumption of wines on the part of residents of the United States." *Time* magazine, however, devoted even less space to the book, describing it simply as an "exhaustive and literate treatise on the choice, care and consumption of the principal wines of France, Germany, Italy, the US, and the rest of the world." The real disaster, of course (and the one that went unremarked in all these reviews, because it was beyond any reviewer's ability to know), was that this encyclopedic effort had been written primarily to support and extend Lichine's business empire—and that business empire no longer belonged to Lichine.

TWELVE

A Changing of the Guard

By the mid-1960s the American love of French food and wine was reaching its apex, but diplomatic relations between the two nations were increasingly testy. With the end of the war in 1945, the United States had helped war-ravaged France keep its people warm and fed, and after that the Marshall Plan had aided France with its economic redevelopment. But by the late 1950s, France's economy was surging and—despite its population of only 48 million and a landmass smaller than that of Texas—it was the leader of the European Common Market. In the fall of 1958, Charles De Gaulle came out of retirement to form the Fifth Republic, and his return to power brought with it renewed French confidence, pride, and hope for the future, as well as renewed Gallic feistiness and pluck. Under De Gaulle, France began to reassert itself on the world stage, often directly in opposition to U.S. foreign policy and interests. Within just a few years the general-turned-president sought to establish nonaligned status for France between the U.S.-led NATO and the Soviet bloc; to end NATO's military presence on French soil; and to end French participation in NATO's military structure. He also poured men and money into France's former colonies in Africa and, much to the irritation of the U.S. government, officially recognized the government of Communist mainland China.

When the Tonkin Gulf Resolution of 1964 broadened the U.S. commitment to winning the Vietnam War, De Gaulle became even more strongly opposed to American interventions abroad. France, he declared, would now "undertake great actions, assume great proportions, and greatly serve her own interest and that of the human race as well."[1] In 1966 his particularly irksome demand that all American soldiers leave French soil led President Lyndon Johnson to ask him if this request included the sixty thousand American soldiers who had been buried there. With that exchange, the honeymoon between the two nations was officially over, and relations between France and the United States resembled, if anything, those of a cranky middle-aged couple.

Paradoxically, American consumer excitement about French food, wine, and fashion was reaching new heights during the early part of the decade. On his 1961 state visit to Paris, President Kennedy had declared that "every man has two countries—France, and his own." In cities and towns across the United States, Americans seemed to agree: French food and French wines seemed to them the finest in the world, and French restaurants the fanciest and best dining that money could buy. France remained America's number one European tourist destination, and Henri Soulé's starchy Le Pavillon remained the grandest restaurant in the nation. Meanwhile, Soulé's new, slightly less formal French restaurant, La Côte Basque, had quickly become the lunchtime destination of choice among American socialites. And the *New York Times* food editor Craig Claiborne remained enraptured by French *haute cuisine* as well, not least because he was just then working closely with Le Pavillon's head chef, Pierre Franey, on developing the French-influenced recipes he was publishing in *The New York Times*, and that he would ultimately gather together in his bestselling *New York Times Cookbook* of 1961.

Throughout his years of writing on food for the *Times*, Claiborne would refer over and over again to French cuisine as the greatest in the world. Although he was born in small-town Mississippi, he felt a profound connection to France and French culture, once writing a friend:

Paris is, of course, my spiritual home. There is the most extraordinary comfort, a mystic relationship that I can't understand nor explain. The view of the garden from my window as I write [you from Paris] is somehow all related to a very real past of which I have no temporal recollection. But the emotional identity is far too profound for fantasy. Not only the garden, of course, but the Seine, the quais, the Opéra, Place Concorde, Place Madeleine—

Alone, I walked back via the Louvre and the small boat basins, stumbling over my joy . . . watching a small child launch a tiny sailing vessel with red sails, marveling at the strict alignment of the arches from the Arc of the Carrousel to the Arc de Triomphe, and having a tremor or two just seeing that Paris sky, unlike any other—anywhere.[2]

Other top food journalists felt the same. In the early 1960s Joseph Wechsberg published *Dining at the Pavillon*, a book linking Soulé's achievements to those of Escoffier at the Ritz, Fernand Point at La Pyramide, and Alexandre Dumaine at the Hôtel de la Côte-d'Or. But even as Wechsberg published it, Soulé's great restaurant was facing substantial new competition, since several of his staff left him in 1960 to open La Caravelle just a few blocks away in Manhattan. Within a year La Caravelle was the new restaurant of choice for the Kennedy clan, with Joseph Kennedy regularly holding court at lunch and dinner. La Caravelle's head chef, Roger Fessaguet, even selected and trained Réné Verdon for his new role as chef to the White House, doing so as a special favor to his best and most loyal client—the president's father.

But ultimately it was Jacqueline Bouvier Kennedy, rather than her politician husband or her vastly wealthy father-in-law, who brought American Francophilia to its pinnacle. "We in America," Julia Child later wrote, "have enjoyed a number of awakenings [to French cuisine]. Our first was certainly sparked in the Sixties by the Kennedys in the White House, with their glorious French food."[3] But of course America's excitement was now, thanks to Mrs. Kennedy, about far more than food and wine. The new first lady was of French ancestry, and made no secret of her preference for all things French. Her striking beauty suggested her French heritage, as did her drawling fluency in the language. And she knew France firsthand, having studied at the University of Grenoble and at the Sorbonne, and having traveled a good deal there with her sister during her debutante years. She also looked perfectly sensational in French couture: Givenchy, Dior, and Chanel were key components to her wardrobe as First Lady.[4] During President Kennedy's official visit in 1961, Mrs. Kennedy appeared at a state dinner at Versailles in an ivory silk cape and matching evening gown embroidered with seed pearls in a pattern of lily-of-the-valley and roses. This fabulous gown by Givenchy quietly evoked the splendor of Marie Antoinette. Shortly thereafter, when asked where and in what era she would have preferred to live, Mrs. Kennedy responded by choosing eighteenth-century France. After returning to Washington, as if to make that fantasy a reality, she invited Stéphane Boudin, the legendary French decorator involved with the restoration of Versailles, to help give the White House its much needed makeover.

❖

But the start of the 1960s also brought with it a changing of the guard, as a generation that had experienced the France of World War II began fading away and a new generation of Americans rose up to discover Paris in its place. A. J. Liebling, long since retired from his work as a war correspondent, was just then coming to the end of a distinguished career at *The New Yorker.* Throughout his later years, Paris had remained his destination of choice, even though his opportunities to return to it were limited; nevertheless, like M.F.K. Fisher, he had returned to it, over and over again, in his mind and in his writings.

Liebling's postwar life back in the United States had seemed to him colorless after the adrenaline highs he had experienced daily in North Africa and Europe during the war. "I have D-Day now for all my life, and the day we got to Paris," he wrote his old friend Joseph Mitchell shortly after being shipped home. "Nobody can ever take them away from me, but nobody can give me another D-Day either."[5] It had been hard for him to go back to everyday reporting. He moved to Chicago to work for a while as an independent journalist, hoping to make more money. But by age fifty he had, by his own account, "failed" as a freelancer, and he returned to *The New Yorker* in humiliation, there to resume his life of perpetual debt. Angered and disgusted by the anti-Communist witch hunts then sweeping the nation, and also by the country's repressive, panic-driven swing to the far right, he voiced his skepticism about American politics and the American press in his "Wayward Press" column throughout the 1950s, cataloguing the failures and inaccuracies of his fellow journalists even as he fretted about America's Cold War politics, blacklisting, red-baiting, and paranoia. But he also continued to write about anything else that interested him, including boxing and good food.

The 1950s may not have been happy years for Liebling, but they were productive, in part because his mentally ill ex-wife, Ann Beatrice McGinn, was still dependent upon him for financial support, and he now had two new dependents to provide for as well. In 1949 he married a beautiful, hard-drinking Kentuckian, Lucille Hill Spectorsky, who came to him with a strong desire for luxury living and a daughter from a previous relationship. Paying for all these women— institutionalized ex-wife, boozing new wife, hapless stepdaughter— meant Liebling needed to write and publish faster and more than ever before. Along with his magazine pieces he published *The Sweet Science*, on boxing, in 1956; *Normandy Revisited*, a stellar reminiscence of his war years, in 1958; and *The Earl of Louisiana*, on controversial Louisiana politician Huey Long, in 1961. These books, and his magazine articles, kept Liebling at his desk late into the night, sometimes overnight. The stress of so many deadlines, combined with lack of exercise and continual overeating and -drinking, ultimately ruined his health.

Liebling published *Between Meals: An Appetite for Paris* in 1962. A collection of surreal comic-gastronomic stories, the book is a mash-up of Liebling's various life experiences of Paris in the early teens, the late 1920s, the late 1930s, and then the 1940s and 1950s. The tales are a unique mixture of fact and fiction, past and present, and they "conveyed so strong a sense of the mingling of time, memory and emotion," his fellow *New Yorker* writer Brendan Gill later observed, "that one could compare Liebling to Proust without seeming to risk staking too bold a claim on his behalf."[6] The comparison is well intentioned but hardly accurate, since Proust is a writer of singular and visionary genius (and Liebling, to his credit, has a sense of humor that Proust entirely lacks). Gill is nonetheless correct in noting the strangely indeterminate nature of time in Liebling's story collection: reading it, one never quite knows what decade is being described, and in many of the stories, as in a dream or hallucination, he seems to be living in several historical periods simultaneously. Liebling's biographer, Raymond Sokolov—himself a journalist of broad scholarship, good humor, and hearty appetites—subsequently noted that:

> More even than *Normandy Revisited*, *Between Meals* is a work of nostalgia for vanished youth, unrecapturable delights, innocence and appetite undarkened by a fat man's guilt. In 1959, Liebling tipped [the] scales at 243 pounds. He was as obese as ever, and degenerating fast from constant overeating, without any serious intention of calling a halt to the gorge that he knew was killing him. But none of the somber side of his life's feast darkens the sparkling memories of *Between Meals*. . . . [The book] has the wistful, bittersweet tone of any memoir written by an old man about the juices of his youth. But the balance of the book is a celebration of Liebling's growth into knowing hedonism. This is why a book explicitly devoted to memories of food ends with a warm portrait of a woman, the Left Bank tart who lived with Liebling in his student digs. She helped him believe in his fantasy of himself as a man about Paris who could wine and dine and wench just like his heroes Villon and Stendhal.
>
>   . . . Liebling had lived his real life by the standards of that pleasure-worshiping, reckless fantasy of the writer's life. At the center of this vision of ideal manhood was the refusal to obey the bourgeois principle of delayed gratification. . . . To eat and overeat was, for Liebling, more than a crude gorge; gluttony was a badge of freedom. His belly was the outward and visible sign of an inward and manly grace.[7]

Liebling felt that overeating was a masculine prerogative, which explains in part the sense of multidimensional time travel that exists in the book, which nearly always favors the hearty-eating France of his boyhood and youth—the France of belly-busting meals and full-figured, Lillian Russell–type beauties—over the increasingly restrained and circumscribed gastronomy of the wasp-waisted forties and fifties. But these gleeful tales of gluttony are a mash-up of locations as well, for though they take place in Paris, they were crafted in New York, and their buzzy, manic, roller-coaster feeling is ultimately far more like a Saturday night at Coney Island than an afternoon in the Tuileries. Moreover Liebling's intense, dreamlike nostalgia for French food and wine is surely connected to his lack of such fine food in the Times Square dives he frequented throughout the 1950s. So just as his stories exist in a jumble of epochs—drawing at once on Liebling's childhood, young manhood, maturity, and then middle age—they are also a loving jumble of Paris and New York.

By the mid-1950s anyone could see that Liebling was dangerously unwell, and that his immoderate eating and drinking were symptomatic of a greater pathology of depression, chronic stress, compulsive overwork, and emotional imbalance. "Liebling's appetite astonished and appalled me," Brendan Gill wrote in his memoir *Here at The New Yorker.* "I saw that he was, in the old saying, digging his grave with his teeth, but there was nothing to be done about it: the pleasure he took in gourmandizing was obviously identical to the pleasure others took in listening to a Chopin nocturne." Gill was far too elegant and refined a character to want to sit across a dining table from Liebling, but he often watched with concern as "Joe" headed out of the office to chow down with Joseph Mitchell. "Mitchell and Liebling often repaired to the Red Devil [Restaurant], where they consumed a variety of repellent, hairy crustaceans, as well as octopus, squid, and other creatures best left, to my mind, to the shallows and deeps from which they had been fetched,"[8] Gill remembered.

> Disheveled, his navel showing through perpetually unbuttoned shirts . . . Liebling at lunch was a monument, a local institution. Young journalists would look on from neighboring tables as he indulged his legendary appetite in a series of martinis, in piles of oysters and double portions of lobster *fra diavolo* and *osso buco.* Waiters loved him; he tipped with a

gambler's largesse. His cronies from *The New Yorker* all remember Liebling's gluttonous performances at various Times Square restaurants of dubious hygiene. [One] recalled watching in awe as Liebling ate an entire broiled chicken at the Red Devil [including the bones.][9]

Through such daily binge eating, Liebling exercised his manly prerogative to live as he pleased. But he was also responding to the deadline pressure, loneliness, and overwork that are the writer's lot, as well as to the sense of entrapment that falls upon any man enmired in debt and unable to look after his family. Food and drink were an escape from that stress: eating (whatever he wanted, wherever he wanted, however much he wanted) made him feel, at least for the duration of a meal, euphoric and free. "I think if he'd been anchored with a family of his own, with a child, he might have taken care of himself," his friend Joe Mitchell recalled.[10]

Lucille Spectorsky turned out to be a hard woman, a bad wife, and a mean drunk, but Liebling remained with her, primarily out of concern for the welfare of his stepdaughter. "Mother drank too much," that stepdaughter, Susan Spectorsky, remembered. "She would scream a lot. . . . Vivien Leigh in the movie of *A Streetcar Named Desire* was a replica of her. She was unstable. With someone like that who needs a constant stream of goodies, no one treat, no one person, is ever enough."[11] Liebling did all he could for both women, even as he struggled on his own with kidney stones and incipient heart disease. In the winter of 1956, aged fifty-two, he attempted to take a health cure, signing himself in at the Bircher-Benner raw foods clinic and sanatorium in Braunwald, fifty miles south of Zurich. But the meager diet of muesli and raw vegetables appalled him, and after just a few days under gray winter skies, he fled across the border to the restaurants of France, subsequently describing Bircher-Benner in a humor piece as "a ruinously expensive para-Buchenwald."[12]

In 1959 Liebling finally divorced Spectorsky to marry the novelist and short story writer Jean Stafford. Brilliant, acerbic, and dazzlingly loquacious, Stafford was every bit Liebling's equal as a writer and character. Behind her significant talent and charm, however, lay a life of psychic and physical misery. Her once beautiful face had been wrecked in 1938 when her first husband, poet Robert Lowell, crashed their car. She never surpassed the early commercial success of her first novel, *Boston Adventure* (1944). In the years that followed, Stafford was plagued by other injuries she had sustained in her car crash, and also by writer's block. In the late 1940s she spent a year institutionalized at the Payne-Whitney Psychiatric Clinic, and during the 1950s and 1960s, she would be admitted to New York Hospital more than forty times for various alcohol-related ailments. Her heavy smoking, meanwhile, brought on chronic bronchitis.[13] But Liebling was rightly beguiled by her wit, her talent, and her bad-girl ways—for she was, in a sense, a female version of himself: hilarious, irreverent, rebellious, and troubled.

The two married at City Hall in April 1959, and afterward held an informal reception at Costello's, a bar on East 44th Street that had long been favored by *New Yorker* writers and staff.[14] While the hard-drinking Stafford took absolutely no interest in cooking and had only a limited interest in eating ("Joe introduced me to horse-racing and food," she later observed), the couple kept a housekeeper, Madella, who could put a meal on the table when needed.[15] Unable to afford yearly vacations in France, the couple instead spent their weekends at a tumble-down little property Liebling had acquired in the Springs, near East Hampton, getting to and from the place by rail and taxi since neither of them could drive. Arriving with sacks full of groceries and liquor (one acquaintance remembers Liebling taking the train out to Long Island with a *zampone** in his lap), they were cherished by their friends—many of them fellow *New Yorker* writers and cartoonists—for their easy hospitality as well as mordant wit.

Liebling's later writings expressed his enduring love of France, and especially of Paris. While his troubled finances kept him at his desk in New York, he nonetheless remained immersed in French culture and politics, and had several close friendships with left-leaning New York–based Frenchmen, including Jean Riboud, a former member of the French Resistance who eventually rose to become the CEO

---

* A stuffed pig's foot, a specialty of Modena. (This memory comes from Helen Rattray, the publisher of the *East Hampton Star*.)

of Schlumberger Limited, the world's largest oil-field services company. During the 1950s Liebling honored the memory of the French Resistance by serving as both translator and editor of an anthology of writings by Frenchmen who had endured the Occupation. He also wrote (disparagingly, humorously, and perceptively) on Sartre and existentialism even as he found a new hero in Albert Camus, the tough, can-do liberal journalist who had edited the underground newspaper *Combat* during World War II, then gone on to author a number of highly influential novels, plays, short stories, and works of philosophy that cumulatively earned him the Nobel Prize. Liebling met Camus while in France researching *Normandy Revisited*, and when the Frenchman was killed five years later in a car crash, Liebling was devastated. "When we last met Camus—in Paris, in November, 1955—he was getting ready to go to Algiers to bring the millionaires and the Moslems together," Liebling wrote in a brief piece on Camus for *The New Yorker*. "He felt the world as close as water on his skin, and never grew the scales appropriate to a Big Fish. He was without insulation—the antithesis of the detached Stranger with whom his name will eternally be associated."[16]

Through Camus's death, and also through Hemingway's suicide in the summer of 1961, Liebling seems to have sensed his own approaching end. By 1963 he had developed acute diverticulitis, a bowel infection that caused him unrelenting pain. His hands, feet, knees, and hip joints had been inflamed for years by gout, but it had now progressed to the point that it limited his mobility. Hoping to lift his spirits, improve his health, and clear his mind, he took Stafford on a 1963 summer trip to France. They spent the first part of that August being chauffeured through Normandy, the Loire, and Burgundy, and then stopped for a while at Jean Riboud's château just north of Lyon. But when they finally reached Paris, the place of his happiest memories, Liebling found the city shut down and silent because of the traditional late-summer holiday of Assomption, and as a result nearly all the cafés and restaurants were closed. Suffering from flu as well as a gut infection, Liebling was unable to eat or drink much of anything anyway, and he returned to New York just as sick and depressed as when he left.

Liebling caught pneumonia shortly before Christmas. Congestive heart failure and kidney failure followed soon after. Stafford, who was with him in the ambulance to the hospital, heard his last words but she could not understand them, except to recognize that they were spoken in French. She later thought he might have been spending those last moments in conversation with Camus.[17] When she buried him at the Green River Cemetery in Springs, she had his black slate headstone decorated with a fleur-de-lys, in simple commemoration of his life-long love of France.

In Liebling's obituary in *The New Yorker*, William Shawn wrote:

> His love for [New York] was not something abstract or general; he knew it and loved it in detail. He walked its streets constantly, and made discoveries about it every day. . . . [But] if New York was Liebling's first love, Paris was his second. Each was his true home. Neither ever disappointed him, and he managed to be faithful to both. . . . He returned to Paris again and again, to be restored and to celebrate the city in his reports for the magazine. . . . Not long after [the liberation of Paris], Liebling received the cross of the French Legion of Honor for his writings about France, and, in a shy way, he was very proud of it. Years after that, he returned through Normandy to Paris, and wrote a remarkable series of articles in which he moved about on three planes of time at once, mingling the present with a past that was present to another past. In a final delirium, as he was dying, he spoke only French, and went back once more to Paris.[18]

Since his anthologized nonfiction is largely concerned with current events, Leibling's best work is today largely unread. Still his various essays, articles, reviews, humor pieces, and war reportage have been duly canonized in a massive edition published by Modern Library, and he remains one of the most insightful, intelligent, and readable American journalists of all time.

Of all his collected works, *Between Meals* has been the most deeply loved by readers since it was first published. "Fair warning: you should not read this delicious book if you get guilt feelings about the intake of too much cholesterol, or a jolly untortured sex life, or gaining weight, or any of the other sensory pleasures against which mid-twentieth century man often seems to struggle," *The New York Times* alerted readers when the book first appeared. "This is A. J. Liebling *en pleine forme*, amiable and enlightening, as he lures us into the wondrous and wicked world of gastronomy."[19] And so the book remains to this day, one of the most delightful accounts ever written of an American gourmand's love for Paris and its many cuisines.

⚜

Even as *Between Meals* drew rave reviews, Julia Child was fast emerging as the great new champion of French home cooking in America. The Childs had packed up and left Paris nearly ten years earlier, in 1953 (departing in the same grand style that they had arrived: "With 45 cases, 5 feet square, 8 trunks and miscellaneous things").[20] Since then she had been working mostly by mail with Simone Beck Fischbacher and Louisette Bertholle on their French cookbook project, coming back to Paris for brief stays whenever her schedule allowed. The Childs took a posting in Marseille and another in the German Rhineland before returning to Washington, D.C., in 1956. There Child continued to hone her skills as a cooking instructor by giving small classes and cooking demonstrations whenever possible (and Beck and Bertholle did the same in Paris). The Childs then took a brief, final posting in Norway before returning to the United States and settling down in a fine home in Cambridge, Massachusetts. With Paul now retired from his work with the government, the duo were able to focus their considerable energies and talents on launching and promoting the new cookbook, which Julia (with the help of Avis DeVoto) had since placed with Knopf.

When the book appeared in October 1961, Craig Claiborne hailed *Mastering the Art of French Cooking* as "probably the most comprehensive, laudable, and monumental work on the subject, [written] without compromise or condescension."*[21] He was just then publishing his own *New York Times Cookbook*—a book with a decidedly French

---

*Although Claiborne described it as "comprehensive," it was only the first of two volumes. It went through eighteen printings before being published in its second edition in 1970, as *Mastering the Art of French Cooking Volume I* (in order to distinguish it from the newly published *Mastering the Art of French Cooking Volume II*).

influence, thanks to Pierre Franey—so his praise was generous, given that the two books were competing for the same niche market. But others also recognized the exceptional collaborative achievement of Beck, Bertholle, and Child. Dione Lucas, author of *The Cordon Bleu Cook Book*, held the book party for *Mastering the Art* at her new, omelet-centric French restaurant, the Egg Basket, and José Wilson, the food and features editor of *House and Garden*, gave the book a sensational six-page spread in that influential magazine. James Beard, by now the Grand Poobah of the American food world, was equally enthusiastic; he rushed to befriend Child and make her a part of his circle. Child and Beck were invited to appear together on the *Today* show, where Beck demonstrated the making of an omelet. But ultimately Child alone would be the book's one-woman publicity powerhouse: after Beck's return to France, Child organized her own national book tour and paid for it out of her own pocket, with resounding success. As she wrote Beck, "The fact that we are now accepted by the big food people is perfectly wonderful—we are now *quelqu'un**—Hooray."[22]

Child's next venture, *The French Chef* television series, initially grew out of her desire to promote the cookbook on Boston public television. But the little show quickly exceeded all network expectations and within months was being broadcast at stations across the country. Blessed with exceptional charisma and innate comic timing, Child was able to utilize all the cooking skills she had acquired in France and subsequently perfected in Washington, D.C., so that when she first appeared before the camera live in February 1963, she did so with utter composure. Paul Child meanwhile used all the skills he had accumulated in his work for the U.S. government to make sure that each of Julia's live presentations ran like clockwork. In time, he would be joined in this organizational work by a group of sophisticated television professionals and kitchen staff, for within the television world the show was immediately recognized as a unique, game-changing phenomenon.

Three years after the show's debut Child captured the cover of *Time* magazine. Her warbly upper-class accent, imperturbable demeanor,

---

*Trans.: somebody.

Julia Child and Simone Beck Fischbacher, photographed together while visiting Jean Fischbacher's family in Chinon, in the Loire, 1952 (Photograph by Paul Child; courtesy of the Schlesinger Library, Radcliffe Institute, Harvard University)

The Palais Bénédictine, Fécamp, Normandy, built by Simone Beck's maternal grandfather, Alexandre Le Grand, the proprietary owner and sole manufacturer of Bénédictine liqueur (Courtesy of the author)

Paul and Julia Child celebrate Paul's fiftieth birthday with a whimsical fancy-dress dinner party, January 1952. (Courtesy of the Schlesinger Library, Radcliffe Institute, Harvard University)

Paul Child's Queen-and-Knave Valentine, 1951 (Illustration by Paul Child / © 2017, the Julia Child Foundation for Gastronomy and the Culinary Arts)

The translator and author Charlotte Snyder Turgeon, Smith College Class of 1934, photographed in her Amherst kitchen. Her diploma from the Cordon Bleu is visible at the right. (Courtesy of the Smith College Library)

One of the first classes held by L'École des Trois Gourmettes (later L'École des Trois Gourmandes), in late January or early February 1952, at 81, rue de l'Université. Simone Beck is at the far right, and beside her is Louisette Bertholle. Julia Child stands just behind the three students enjoying their fine lunch. (Photograph by Paul Child; courtesy of the Schlesinger Library, Radcliffe Institute, Harvard University)

Beck, Child, and Bertholle give a dinner for Curnonsky (at center) chez Bertholle, February 1953. (Photograph by Paul Child; courtesy of the Schlesinger Library, Radcliffe Institute, Harvard University)

Sir Francis Rose (center), illustrator of *The Alice B. Toklas Cook Book*, flanked by his adopted son, Luis Rose (left), and his friend Samuel M. Steward (Courtesy of the Estate of Samuel Steward)

The artist Brion Gysin and his Dreammachine; the Beat Hotel, Paris, 1957. Gysin's hashish fudge recipe provoked an international scandal when published in *The Alice B. Toklas Cook Book*. (© Harold Chapman / TopFoto / The Image Works)

Alexis Lichine (Photograph by John Engstead; courtesy of Sacha Lichine)

Château Prieuré-Cantenac. Lichine purchased it for $16,000 in 1951 and renamed it Château Prieuré-Lichine in 1953. (Photograph by Guy Charneau; courtesy of Prieuré-Lichine)

Château Lascombes, which Lichine purchased for $70,000 in 1952 with the assistance of thirty-five high-profile investors, mostly American. Lichine retained a 25 percent stake in the operation and full control of the château's winemaking. (Courtesy of Château Lascombes)

One of the Lichine
billboards that
outraged the Bordeaux
wine establishment

(Courtesy of Sacha Lichine)

Joseph Wechsberg (far right) and Alexis Lichine (second from right) confer with fellow winemakers in the vineyards of Château Lascombes, 1958. David Rockefeller's flagpoles from the U.N. Plaza can be seen in the background. (Courtesy of the Estate of Arnold Wechsberg)

Arlene Dahl and Alexis Lichine (Photograph by the *New York Post* archives; courtesy of Getty Images)

Maître d' Martin Decré, chef Pierre Franey, and restaurateur Henri Soulé at New York's Le Pavillon restaurant (Courtesy of Claudia Franey Jensen)

Poppy Cannon and her children at Breakneck Hill

Left to right: Janet Flanner, James Jones, Thornton Wilder, and Alice B. Toklas attending a reunion at Sylvia Beach's famous bookstore, Shakespeare and Company, March 1959. (Photograph by Loomis Dean / The LIFE Picture Collection / Getty Images)

Jackie Kennedy, Charles De Gaulle, and André Malraux at Versailles, June 1961.
President John F. Kennedy can be seen just behind them. (AP Images)

Jean Stafford (left), a waitress, and A. J. Liebling in a New York restaurant (Courtesy of the A. J. Liebling Papers, Cornell University)

Julia Child and Charlotte
Snyder Turgeon give a
lighthearted cooking
demonstration together;
Smith College, 1964.
(Photograph by Margaret Sussman;
courtesy of College Archives, Smith
College)

The ruined house at Solliès-Toucas in 1961, around the time that Richard Olney purchased it (Photograph by Richard Olney; courtesy of Byron Olney)

Olney in his Provençal kitchen

(Courtesy of Byron Olney)

Elizabeth David in her London kitchen (Photograph by Cecil Beaton; © the Cecil Beaton Studio Archive at Sotheby's)

Richard Olney in his garden at Solliès-Toucas (Courtesy of Byron Olney)

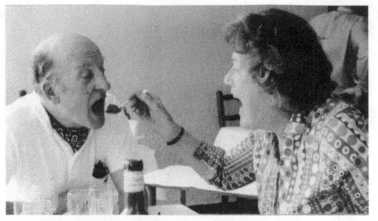

Julia Child feeds Paul Child during a visit to Richard Olney's house in June 1973. (Photograph by Suzy Paterson; courtesy of the Schlesinger Library, Radcliffe Institute, Harvard University)

Olney and Simone Beck in Richard Olney's garden, June 1973 (Photograph by Paul Child; courtesy of Byron Olney)

Julia Child and Richard Olney share a glass of wine at Solliès-Toucas. (Photograph by Paul Child; courtesy of Byron Olney)

and very evident love of a good laugh made her the perfect (and perfectly relaxed) cooking instructor for American homemakers tentative yet curious about French cuisine. "No matter if she breaks the rules, her verve and insouciance will see her through. Even her failures and *faux pas* are classic," *Time* gushed. "So good is she that men who have not the slightest intention of going to the kitchen for anything but ice cubes watch her for pure enjoyment."

Time credited Child's popularity to increasingly cosmopolitan American appetites, for "a decade ago, the typical [American] market offered half a dozen cheeses [but today the figure is more like] at least 50." It also noted the influence of tourism: "the postwar travel boom [has] brought millions of US tourists back from Europe with their tastes broadened and sharpened by what they [have] eaten there." Even the American housewares industry was partly responsible, *Time* maintained, for "a host of kitchen aids, from dishwashers, pressure cookers, blenders and deepfreeze units [as well as] the latest nonstick Teflon pans [are now] taking the drudgery out of cooking." But French cuisine ultimately received a little bit of credit for Child's success too: "what really makes [Child] just about everybody's chef of the year—and the most influential cooking teacher in the US—is that her specialty, French cuisine, is the central grand tradition for the growing multitude of home gourmet cooks." The profile ended with Child stalwartly pledging allegiance to the cuisine of *la Belle France*: " 'I will never do anything but French cooking,' she says with Francophilic fervor."[23]

Child's second book, created specifically as a tie-in to her television show, established once and for all the effectiveness of televised food programming upon cookbook sales. Robert Gottlieb, the new head of Knopf, gave *The French Chef Cookbook* (1968) a massive printing of 100,000 copies. Although the book contained material recycled (in a simplified version) from *Mastering the Art*, the first printing nonetheless sold out almost immediately, with Knopf easily recouping its investment.

Unfortunately, the Childs were now so busy with television work that return visits to France became increasingly difficult. When they did manage to get away, they were exhausted and needed rest. Luckily they were able to retreat to Domaine de Bramafam, an estate that the sisters of Simone Beck's husband, Jean Fischbacher, had inherited in 1958, and that the sisters (who had children) subsequently leased to the Fischbachers (who were childless) for their lifetime. The fine old *mas* and its several outbuildings sat on a twelve-acre property of olive trees and vineyards in the quiet hills above Cannes. The Childs liked the place so much that the Fischbachers in turn offered them a life tenancy there, with the Childs paying the construction costs of the new little house designed exactly to their specifications in lieu of rent. "We've no plans to come abroad this year," Julia Child wrote a new epistolary acquaintance, the British cookbook author Elizabeth David, in 1964. "But [we] shall probably do something next year, as we are planning a little house in the S[outh] of France (*entre Cannes et Grasse*), on a bit of Simca's property. Divine and peaceful and *Provençale*. We hope our friends will use it often. We find that we are, after all, partly European, and just must return."[24] A year later, in another note to Elizabeth David, she explained, "we mean to spend 3–4 months there every winter—lucky us. I think it is the only way to have a peaceful working time, and a painting time for Paul."[25]

✦

Back in Paris, meanwhile, the 1960s were proving exceptionally difficult for Alice Toklas. In the aftermath of *Aromas and Flavors of Past and Present*, she continued to struggle with her memoir. With the occasional assistance of a typist and regular bulk shipments of Pall Mall cigarettes from Robert Lescher in New York, she finally managed to complete the draft, and the small advance she was paid for it proved of greatest importance to Toklas during 1960, when her remittances from the Stein estate came to an absolute standstill, leaving her, in her own words, "down to bedrock." The situation worsened when Toklas returned from an extended trip to Rome in June 1961 to find that Gertrude Stein's painting collection had been seized and removed from the apartment as the result of a swift legal action taken by Allan Stein's widow, Roubina—who felt, perhaps rightly, that Toklas had neither protected the works during her prolonged absences from the place, nor insured them properly.

When *What Is Remembered* was finally published, in 1963, its narration (like that of *The Alice B. Toklas Cook Book*) bore an uncanny resemblance to the voice summoned by Stein thirty years earlier in *The Autobiography of Alice B. Toklas*. One reviewer thought it "oddly dotty, oddly delicious . . . a complement to Gertrude's *chef-d'oeuvre*," while others, including Toklas's longtime supporter Joe Barry, simply used the book's publication to commemorate Toklas's devotion to Stein during their nearly forty years of living and working together. But just six weeks after its publication Toklas was served with an eviction notice. After many years, her landlords had finally won back their apartment through the French courts. Toklas had no intention of leaving her apartment of twenty-five years without a fight, and through various actions she staved off the eviction for a year as friend after friend (including André Malraux, France's first minister of cultural affairs) attempted various intercessions on her behalf. Ultimately, however, the eviction was upheld, and in 1964 she was out. A group of concerned friends then rallied together and found her a small apartment more than three and a half miles down the Seine, in the far reaches of the Fifteenth Arrondissement. There Toklas would spend the last three years of her life, living for the most part on charity monies collected on her behalf by Janet Flanner. Toklas's faithful *femme de ménage*, Madeleine Charrière, who had been with her since 1950, stayed with her to the end, and when Toklas died in March 1967, she left Madeleine a gift of what money remained—but not the continuing royalties from her two cookbooks, which she gave instead to her priest.*[26]

Following a small funeral service at the little parish church of St. Christophe, Toklas's body was interred beside that of Gertrude Stein at Père Lachaise. The headstone of their shared plot seems at first glance to bear only the name and life dates of Gertrude Stein, but not so: Toklas had arranged (with characteristic discretion) that her own name and life dates appear instead on its reverse.

---

* The will, which was written in French, also left several small gifts and mementos to old friends.

THIRTEEN

Olney Stays On

Richard Olney came back to Paris in the fall of 1959, having spent two rather unhappy years in New York. He had worked for a while at Brentano's bookshop there, taken some side gigs as a decorative painter, and continued his work as a fine artist. But even as he did so, he realized that life in the States was not for him. Many of his New York friends had fallen into lives of alcoholism and drug addiction in the past decade, and New York—dirty, ugly, and so frantically busy— seemed to him to lack all *douceur de vivre*. Having kept the lease on his little apartment in Clamart, he moved back there with his American-earned savings in his pocket, determined this time to remain in France for good.

For a while his painting seemed to be gaining recognition, and he had hopes of making a living as an artist. During the later 1950s he exhibited steadily at group shows held by reputable Parisian galleries, and was included in salons* in both Paris and London. In 1960 an old friend, the well-to-do young aesthete turned art dealer Robert Isaacson, gave him his biggest break yet: a one-man show at his gallery on

---

*Olney showed in the Salon Nationale of 1955 (at the Musée d'Art Moderne de la Ville de Paris), and at the Salon de la Jeune Peinture (at the same museum) in 1955, 1956, and 1957.

East 66th Street in New York. It opened in February 1961 to good notices in *The New York Times* and *Art News*. Shortly afterward Olney was given a substantial two-year grant from poet James Merrill's Ingram Merrill Foundation.*

That spring, Olney took a vacation in the South of France with his youngest brother that changed the course of his life:

> Byron and I decided to spend some time [that spring] near Toulon. . . . We rented [a little house] for a spectacular month of April . . . [and a friend of a friend showed us] an abandoned property in the hills of Solliès-Toucas overlooking the valley of the Gapeau River. Cherry orchards transformed the valley into a blanket of white blossom in early April, the ground of the hillsides formed a tapestry of the blues and violets of flowering wild thyme, punctuated by bushes of wild rosemary, feathery shoots of wild fennel and the spring growth of oregano and winter savory—the poetry of Provence was in the air. . . . I fell in love.
>
> The house, whose foundations bore a cornerstone dated 1859, rose sheerly from a high dry-stone wall grounded on a lower terrace; it was a shambles of rotted timbers, collapsed tile roofs and cracked walls. . . . Beyond, three hectares— about seven acres—of dry-stone terraces, built over the centuries, planted with olive trees that had been neglected for fifty years, reached to the summit of the hill.
>
> . . . [I was told] I could have the property for a million old francs (about two thousand dollars). . . . I deposited half the [asking] price with [the agent]. Bernard [Hassell] . . . upon hearing of the Solliès discovery, proclaimed that, since he had introduced me to [the friend who had introduced me to the agent], he had a right to be co-proprietor.[1]

---

*Olney met Merrill in New York during the late 1940s. Isaacson was romantically involved with Merrill during the late 1950s. Merrill would subsequently come to dinner in Clamart with his lover David Jackson in 1963.

Olney had used the money from the Ingram Merrill grant to make the purchase, which would otherwise have been impossible for him.

Another trip, this one taken the following fall, proved equally significant: Olney joined the *Cuisine et Vins de France* wine-tasting trip to Bordeaux, thus beginning a decade-long professional relationship with the magazine. He recalled that Bordeaux trip as:

> An overwhelming experience. Year after year, the formula was the same: a Thursday evening buffet-reception in the city of Bordeaux with hundreds of wines to taste, at which the proprietors at all the principal Bordelais vineyards were present. Each succeeding morning, a bus picked us up in Bordeaux to visit Graves and Sauternes; the Médoc; and Saint-Émilion and Pomerol, not necessarily in that order. The first vineyard visited each morning served an abundant *"casse-croûte,"** sausages or steaks grilled over vine embers, charcuterie and cheeses. Three properties were visited each morning; at morning's end a "commanderie" chapter (Le Bontemps du Médoc et des Graves, Le Bontemps de Sauternes et Barsac, Les Hospitaliers de Pomerol; La Jurade de Saint-Émilion) was held, with the dignitaries done up in their grand, pseudo-medieval robes, at which several members of the tour were ritually enthroned. Lunch was catered at a château, preceded by an aperitif of white Graves or Champagne and accompanied by three or four wines, the last of which was always an old vintage of the receiving château. There were three afternoon visits and the first two evenings were free for groups of friends to check out the restaurants of Bordeaux; Sunday evenings, we had dinner at a château, the tour winding up after midnight.

On the first day of the tour, Olney was seated beside a journalist, Michel Lemonnier, who was then on the staff of the French magazine

---

*Literally "break [a] crust [of bread],"—that is, a snack.

Finance and also a monthly contributor to *Cuisine et Vins de France*. Fascinated by Olney's intelligent conversation, he recommended Olney to *Cuisine et Vins de France's* editor, Madeleine Decure, and to her second-in-command, Odette Kahn. The two women then invited Olney and Lemmonier to back-to-back dinners, seducing Olney on the first evening with a Château Margaux 1928 and on the next evening with a Château Latour 1929.*

In short order Olney became the object of much curiosity at the magazine. As he later remembered,

> A few days later Michel came to dinner in Clamart. He had suggested a pot-au-feu, the symbol of ultimate gastronomic simplicity. I prepared an oxtail pot-au-feu, discarded the vegetables and bouquet garni, put the oxtail aside for a future meal and, with the broth, prepared a pot-au-feu with boned, tied-up beef shank, and another bouquet, adding little carrots, turnips and potatoes toward the end; a quartered, blanched cabbage was braised apart in fresh thyme and bay-leaf. Michel wrote an article for *Finance* about the most fantastic pot-au-feu of his life, which was [subsequently] quoted in *CVF* [*Cuisine et Vins de France*] and my pot-au-feu became famous in French gastronomic circles.[2]

Olney had another new acquaintance invite himself to lunch shortly thereafter: Simon Arbellot, head of the Kleber-Colombes Guide Touristique and one of Madeleine Decure's most important advisers† at *Cuisine et Vins de France*. Meeting him at a *CVF* function, Olney had been delighted by this elegant man-about-town (com-

---

* Both wines are *premier grand cru classé* Bordeaux, the Margaux of the Margaux AOC and the Latour of the Paulliac AOC. Similarly aged bottles of these wines would today sell for approximately $400 and $350 retail, respectively.

† Madeleine Decure would later describe Arbellot as one of four mentors who guided her at the time she cofounded the magazine with Curnonsky in 1947—the other three being the chef Gabriel Dumont-Lespine, *chef cuisinier* of Maison Félix Potin; J. R. Roger, *CVF's* first wine consultant and expert; and the scientist-gastronome Édouard de Pomiane, "a great genius and humanist whose wit and civility delighted me, and who cooked with perfect style" ("L'Allocution de Madeleine Decure," *CVF*, March 1968, p. 33).

monly referred to at the magazine as *"le joyeux convive"**), describing
him as "an old fashioned charmer, with a monocle that tumbled regularly from his eye and a wealth of anecdotes." Arbellot—who was
just then writing Curnonsky's biography—"arrived bearing a terrine
of foie gras, a bottle of Clos des Mouches† 1952, a bottle of Château
d'Yquem 1954 and a bottle of Cognac 1914. I prepared a pheasant
salmis (rare roast pheasant hen, cut up, skinned, smothered with thickly
sliced black truffles, a few drops of cognac and a game bird velouté)
and the same old apple pie that I had been making since childhood;
served the Clos des Mouches with the foie gras, Ducru-Beaucaillou
1947 with the *salmis* and the cheeses, and the Yquem with the apple
pie. Simon [subsequently] devoted one of his monthly *CVF* articles to
the lunch in Clamart, making it sound very grand."[3]

In short order, as Olney later wrote, "Madeleine [Decure] began
to gather me into all the functions organized for the staff of *CVF*.
She, Odette, Michel and I traveled to Burgundy for a vertical tasting
of La Tâche at the Domaine de la Romanée-Conti. We were received
by Aubert de Villaine,‡ then twenty-two and seductive by virtue of a
combined shyness, intelligence and respectful courtesy. [And] Simone
("Simca") Beck, who was a loyal member of 'Les Amitiés Gastronomiques Internationales,' invited us to a reception to celebrate the
publication of *Mastering the Art of French Cooking*. Nearly everyone
present was American; I remember meeting James Beard."[4]

Olney's attraction to Simone Beck Fischbacher was immediate
and lifelong, for many reasons: They shared a sense of humor, a love
for French culinary culture and history, and a passion for hands-on
cooking. Not least, they had a mutual enthusiasm for fine French
wines. As Beck would recall in her memoirs, "Richard . . . is surely
one of the best French cooks I know, in some ways a genius. I was in
close contact with him ever since he was a young man in Paris, writing for *Cuisine et Vins de France*. During the 1960s and 1970s Julia and

---

* Roughly, "the merry guest."

† A Beaune *premier cru* vineyard (Burgundy).

‡ Today codirector of the Domaine de la Romanée-Conti. After this early introduction, Olney
maintained a lifelong friendship with de Villaine and with his wife, Pamela (née Fairbanks), an
American from Santa Barbara, California.

I were able to spend more time with him, since we had all [by then] made our main homes in Provence. . . . Richard's house [has served as an] inspiration for much of his brilliant food writing. . . . I've often been over to see Richard on my own, just for a breath of fresh air on the cooking scene and to pick his brain. . . . I think Richard has always served me the best wines I've ever drunk, and right out of that picturesque little cellar under the rocks."[5]

Olney thought Beck a Frenchwoman of great style, intelligence, and forcefulness of character. He also respected her for her lifelong immersion in French cuisine, which connected her directly not only to Pellaprat but also to many other grand figures of the culinary past. For example, while Olney worshipped chef Alexandre Dumaine of the Hôtel de la Côte-d'Or, his first visit there had only taken place in the mid-1950s, but Beck had been going to that restaurant in Saulieu since the year Dumaine opened it, 1932, and had patronized it regularly ever since. Moreover, from 1922 through 1932 she and her parents had routinely dined at the Hôtel de la Poste just down the street,* whose chef-owner, Victor Burtin, had been one of Dumaine's early mentors.

He also admired her for her toughness. "To several generations of Americans, Simca is a legend—*La Grande Dame de la Cuisine Française*," Olney would later write. "[But] beneath the cloak of legend lies a rock bed of *la vieille France*. [She has] a respect for tradition coupled with a fascination for all that is new, a formal correctness of speech often seasoned with rather astonishing expletives, a fierce loyalty to friends, a determination that knows no bounds and sometimes irrationally refuses to recognize any barriers." In the years to come she would invite him to stay and cook with her for days at a time at her charming old farmhouse at Domaine de Bramafam, Le Mas Vieux, sending her own chauffeur to collect him since he did not drive. Olney in turn loved having her come to lunch in Solliès-Toucas: she not only appreciated all he had created at his modest garden-home but also delighted in his correct pairing of fine wines with good foods, which for Olney was a preoccupation that bordered on obsession. His informal

---

* Beck and her parents had dined so frequently in Saulieu because it was a convenient overnight stop for them between their Norman château and their villa in Cannes.

patio lunches for Beck at Solliès-Toucas routinely began with Champagne, continued on to a still white wine with the *entrée*, and then proceeded to two red wines (always from the same region) with the *plat* and the cheese. The meal then came to its conclusion with and an old Sauternes served "either with the dessert or in the guise of a dessert." The greatest difference in their opinion about French wine was also a very basic one: Olney's all-time favorite wine was La Tâche, among the finest of Burgundies, while "Simca's greatest passion among wines [was] Château Margaux."

❧

Just a few months after making his down payment on the property above Solliès-Toucas, Olney published his first small article in *Cuisine et Vins de France*. He was surprised and gratified to receive a warm reception for that piece among his French friends: as he soon discovered, the magazine, though modest by American standards, was a singularly important publication in the French culinary world. As he wrote in his memoirs,

> In 1961, except for professional organs, *Cuisine et Vins de France* was the only food and wine magazine in France. [And] *La Revue du Vin de France*, the wine review founded in 1927 by Raymond Baudoin . . . had just been rescued from oblivion by Madeleine Decure; [as a result] the two reviews shared the same roof and policies [and I was ultimately asked to write for both]. *CVF* [was] founded in 1947, with Marcel Honoré's backing, by Madeleine Decure and Curnonsky. Madeleine, then in her twenties, was Monsieur Honoré's mistress. . . . [And] Curnonsky . . . was mainly a figurehead; until his death in 1956, he wrote [only] a brief monthly editorial, setting down (his) gastronomic laws and cursing those who broke them.[6]

While the work was not remunerative, Olney's association with this unique and highly regarded publication brought with it a number of incomparable perquisites—most notably, outings to France's finest restaurants and regular trips to its greatest wine regions, during which the magazine's writers and editors were given full access to the greatest domaines and châteaux, with extensive tastings of their best vintages. And because all subscribers to *CVF* were automatically invited to join a food club called Les Amitiés Gastronomiques Internationales—which organized monthly meals in Parisian restaurants—Olney was also asked to attend (and help host and translate at) these truly opulent meals, which included "special 'theme' dinners, for which evening dress was obligatory, in grand establishments like Laserre, Lucas Carton, Taillevent and the original Prunier, in the rue Duphot." He also helped host the "annual three-day visits to the Bordelais vineyards and irregular two or three day visits to the vineyards of the Touraine,* Alsace, Champagne, the Côte-d'Or, Beaujolais, the Côtes-du-Rhone, and Provence. Monsieur Honoré was president of 'Les Amitiés' . . . [and since he owned the magazine, he housed it in his office building on the Place Beauvau†—just as he housed Madeleine Decure there, too, in] a tiny airless flat . . . whose only window was in the 'cuisinette.' "‡

Like Olney, the two little magazines operated on a shoestring budget. "Financially, neither *CVF* or *RVF* broke even," Olney wrote in his memoirs, "but M. Honoré made up the deficit and Madeleine was having a very good time. The restaurateurs loved these organized dinners [such as La Paulée§ de Paris at the Taillevent]. And the vineyard proprietors, at a time when even the most celebrated were unable to make ends meet, were grateful and enthusiastic supporters of the two [magazines] and willingly offered their wines [for the gatherings]." Olney had little money but he was articulate and well mannered, and he was accustomed to conversing intelligently in two languages. Several of the people he met through the *CVF* dinners would eventually become good friends: the pastry chef and caterer Gaston Lenôtre, the

---

* The area immediately surrounding Tours, in the Loire.
† A chic Parisian address, just a few yards down the street from the Élysée Palace on the rue du Faubourg Saint-Honoré.
‡ That is, kitchenette.
§ La Paulée de Meursault is a traditional Burgundian end-of-harvest lunch celebration, essentially a feast for all who have been involved in the making of the wine. (The word derives from the French for sauté pan, *poêle*.)

chef Pierre Troisgros, and Alex and Andrée Allegrier, owners of the historic three-star Paris restaurant Lucas Carton.

Through the magazine, Olney also met and got to know the president of Le Club des Cent, Pierre Mouquet. When Mouquet (and other members of the club) mentioned reading about Olney's pot-au-feu, Olney boldly invited them out to Clamart to give it a taste. Although the club included some of the finest and most demanding palates in France—each member was, according to Olney's friend Naomi Barry, "a master of food and wine and each of them [was able to] professionally prepare a menu, as well as enjoy the results"[7]—Olney worried more about how these wealthy Frenchmen would react to his shabby studio-home, for "except when going out, I dressed in rags and received in rags . . . my studio-dining room was a shabby little affair from which the lingering scents of turpentine and oil paints were never absent." But the evening was nonetheless a triumph, perhaps because of the novelty. "It was a mystery to me how people from worlds so foreign to mine could be so charmed," he later wrote. "[But] the pot-au-feu was a great success." A few days later, Olney's friend Georges Garin told him that Mouquet "had queried him at length about my antecedents, my bank account and so forth, hoping that I might be elected a member [of Le Club des Cent.] Garin said, 'Richard? . . . Ridiculous! He's nothing but a penniless painter.'" ("Of course he was right," Olney subsequently recollected, "but I would have preferred to answer for myself.")[8]

⚜

Garin, a Burgundian chef recently arrived in Paris, was quickly becoming Olney's closest friend. Their introduction had come about through Michel Lemmonier, who recommended that Olney try Chez Garin, a new restaurant on the Left Bank at 9, rue Lagrange. Garin had formerly run a hotel-restaurant in the little town of Nuits-St.-Georges in Burgundy, where he had also catered many of the Confrérie des Chevaliers du Tastevin banquets at the Château du Clos de Vougeot. Intrigued, Olney invited Mary Painter to the restaurant (she had just moved back to Paris from Washington) and the two found the food outstanding. At the end of the meal, the middle-aged Garin came out of the kitchen to say hello. Olney later recalled him as having "moist rosebud lips and an over-ripe look to the fleshy face [that] betrayed a gourmand nature. Barrel-shaped torso, slightly humpbacked, head set forward, shoulders thrust forward, elbows turned out . . . when wrapped tightly in chef's whites and apron, he cut an impressive figure."[9] The three lingered late into the night, talking mostly about food and wine.[10]

An emotionally complicated relationship soon developed, with Garin (who was married) falling in love with Painter even as Olney became his confidant, adviser, and best friend. The situation made Olney uncomfortable because he was no fan of infidelity and he did not like being drawn into sexual duplicity. To make matters worse, Garin was a hard-drinking man whose paranoid tendencies worsened when he drank, and since Painter too had a drinking problem, the pair tended to reinforce each other's bad behavior. Toward the end of his life, Olney would observe that his good friend Garin (whose ashes he would ultimately scatter over the garden at Solliès-Toucas) had been "sentimental, irascible, jealous, possessive, generous, unprincipled, and devious. When not being obsequious with the Duke and Duchess of Windsor" and other clientele, who included Marlene Dietrich and Prince Philip, Garin was "gruff." Often his "unprintable obscenities . . . soared loud and clear" into the dining room from the kitchen, "silencing all conversation." The chef's heavy drinking extended into working hours. Olney noted that "Garin tasted every wine before it was poured," habitually joined guests for Champagne, whiskey, or Cognac after their meal, and would have a whiskey after the restaurant closed before heading off to Les Halles where, after doing the marketing for the restaurant, he would gossip with friends over tripe and Beaujolais, or else go on to a club called the Castel, or else to Montparnasse to eat oysters at the Coupole. "He was always in the restaurant by 8 AM and after a night of [this sort of] 'relaxation' he [always] needed several glasses of *pastis* to pull himself together."[11]

Garin would probably have fit in very well with Olney's other hard-drinking friends—but apart from Mary Painter, that gang had now pretty much broken up. James Baldwin was spending most of his time in New York, both as a literary figure and increasingly as a leading spokesman for the black civil rights movement. On a recent visit to Paris he had reached out to Olney, inviting him to back-to-back dinners at the home of novelist James Jones. But their two evenings at the Joneses had been rough gatherings of contentious writers who smoked a lot of hashish, drank heavily, and hurled insults at one another, leaving the (catered) food ignored and the wine unappreciated. It was much more Baldwin's scene than Olney's. In one instance, Olney recalled, "The evening disintegrated into a drunken, pot-smoking brawl."

Olney's housemate, the Harlem Renaissance painter Beauford Delaney, meanwhile, had suffered a psychotic breakdown in the summer of 1961 while aboard a ferry bound for Greece, and jumped overboard. "He was saved and delivered to a hospital in Athens," Olney recalled, but "he continued to hear voices and [so] slashed his wrists with a razor blade."[12] Upon returning to Paris Delaney moved in with Olney for a while—thinking his own studio occupied by evil spirits— but the arrangement could not last. Delaney's friends found him a little studio on rue Vercingétorix, alongside the railroad yards behind the Gare Montparnasse. Delaney would subsequently spend many years in and out of French public hospitals before dying in a French public asylum in 1979.

Olney faced great problems of his own in 1961 when his lover, Bernard Hassell, turned physically abusive. Partly the problem came out of financial desperation, for Hassell was in the country illegally, and lacked education and work skills, so was constantly short of money. When Olney did not have it, Hassell would menace or beat him until he found it. Verbal threats and intimidation had been taking place for several years, but during the summer of 1962, the violence escalated; Hassell showed up unexpectedly at Solliès-Toucas while Olney was hosting his brother James. "He wanted to tear the house down and start over again, he didn't want to be co-proprietor, he wanted all the property in his name, and so forth," Olney later remembered. "His method of expressing his irritation consisted in battering at me with his fists." In the hours following the assault, the Olney brothers abandoned the house for Paris, stopping along the way in Saulieu to "repair [our] shattered nerves and make up for [James's] ruined birthday dinner" by visiting the Hôtel de la Côte-d'Or. "It was Bastille Day, [and] Dumaine prepared [us] a perfect meal," Olney remembered. "We drank another bottle of La Tâche 1951, among others." This was one of the last meals Olney would ever enjoy from Dumaine, who retired two years later at the age of sixty-nine.

That fall, Hassell continued to menace Olney and cause scenes. Joining the *Cuisine et Vins de France* Bordeaux wine tour along with Mary Painter, he became drunk and aggressive, picking fights and tossing insults at others on the tour. (Olney subsequently banned him from outings to vineyards.) A few months later the threats and violence were such that Olney arranged to transfer all the Solliès property into Hassell's name, on the understanding that once the transfer went through, Hassell would never again contact him. But when offered the property, Hassell suspected a legal trick and he refused to sign the papers.

The extortion, psychological abuse, and physical harm that Olney subsequently suffered was something he himself could barely understand, much less explain to his concerned brothers. "I have [recently] had to pay a 65,000 franc fine to keep [Bernard] from being expelled from the country [after] he was picked up by the police for having sex in a turkish bath," he wrote his brother James in the fall of 1963. "I am hopelessly in love with Bernard . . . [despite the fact that] he is ruthless, promiscuous, and a whore. . . . My state of mind . . . is far from logical, for . . . what I want more than anything else is to go back with him and I almost certainly will not have the *volonté* [will-power] to maintain [our] separation."[13] Olney's brother Byron—who had also experienced Hassell's rage firsthand—sensed that Richard stayed with Hassell out of a sense of commitment: "Richard believed in fidelity," Byron later explained. "It broke him up when marriages fell apart. So far as Richard was concerned, Bernard was his partner, just like our parents had been partners. He felt that he and Bernard were together through thick and thin."

In the middle of all this misery, Olney began building his long association with *Cuisine et Vins de France*. His work there earned him the attention and respect of his fellow writers, and also their friendship.

One of these writers fondly recollected the American's *"atelier bohême et accueillant,"*[14] as Olney had these new friends over often. He was, in fact, something of a phenomenon at the magazine, for he wrote well, brought imagination, intelligence, and wit to his food and wine selections, and his research and recipe-testing were impeccable. Later that same year, he was invited by the magazine to take two trips to the south, doing in-depth wine tasting and reporting across the Beaujolais and then Provence. In the process he dined not only at Paul Bocuse's L'Auberge du Pont du Collonges near Lyon but also at André Hiély's classic three-star Chez Hiély† in Avignon, one of the great restaurants of Provence.

Through daily exposure to these contemporary French chefs, dishes, menus, and food ideas, Olney began cooking more elaborately at home, and also to work with more costly foods—notably, truffles, of which he was inordinately fond. Very much an autodidact, Olney loved the challenges inherent in cooking with these magical new materials. Meanwhile, his absurdly limited kitchen space and thrift-shop *batterie de cuisine* made the testing of each menu a tour de force of mind-over-matter imaginative play—particularly so since he had received no formal training. "To be a good cook you do not have to be trained," he would later tell an interviewer; "too often professional training leads to a professional deformation. You [simply] have to have a passion for sensuous experience and for the rituals of sharing at table." Certainly Olney had both those things; he also had a lifetime of experience in working improvisationally with his hands, beginning with his rural Iowa boyhood and continuing right up through his decades in the art studio. In taking this no-nonsense, anyone-can-do-it approach to cooking, he began to realize the importance of informed critical and aesthetic judgment to the home cook, whatever the space one happened to occupy, and whatever one happened to be cooking. It was, in that way, like creating art: "you, the cook, must also be the artist," he would write in *Simple French Food*, "bringing

---

* Trans.: Welcoming bohemian studio.
† Formally known as Lucullus, Chez Hiély, founded just before the war, held a Michelin three-star rating throughout the postwar era.

understanding to mechanical formulas, transforming each into an uncomplicated statement that will surprise or soothe a gifted palate . . . for such is creativity, be it in the kitchen or in the studio." •

Byron Olney later suggested his brother's achievements as a resourceful self-taught author-cook bore comparison to other surprising achievements within their immediate family—from John (who left the U.S. Army to become a self-directed research neuroscientist) and James (who became an internationally recognized Yeats scholar and author) to Byron himself (who apart from becoming a cardiologist would also build his family's Minnesota home entirely by hand). From their small-town beginnings, each of these Olney brothers had made his way in life via self-instruction and inner direction, as had their equally resourceful and intellectually curious father, who was after all a self-made businessman. In Byron's words,

> [Richard's] interest in food was just a part of his natural curiosity. . . . His knowledge of food, like most of what he knew and valued most, was acquired on his own by reading and experimenting. There was never any formal education and training. He was born with the ability to completely master and devour anything that fascinated him enough. Mother and Father were intelligent, educated and tolerant people who set an example for him by having strong principles and living their lives accordingly. . . . Fortunately the home [we] grew up in allowed him the freedom to go his own direction. . . . Father and Richard . . . [both had] clear perceptions of right and wrong and good and bad, scrupulous honesty, an intense work ethic . . . [as well as] a recognition of the importance of knowing oneself and living accordingly.[15]

Unlike his very conservative Midwestern father, Olney had chosen a life that valued sensual self-indulgence over security, and this choice had distanced him from both of his careful, thrifty, unassuming parents. As the relationship with Hassell came to an end, Olney seems to have felt a resurgent need for connection, both to his family and to his close friends. Hospitality—food, drink, good conversation, and time spent at table—now became a central way for him to maintain that sense of connection.

Garin became closer to him during this time. Olney began inviting the chef out to Clamart for meals that were also exchanges of ideas and inspiration. On Garin's first visit, for example, Olney gave the chef and his wife a "simple" springtime lunch that began with an *entrée* of artichoke hearts stuffed with chicken-liver mousse and served atop a tomato mousse, followed by a *plat* of sautéed ortolans.* Then came a cheese course and, finally, an exceptionally delicate springtime dessert of fresh green almonds (peeled at the table to reveal their gelatinous interiors) accompanied by cherries fresh from the tree. Good wines were served throughout, adding an enveloping sense "of well-being and ritual communion" through which the two men came to know and love each other.

The ortolans had been costly, but the lunch had not been a showcase of technique; rather, its genius lay in Olney's thinking-out of how a fine spring afternoon might best be enjoyed at table. The place, the time, the season, and the underlying awareness of French culinary traditions had all been taken into account in the formulation of the menu. There had been a bit of fuss in the *entrée*, luxuriousness in the *plat*, and an exquisite simplicity in the dessert. Garin, duly impressed, reciprocated by inviting Olney (and his brother James) for a fine meal at the restaurant, one featuring some knockout wines: Veuve Cliquot 1952, a Clos Blanc de Vougeot 1949, a Nuits-St.-Georges 1949, a Corton Clos du Roi 1947, and a 1904 Cognac.[16] Hospitality exchanges of this sort would continue all through the sixties, providing sufficient pleasure and gastro-intellectual stimulation to both men so that within a few years Garin bought a property near Olney's in Solliès-Toucas and placed Olney in charge of its renovation. The two friends clearly planned to dine with each other well into old age.

Unlike Garin, Olney was no chef or restaurateur; his specialty was fine home cooking. His success at *Cuisine et Vins de France* was based, at least in part, upon his very peculiar (to the French) identity

---

* Although most people associate the eating of ortolans with the fall game season, there are two ortolan seasons, the other (as here) taking place in spring.

as a nonprofessional male home cook from the United States. His gender, nationality, and lack of any professional affiliation set him far apart from the others who contributed recipes regularly to the magazine, some of whom were Frenchwomen homemakers, and others of whom were Frenchmen in the cooking professions. (The magazine's regular cooking features were mostly written by women, some of whom, like Jacqueline Gérard, went on to be successful cookbook authors: *Cuisine Pratique, par Vérène, Cuisine Contre la Montre,** *La Cuisine des Débutantes,*† and *Les Récettes de Morena.*) But the tone of Olney's writing also set him apart from other contributors, since his prose was unusually elegant and precise.

In 1964, three years into writing for the magazine, he was given his own monthly feature, *"Un Américain (Gourmand) à Paris: Le Menu de Richard Olney,"* which ran for more than a decade. In each of these columns, Olney stressed the importance of creating menus of balance, harmony, and restraint, in which each course (and its accompanying wine) went well with the other courses (and their accompanying wines)—thus creating a well-thought-out, aesthetically pleasing, and unified artistic whole. Olney would also provide several wine choices for each course of each menu, so that each of his menus could be adjusted to suit varying budgets and occasions.

The foods Olney selected for his menus were dependent in part upon the importance of the meal, in part upon the significance and preferences of the guests, and in part upon the time of year and place. The wine choices were as well. But as Olney also demonstrated, a fine wine could be served with a simple meal to great effect; and a playful or imaginative wine pairing could transform a relatively simple course (and meal) into something far more interesting and thought-provoking. Take, for example, the dessert pairing of a humble prune *flaugnarde* with either a Banyuls‡ or an Alsatian *grand cru* gewürztraminer. In the first instance, the rich, plummy, mouth-filling flavor and long finish of the dark and syrupy Banyuls were set off by the

---

* Trans.: Cooking Against the Clock.
† Trans.: Cooking for Beginners.
‡ An AOC fortified wine, rich and sweet and similar to a port (but slightly lower in alcohol), made in the Roussillon, in the southwest.

simple and sympathetic flavor of the prune-studded *flaugnarde*, with its not-too-rich texture, somewhere between that of a custard and a cake, combined with the lingering aftertaste of the prunes. In the second instance, however, the full, floral nose of the gewürztraminer took the pairing of the *flaugnarde* in another direction, this time contrasting the rich, honey-and-spice nose of the gewürztraminer (and its balancing lightness and acidity) with the dense, plum-jam texture and flavor of the dessert. The pairing of the *flaugnarde* with the Banyuls was particularly appropriate culturally—both the dessert and the wine came from the southwest of France—while the gewürztraminer brought by comparison an element of novelty, luxury, and surprise.

Olney took an interest in ingredients that were to most Americans unusual, even exotic, but that were less so to the French. His menus often called for offal, uncommon poultry, overlooked seafoods, and home-grown (or home-foraged) herbs, greens, and vegetables. Pigeons, mackerel, sea urchins, crayfish, winkles, raw baby artichokes, truffles, purslane, dandelions, tripe, calf's brains, and lamb kidneys were the everyday stuff of his features. But *CVF* readers, unlike American cookbook readers, were in no way put off by such things; on the contrary, they took a lively interest. In a short piece extolling the virtues of sorrel, Olney would suggest improving two dishes that were basically exotic (to Americans) to begin with—the first, a gratin of calf's brains; the second, a dish of fresh sardines roasted in white wine—and then make them even more exotic (and interesting) through the addition of sorrel. The cream sauce of the first would be turned gray-green by the addition, and become bracingly acidic—an acidity that would contrast well with the richness of both the cream used in the dish and the creamy texture of the cooked brains. In the second preparation, the oily little sardines would be given "shirts of sorrel" that made them ever more dainty and appealing, even as the sorrel lent the fatty fish a contrastingly tart, lemony astringency.

Although many of the ingredients Olney explored in his features were inexpensive—calf's brains and sardines are two good examples, as is sorrel—he took pleasure in occasionally presenting dishes of luxurious, even shocking excess. One such menu proposed a celebratory meal opening with a ragout of fresh truffles in red wine. The idea came out of a rather bizarre conversation Olney had recently enjoyed with a truffle merchant in the Vaucluse, who told Olney that he rarely enjoyed truffles due to their astronomical cost, but then paradoxically added, *"Les dimanches, on les fait cuire avec une bouteille de Châteauneuf."**

Each course of the ensuing, peasant-inspired, luxury menu—which, after the ragout, continued with a grilled shoulder of mutton and green beans, then a cheese course, then a sensational *riz à la Maltaise*[†]—called for a wine of real substance. He began with a relatively affordable Domaine Tempier (Bandol)[‡] to accompany the truffle ragout (and called for the same red wine to be used in the braising of the truffles), but then progressed to a Château Haut-Batailley (a *cinquième cru classé* Pauillac) for the lamb and green beans, followed by a Château Latour (a *premier cru classé* Pauillac) to take pride of place among the cheeses. Diners could then linger over glasses of Château Filhot (a *deuxième cru classé* Sauternes), a celebrated dessert wine that set off the elaborate orange pudding to perfection. In today's dollars, the cost of materials for such a meal verges on the absurd: the four bottles of wine, similarly aged, would cost roughly $450 retail, and the additional bottle of Bandol needed for the ragout would bring the tally (for wine alone) to $500; the 300 grams of fresh black truffles required for the dainty ragout, meanwhile, would cost upward of $600.[§]

When later in his career Olney began creating menus for *CVF's* sister publication *Revue du Vin de France*—doing so in English, for what the publishers hoped would be a growing readership in Britain and the United States—he purposefully toned down the complexity of his recipes, and in many instances worked with ingredients that were far less costly, exotic (to Americans and the British), and difficult to acquire. He would continue to do this in his second book, *Simple French Food*. Nonetheless, throughout his career he would feel—as

---

* Trans.: Sometimes on Sundays we cook them up in a bottle of Châteauneuf du Pape.
[†] A rich, orange-flavored rice pudding (made in part with a Bavarian cream), usually molded, decorated, and sauced.
[‡] Relatively affordable then, but not today, since Domaine Tempier Bandol has become highly sought after in the United States.
[§] Garin loved this truffle recipe so much that he placed it on his restaurant menu as *ragoût de truffes de Garin*. Shortly thereafter, *Le Monde's* famously grouchy food critic Robert J. Courtine hailed its brilliance even as he decried its vast expense.

many French do—that luxury foods and fine wines fully merit their price, and that choosing to spend extravagantly on good food and truly fine wine is simply a matter of opting for quality over economy. (He practiced what he preached: although he otherwise subsisted on next to nothing, Olney was a regular purchaser of extravagant meals, luxury ingredients, and fine French wines of every sort.) Then again, he was hardly alone in his taste for culinary luxury during these years, as *CVF's* other monthly features attest: *"Les Restaurateurs Nous Confient Leurs Bonnes Recettes"* gave readers the latest and most advanced restaurant recipes, while *"Les Gourmandises"* took a careful look at elaborate pastries and sweets. *"Explorons Nos Vignobles"* meanwhile described the quality and desirability of France's finest wines, and *"Paris à Table"* and *"Carnet Gourmand"* presented news and menu ideas from France's top restaurants.

In the end, however, Olney's imaginative writing on fine food and fine wine is based primarily on his respect for French culture and his long-standing interest in French gastronomic history and traditions. Luxury ingredients and elaborate preparations had been a celebrated aspect of that history since at least the days of Vatel, three hundred years earlier, and even though peasant and bourgeois cooking traditions were the mainstay of the nation, these luxury traditions remained a subject of widespread interest among the French. *CVF* was doing its best to reflect and represent all those various French food cultures and traditions—even if, for the most part, the average French reader could only dream of dishes so fine, rarefied, and extravagant as a black truffle ragout. While back in the United States Julia Child routinely emphasized economy cuts and affordable French wines in her *French Chef* TV series (partly because the American public would not have had it otherwise, but partly also out of Child's desire to connect with mainstream America on its own terms), budget cooking was not at all what she had responded to during her first years in Paris, nor was it what she (and Beck and Bertholle) had written about in the first volume of *Mastering the Art of French Cooking.* In fact, when her coauthor Simone Beck Fischbacher was addressing the Parisian food world of 1962 through the pages of *Cuisine et Vins de France* (doing so to promote the publication of *Mastering the Art*), she selected some of the cookbook's most extravagant recipes to showcase the book, most notably *caneton à la d'Albufera,** a 150-year-old recipe for roast duck that featured a stuffing of foie gras and truffles as well as a costly and elaborate *sauce financière*.

⚜

The idea for Olney to write a French cookbook for Americans came about not so much through his own personal ambitions as through the insistence of his friend (and fellow wine enthusiast) Sybille Bedford. A novelist, journalist, and reporter, Bedford had been born in Germany to German parents and was then raised on the French Riviera by her mother and stepfather. Although unapologetically lesbian throughout her life, she had married an Englishman as a means of emigrating to the United Kingdom to escape internment (as a half-Jewish German national) in World War II. Olney had come to know her through her partner, American-born Eda Lord, M.F.K. Fisher's high school class-mate and first love. Olney had befriended Lord in Paris in the early 1950s, and after Lord subsequently set up house with Bedford in London in 1956 (the two had first known each other in Berlin, and corresponded throughout the war), Olney went over to England to visit them. There he discovered in Bedford a kindred spirit: a writer-artist of formidable intellect who had a lifelong passion for French food and wine. Bedford was then a well-established legal reporter who had also published a delightful book about her travels in Mexico, but it was really the pub-lication of her astonishing autobiographical novel *A Legacy* (in 1956) that brought her enduring literary acclaim.

In the early 1960s, Lord and Bedford had been invited by a longtime friend, the British publisher and socialite Allanah Harper, to occupy the garden-floor apartment of Harper's home, Les Bastides, in La Roquette-sur-Siagne, about seven miles from Simone Beck

---

*The dish is named after Maréchal Louis-Gabriel Suchet (1770–1826), whom Napoleon named Duc d'Albufera in 1812. Its first version, *poularde Albufera,* created by Adolphe Dugléré, a pupil of Carême, was served at the Café Anglais. But Beck developed the École des Trois Gourmandes recipe from a second version (as described in the *Larousse Gastronomique*), which specified roasting the stuffed duck with bayonne ham, braising it with Madeira, then carving and serving it with mushrooms and a *sauce financière* (which is a velouté-based sauce flavored with truffles, Madeira, and *foie gras*).

Fischbacher's Domaine de Bramafam. There Bedford had continued work on her biography of Aldous Huxley while Lord worked on her fiction (having published two novels, she was now writing a third). In time, Lord and Bedford met and dined with Paul and Julia Child. Bedford enjoyed Julia Child's company but remained relatively unimpressed by her gastronomic prose, particularly in comparison to that of her friend the cookbook author Elizabeth David. "We saw a good deal of Julia Child and her husband this winter," Bedford wrote David in May 1967. "I liked them both very much indeed; she had a great charm and an endearing vast unflappability. We really took to them. But . . . as a cook, or writer on food, *ce n'est pas quand-même que cela.** What do you think. . . . There's gusto and ability and hard work. But true taste? Compared to you, it's a Hovis advertisement against a Chardin."†17

Bedford felt differently about Olney's writing, for she felt that his engagement in French food, French wine, and French culture was not only practical but also deeply felt and deeply informed. Olney also impressed Bedford with his wine knowledge and wine collection; the two frequently lingered together over a bottle (or two, or three) while Lord, a recovering alcoholic with a compromised liver, sat by drinking instant coffee. Bedford later described Olney as "a painter, a passionate oenophile, a very bright light indeed in the international cookery world . . . an American from the Midwest who has spent most of his adult life in France, where he is held in much affection and esteem."18 Since Bedford had studied wine seriously since childhood—having been introduced to it by her aristocratic but emotionally remote father, also a fanatical wine collector and oenophile—she brought total focus and commitment to the activity, as well as a lifetime's worth of tasting experience. She described tasting wine with Olney in Bordeaux this way:

We look, we inhale, we draw in our mouthful: we chew, we *think*. It is a slow process (one is standing, if not always stand-

---

*Trans.: That's not really all it takes.
†Hovis is a bestselling (and widely advertised) packaged bread in the United Kingdom; Jean-Baptiste-Siméon Chardin (1699–1779) is the great French master of still life and the domestic interior painting.

ing still), utterly absorbing and near an ordeal—the raw tannin [of the immature wine] puckers the inside of the cheeks, rasps the throat like claws, while at the kernel one finds a notion of . . . what? Texture, structure, multiplicities of scents, analogous tastes; [one] divines staying power, future harmonies. How? It is a mysterious process, essentially private, individual—who can ever get inside someone else's palate?—*and yet*, there are rules, measures of consensus, codes of communication. [While much about wine is decided by machinery these days,] live individual [taste-]testing by human beings is still an essential pointer at every stage of the making, upbringing, and preservation of wine. What makes a credible, an effective wine taster? Attention, memory and, I would say, a natural gift, an inherited palate, subsequently trained. There must be interest, love; also a willingness to understand nature.[19]

These were the sorts of wine-tasting experiences Olney had been having in wine cellars across France since the early 1950s, and that his position at *CVF* had enabled him to pursue in a far more comprehensive way from 1961 onward. So when Bedford and Lord moved from England to the South of France in the mid-1960s, it was only natural that Bedford, equally impassioned about wine, should regularly come share his table and cellar—and that Olney should be enraptured by her good company and brilliant conversation. "Sybille was at first intimidated by the goat-path up the hillside," Olney later noted, but then ultimately

She was seduced by the atmosphere, the wines, and the simplicity of the food. . . . In her [many] autobiographical novels . . . a passion for the table, for freshly plucked or dug vegetables and creatures pulled from the sea the moment before being eaten[—]alive, grilled or sautéed[—]is woven through the treacherous tales of imperfect love, heartbreak and desolation, a steadying and voluptuous thread of joy. The ritual litanies of classified Médocs, noble Burgundies or friendly little Italian wines that don't mind being warmed up on a trip to the beach and cooled down with an ice cube, are marvelous.

Knowing the scarcity of really good writing on the subject of French food and wine by American writers for American readers, Bedford was puzzled that Olney should not care to publish there on the subject. And she felt passionately that he really *ought* to, given his hands-on abilities, his vast knowledge of French foodways, and his place within the contemporary French food and wine establishment. Having already read his food and wine writing in French, she appreciated his innate ability with language. She too was a remarkable prose stylist, and like Olney she was as comfortable in French as in English.

As it turned out, Bedford was not to be denied. As Olney recalled,

> Sybille was not the first friend to suggest I write a cookbook. I had never taken the idea seriously but Sybille did. She asked me to contact her friend, Evelyn Gendel* (to whom *A Legacy* is dedicated) at Simon & Schuster. Evelyn introduced me to the food editor, Pat Beard [in December 1966] who seemed interested. Sybille must have paved the way for I had nothing to show except some articles in French which no one could read. Pat asked me to bring in some sample material before returning to France.[20]

Pat Beard also stipulated, much to Olney's surprise, that this sample material be typewritten and in English. "My articles for *CVF* [had always been] handwritten," he later wrote. "I saw no reason for a painter to master the typewriter. S&S didn't agree." Olney had his sister Elizabeth type up the material on his behalf and send it "to Pat Beard, who was pleased. We had lunch at the Lutèce†. . . . John

---

* Although married, Gendel had a significant romantic affair with Bedford; the two became close in 1952 in Rome. (Gendel went on to work as a writer and editor after her return to New York.)
† Lutèce, at 249 East 50th Street, opened in 1961 by the Alsatian-born chef-owner André Soltner, was a leading French restaurant in the United States for the next thirty-four years.

Schaffner, whom I had known twenty years earlier [in New York], joined us. It was agreed that John would be my agent. I sailed, March 9, [1967] on *Le France*, bought a typewriter in Toulon, and learned to poke at a French keyboard."[21]

❧

What Olney would attempt in his first book would be to present American readers with the most up-to-date ideas about French cooking and dining—and menus ranging from the simple to the complicated, the modest to the grand—without any of the shortcuts, simplifications, or substitutions then so common among American cookbook writers, and at that time virtually mandated by American publishers. But even as he did so, he maintained that good French cooking and good American cooking were not all that different:

> Good and honest cooking and good and honest French cooking are the same thing. Certainly there are national dishes . . . but it is comforting to realize that the principles of good cooking do not change as one crosses frontiers or oceans and that the success of a preparation depends on nothing more than a knowledge of those principles plus personal sensibility. . . . A menu composed of preparations that are not in themselves French may remain totally French in spirit, for it is the degree to which a menu is based on a sensuous and aesthetic concept that differentiates a French meal from all others. It may be served under the simplest and most intimate of circumstances, but its formal aspect is respected, and its composition—the interrelationships and the progression of courses and wines—is of the greatest importance.

Olney's ideas about menu composition were in line with the dialogue on food that he had tapped into through his years of restaurant-going in France, and also, of course, through his years at *Cuisine et Vins de France*. But they also reflected his own participation in that dialogue, since his magazine articles had been based in large part upon his passion for—and encyclopedic awareness of—nineteenth- and twentieth-century French gastronomy,* food writing, and culinary history, from Grimod de la Reynière to the present day. While his sensibility owed a great deal to the dining he had done throughout France over the previous decade, his aesthetic was really shaped by two main culinary figures: Escoffier and Curnonsky. The latter had championed French provincial cooking as it was creatively reinterpreted in restaurants across France during the first half of the century, and Olney's admiration for the suave complexity of this so-called simple cooking—combined with his appreciation of the culinary artistry (and work) that such "simplicity" demanded—are reflected in his words about Curnonsky in *Simple French Food*:

> On [Curnonsky's] banner were inscribed Escoffier's famous two words[†] but [Curnonsky] has bequeathed us, as well, a number of maxims of his own fabrication. . . . Coupled with the knowledge that Curnonsky's passion for the garden-fresh vegetable and the farm-kitchen stew failed to temper his admiration for the apparently involved refinements of the classical French tradition, the [following] aphoristic pronouncements [by Curnonsky] may shed a bit of light on what "simple food" means to a relatively complicated (gastronomic) intelligence [such as his]:
>
> *En cuisine, comme dans tous les arts, la simplicité est le signe de la perfection.* (In cooking, as in all the arts, simplicity is the sign of perfection.)[‡]
>
> [But here it is also necessary to note that] the simplicity that Curnonsky . . . [had] admired in cooking was, above all,

---

* Just to be clear, *gastronomy* is defined as "the practice or art of choosing, cooking, and eating good food" (*New Oxford American Dictionary*).
† Escoffier's "famous" two-word dictum was "*faîtes simple*"—that is, "do it simply"—something Olney took for granted that American readers would know (but that most, of course, do not). Taken in its original context, the meaning of Escoffier's oft misunderstood phrase becomes clear: "We must be ingenious. We must see that it is not error, only a challenge and a truth, that simplicity does not exclude beauty. '*Faîtes Simple*' " (Escoffier, *Guide Culinaire*, introduction to the second edition, Feb. 1, 1907).
‡ This is Olney's translation (as is the instance below), included here just as it is written into his text.

the simplicity of art, [which is to say,] the purity and the spontaneity of the effect justifying any means.

And [another of Curnonsky's aphorisms]:

La cuisine! C'est quand les choses ont le goût de ce qu'elles sont. (La cuisine! That's when things taste like themselves.)

This is none other than the artist's precept, "Respect your medium," transposed into the world of food.[22]

The complexity of Olney's writing here (and also the relative complexity of his cooking, particularly in *The French Menu Cookbook*) is not a complexity Olney had created for its own sake. Rather, it is a faithful rendering of the French culinary complexity (of thinking, of instruction, and of practice) that had surrounded him in France for more than a decade, and in which he was now a happy participant, both through his work at *CVF* and as a home cook. Olney was speaking about French cooking with and among the French every day; in addressing Americans, he did not want to create "easier" or "Americanized" French cooking, as Julia Child did. Instead, he wanted to invite his readers into a more challenging (but, ultimately, more liberated) *French* way of cooking—thereby creating food that was authentically "simple" (but not always "easy") and authentically "French" (not "Franco-American"). Perhaps the best analogy for this concept of "simple but not necessarily easy" can be drawn from the world of haute couture, where a dress of ravishing "simplicity" will sometimes require many fittings and hours of stitching to create.

Ultimately Olney's faithfulness to French foodways would result in writing that is more highly valued in Europe (particularly Great Britain, where he is often compared with Elizabeth David*) than in the United States. But since he never set out to achieve mass popularity among American home cooks, Olney was not overly interested in walking them through recipes, or for that matter in providing them

---

*Consider, for example, Elizabeth David on *faîtes simple*: "What a Frenchman intends these words to mean may not be quite the same as what an English cook would understand by them. They mean, I think, the avoidance of all unnecessary complication and elaboration: they do *not* mean skimping the work or the basic ingredients, throwing together a dish anyhow and hoping for the best. That is the crude rather than the simple approach" (David, *French Provincial Cooking*, p. 17).

with less than satisfactory American ingredient alternatives—sensing, rightly, that those motivated to attempt authentic French recipes would ultimately find their own solutions and/or compromises. Within the smaller community of thoughtful, dedicated home cooks, and also among the community of highly skilled professional cooks, his cooking (and writing) would ultimately be cherished for its uncompromising faithfulness to the French original.

✤

Composing his first cookbook took Olney approximately a year even though he incorporated many menus and recipes he had already created for *CVF* into the project. He began with an elegant introduction explaining to American readers the ideas and principles that informed French menu composition. He then devoted thirty-three pages to a discussion of French wines—a good indicator of how essential wine was (and remains) to French menus. Next came forty pages on "Mechanics, Aromatics, and Basic Preparations." The heart of the book followed: a series of menus and recipes, with the menus ranging from formal to informal, festive to simple. These menus were broken down into four sections, one for each season of the year—freshness and seasonality being, to the French mind, an essential component of thoughtful menu planning.

But even as he was creating this extraordinary first book—one which forty years later would be named by a panel of British experts as the number one cookbook of all time*—Olney was in a period of personal transition. His relationship with Bernard Hassell was coming to an end, and (though he did not yet realize it) he was also coming to the end of his time in Paris. As James Olney later remembered,

---

* Assembled by *The Observer Food Monthly*, the judging panel included Raymond Blanc, Bill Buford, Rachel Cooke, Monty Don, Fuchsia Dunlop, Fergus Henderson, Mark Hix, Simon Hopkinson, Atul Kochar, Prue Leith, Thomasina Miers, Tom Parker-Bowles, Jay Rayner, and David Thompson. Their "Top 50 Cookbooks of All Time" included Olney's *French Menu Cookbook* in first place, directly followed by Elizabeth David's *French Provincial Cooking* (1960). *Mastering the Art of French Cooking* came in at #21, Escoffier's *Guide Culinaire* (in its English translation) at #24, and Édouard de Pomiane's *French Cooking in Ten Minutes* at #41.

[Richard's] move [to Solliès] occupied a span of some five or six years during which he was back and forth between Paris and the south of France . . . not quite abandoning Clamart but not yet fully established in Solliès either. Meanwhile Mlle. Marty was becoming ever more despondent as the finality of the decision was borne in upon her and as she became convinced that the exhilarating days were over when Richard, Bernard, Jimmie [Baldwin], Beauford [Delaney] and Company—an acting troupe in their own right—could be counted upon to supply an excitement at 68, rue Paul Vaillant-Couturier to be found nowhere else. . . . After he completed *The French Menu Cookbook* in 1968 . . . it became pretty clear to Richard and to others that Clamart and painting were of the past, replaced by the effort of restoring Solliès and engaging himself fully with writing about food and wine.[23]

Like many breakups, the breakup with Hassell took place gradually, then all at once. It had been set in motion as early as fall of 1963, when Olney returned from a wine tour in Bordeaux to "a hysterical three-hour scene [of] screams and threats [in which Bernard swore that] never in life would he allow me or any member of the Olney family to set foot on [the Solliès] property again, he was going to tear down the fireplace, the doors, everything that had my touch on it."[24] Then during the winter of 1964 to 1965, Olney returned from a trip to the United States to discover that Hassell had moved a French photographer into Beauford Delaney's old flat, then broken the lock on Olney's wine cellar, drunk or sold off all the wine, and " 'sold' the cellar [space] to the photographer to be used as a darkroom. I had no more wine [to store there], but I was cross; [so] I put the photographer's equipment out, replaced the lock, and invited Bernard to move out of Clamart to the clamor of screams and insults." When Hassell absolutely refused to vacate the Clamart studio, Olney left Paris for Solliès-Toucas.

A few months later, while Olney was visiting Paris on business and staying with Mary Painter, Hassell stalked and attacked him. "Robert Isaacson [my New York art dealer] was in town and we had

arranged to meet at the flat of our friend, John Hohnsbeen.* Bernard
must have followed me for I had just arrived when there was a knock
on the door. John opened it and Bernard burst in, flailing his fists at
me. Robert and John were stunned; I had no idea what the problem
was but I left with him to escape further embarrassment. [Bernard] was
irate because he wanted money . . . Mary [Painter] agreed to lend me
the money" to pay Bernard to keep away from Olney and to drop his
claim on the Solliès property. However, after taking that money,
Hassell subsequently "denied having sold me his portion of the property. I hired a lawyer, Bernard was uncooperative [and] refused to
appear in court, and [ultimately] the court decision [about the Solliès
property] was in my favor."[25]

     To avoid any more dangerous encounters with Hassell, Olney told
Mlle. Marty that he was moving out for good. But she begged him to
keep his studio out of friendship for her. Therefore, for the next several years he paid her a small amount and kept his paintings, art
supplies, books, and other belongings there, even while staying at
Painter's apartment "to avoid scenes with Bernard."[26] When Mlle.
Marty died very unexpectedly in the spring of 1968, Olney was on an
extended visit to his brother James in Liberia. Upon his return to
Solliès-Toucas, Olney received the news of her death, and immediately took the train to Paris to see about his things in Clamart. But
he got there too late: Hassell had already gained access to the studio
through other tenants in the building. The apartment had been ran-
sacked and Hassell had taken away everything of value, including all
the paintings, drawings, and sketches that Olney had kept in storage
there. Doubly devastated by the loss of Mlle. Marty and the loss of so
many years of artistic production, Olney left the Clamart studio for
good, and his relationship with Hassell at last came to an end.

---

* John Hohnsbeen curated for Peggy Guggenheim, and was a longtime partner of the architect
Philip Johnson.

FOURTEEN

M.F.K. Fisher and
The Cooking of Provincial France

The mid-1960s were good years for M.F.K. Fisher professionally: a younger generation of food-oriented readers were discovering her books of the 1930s and 1940s for the first time, and responding with enthusiasm. Donald Friede had skillfully repackaged these earlier books as *The Art of Eating: Five Gastronomical Works of M.F.K. Fisher* in 1954, and they remained in print in that omnibus volume for more than a decade. But she published no new book-length work until 1961, when she came out with a slim compilation of folk cures and remedies entitled *A Cordiall Water: A Garland of Odd and Old Receipts to Assuage the Ills of Man or Beast*. (An even slimmer book of 125 pages, *The Story of Wine in California*, published by University of California Press in 1962, was in Fisher's own words "a blatant ADVERTISEMENT"[1] commissioned, overseen, and paid for by a consortium of California wine producers.) Even so, writing remained central to Fisher's existence throughout the 1950s and early 1960s, as her many journals, letters, stories, and papers make clear.

Fisher took two extended trips to Europe during the 1950s in an attempt to reconnect with her earlier life there, and to forge ahead as a novelist and short story writer. The first trip was in the fall of 1954, when having inherited some money from her father's estate, she returned to Aix-en-Provence. After placing her two young daughters in a convent boarding school, she took a furnished room off the Cours Mirabeau and set to work writing fiction and magazine articles.[2] However, by early spring, she was fed up with rooming-house life, and moved (with her daughters, whom she had taken out of school) to a primitive little farmhouse three miles outside of Aix. There, near the village of Le Tholonet, Fisher continued to struggle with her writing, experiencing more of the depressive episodes she had known throughout so much of her life. (Others in her family had similar mental and emotional issues,* most recently her sister Anne, who as she aged had relied on a combination of scotch and paregoric[†] to get herself through the day.)[3] Describing the loneliness of Le Tholonet in "Two Kitchens in Provence," a story written more than a decade later, Fisher lingered over the memory of food that spoiled in her kitchen (which had no refrigerator), finding it emblematic of her own fragile state: "a couple of times I found myself facing one withered lemon, a boiled potato, and a bowl of subtly rotten green beans for supper," she writes at one point. Coming back from the market, she knew "the fish would spoil by tomorrow, the chops would be practically incandescent in thirty-six hours, and the tomatoes would rot in twelve." Later she describes "a bowl of berries delicately veiled with a fine gray fuzz," and in the last moments of the story recalls, "I would lift the lid from a pot of leftover ratatouille—was it really all right, or did I catch a whiff, a hint, of death and decay in it?"[4]

Upon her return to California, Fisher's life took a turn for the better, as she began a romantic relationship with a high school English teacher named Marietta Voorhees. Remembered by one former student as "a strict disciplinarian who understood that a ruler could be used for more than measuring," and by another as "a tough old bird,"[5] Voorhees may have been a no-nonsense educator, but she was also deeply interested in the arts: she directed an amateur theatrical group called the St. Helena Players, and was friendly with the novelist and

---

* Fisher's mother, father, brother, and sister Anne all exhibited symptoms of depression. (For this and more on depression in the Kennedy family, see Reardon, *Poet of the Appetites*, p. 369 and elsewhere.)

[†] A strong opiate medication meant for the treatment of diarrhea, but subject to abuse.

short story writer Jessamyn West, a local neighbor.[6] While Fisher had enjoyed a number of sexual liaisons with women before meeting Voorhees, she had never before had a sustained romantic relationship with a woman, and for a while doing so brought her some contentment. The two were together from 1957 on, and jointly occupied a house, sharing it until their breakup in the mid-1960s.[7]

⚜

In December 1960, Donald Friede invited Fisher and her daughters to spend the Christmas holidays in Paris. Even though the city was notoriously cold, damp, and dark in December, there was much pleasure on offer at its fine restaurants, and Friede, who was now wealthy thanks to his inheritance, enjoyed splurging on good food and wine. Meanwhile his current wife, a literary agent, took an interest in the girls. Fisher's journals record a festive lunch for the group held at the restaurant in the Eiffel Tower,[8] which although a tourist trap, was also a sensationally amusing one, particularly for the children. There was an equally festive dinner at a Russian restaurant, enlivened by balalaikas and vodka. An afternoon at luxurious Prunier in the company of the newspaper columnist Art Buchwald was followed by a dinner just a few hours later at the Taillevent. There Fisher surprised her ex-husband by ordering a "*boudin**" [much] to D[onald] F[riede]'s disgust—I think I ordered it a little to shock him. . . . We drank a 1945 Bordeaux, whose name I forget, and then a '43 Haut-Brion,[†] very fine, in magnums (of course!). . . . [and] not even D[onald's] state of cosmic misery could spoil [the meal] completely." Recycling the memory into fiction, Fisher would describe it as having taken place during "the worst Christmas I ever spent in Paris," in the company of "two very wealthy and unhappy dear friends," neither of whom wanted or appreciated wine, leaving Fisher to savor a noble Chambertin on

---

*A kind of cooked sausage. Fisher doesn't specify what kind of *boudin*—perhaps relishing the perversity of having ordered a humble sausage in one of the world's great restaurants. Given the time of year, however, it was probably a *boudin blanc de Rethel*, a celebrated gastronomic specialty of the Ardennes that is customarily served at Christmastime and accompanied by Champagne.

†A rare and expensive proposition: if one could find it, a magnum of Haut-Brion of comparable bottle age (seventeen years) would today cost approximately $1,000 retail.

her own. She would similarly transform the family meal at the Eiffel Tower into a story about a romantic tryst with a former husband.[9] Here, as throughout her life, Fisher created a childlike alternate reality in which her own experience lay at the center of everything, and she understood and appreciated not only the exquisite complexity of a particularly charged moment or situation, but also the brilliant flavors of world-class cooking and vintage wines.

Fisher concluded that vacation with a short visit to Aix, subsequently incorporating her impressions of the city into *Map of Another Town* (1964), which was later repackaged (along with *A Considerable Town*—her 1978 book about Marseille) as *Two Towns in Provence* (1983). But she earned little from the Aix book and was struggling to keep solvent. To raise funds she sold the house that she had occupied with Dillwyn Parrish—her "90 acres of rocks and rattlesnakes over near Hemet"[10]—and spent some time in spring of 1965 in Nevada with her troubled, hard-drinking sister, Anne, whose health was now failing. There Fisher found herself losing entire days to "drinkies," for the two started tippling before lunchtime and would continue that way until arriving at what Anne described as "the evening block-buster"— a nightlong binge on the sweet, powerful gin-based "One Two Three" cocktails (Campari, dry vermouth, and gin)* that Fisher adored.[11] Henry Volkening, her new agent, had recently negotiated a contract with *The New Yorker* for Fisher to write a series of articles on culinary writing and culinary history,[12] but Fisher simply could not bring herself to start them. "I am here to work, to pull myself out of a pit of nonexistence," she wrote in her journal. "This [drinking with Anne] is deliberately destructive or at least dangerously careless of me, and in some ways it would be better if I let myself break a leg, instead of masochistically risk breaking my present lucrative arrangement with the magazine. I am defying reality."[13]

But even as Fisher was fretting over her lack of productivity, her writings on food and travel were increasingly sought out by Ameri-

---

* Fisher's love of this cocktail was such that, as Joan Reardon reports in *Poet of the Appetites*, when she "died in her own bed as she had wished, [her caretakers] made 'One Two Threes,' placed one by her bedside, and raised their glasses in a final toast" (p. 452).

cans excited about France and French cooking, and editors were taking note. Much to her surprise in May 1966 Time-Life Books contacted her agent with a substantial offer for a new project. They wanted her to participate in something the company described as "the most mammoth venture of its kind in the history of publishing":

> Time Life Books is today officially introducing "FOODS OF THE WORLD," the first illustrated library of International Cooking. The initial title in the series, *The Cooking of Provincial France* . . . contains a concise history of the country's cuisine, and is replete with information on local food specialties, cooking implements, eating and shopping habits and the origins of dishes—along with scores of recipes with step-by-step pictures and directions, showing how to prepare the most famous, or lesser known, but always unique, characteristic, and delicious dishes of the country's cuisine.
>
> Written and directed by the world's foremost food and cooking authorities, the important new "FOODS OF THE WORLD" library will be comprised of a multi-volume series of hard-bound books intent on making cooking a new delight, reading a rediscovered pleasure, and producing even the most special of international specialties virtually mistake-proof for the average homemaker.[14]

Each of these books—which were to be produced under the direction of a series editor, an assistant editor, and an in-house staff of thirty—was planned as a combination of text, heavily captioned photography, and step-by-step recipes, with the same recipes then reproduced in a second, smaller, spiral-bound paperback suitable for kitchen use.

Fisher's agent was eager to sign Fisher for the first volume in the series, but Fisher had doubts about her ability to write what Time-Life wanted. The fee being offered was so spectacular, however, that she allowed herself to be persuaded. The forty-thousand-word text*

---

* Approximately 160 double-spaced typewritten pages.

was to be composed under the editorial direction of Michael Field, an ambitious, New York–based cooking instructor and author, with Julia Child consulting with Time-Life's staff on the book's one hundred recipes. In Fisher's correspondence with friends and relatives, she seemed sure that Time-Life's editors, its legion of support staff, and the consulting services of Michael Field and Julia Child would shield her from any potential embarrassment or gaffe. "They are very serious and dedicated and grim [at Time-Life]," she wrote her aunt. "I hide my inner jaunty detachment. I get a fat sum, which [at first] seemed 'wrong' for me, for I have never dealt in such terms."[15]

In the weeks that followed, Time-Life's editors laid out the structure and focus of the book. Chapter 1 was to answer the deceptively simple question "What is provincial French cooking?"; chapter 2 was to focus on the miracle of the French housewife, and look at the relatively modest and limited kitchen in which she functions; chapter 3 would then move on to discuss hors d'oeuvres, in which Time-Life specified that "both Mrs. Fisher and Mrs. Child [were to] make the point that imaginative and artistic garniture come as naturally to a French housewife as laying a napkin on a table." Other sections of the text would describe "French Provincial Kitchens," "A Family Celebration," "Market Place," "A Picnic," "Small Country Inn," and "Food Habits of the Provinces." Interspersed here and there would be individual color pages on topics such as "bread," "basic salad dressings," "herbs," "garlic," "wine," "cheeses," "pâté," "truffles or snails," "cider in Normandy," "mushrooms," "mustard," and "garnishing." Yet even as the editors dictated the content, they maintained high expectations of Fisher as a prose stylist, storyteller and food expert, describing her to their subscribers as "one of the wittiest, most common-sensical and fluent of the great modern gastronomes. She acquired much of her kitchen wizardry in southern France. . . . Few English speaking people know the subtleties of French cooking as well as Mrs. Fisher."[16]

❧

Fisher's accounts of how she spent her summer of 1966 in France vary. Her Time-Life expense reports for the trip lay out its particulars, with hotel and restaurant bills clearly marking off her days and whereabouts. Eighteen years later, however, she published a highly readable account of that same visit, describing the unexpected friendship she developed with Janet Flanner in Paris, and also describing how she almost met Alice Toklas (but didn't). The piece would ultimately be published as a foreword to a thirtieth-anniversary reissue of the *Alice B. Toklas Cook Book*, published in 1984—the same reissue that would feature Simon Michael Bessie's misleading "Happy Publisher's Note to the New Edition," with its spurious dialogue between author and editor.

Fisher begins the piece by noting "Miss Toklas has been an integral part of my life (sensate, thinking, sensuous, spiritual) since I was in adolescence. And when I was 21 and newly married, I could have met her." She then explains, "My husband and I stopped in Paris in 1929 . . . and we had an 'introduction' to Miss Stein and Miss Toklas, but I could not bring myself to present it. I could not walk around the corner with the letter in my hand."[17] But while Fisher kept exceptionally (almost obsessively) detailed records of her life from girlhood onward, there is never any mention of that supposed letter of introduction—or even of the possibility of an introduction to Stein and Toklas in 1929—except in this one piece of writing, which Fisher wrote in 1984 at the age of seventy-six. Fisher's assiduous biographer gives the story no credence, in part because Fisher's own records of her 1929 honeymoon quite specifically note that the Fishers spent less than a week in Paris, at the end of September, staying at a hotel just off the quai Voltaire. That hotel might, with some exaggeration, have been considered "around the corner" from the Stein-Toklas apartment at 5, rue Christine (it was more than half a mile distant); but in 1929 Stein and Toklas were still residing on the rue de Fleurus near the Luxembourg Gardens, roughly a mile away. (Stein and Toklas moved to the rue Christine apartment only in 1937.) "I often walked past her door," Fisher writes, "and knew she was behind it." But that too is impossible, not only because of the distance between Fisher's hotel and Toklas's front door, and not only because Fisher was only in Paris for a week, but also because Toklas was not in Paris that September. She and Stein had remained at Bilignin through October, as they would every year. (And letters to Stein and Toklas from September and October of 1929 bear out that fact conclusively.)

On top of all this it is really impossible that Toklas could have been, in Fisher's words, "an integral part of my life (sensate, thinking, sensuous, spiritual) since I was in adolescence," for the simple reason that Toklas was entirely unknown in the United States in the 1920s, which were the years of Fisher's adolescence. Stein's *The Autobiography of Alice B. Toklas*, the book that introduced Toklas to American readers, was only published in 1933. Before 1929, Gertrude Stein was herself barely known in America,* and Toklas not known at all.

Fisher then moves forward in time, noting that "in about 1938, my second husband and I . . . decided that we could afford, for a year or so, to rent two small rooms in the servants' quarters of the old Hotel Continental in Paris, high in the attics above the Tuileries,"[18] and goes on to say that when she returned to Paris alone in the "summer of 1967," "I asked to be lodged in the attic rooms my husband and I had planned to live in. . . . [And] in the next room, where [my husband and I] had meant to sleep, lived a trespasser, a stranger who became my good true friend, an elderly writer named Janet Flanner."[19] But again this is not strictly true, since Flanner was no "stranger"— Fisher had met her and got to know her in California a few months earlier, at the home of Fisher's very good friend Hildegard Flanner Monhoff, Janet Flanner's sister—who lived just over the hill from Fisher in Calistoga.† And of course, Fisher is also mistaken about dates: she returned to Paris not in the summer of 1967, but the summer of 1966.

While it is difficult to know why Fisher should have wanted to tell so many lies in her foreword to the *Alice B. Toklas Cook Book*, it is

---

* Stein had only two books published in the United States before 1929. *Three Lives* had been published by a vanity press (Grafton Press) in an edition of 500 copies, while *Tender Buttons* had been published by a small obscure firm, Claire Marie Publishers. *The Making of Americans* was published in 1925 in Paris, but in an edition of only 500 copies, by Contact Press. (The later, more visible republication of *Three Lives* came only after the 1933 success of *The Autobiography of Alice B. Toklas*.)

† There can be no doubt about this meeting: as Fisher herself wrote, "There were many good things [that happened last year] . . . the main one, quite probably, was meeting you at the Monhoffs' and then [being so near you] in Paris" (Fisher to Janet Flanner, Feb. 24, 1967, in *M.F.K. Fisher: A Life in Letters*, p. 242).

not difficult to understand why Fisher was intrigued by Janet Flanner. Like Eda Lord, Flanner was a woman writer of talent who had managed to establish herself in Europe for good, something Fisher herself had always wanted to do. Flanner had achieved great and enduring success as a longtime correspondent for *The New Yorker*, something Fisher would never manage. Perhaps most important, Flanner was (again, like Lord) openly lesbian, something that Fisher, despite her own significant and lifelong lesbian desires and activities, would never own up to publicly.

Fisher moves on to describe the intense friendship that quickly sprang up between the two women. Of the spartan, writerly furnishings of Flanner's room, Fisher makes a point of noting that it always had "a big fading garden bunch of roses or field flowers brought each weekend from her lover's country house." (But again, this is not quite true; that country house belonged to Noel Haskins Murphy, who had only had a brief fling with Flanner thirty-seven years earlier; since then they had been friends, and Flanner had been far more deeply involved with two other women: Solita Solano and Natalia Danesi Murray.) Fisher also described Flanner's "little bathroom always hung with a drying elegant nightgown or some tiny high-style panties."[20]

In short order Flanner, like an enchantress in a fairy tale, imperiously sets Fisher to doing various tasks and chores on her behalf. Of this period of psychosexual thralldom, Fisher writes, "I spent most of that summer happily puffing around Paris on errands for her . . . [but in doing so] I was more alive and happy than I'd ever dreamed of." Again, this statement does not square with Fisher's travel diary, which shows Fisher was only in Paris for ten days—not for "most of that summer." In addition, as her biographer Joan Reardon notes, "Much as she would have liked to explore the city at leisure, Fisher spent most of her [ten days] in Paris hard at work on setting up and photographing the 'stories' on which the Time Life book would depend."[21] Fisher's receipts, meanwhile, show that she spent only eight days (June 19 to 27) at the Paris hotel where Flanner resided.[22]

Fisher now turns again to the subject of Alice Toklas, writing, "[Flanner] refused to *include* me, even vicariously, when she went several times a week to the clinic in the suburbs where Alice B. Toklas lay like a sightless, speechless vegetable." According to Fisher, Toklas was incapable of receiving guests: "By 1967 I . . . had shed some of my first timidity [about meeting Toklas], but she was hospitalized, too remote ever to welcome me as she might once have done."[23] Once more, these statements do not square with fact, for Fisher's visit to Paris took place in 1966, not 1967—and if Fisher had actually been there in the summer of 1967 (which she was not), Toklas would have already been dead. More important, Toklas was not hospitalized in 1966; she was living in her little apartment in the Fifteenth Arrondissement. And she was not moribund either: her personal and professional correspondence remain active until February 1967, a month before she died.

✤

The fact that Fisher was more interested in telling a good story than in telling the truth can hardly be held against her. She was in the business of telling good stories, and throughout her life her way of telling a good story was always to embellish and alter fact until it satisfied the very different requirements of fiction. But while one might argue that Fisher, like anyone, was subject to the vicissitudes of memory (or, alternately, inclined to arrange the facts of her life as she liked to remember them), there is so much outright (and creative) lying going on in Fisher's tale of her summer in Paris that a mere lapse of memory seems unlikely. There is, however, a very real *emotional* truth at the heart of this vast heap of careless fabrications: namely, that Fisher was attracted to these two lesbian women of character and substance, and wanted to be among them, but they did not care to include her, and her being excluded by them hurt her. What is truly disturbing, and ultimately inexcusable, is that Fisher should have presented this story as fact and then published it as a foreword to *The Alice B. Toklas Cook Book*.

According to Fisher's biographer, Fisher's lifelong habit of lying became particularly compulsive (and bothersome, and pathetic) in later life, when she would routinely "lead interviewers into a morass of misinformation" and "strained [their] credibility with fabricated stories."[24] Through lies and other sorts of game playing she could command a good deal of attention from people depending upon her for information, and at the same time assert her own place in literary history. In this instance, she pulled it off beautifully, for not only did she publish the foreword in the Toklas volume, but her new agent, Robert Lescher (Toklas's former editor at Holt), also sold it to *Vanity Fair* magazine for a very tidy sum.[25]

The foreword appeared in print a full decade after publication of James Mellow's acclaimed *Charmed Circle: Gertrude Stein and Company*, which gave all the facts about Toklas's later life that Fisher got wrong. Many other fine Stein-Toklas biographies, memoirs, and letters collections were also available for Fisher to consult—works by John Malcolm Brinnin, Donald Gallup, Howard Greenfield, Gilbert Harrison, Janet Hobhouse, Frederick John Hoffman, W. G. Rogers, Linda Simon, Elizabeth Sprigge, Samuel Steward, Allegra Stewart, and Donald Sutherland. Fisher might have got her story straight about her near meetings with Toklas in 1929 or 1966, if only she cared to do so. But apparently she just couldn't be bothered to look up the facts.

⚜

After her ten days in Paris working with Michael Field, Fisher spent a day in Dijon before continuing down to Aix-en-Provence for two weeks, where she stayed at the luxurious Hôtel du Roi René, with the bill paid by Time-Life. She then met up again with Michael Field, to whom Paul and Julia Child had lent La Pitchoune, their new little home at Simone Beck Fischbacher's Domaine de Bramafam.* The three-bedroom cottage had only just been done up the year before. The Childs had lived and worked there with Beck for much of that winter and spring, with the two women developing and testing recipes for their long-delayed *Mastering the Art of French Cooking Volume II*; when the Americans departed that May to resume their television work in Boston, the house was free for the use of Field, his wife, and Fisher.[26]

Field was an odd choice for an editor on a book about French

---

* Alternate spelling: Domaine de Bramafan, which is how the property and its road are spelled on French road maps and on websites such as Google Maps.

provincial cooking. A former classical pianist, he had devoted himself to writing about food and restaurants since quitting the concert stage in 1964. He also taught cooking courses out of his home. *The New York Times* would later describe him (in his 1971 obituary) as "a nervous, intense live wire of a man . . . [who] attacked the subject of good food and the cooking of it with literate, no-nonsense zest."[27] By the time of his first meeting with Fisher, he had published two books, *Michael Field's Cooking School* and *Michael Field's Culinary Classics and Improvisations.* He was no specialist in French cuisine, but he was an enterprising fellow, and he had somehow hustled his way into Time-Life, which hired him at top dollar despite the fact that he was just then in the middle of completing his third book, *All Manner of Food.* Simone Beck, who first met him at Bramafam, was dismayed at his lack of knowledge about French cooking* and kept her distance.[28] Fisher, meanwhile, took time away from Field and his wife by visiting her old friend Eda Lord (and Lord's partner, Sybille Bedford) in nearby La Roquette-sur-Siagne.

Fisher had reunited with Lord, her high school flame, just a few years earlier in Aix, just as she was ending her relationship with Marietta Voorhees. Both then and now Fisher was captivated by Lord, even as she was irritated by Bedford.† Bedford, for her part, quickly came to the conclusion that Fisher was vapid and ill informed.[29] Upon hearing about Fisher's new book project, though, Bedford became intrigued; she was good friends with Elizabeth David, whose *French Provincial Cooking* had been published to universal acclaim six years earlier—and the two projects seemed, on the face of it, to have an awful lot in common.

Bedford had first met Elizabeth David in person in 1963, after

---

* In her memoir *Food and Friends*, Beck (who is otherwise quite discreet about her impressions of people) describes Field as "clever in many ways but he'd never had any formal cooking instruction. . . . I was flabbergasted when one day he asked, 'could you show me how to make a brown *roux?*' That's sort of like a science writer asking, 'what's the composition of water?'" (p. 242).

† Fisher wanted to break the couple up. Richard Olney wrote his brother James in 1970, "Eda and I passed an afternoon with M.F. [Fisher], who launched into an interminable and pointless tale about an 'institution' near her California home where [sexual] 'deviates' were kept under guard. . . . [She later] asked to see me privately. 'Sybille,' she confided, 'is very bad for Eda. We must work together to separate them.' I told her I was not into breaking up friends' love relationships. She was not pleased" (Richard Olney to James Olney, Dec. 18, 1970, quoted in *Reflexions*, pp. 127–28).

writing her a fan letter—David, as it turned out, was a great fan of Bedford's *A Legacy*.* Their friendship was therefore immediate and lasting, with the two frequently meeting for lunches and dinners in London, usually to commiserate about the difficulty of writing well—an activity Bedford once described to David as "all anguish and stone-heaving work."[30] David, for her part, had been "stone-heaving" on gastronomic subjects since publishing *A Book of Mediterranean Food* in 1950. Her other fine, highly readable, painstakingly researched books included *French Country Cooking* (1951), *Italian Food* (1954), and *Summer Cooking* (1955). But the greatest of all her books was undoubtedly *French Provincial Cooking* (1960).

Unlike the Time-Life project, which would struggle unsuccessfully to define its subject, and in many instances feature recipes more commonly found in hotel dining rooms than authentic provincial homes, Elizabeth David's masterly and comprehensive work of 493 pages had been clear and straightforward about the nature of French provincial cooking, deftly describing it as "not rustic or peasant cooking . . . [but rather] sober, well-balanced, middle class French cookery, carried out with care and skill, and due regard to the quality of the materials, but without extravagance or pretension." David had adored this style of cooking since her student days in Paris, when she had lodged with a supremely well fed upper-middle-class family there. In her research on the subject, she rightly credited the preservation and documentation of French provincial cooking to the concerted efforts, starting in the 1920s, of Curnonsky, Marcel Rouff, and a number of other distinguished Frenchmen and -women of letters, all of whom had worked (along with innumerable regional chefs and restaurateurs) to preserve these local cooking traditions at a time when the new style of international restaurant cuisine (or "hotel cooking") threatened it with obliteration. Even as she wrote about it, however, David

---

* David wrote Bedford, "How immense in me [is the] admiration and love for your own beautiful books. Two copies of *The Legacy* [*sic*] are always near me—one in my bedroom, one near my work table. The passage about Mélanie and the *loup de mer* I know by heart like I know [Lawrence] Durrell's piece about black olives from *Prospero's Cell*—all the same I still want to get the sensation of actually reading them on the printed page" (David to Bedford, Sept. 8, 1963, in Artemis Cooper, *Writing at the Kitchen Table*, p. 228).

was leery of the various manifestations of provincial cuisine on offer in the France of the late 1950s, noting that "there are a few restaurateurs in France today [who are] willing to barter their birthright of taste, moderation and simplicity in cooking for the cheap publicity and quick profits of showy food served in and out of season to gullible customers with more money than sense."[31]

Julia Child, too, was awed by Elizabeth David, describing her as an "authority" whose "immense research, historical documentation, and on-the-spot verification [made her] large and authoritative book *French Provincial Cooking* [an immediate] classic . . . [as well as] fine reading and learning." Child admired David not only for her incisive prose but also for her very obvious love of cooking. "You realize, once you start on a dish, that this is a book for people who really want to cook, written by a person who really is a cook, a person who visualizes your every move. . . . [It's] a timeless treasure."[32] Richard Olney, who came to know Elizabeth David through his brother James, was equally impressed: in Olney's words, "simply being in Elizabeth's presence was magical. She was witty and literate. Her observations about people were often scathing, but only because they were so devastatingly accurate— they were funny, never cruel. She was generous and kind."[33] All three—Olney, Child, and Bedford—found in Elizabeth David that rare combination of writer-scholar-critic-cook who took infinite care to get her details exactly right while making the whole complicated business of writing well about French cuisine appear both effortless and a joy. "Perhaps what captivated us at the outset," Bedford later wrote about David, "was her artist's eye, her own perceptions of the forms and textures of food. . . . How often in her actual recipes we are seduced by that carefree touch, that alchemization, as it were, of a drab and messy task into the neat, the swift, the graceful."[34]

Fisher, whose first order of business was writing a text that would pass muster with the editors at Time-Life, now began to realize through her conversations with Bedford and Lord that she also faced another, far greater challenge: namely, writing a book on virtually the same subject as Elizabeth David's without seeming like a dunce by comparison. In fact she seems from the outset to have resigned herself to the fact that, in the end, there would be no possible comparison of the two projects, writing Julia Child, "this book [of ours] is 200 pages of text and pictures and methods and so cannot possibly hope to cover French 'home cooking' as Mrs. David's book did."[35] When Fisher left France to return to the States on August 3, she stopped off in Boston, where she met Paul and Julia Child for the first time, and stayed with them briefly in Cambridge before they headed up to Maine on vacation. As Child would recall to Fisher a decade later, "I so well remember meeting you at the airport . . . we were expecting a diminutive creature, but you were a nice big girl."[36] However, Julia Child at first seems not to have known what to make of this "nice, big girl"—for although both big girls hailed from Southern California, their backgrounds and life experiences were worlds apart: Child, happily married, independently wealthy, highly productive, and a celebrity; Fisher, very much alone, with money troubles, a family history of depression and suicide, a compulsion for telling lies, and a drinking problem. Paul Child nevertheless seems to have been smitten with Fisher. And in fact the two had much in common: life-defining experiences in France during the late 1920s, identities as artist-gourmands; strong sex drives; and a fine, flirtatious way with the opposite sex. The two were also close in age: Fisher was only six years younger than Paul Child (as opposed to Julia's ten). As a result, Paul Child, not Julia, would often draft the couple's chatty letters to her.

Julia Child had growing concerns of her own about the Time-Life project, ones that predated her first glimpse of M.F.K. Fisher or her manuscript, since she had been in regular contact with Simone Beck over the summer. "Recently we have finally met Mrs. M.F.K. Fisher," Child wrote her editor at Knopf, Judith Jones,* that September. "She is doing the writing for the Time Life French cookbook for which Michael Field is the overall editor, and I am the somewhat reluctant consultant. . . . An interesting woman, about 58 but looks more, and takes more knowing than we had time for in the 3 days we were together here [in Cambridge] and on the way to Kennebunkport. She spent a week with the Fields in our house in Provence, and I have

---

* Jones, who had edited *Mastering the Art of French Cooking*, was not involved with the Time-Life book; Child was just then working with her on *Mastering the Art of French Cooking Volume II*.

a feeling they didn't get along with utter bliss. We liked her: she's interesting, one feels she has 'lived', and she is a thinker-feeler with certainly a graceful writing style."[37]

❖

Because Fisher was under great pressure to complete her text quickly—in fact, by October—she visited only three of the eleven French "provinces"* she was to profile in her book (the Île de France, the Côte-d'Or, and Provence). For the rest of the project, she apparently cobbled together impressions from books, maps, culinary guides, photographs, and old magazine articles. As with the Brillat-Savarin project and her various anthologies, she was once again appropriating work done by others and "serving it forth" it in her own inimitable style. This time, however, she had a problem when the manuscript reached the publisher. Even though none of the editors on the project at Time-Life knew much about French cooking or French culture, they did know enough about publishing nonfiction to know that Fisher's manuscript was not fit to go to press.[38]

Fisher's New York editor, Dick Williams, looked over the material with his colleagues, then sent it out for review to both Julia Child and Waverley Root, whose *The Food of France* had been published to good reviews in 1958. Root responded directly to Time-Life about his concerns. The Childs, meanwhile, wrote Fisher a letter that diplomatically registered only a few of the many issues they had with the book. "I have read {the manuscript} and written {this editorial letter} as though you were not O*U*R F*R*I*E*N*D*, which seems the sensible thing to do," it began, since the couple had no desire to hurt her feelings or drive her away.[39] But in fact they knew the manuscript was an embarrassment: Simone Beck had written a devastating series of memos on it (in French) which she gave to Child to review. The first of them (twenty-seven single-spaced typewritten pages) simply addressed the many errors in fact in the manuscript's opening pages.

---

* The use of the word "province" is problematic to the French. Even as various regions of France have maintained their distinct cultures and identities, they have not been "provinces" since France was reorganized into *départements* in 1791, in an effort to eradicate ancient feudal and aristocratic claims to the land.

What all the memos from Beck make perfectly clear, however, is that no French person could read through Fisher's relatively brief text without finding it just plain wrong about countless things. The Childs, however, merely wrote Fisher that while they enjoyed her way with language and her storytelling abilities, they were a little concerned about Fisher's views on the American way of living, eating, and cooking—they were uncomfortable, they wrote, with anything that "degraded the red-blooded American way of life."[40]

✤

Fisher's first draft of the manuscript has not survived, but even after that draft was heavily edited and then published in its 1968 version, it remains highly problematic. Its opening paragraph, for example, takes a distinctly odd approach to celebrating the glories of French cooking. "To nine out of ten of us," Fisher begins,

> "French Cooking" means an elaborate and expensive way of complicating or at least masking foods with sauces. (When I stopped in Scotland with my young children after a long stay in Provence, elderly and rather insular friends exclaimed in wonder at how well we seemed to be, "in spite of those dreadful thick rich concoctions covering everything and making one bilious, not to mention gouty.") Unfortunately "French cooking" can also mean mediocre or poor or dishonest cooking, served with pomp in pretentious restaurants everywhere, including the city of Paris itself.[41]

This delicious series of put-downs is followed by a second paragraph no less critical, this time about French bodily hygiene:

> The food these Frenchmen have fed on for hundreds of years has irrevocably shaped the ways they look, feel, and think. (A fine-nosed Swede who has lived for a long time in Paris once said to me, "I can tell immediately and with my eyes closed when I am next to a man in the Métro, what province he is from. Garlic? Provence! Apple Brandy? Normandy! Sauerkraut?

Alsace! It does not matter how long ago he left home: he is *made* of it!" My friend then shuddered a little, being Swedish and therefore fastidious about odors not his own.)[42]

Simone Beck's response to this nonsense is remarkable for its diplomacy. In the case of the smelly Frenchmen on the Métro, for example, she simply points out that neither Calvados nor choucroute will make a person stink, doing so with a dignified formality that itself stands as a reproof: *"On ne peut dire que le Calvados ou la choucroute aient des odeurs qui signalent leur consommateur du loin,"* she wrote, adding, *"Il faut faire attention à ne pas choquer le lecteur français."* She seems to have wanted, whenever possible, to prevent Fisher (or perhaps more accurately to prevent Julia Child, whose name was attached to the book) from making such heinous errors of fact: *"Pour faire admettre le tout, il faut que le volume consacré a la cuisine française, soit absolument sans défaut, et ne puisse être critiqué pour une erreur de détail,"* she wrote. *"Il faut éviter toute possibilité de critique qui rejaillirait sur l'ensemble de l'ouvrage."** To help forestall that eventuality, she followed up her first long memo with seven more memos, each between seven and fifteen single-spaced pages, pointing out more errors.

Fisher's published text is full of cheap shots as well as mistakes. In her account, the food-obsessed French have a bloodthirsty proclivity for devouring small animals and "innards," and also for savoring various ripened, fermenting, or half-spoiled foods. Another favorite theme of the book is the low standard of cleanliness among the French, both in the kitchen and out. In her introduction to a chapter on soups, for example, Fisher writes, "there is a legend, still firmly fixed in our romantic and therefore somewhat impractical minds, that an enormous black kettle sits at the back of every provincial French stove, continuously brewing its own delectable botulism day after day. Bones, crusts, carcasses are tossed into it, simmering 'a simple little soup of the country.'" And her chapter on fish notes that

---

* Trans.: To be perfectly frank, a book dedicated to French cuisine must be absolutely without faults, and must not be able to be criticized for an error in detail. One must avoid any possibility of criticism that would reflect badly upon the work as a whole.

"people who are not French have long been astonished by the behavior of people who are. This is especially true of table habits: a Frenchman will look for, and then prepare and eat with enjoyment, certain foods which to Anglo-Saxon palates are plain outlandish. . . . Snails are a good example."[43] (Interestingly, Fisher here classifies *escargots* as fish, although these edible snails live on dry land and are a specialty of landlocked Burgundy.) The chapter on meats expresses a similar ill-informed disgust about the French consumption of offal: "an interesting facet of the common-sense thriftiness of the French is their attitude toward what Anglo-Saxons refer to more or less disdainfully (or disgustedly) as 'livers-and-lights' or 'innards.' We are inclined to think of them as economy meats, to be coped with gastronomically, if at all, when the next paycheck seems dangerously far off. In France, however, innards are treated . . . respectfully."[44] Under the subheading *"Innards: Disdained Here, Honored There,"* she then adds that "kidneys, if cooked correctly, need not be tough and smelly. Sweetbreads and brains need not be soft, sickish reminders of our puzzling glands and cerebral confusion. Liver need not be considered solely as a revolting remedy for anemia."[45] To Fisher, even French vegetable dishes were suspect, since many were kept on from meal to meal: "a ratatouille improves with age . . . and can be reheated or served cold for several days . . . this gift of happy reappearance at the table is common to many dishes made by French housewives."[46]

When not describing the disgusting and unhygienic nature of French foodstuffs, Fisher was, oddly enough, serving up a lot of romantic nonsense about France. In a section on bread she asserts that nearly every town and village in France has its own distinctive way of making bread, and concludes, "Myself, I know of only one village in all of France without its own bread, and that is Le Truel in Aveyron, on the wild banks of the Tarn. By now this situation may have changed, but—when last I heard—all the bread had come from neighboring places for many years, since the startling suicide of a baker who was felt to have betrayed his trade and his village by leaving so unexpectedly, with nothing edible in his ovens."[47] Her comment about each village having its own special way of making bread was, of course, untrue: the varieties of French bread are relatively limited, and there are more than 36,000 *communes* in France (with roughly twice as many villages). Moreover, and despite the bizarre non sequitur of the "startling suicide of a baker" in Le Truel, that little town is hardly unique in France for having no bakery.

In other passages, Fisher was oddly simplistic and/or reductive, as if explaining France to children: "The people of Normandy are strong and brave . . . they eat well, work hard, and are courageous,"[48] she notes at one point, and at another observes that "Alsatians are very thrifty, shrewd people, which is probably why they place the pig second only to the profitable goose in their economy."[49] The logic here is inherently flawed; not all Alsatians are thrifty and shrewd, and the Alsatian culinary preference for goose and pork is determined by Alsatian culture and history, not by the regional obsession with penny pinching. Such nonsensical statements crop up throughout the book: "Some people think it is the rich soil of the riverbanks of the Ile-de-France that gives [its foods] th[eir] special savor, but generations of artists, and the sensitive inhabitants themselves, believe that it is the sky, rather: tender and luminously gray, or a clear, kind, blue, never cruel."[50] (Who exactly, one might ask, are these "artists and . . . sensitive inhabitants" of the Île-de-France, who believe that their meats, cheeses, and vegetables have been flavored by a sky that is "clear, kind, blue, [and] never cruel"?) She concludes with a similarly silly (and untrue) statement about the people of the Gironde: "It is possible for the people here to choose [their way of life], rather than have their [life] patterns thrust upon them," she writes. "They can be wine makers, farmers, hunters. They can raise geese. They can hunt truffles. They can fish, or cultivate oysters, or make cheese. They can raise greengage plums."[51] Again, the logic here is almost beyond comprehension: Why are the people of Bordeaux more at liberty than others "to choose [their way of life], rather than have their [life] patterns thrust upon them"? Few people engaged in agricultural pursuits get to choose between spending their lives hunting truffles, cultivating oysters, making cheese, or raising greengage plums—particularly in France, where farmers are born into family businesses or landholdings. In sum, although Fisher's words might have looked stylish and romantic on the page, they were far from accurate, or even logical—

which was problematic, since she had been asked to write a book of nonfiction.

⚜

After being very heavily marked up by the editors of Time-Life, the draft was returned to Fisher with a request for a rewrite. But Fisher instead responded with the melodramatic statement that she was removing her name from the book and withdrawing utterly from the project, telling Dick Williams that his staff were henceforth free to "depersonalize" the thirty-eight-thousand-word text and make it entirely their own. She followed up this letter of resignation with a note to Paul and Julia Child thanking them for their friendly assistance and likewise informing them she was done.[52] But in a letter to her agent, Henry Volkening, Fisher wrote that her real intention was to throw the Time-Life corporate offices into a panic at losing the author for the first book in the *Foods of the World* series.

But then two other things happened. The first was that Fisher found herself in urgent need of money because her daughter Anna, who had grown up with significant emotional and addiction problems (and would ultimately be diagnosed with manic depression), was now endangering the life of her two-and-a-half-year-old son through neglect. Matters came to a head in August 1967, when the boy was found wandering, filthy and alone, along a six-lane highway, and subsequently placed in juvenile protection.[53] As a result, Fisher needed to take in both daughter and grandson, and also pay their debts. Fisher's sister, Anne, meanwhile, turned out not to have left Fisher any money when she died—money Fisher had been counting on inheriting—and in January 1967, Anne's husband hanged himself, further complicating family, estate, and inheritance matters.[54] Faced with her daughter's debts, increased money worries, and yet another suicide in the family, Fisher began to rethink her withdrawal from the Time-Life deal—both because there was still a hefty final payment coming her way if she kept her name on the manuscript, and also because her future career was sure to suffer if she developed a reputation for stiffing her publisher.

Even as she began to reconsider, however, Time-Life went into action: its executives did not want to lose the celebrity name with which they had launched the *Foods of the World* series. So, disappointed as they were with her manuscript, the project managers, to avoid jeopardizing the entire multivolume undertaking, patched the thing up as best they could, and handed it back to Dick Williams. Williams flew out to California with it, where he humbly begged M.F.K. Fisher to reconsider her decision. Fisher reviewed the manuscript, perversely vetoed a large number of the proposed copyediting corrections, but then agreed to keep her name on the book.[55] "I spent two harrowing days going over every directive, from him, Julia Child, Waverley Root [and many others, and then I] wrote ten pages of comments, mostly saying 'Omit//cut out . . . agree//do as you wish . . .' and mailed them this morning," she wrote her friend Arnold Gingrich. "Williams called and wanted to come out at once and spend no matter how long to 'rewrite' with him. I refused flatly. So he is accepting my list, and *himself* rewriting. Then he is sending me his copy. If I think it still sounds enough like Fisher . . . I'll go along. . . . Poor guy . . . I think he is desperate."[56]

❧

The first public denunciation of *The Cooking of Provincial France* came from the most powerful voice in American food journalism, Craig Claiborne of *The New York Times*, shortly after the book crossed his desk in February 1968. "It is said that the popularity of Americans in France is at its lowest ebb in history," his piece began. "After the Gauls read *The Cooking of Provincial France* by Time-Life Books, things are very likely to get worse":

> For months the projected series of Time-Life Books on *Foods of the World* has been the talk of the world of food. The volumes are reportedly financed by one of the largest budgets in cookbook history . . . [and] those who have lent their names to the project include Julia Child, M.F.K. Fisher, [and] James Beard. . . . The project could have been a grail-like monument to good taste. On the other hand, if *The Cooking of Provincial France* is a sample of what's to come, now's the time to mourn in the name of Georges Auguste Escoffier, Carême,

Vatel and Ali Bab. . . . At best, this book is the most dubious sample of the regional cooking of France. . . . [It falls] embarrassingly short of the scope and imagination that a work of such promised value could have provided.

Claiborne focused less on Fisher's gaffe-ridden text than on the recipes: "One suspects these recipes were in somebody's files and were—in their opinion—just too good to resist including," he wrote. And indeed, many of them (such as the *Homard à l'Américaine* recipe) bear a striking resemblance to recipes in *Mastering the Art of French Cooking*. "No effort has been made to relate the provinces to the origin of the recipes. The volume, while ignoring [many] regional treasures . . . includes . . . such mundane dishes as roast chicken.* It also details how to boil artichokes and asparagus! When I need to know how to boil asparagus I can borrow Fannie Farmer."[57]

Claiborne's scorched-earth review appeared the same day that Time-Life threw its deluxe book party to launch the series at Manhattan's Four Seasons restaurant. The journalist Nora Ephron subsequently wrote a gleeful *New York* magazine article using the occasion to profile the gossip-ridden, jealousy-plagued, backstabbing world of the newly emerging American food establishment, since the critical failure of the book on the very day of its magnificent launch party made a perfect set piece for her malicious group portrait. In Ephron's version, the failure of the book (which she saw as both a total failure and a trivial failure, given the deplorable state of the world in 1968) fell not on M.F.K. Fisher (who, like Julia Child, knew enough to be discreetly absent from the party), but rather on Michael Field, "the bird-like, bespectacled, frenzied gourmet cook and cookbook writer" who had taken charge of the production, and (according to Ephron) earned a fortune in doing so. While delighting in the "bitchy, gossipy, devious" ways of the new American food establishment, Ephron (who was herself being bitchy, gossipy, and devious) registered no real opinion about the quality of the book in question, except to point out

---

*The Time-Life editors had intentionally chosen French foods likely to appeal to an American appetite. The first five recipes, for example, were for *soufflé au fromage, saucisson en croûte, quiche au fromage*, "omelette," and *crêpes fourrées gratinées*.

its most glaring and undeniable fault: namely, its cover illustration—which, though captioned a soufflé,* was in fact a meringue baked in a dessert ramekin. Further into the article, however, Ephron did quote Craig Claiborne (who, she had implied, was waging a jealous vendetta against Michael Field) as exclaiming, "I don't give a good Goddam about Michael [Field]. . . . The misinformation! The inaccuracies in that book! I made a stack of notes thicker than the book itself on the errors in it. It's shameful."[58]

In the world of cookbook publishing, an extremely bad review in *The New York Times* is a rare thing (since few cookbooks are reviewed there), and presumably this one should have been enough to send *The Cooking of Provincial France* off to the remainder bin posthaste. But this particular book was the first of a large, ambitious, and heavily financed book series being marketed by an international corporation that had already presold a first printing of fifty thousand copies to its subscribers. As the lead volume in the series, it was simply too big and too important to fail. (Instead, Time-Life would "serve it forth," then quietly withdraw the 1968 edition several months later, to revise and correct it as much as possible before rereleasing it in 1969.)

⚜

Nevertheless, the story of the book was not yet over, because Time-Life was also about to publish the book in German and in French. Amazingly, no one at the company seems to have anticipated an adverse reaction to the book in France, even after Claiborne's review. Instead, Time-Life entered Paris with all flags flying and launched the cookbook series with a lavish party-to-end-all-parties, erecting an enormous striped circus tent in the former cheese pavilion of the soon-to-be-demolished Les Halles,† and hiring top Parisian chef Gaston Lenôtre to create the five different buffet stations to show off five

---

* This caption for the cover photo appears on the copyright page of *The Cooking of Provincial France*: "The cover: a dessert soufflé, delicately puffed and golden brown on the peak, is a perfectly achievable French dish—if done right."

† The French government had decreed the relocation of the great wholesale market of Les Halles as early as 1959. The last market day took place ten years later, on February 28, 1969. The iron-and-glass pavilions of Les Halles, engineering marvels of their day, were destroyed to facilitate an urban redevelopment scheme in August 1971. A single pavilion was preserved in pieces, however, and

different cuisines of the world: French, Italian, Chinese, Scandinavian, and American. Celebrities, statesmen, and jet-setters were invited to this extravagant buffet as a way of attracting European publicity; attendees included Maurice Chevalier, Mrs. Moshe Dayan, Baron Alain de Rothschild, Bernard Lanvin, the Maharanee of Baroda, and a goodly number of what one journalist referred to as "[fashion] models in see-through dresses." The gathering quickly devolved into a feeding frenzy: "quite frankly the French buffet looked and tasted the best," the *International Herald Tribune* reported; "With a menu including *caneton à l'orange* over *mousse de foie gras*, fresh salmon from the Loire, Florens Louis Champagne and a Château La Mission Haut-Brion '04, it's little wonder that the French buffet ran dry very early in the game."[59]

The *New York Times* Paris correspondent John L. Hess happened to be at the party—and being, along with his wife, a great fan of French cuisine, he took home a copy of the new French-language edition of the book. *Newsweek* carried an account of what happened next:

> The guests dined on an international variety of dishes that ranged from old-fashioned chicken pie to Ch'un-chuan (Pâté Imperial [*sic*]*), scampi alla grilla [*sic*], sauté de lapin and clam chowder. Not a few of the diners remarked that the book—written by such U.S. authorities as Mrs. M.F.K. Fisher, Michael Field and Julia Child—was clearly assured of success because the editors had the rare good judgment to have a commentary and footnotes supplied by no one less than Robert J. Courtine. . . . Then they took their gift copies and went their various ways, [with *New York Times*] correspondent [John] Hess [going] home to his French-speaking wife, Karen, who is perhaps the best American cook in Paris. She started reading and then started laughing.

---

subsequently reconstructed in Nogent-sur-Marne, in the eastern suburbs, where it has been renamed the Pavillon Baltard, after the architect who designed and built Les Halles from 1853 to 1870.

* A spring roll. The correct spelling is *pâté impérial* (it is also known in France as a *rouleau impérial*, and more commonly as a *nem*, after its Vietnamese name, *nem rán*).

Not long thereafter, the account of what made Karen Hess laugh appeared under Hess's byline in the *Times*, under the headline "Time-Life Cookbook: It's Self-Roasting." So it was, because Courtine's foot-notes turned out to be a witty and sometimes vitriolic attack on the book's more pretentious and egregious errors.[60]

As Hess himself reported,

A book that pans itself has been published, inadvertently it would seem, by Time-Life, Inc. . . . [which recently saw fit to engage] at a substantial fee—the only kind of fee mentioned in the project—France's most feared gastronomic critic, Robert J. Courtine, one of whose pen names is Le Grincheux—the surly one [to write the book's French introduction and foot-notes.] *La Cuisine des Provinces de France* [has since] become an item for collectors of curiosa, [for] the notes are a running heckling commentary on the book.

Courtine was a self-described "militant gastronome," a right-wing Frenchman (and monarchist) who had begun his career in journalism as a member of the anti-Semitic political movement Action Française. During World War II he had supported the Vichy regime, and sub-sequently paid the price for his collaboration, receiving a sentence of ten years' hard labor. Although released from prison after only two years, he was permanently banned from expressing his political views on French airwaves, and so, in returning to journalism, he took a job as a restaurant and food critic, writing on French gastronomy for *Le Monde* under the pseudonym La Reynière.* Starting in 1956, he pub-lished several dozen highly respected books on food and wine, including the 493-page *La Vraie Cuisine Française* ("True French Cuisine"). As that title suggests, Courtine understood French cuisine as a vital ex-pression of French national and cultural identity, and therefore wor-thy of greatest possible consideration and respect.

While Hess and *Newsweek* subsequently made Courtine sound like an impossible old curmudgeon, he was relatively young at the time of

---

* After Grimod de la Reynière.

the scandal (fifty-one) and his introduction and footnotes to the book, as well as his published statements about them after the fact, make him seem, if anything, like a man with a good sense of humor who had simply written what needed to be written. That he had sabotaged Time-Life's publication was an unlikely conclusion to the fun he had had with the project; but surely the fault for that colossal and very expensive blunder lay not with Courtine but his corporate overseers. As a conservative nationalist turned obsessive culinary expert, Courtine did not attempt to explain to the French reading public that the book they held in their hands was badly written and ill-informed, because he had not been allowed to do so. In fact, he had not been allowed to change or edit any of the text, for Time-Life had paid an American celebrity a great deal of money to write it. So he simply did what he had been asked to do.

His footnotes are, in their way, a model of restraint. Nearly any French person who cared about cooking would have noticed and exclaimed at the blunders Courtine calmly footnoted (as Simone Beck's eight lengthy memos testify). For example, when the book had described Breton *cotriade* (a fish, potato, and onion soup similar to a chowder) as highly spiced, Courtine had not exclaimed, as most Frenchmen would, that nothing in Breton cuisine is highly spiced—for Brittany is ethnically Celtic, with bland celtic cooking traditions. Rather, he simply noted that "*cotriade* is in fact not at all spiced."

In her section on Champagne, Fisher had written "sparkling champagne . . . [is] costly, and it is impossible to imagine using it in cooking. Recipes which call for 'champagne' should never be made with the sparkling wine if they are to be heated in any way."[61] But again, that simply wasn't true. French cooks had utilized sparkling champagne in their cooking for at least a hundred years, as the *Guide Culinaire* (and innumerable other French cookbooks) made perfectly obvious. (So too, for that matter, did Alice Toklas's modest chapter on cooking with champagne in *Aromas and Flavors of Past and Present*.) "A dish *à la Champagne* certainly does use bubbly wine," Courtine wrote in his footnote, "that's what it's about."

To Fisher's suggestion that one could get fresh mountain trout and crayfish in any mountainside restaurant or *auberge*, Courtine pointed out (again, discreetly, via footnote) that the taking of such fish had been outlawed for years as a conservation measure—something Fisher might have realized had she not been relying on her memories of 1929 and 1938 to write the book. (In fact, Parisians had been relying on Russian and Silesian imports of crayfish since the earliest years of the twentieth century.)[62] And to Fisher's suggestion that Roquefort cheese made a choice accompaniment to the best and finest of wines, Courtine didn't point out that no wines are improved by such a pairing; he simply noted "to recommend a great wine with Roquefort is a grave error," something any wine-loving Frenchman already knew. Likewise in Fisher's section entitled "The Terrine: Key to the Cuisine," where she had stated that "serious French eaters—which means serious Frenchmen—often gauge the standards of almost any kitchen, whether great or modest, by its *terrine* (or *pâté*) *maison*, the special product of the house or restaurant," Courtine suggested that rather than judging "the quality of a restaurant on the *terrine maison*," a gourmet was much more inclined to "shun it like a plague." He wasn't being bitchy, since a chilled slab of terrine or pâté is a relatively dull and greasy way of starting a meal, and rarely (if ever) the preferred starter in a French restaurant of quality, not least because terrines are so commonly available at a *traiteur* (or *charcuterie*, or market stall), and therefore more the sort of thing an average Frenchman would routinely eat at home.*

In her chapter entitled "Poultry: Those Foolproof Fowl," Fisher had written "wild birds, because of their diet and the strenuous lives they lead, are tougher, dryer, and more flavorsome than most tame ones, and they must be cooked somewhat differently, in a fashion likely to involve slow simmerings rather than roastings."[63] Courtine's footnote here was simple: "Except partridge, pheasant, quail, etc." Again, he wasn't being arbitrary: according to Escoffier, Montagné, and virtually all other French culinary authorities, a fast high-temperature roasting is the preferred and recommended method of cooking these treasured, dainty, expensive morsels, from woodcock and ortolan to

---

* In *From Julia Child's Kitchen*, Julia Child herself would soon observe that a pâté is "no more difficult and only slightly more expensive than the average American meat loaf" (p. xiii).

lapwing and wild duck.* Courtine made a similarly matter-of-fact comment when, near the end of the book, Fisher recounted a favorite story about going to dinner in Marseille with a friend who despised garlic. After declaring he would allow none of it in his salad, he had ultimately loved the salad he was served—into which, at Fisher's instigation, the waiter had slipped three cloves of finely chopped garlic. Considering the story critically, Courtine wrote in his footnote, "It seems doubtful to me that the garlic taste would quite disappear." And of course anyone who has ever eaten just one clove of finely chopped raw garlic would surely agree.

Courtine also very calmly corrected a number of basic recipes in the book, including the ones for mayonnaise and *sauce hollandaise*, doing so in accordance with Escoffier (who used no cream in his hollandaise[†] and no mustard in his mayonnaise[‡]). But ultimately he chose simply to shrug at the vast cultural divide that existed between France and the United States, and perhaps always would. "Think what a cookbook on America might be," he suggested to his readers, were it "written by a scrupulous and food-loving Frenchman."

Newsweek recounted the subsequent fallout:

> The first reaction on both sides of the Atlantic was a number of red faces. In New York, Time Life editors admitted that they had not had Courtine's footnotes translated until after the French edition was ready for publication, and suggested that the Paris office had been derelict in letting them slip through.
>
> Then everyone concerned set about putting the best possible face on the affair. "I did not intend to be mean or make

---

* There are a few exceptions to this rule, as with the eye-catchng *perdreaux en chartreuse*, in which an aged partridge (a *perdrix*) is slow-cooked with cabbage to give its flavor to the vegetable—but that aged bird is then simply discarded and the cabbage (after being arranged in a mold with other delicate cooked vegetables and some sausages) is unmolded onto a platter and topped with quickly roasted young partridges (the *perdreaux*) (Escoffier, *Guide Culinaire*, p. 591).

† Escoffier specifies that hollandaise sauce is to be made of butter, egg yolks, vinegar, salt, pepper, and lemon juice (*Guide Culinaire*, p. 22).

‡ Escoffier specifies using vinegar, not mustard, which creates a lighter and more delicate mayonnaise (*Guide Culinaire*, p. 49).

mischief," says Courtine, adding slyly, "I don't say that this book is good or bad. I say it's interesting because of its errors. It's fascinating."

Finally, the publishers inserted in each of the more than 10,000 copies of the book that are being distributed in France a letter from New York editor-in-chief Maitland A. Edey. "Although sometimes a little harsh, his [Courtine's] remarks are not any the less judicious," wrote Edey. "In addition, they have the advantage of adding more value to a work which, in itself, is already fascinating."[64]

And Hess of *The New York Times* noted:

Mr. Courtine in a telephone interview confirmed that he had received reproaches from Time-Life since the book appeared, but said he couldn't imagine why. He had done the job he was paid for, he said. "I think it's rather amusing," he said. "I hope they'll see it that way too."

In New York yesterday, [Dick] Williams, editor of Time-Life's *Foods of the World* Library, said that "no heads have rolled, are rolling or are about to roll." . . . [And] reached by telephone at her home in St. Helena, Calif[ornia], Mrs. Fisher said, "I feel Mr. Courtine has a right to his opinions. I don't think the book is important in France. If I were French, I wouldn't give it the time of day. Even if I were American— and I wrote the introduction, after all—I wouldn't."[65]

Fisher was being jaw-droppingly disingenuous here: she was not the author of "the introduction," she was the author of the book. But she was once again doing what she did best: spinning a tale featuring herself as blameless heroine. Time-Life's editors were furious at Fisher for her disinclination to acknowledge the book as her own, but by then, of course, there was nothing they could do.

To those readers who cared about responsible, well-researched food writing, however, Fisher's failure was clear. "That Grande Cuisine Volume of Time-Life," Sybille Bedford subsequently wrote Elizabeth David. "What an expensive mess they make of their 'projects.' Well, projects are doomed; there are only books written by solitary individuals. M.F.K. Fisher sent a copy to Eda. One did not know what to say to her."[66] And after Bedford and Lord invited Richard Olney to dinner with Fisher a year later, he was even more candid in his assessment, writing to his brother James several days afterward,

> As for M.F.K. Fisher, she remains sweet but is essentially empty-headed, has no palate (eats practically nothing and drinks tumblers-full of sweet vermouth all day) and her writing is silly, pretentious drivel. I had never read her until these last days when Eda piled the books in my arms before going to bed each night. She had already asked me several times what I thought of M.F.—who is, after all, her old school chum and friend of fifty years. I kept saying, "very nice, ever so sweet, I like her very much. . . ." [But] Eda insisted on knowing what I thought of the books. I mumbled a few embarrassed inanities before blurting out that they were trash. She breathed a sigh of relief (as if to say, "It's about time!") "I'm glad you feel that way," she said. "Of course, I agree."[67]

FIFTEEN

Olney in the Var

By the time he looked through M.F.K. Fisher's *The Cooking of Provincial France* at Sybille Bedford and Eda Lord's house, Richard Olney had been established full-time in Solliès-Toucas for about two years. His little ruined shepherd's cottage had kept him very busy during that time, in large part because he had done most of the restoration of it himself, bit by bit. The one-bedroom home featured a combination kitchen and hearth as its main room, but the real gathering place for company was the terrace just outside, which featured a dining table tucked into a combination of sun awning and grape arbor. Early on Olney strung it with the multicolored lights suggestive of a provincial *guinguette*,* and it was under these festive lights that Olney and his friends spent the majority of their time, enjoying conversation and meals in the fine, dry, herb-scented Provençal air.

Reconstruction and improvement of the house and grounds would continue for more than a decade. There were some occasional setbacks—as in the spring of 1968, when an old retaining wall under the east side of the house collapsed, turning the bedroom into a vast heap of rubble. But the kitchen, the center of all activity, held strong.

---

* An open-air restaurant and dance hall.

It had recently acquired a substantial *batterie de cuisine*, thanks to old friends in Clamart who were closing their café-restaurant and getting rid of their ancient, oversize copper pots. When hung from the wall, these gleaming pots and pans of an earlier time became the room's main decorative feature. And in the summer of 1964, with the assistance of his brothers Byron and James, Richard built the great corner fireplace that would henceforth define the room. Out in the garden there were all sorts of other projects in various stages of development, including a swimming pool on one of the olive terraces above the house, created in a quarried-out rock basin that had formerly been used for watering livestock. The pool took four days and nights to fill using a simple garden hose, but its cool clear water proved refreshing in the oppressive heat of summer. Likewise, as Olney recounted, "at the southwestern corner of the terrace, sheltered from the southern and western sun by rock walls, Garin, with a dramatic gesture, swung a pickax, pierced the earth, and decreed, 'Your wine cellar will be here.' . . . Nearly six years later it was finished."[1]

Guest accommodation remained minimal and rustic throughout the 1960s, so much so that the place sometimes felt like a campsite. "I had not yet brought water from the far end of the terrace [in]to the house, [so] toilet duties were performed on the hillside," Olney would later recall. "Cooking was done on a single gas ring attached to a bottle of butane gas, meats were grilled over bonfire embers, and one bathed out of doors with a hose." The house had no telephone, nor even a road leading up to the property—only an ancient, steep, and narrow footpath right-of-way. Still, there was plenty of room for anyone who cared to visit: with seven glorious acres of terraced olive groves rising upward from the house and looking out over the Gapeau Valley, friends were welcome to pitch a tent anywhere they liked, or simply sleep out under the stars. For those who needed more luxurious accommodation, there were simple *chambres d'hôtes* down in the village, and later a very basic motel. A second bedroom would be built onto the house in subsequent years, and in time an artist's studio, one that could also double as a bedroom. Ultimately a deal would be struck with a neighbor to create a steep driveway leading to a tiny parking area just at the head

of the property—even though Olney himself did not drive and had
no car.

From season to season, but particularly in summer, the gaily lit
terrace before the house hosted something akin to the "Saturday Night
Function" of Clamart days. And because getting to the house took so
long, Olney's guests (who came not only from Paris but also from
Britain and the United States) would routinely stay a week or two,
creating a nonstop house party during the warmer months. Olney's old
phonograph and ever expanding collection of *bal musette* and jazz
LPs provided music both indoors and out. Work on the house and
garden was always a part of any visit, but for those disinclined to
work, there were also shady nooks for reading, talking, or simply enjoying nature. The thyme-scented air floating up off the steep, sun-
baked hillsides, combined with the modest parterres of flowers and
herbs that Olney laid out below the dining terrace, provided ongoing
delight to the senses. So too did various daily experiments in the
kitchen, and various rare and interesting bottles emerging cool and
well-rested from the deep, dark wine cellar.

Visitors came even in winter. Provence can be cold, windy, and
bleak during that season, but unlike Paris, it is neither damp nor dark,
and in fact the little house with its southeastern exposure remained
sunny and bright pretty much all year long. The garden, though dor-
mant, remained formally beautiful, and was sheltered from the mistral
by the steep cliffs and olive terraces rising up behind the property to
the north and west, making it a good place to sit out and enjoy the sun.
Georges Garin spent the month of February 1966 with Olney in Solliès-
Toucas, recovering from a near nervous breakdown. The two friends
passed many an afternoon puttering around the intimate little kitchen
together—cooking, drinking, talking about food and wine. The large
stone hearth kept the place toasty warm even on the coldest of days,
and proved a great place to experiment with old-fashioned cooking
techniques. "Garin loved working there, in particular, grilling," Olney later recalled. Along with various meats roasted upon a brazier,
they prepared *gigot à la ficelle*, a whole leg of lamb suspended by a
string before the blazing fire, slowly twirling back and forth in front
of the flames. Another favorite was *truffes sous la cendre*, a whole black

truffle wrapped in pork fat, then tightly sealed in several layers of greaseproof paper and left to cook half an hour in the ashes of the hearth.

❧

In the summer of 1967, Olney had barely returned from the United States with the contract for his first book, *The French Menu Cookbook*, when Garin came to live with him again—this time for the entire month of August. Ostensibly he had come to recover from a minor operation, but in fact he arrived with Mary Painter, and clearly the two wanted to relax and make love in a place far away from Garin's wife. Because both were prone to heavy drinking and dramatic, even violent outbursts, the month was not an easy one, particularly since Olney was just then drafting his manuscript. Garin's sudden, bizarre fits of rage, combined with the couple's drunken antics, both amorous and otherwise, disturbed and occasionally disgusted Olney. As he later wrote, "It took me a long time to understand—and I was never able to accept—that for Garin, violent, irrational quarrels were an essential element in a bosom friendship."

Olney tried hard to make his contractual deadline of September, and doubtless he was grateful to have Garin with him as a sounding board and adviser that summer, despite all the brawling and commotion. But because his guests proved so distracting, he needed to wait until they left to complete the work, which took him well into the fall. When his publisher accepted the manuscript and paid the remainder of his small advance, he spent it immediately on a La Cornue cookstove. But because there was no road up to the house, the massive iron stove could not be delivered; ultimately it needed to be hoisted up the narrow, winding footpath by a crew of local workmen.

The simplicity of Olney's living conditions, the sophistication of his palate, and the constant presence of guests arriving for indeterminate visits (often bearing lavish gifts of luxury foods and wines) meant that Olney's writing continued to be informed at both ends of the socioeconomic spectrum. Much like Alice Toklas, he was a hands-on, do-it-yourself cook, gardener, and homemaker living on the tightest of budgets; at the same time he was also a deeply cultured, widely traveled, and exceptionally well-read host-gourmand with a great enthusiasm for complex kitchen projects, luxury ingredients, and fine wine. Moreover, and despite his American background, he adhered to the French way of doing things, embracing the inherent logic of traditional (and often thrift-oriented) home cooking practices, even with those recipes featuring the most expensive of ingredients. So Solliès-Toucas became a sort of cooking laboratory, one in which traditional French food-preparation techniques were undertaken with the above-average (French) home cook in mind.

In presenting French cooking to American readers in his first book, Olney went to great lengths to disambiguate the term "French cuisine," noting that it might take several distinct forms:

> Classical French cooking, that which from the beginning made France's reputation abroad, is naturally eclectic. It was, and is, created by men—professional chefs. It is refined and, in execution, often involved. In the hands of a loyal artisan it can be very good indeed; in the hands of a great chef it can be sublime. . . .
>
> In contrast to the classical cuisine of professional kitchens [there] are the traditions of regional cooking—as various as the provinces are numerous, but all related in character in the sense that each is the direct outgrowth of the combined wealth and poverty of the immediate countryside and the limitations of the kitchens. It is essentially peasant cooking, elaborated by generations of peasant women who were never far from the kitchen and whose imaginations were forced into flower through necessity and limited means. [And there is also *cuisine bourgeoise*, though] as a rigidly defined aspect of a way of life it no longer exists as a category apart. It is richer than regional cooking in the sense that it uses more expensive products, yet it is also less imaginative . . . [and] much in it has been borrowed from professional classical cuisine. The food prepared by Françoise and caressingly described by the narrator in *À la Recherche du Temps Perdu* is exemplary *cuisine bourgeoise*.[2]

Even as he completed his first cookbook, Olney found himself drawn more and more to this "essentially peasant cooking"—especially that of Provence. He loved *haute cuisine* but no longer saw the point in attempting it at home; and at any rate he was living closer to nature now, and the ingredients he had most ready access to were Provençal ingredients. In simplifying his cooking practices and connecting them to the place in which he lived, he only regretted that his little property was not more capable of sustaining a proper garden. But the olive terraces were essentially beds of rock and gravel, and no matter how much he improved his soil, he would still lack adequate water for its necessary irrigation. He did, however, raise his own poultry (mostly for eggs); he foraged; he grew his own herbs; and just as in Clamart, he did his marketing every couple of days, this time walking a half mile down to the village for meats, fish, fruits, vegetables, and fresh milk and butter from a modest village dairy. This new way of life would ultimately inform his second book, *Simple French Food*, precisely because it was this better sort of French home cooking that seemed to him most worth sharing with American readers:

The eating habits of the peasants and the working classes [in France] have not noticeably altered in the past twenty or thirty years. They remain oblivious to food trends and fashions, loyal to the regional cooking of their mothers and grandmothers. One of the great moments of the working day is the morning *casse-croûte*, a charcuterie, cheese, and wine break after the first couple of morning working hours. Lunch is typically a simple hors d'oeuvre—crudités or a salad—followed by a stew, *gibelotte** or other, or a *grillade*,† and cheese, possibly fruit, [and] ordinary red wine. And supper is simple—soup, cheese, and wine—for they do not believe in going to bed on a full stomach (it causes nightmares). Except in white wine regions, white wine is looked upon with suspicion, whereas red wine is considered to be a necessary aid to

---

* A stew of rabbit in white wine.
† A generic French term describing grilled meats of various sorts.

digestion. The weekly celebration at table is the Sunday lunch which may be built around a pot-au-feu, a roast leg of lamb, a *daube*,* etc. and accompanied by a better-than-usual wine.

Both *The French Menu Cookbook* and *Simple French Food* would give Americans a sense of French food as it is cooked and presented by good French home cooks, using French ingredients, and relying on the characteristic French sense of order, harmony, logic, proportion, and restraint to make meals memorable. "Our greatest debt to the French, in terms of the table, lies in their concept of a menu, as it has evolved over the last century with progressively greater simplification: a composition of a few dishes and a few wines, intimately interrelated, to create a dramatic and harmonious entity, an ephemeral but unforgettable work of art when the composition is successful."

Olney had no particular agenda or ulterior motive in the writing of either of these books: he was not selling himself as cooking instructor, cultural anthropologist, or connoisseur of fine dining. He had no interest in celebrity either. Rather, he was sharing an enormously complicated body of cultural and gastronomic information that had long fascinated him, doing so for readers minimally acquainted with it, but eager to learn it. He had too great a respect for his subject to oversimplify it or "dumb it down," but he also did his best not to make it seem overly complex. In *The French Menu Cookbook*'s section on French wine, for example—about which Olney might very well have gone on interminably, given the depth and breadth of his hard-won knowledge—he simply wrote:

> To analyze a wine, the taster takes no food, for the palate must remain virgin, unaffected by other flavors. But wine's principal role is to give pleasure, and that role is best played at table in the context of a menu. . . . Any wine that is honestly made can be perfect of its sort; the line separating great wines from others is tenuous—mostly a matter of complexity, something more easily sensed than defined. A great wine partakes of the same mystery and inspires the same awe as a

---

* A covered, slow-cooked stew (usually made of beef) with a liquid base of red wine.

work of art. . . . [But as a general rule] the proportion of wines characterized as fine, great or noble is infinitesimal by comparison with the others. [In fact] many wines are best drunk as young as possible and without too much thought.*[3]

Later in life, Olney would be asked to clarify his position about French food and wine because some (American) critics had suggested his writings were too challenging and alien, while others thought him too disconnected from the American kitchen to address American home cooks in any meaningful or productive way. In an informal letter to a fellow food professional, he attempted to explain how his love of French food and wine was intimately related to his life in Solliès-Toucas:

My approach to the table is not very complicated. All I ask of food is that it taste good and that it be kind to the wine that accompanies it. I don't care whether the food is called French cuisine or not. I am often asked, "If that is the way you feel about food, why is it so important that you live in France?" The answer is not easy and probably never very clear—I feel at home in France; I like the French mind and wit, "*l'esprit malicieux*";[†] I like an atmosphere in which, whenever one sits down to a meal, however simple, it is conceived as an aesthetic experience in which wine always has its place; I like to be able to furnish my cellar with wines that are delivered to me directly from the vineyards at which I have first tasted them. More specifically, I love the hillside on which I live, the fireplace in which I cook, the grape-arbored terrace on which I eat for half the year, the quality of the Provençal light, the wild herb scents which permeate the air, and the presence of olive trees in the landscape.[4]

---

*Olney here echoes Édouard de Pomiane, who in *Cooking with Pomiane* wrote (with characteristic charm), "I frequently drink those marvelous wines which are called '*petits vins.*' . . . They have the charm of a young face, flushed, smiling and radiant. The great wines of France have the distinction of an eighteenth-century marquise. The little wines, the gaiety of our beautiful country girls. One can love both of them. And indeed, don't they say that the Pompadour dressed herself as a village maiden to please Louis XV?" (p. 269).

†Trans.: Mischievous wit (not, as one might think, "malicious wit").

If Olney's earlier years in Paris had been characterized by his long-running (and occasionally explosive) bohemian-expatriate, multiracial, multiethnic house parties in Clamart, his new life in Solliès-Toucas was characterized by evenings that were far more subdued. In this quiet and remote place, Olney surely faced new challenges, but most were work-related. His solitary days consisted of reading, writing, painting, chores, and various forms of creative or remunerative work. His greatest struggle was with loneliness: he was by nature introverted, and paradoxically found company exhausting even as isolation depressed him. Dinners, when he had company (and he worked hard at cultivating friends as dinner guests), were a relief from that daily loneliness: full of spirited and informed conversation, warmth, and good feeling. Many of his new friends, being equally devoted to the pleasures of food and wine, were just as interested as Olney in the preparation and enjoyment of a good and imaginative meal, or the sharing of a particularly fine and distinctive bottle of wine. So these mealtimes often had a collaborative or participatory feeling, with a great deal of excitement and discussion about what was being prepared, and how, and how it might best be served and enjoyed.

Olney's friend Michel Lemmonier began visiting Solliès in 1964, when the house and garden were not much more than a work site. But from the very first moment he was enraptured. He wrote about the place several times for *Cuisine et Vins de France*, and in one piece in particular he praised Olney as an extraordinary combination of cook, artist, and writer who gave the place its heart and soul. Since this "*Américain (Gourmand) à Paris*" was now a minor celebrity at *CVF*, Lemmonier took pains to describe his new life in Provence:

> We are walking up an endlessly long stone stair set among terraces of olive trees, almond trees, [amid] bushes of rosemary and thyme [and] all those [other] plants whose names are also the names of perfumes. And then, *voilà!*—here we are, in the midst of an exceptionally well cultivated terrace garden, arranged as what might be called a *jardin de curé*—a wonderful tangle of herbs, kitchen-garden vegetables, and flowers. Richard Olney is usually right there in the middle of it all, hand on

spade, or else he is at work before the great stone fireplace that was for a long time his only cooking fire, simmering the stocks and preparing those dishes that it will soon be our great pleasure to consume.

Often at this house we come across friends we have in common, or else others who are soon to be new friends—many among them restaurateurs who are visiting Richard while in the midst of their own summer holidays. . . . Take, for example, the unexpected silhouette of Georges Garin, as I had never before seen him in Paris—having abandoned his chef's toque and white smock, he has merely a simple bandana covering his head, and he is standing with Olney over their many pots—nostrils flaring, eye attentive, his mouth at one moment full of patient and indulgent explanations, and at others imperious and delivering ultimatums at this partycrasher (me) who keeps asking impertinent questions.

. . . One would need to make a long list of all those meals, both simple and elaborate, that have been prepared in this kitchen, a kitchen just as bohemian as the one in Clamart, and one equally just barely functional—particularly when compared to the elaborate kitchens one sees in glamorous magazines. Nonetheless all the objects in the kitchen are of beautiful material, form, and utility. . . . And amid all our laughter and our joking, what an interminable lot of dishwashing we have done here!

. . . These [were] simple, perfect meals. Sometimes they were menus that have appeared [in Olney's column] in the pages of this magazine. Extraordinary among the dishes were soups including an *aïgo boulido rustique*, a noble *potage Germiny*,* and a cream of artichoke soup thickened with ground hazelnuts. And then such lovely main dishes: *rouget de roche* marinated

---

* *Aïgo boulido rustique* is a traditional Provençal soup: boiling salted water is flavored with sage leaves, bay, thyme, and a handful of crushed garlic cloves, then strained and poured over dried bread crusts. (More sophisticated versions, such as the one featured in *The French Menu Cookbook*, feature a liaison of egg yolks, Parmesan, and olive oil.) *Potage Germiny* is a stock-based cream of sorrel soup, enriched with egg yolks and crème fraîche.

with wild fennel and olive oil and then grilled over vine branches; *loup de mer* in a sauce of sea urchins; delicious wild asparagus; the unique and incomparable Marseillaise *pieds et paquets*; and of course mushrooms—whether *cèpes à la borde-laise*, or else *lactaires délicieux*, one time grilled over the fire, another time served over artichoke hearts braised in white wine. Another time it was veal medallions braised and served over a puree of sorrel, and yet another time it was a shoulder of lamb, marinated and then grilled with zucchini. Or a chicken fricassee in the style of the Vaucluse, or a *salmis* of thrushes, which evoked for us one more time the fine article on the subject of [Olney's] *salmis* written by Simon Arbellot—or else a *mousseline* of chicken,* of such a high and rare tradition and perfection. . . .

Such wines we had, as well—we drank them, discussed them, and appreciated each one of them as accompaniments to these marvelous dishes. Take, for example, a simple wine we sampled from a vineyard right nearby—with an interesting aroma of licorice, it was full of personality—a remarkable find, particularly if you have had the wisdom [like Olney] to buy it in a demijohn and bottle it up yourself! Or else perhaps it was a wine made by one of the greatest of our *grands seigneurs*: Château Cassevert[†] '62, or a Château Bouscaut,[‡] both the red and the white. I fondly remember as well a 1964 Clos de la Roche[§] made by Charles Rousseau,[¶] already full and beginning to bloom, beautifully harmonious, with aromas of amber and musk growing deeper as we drank it, and with a particularly long finish . . . and also a 1950 Château d'Yquem.

[All of this we enjoyed to music from Olney's collection of old French recordings, including] songs by Fréhel and

---

* A rich, light chicken mousse made with whipped cream and stiffly beaten egg whites.

[†] A *grand cru* Saint-Émilion.

[‡] Once a *premier cru* Graves AOC, Château Bouscaut is today part of the Pessac-Léognan AOC (established in 1987).

[§] A Burgundian *grand cru* AOC, located in the *commune* of Morey-St. Denis.

[¶] A well-known Burgundian winegrower and producer.

by Damia,* warbling into the night off an old portable phonograph . . .

. . . This same table out on the patio that we set each night with such pleasure, we have often found in daylight covered with pots and pans, papers and a typewriter—and yet at other times with tubes of paint and paintbrushes—bringing together in a great, symbolic disorder the three great talents of this "American in France"—for both his painting and his writing have the same virtue as his cooking: simplicity; yet with refinement and sensuality. And his canvases breathe with the same *joie de vivre* as the enchanting countryside that surrounds us.

An "American in France"? Rather, I'd call him "an American Frenchman." An unassuming guy, the kind just as likely to turn to you in the kitchen and say "my pot runneth over" or "unfortunately it flopped," shaking his head and smiling at his wasted effort. Need I tell you that, when he does so, we respond by shaking our heads and smiling fondly as well?[5]

Lemmonier's suggestion that Olney lived in a *jardin de curé* is one of the more telling details of his loving tribute, since it suggests how completely Olney had embraced this discreet and quintessentially French aesthetic. A *jardin de curé*—literally, a "curate's garden"—is a particularly French style of garden: modestly scaled and containing a mixture of flowers, culinary and medicinal herbs, vegetables, a grapevine, and perhaps some fruit bushes or trees, it is conceived as a primarily meditative space. Not as highly productive as a *potager* nor so formal as a cloister, the *jardin de curé* is a place to putter, work, and think. The French passion for privacy and discretion is reflected in this intimate, informal style of gardening; so too is the French understanding of the importance of contact with nature to the proper functioning of the mind, body, and heart.

While anyone visiting Olney's garden would instantly recognize it as a highly personal space, it was also typically Provençal—and

---

*Two great French singers of the *chanson réaliste* style; both inspired Édith Piaf.

specifically of the Var, because of all the departments within the administrative region known as Provence–Alpes–Côte d'Azur, the Var is by far the most humble. Olney's house was small even by French standards, and while its little garden featured a walk-in aviary and chicken run, a gently dripping fountain, a persimmon tree, a wine cellar hewn from solid rock, and, at the center of it all, an outdoor dining area shaded by grapevines and strung with those old-fashioned colored lights, it was at the same time entirely unpretentious. On the contrary, it was intimate and homey. Early on there had been a view from the house down into the valley toward the Mediterranean, but much of that view disappeared as various trees and shrubs grew up around the house and garden, increasing its sense of seclusion and privacy year by year.

The neighborhood, too, was humble. Solliès-Toucas lies just north of Toulon, an industrial port and naval base that has a largely working-class population. Even during Olney's lifetime, the city had begun to sprawl outward, turning the once sleepy countryside into a world of modest, dusty, sunstruck suburbs crisscrossed by highways and strip malls. Unlike the fashionable nearby coastal resorts of Hyères, St.-Tropez, and Ste.-Maxime, Solliès-Toucas is far from the sea, on the way to nowhere, and holds little interest for the Parisian or international tourist. Simone Beck's Domaine de Bramafam, a few hours' drive over the mountains, was in another world entirely, since it lay in a manicured neighborhood filled with luxury hotels and Michelin-starred restaurants favored by the wealthy, so close to glittering Cannes and Cap d'Antibes. Solliès-Toucas was, in a sense, just the opposite: as some might say, a Provençal Clamart.

❧

Lemmonier's response to Olney's little garden in the Var was not just a response to a friend who was managing to live well on modest means. Rather, he seems to have been saluting Olney's realization of a French ideal, one in which freedom and creativity are made possible through a return to the simple life. The idea goes back to Rousseau and the Enlightenment, and also to the back-to-nature fantasies of Marie Antoinette at Le Hameau, in the gardens at Versailles. That fantasy continues in French culture well into the Romantic era, and then can be found, more locally and more recently, in the Provençal writings and dramas of Alphonse Daudet, Fréderic Mistral, and Marcel Pagnol. One of the reasons Olney was so very much at home in France was that his own vision of a fully realized life was in line with this French ideal. A man of culture, he was also an artisan and a laborer, always ready to roll up his sleeves and get to work, whether in the kitchen, the garden, the studio, or at the typewriter. And if he felt at home amid the left-leaning, working-class culture of the Var, it was probably because he too had grown up in humble circumstances and felt no shame or indignity in living simply. Despite his cultivation and intellect, he had worked with his hands for most of his life, and the living he had made for himself, while modest at best, was not much worse than the life his parents had known back in northwestern Iowa. So the place and people suited him. To Lemmonier (and to other Frenchmen who knew and admired him) Olney seemed to be living a free and complete life: one in which the ascetic had reconciled with the sybarite, the intellectual with the sensualist, the artistically ambitious city dweller with the simple, nature-loving country boy.

But Olney's return to the Simple Life had been undertaken in the French way. Unlike Thoreau—grimly counting his beans alone at Walden Pond—Olney had created at Solliès-Toucas a home that embraced both social life and pleasure, even as it was largely a place of solitude and solitary work. He had retreated from Paris to a life of relative obscurity, but he continued to eat and drink well there, to live comfortably in a garden setting, and to receive a seemingly endless stream of friends and colleagues to his home as guests. "Richard lived a solitary, orderly life [and] he disliked leaving his hillside," the British cookbook editor and writer Jill Norman later observed, "but friends were always welcome: he was generous, thoughtful, forever hospitable. He . . . had no radio or tv, [but he] wrote . . . regularly to his four brothers and two sisters in the States and to friends all over the world: fellow writers Elizabeth David and Sybille Bedford, [and later] chefs Alice Waters and Jeremiah Tower, Simon Hopkinson*, and most of

---

* Simon Hopkinson (1954–) made his name as chef at Bibendum, the top-floor restaurant in the historic Michelin building on Fulham Road, London. Today he is a leading British food writer, television presenter, and critic.

France's greatest winemakers and restaurateurs. He was enormously admired and respected by the French gastronomic community." As a result, artists, cooks, cookbook authors, editors, journalists, winemakers, chefs, novelists, and poets all found their way to his door, and would continue to do so for decades to come. But the best-loved visitors were certainly Olney's brothers and sisters, their spouses, and their children.

Over time, a new kind of collaborative, loose-knit "family" began to come together at Solliès-Toucas—including not just the Olneys, but winemakers Lucien and Lulu Peyraud from nearby Domaine Tempier in Bandol (Olney had been friends with Peyraud since meeting him at the Salon des Arts Ménagers in 1953), and many other longtime colleagues and associates. And the feeling there was much like that of the house in which Olney had grown up: it was a place where the door was always open. James Olney would later write to Sybille Bedford, "Strange though [Richard's] odyssey may have been, it nevertheless had about it a remarkable continuity and internal logic, an integrity and oneness. And the source of this continuity and oneness was undoubtedly Richard's mother and father—*our* mother and father—and Marathon [Iowa] itself. . . . You could take Richard out of Marathon but you could never take Marathon out of Richard."[6] Olney's friend and fellow artist Jane Wilson, who had first met him at the University of Iowa, agreed with that notion, later writing, "whenever I read Dick [Olney] I have an overwhelming whiff of Iowa farm cooking over-laid with artful hands of plain daily know-how . . . and for some reason [I] think on farm grandmothers doing what they do, day-in-day-out."[7] Olney's cooking, gardening, and homemaking efforts also bear comparison to those of Alice Toklas at Bilignin. Toklas's many years of hard work in the château's garden, kitchen, and dining room ultimately turned a furnished country rental into an authentically welcoming home—not only for Stein and Toklas, but for their many visiting friends.

Unlike Marathon or Bilignin, however, Solliès-Toucas was a place where guests actively contributed to the running of the house, doing so in their own free-form way. Like any kitchen, this garden-home was a place devoted to work. And just as in the closing scene of

Voltaire's *Candide*, when Candide and companions finally settle down to a life of quiet labor and "the whole little society entered into this laudable design, each one according to his or her different abilities," so too did Olney's family and guests set to work in Solliès-Toucas. Olney's family correspondence records many such activities over the years. Richard and his brothers turning the compost heap, excavating the future wine cellar, reconstructing a collapsed wall. Olney and Garin devising the evening's menu, then preparing it. Friends dropping by unexpectedly with a case of wine and some freshly caught seafood for an impromptu lunch. Houseguests foraging for purslane or wild asparagus; harvesting, drying, and processing herbs; making homemade herbal vinegar in Olney's *vinaigrier*. The stacking of wood. The hike down to the village for provisions. The cleaning and preparing of the fresh produce and meats or poultry for the evening meal. There were tiresome, thankless, repetitive activities too: the washing and drying of dishes and glasses; the cleaning of the house; bookkeeping; bill paying. But then, also, swimming, reading, painting, listening to music; or else simply sitting over a cup of coffee or a glass of wine or an after-dinner drink. And, above all, plenty of good conversation, most of it taking place around the dinner table, sometimes long past midnight.

Within just a few years, a new generation of young Americans would be doing something similar back in the United States—creating communal living and working arrangements that both challenged traditional notions of family, home, and work, and at the same time suggested a more thoughtful way of living in harmony with nature and with one's fellow man. These American experiments in living would, in time, produce some extraordinary cooks, cookbook authors, artisanal food and wine producers, and even some great restaurateurs. But in Solliès-Toucas it was already happening, in a free-form cross-cultural experiment in bohemian *savoir-vivre* where, like the table on the patio, the focus of attention was, naturally enough, the reasoned enjoyment of good food and wine.

SIXTEEN

The End of the Affair

Olney's move to the South of France in 1968 was hardly unique. By the late 1960s, many other Americans were venturing south, including Olney's good friend James Baldwin, who moved to St.-Paul-de-Vence in 1970. Of course, the Côte d'Azur had been attracting summertime visitors since the 1920s (and wintertime visitors since the previous century), but now Provence was attracting Americans as well, for starting in 1959, the French Tourist Board had hired the Madison Avenue advertising firm of Doyle, Dane, Bernbach to promote Provence heavily among Americans. Though mostly landlocked, the region featured good food and wine; fine hotels; a bright, dry, and salubrious climate; as well as welcoming locals and a very relaxed way of life. As a result, the region's sleepy, inexpensive, somewhat derelict villages and towns suddenly seemed far more attractive and welcoming than cold, gray, overcrowded Paris. Films set in the South—such as Roger Vadim's *And God Created Woman* (1956), starring Brigitte Bardot in St.-Tropez, and Otto Preminger's *Bonjour Tristesse* (1958), set on the Côte d'Azur—also helped promote the seductive beauty of the Midi.

Social unrest, meanwhile, was making Paris less attractive to moneyed Americans. In May 1968 a protest over the failings of France's higher educational system escalated overnight into the city's most intense street fighting since August 1944. Beginning at the Université Paris Ouest Nanterre (a branch of the Sorbonne in a poverty-stricken suburb), these demonstrations spread quickly to the Sorbonne itself, in the heart of the Left Bank. When French police occupied that historic university for the first time in its history, students were quickly joined by left-wing sympathizers from France's major unions, creating a massive, city-wide riot that suddenly threatened to topple de Gaulle's Fifth Republic. Riot police responded by arresting six hundred people within twenty-four hours. The next morning angry demonstrators hurled cobblestones, chopped down trees, threw homemade bombs, and set cars on fire. The French forces retaliated with nightsticks and tear gas. A day later, in protest of this unprecedented use of force against unarmed citizens, thirty thousand students marched arm in arm up the Champs-Élysées singing the Communist "Internationale." Strikes and demonstrations then spread to a dozen cities across the country, shutting down the nation's transport system, social services, tourism industry, and eventually the entire French economy.[1] For the rest of the summer, antibourgeois, anti-imperialist, and anti-American rhetoric was shouted from the rooftops.

While the May 1968 riots made headlines around the world, coverage was particularly strong in the United States. Because of the Vietnam peace talks then taking place in Paris, American cameramen and reporters were on the scene and able to catch the violence, chaos, and destruction as it happened. In the days that followed, American print, television, and radio journalists reported on Maoist, Trotskyist, and Communist revolutionaries addressing mobs across the city, many of them denouncing U.S. capitalism and American imperialism.

This new French hostility toward the American way of life came just as the United States was experiencing terrible social and political problems of its own. The year of 1968 had begun with the Tet Offensive. The assassination of Dr. Martin Luther King, Jr., in April had then triggered riots in Washington, Chicago, and Baltimore. Robert F. Kennedy was assassinated in June, and in August antiwar rioting at the Democratic National Convention brought bloody retaliation from the Chicago police. Small wonder, then, that few Americans wanted to vacation in equally unstable (and leftist, and anti-American) Paris.

At any rate, the city's great popularity among American tourists, which had by now lasted from the early 1950s through the late 1960s, could not sustain itself forever. Or, rather, its popularity was undergoing a demographic change. Until 1957, the majority of American tourists coming to Paris had needed to spend more than a week crossing the Atlantic by ship, then had to make their way to Paris by train—which limited the number of Americans who could afford to visit, and made such visits a rare treat. But by the mid-1960s there were direct flights to Paris from major cities all across the United States, and Paris was within easy reach of many Americans. Budget and package tourism now began to degrade the experience of Paris (and other major European capitals) even as it overwhelmed the city center with throngs of American visitors. At the same time, the city's appeal to top American spenders began to diminish, for Paris had lost its air of exclusivity, and felt more and more like a tourist trap. Dreaming of rare new adventures in harder-to-reach places, luxury-oriented tourists began to jet elsewhere for their fun.

Paris also suffered a different kind of public relations setback in the late 1960s, as many American leftist and countercultural movements set up provisional headquarters there. As Henry Pillsbury, former director of the American Center in Paris, later recalled, "in the wake of May 1968, [we were] often at the mercy of young political power-brokers; every possible group, notably the Black Panthers, laid claim to the throne. It was the heyday of the cheap charter flights . . . there was a lot of hanging out in the lounge and restaurant [at the American Center], it was hard to control."[2] Pillsbury's wife, Judith, similarly remembered scores of American draft dodgers adrift in Paris during that time, avoiding service in Vietnam by living on remittances, many drinking or on drugs, crowding into the American Center daily for use of its free showers and toilets.[3]

Film representations of France and French cuisine during the period record this gradual shift in mood. Unlike the sunny, rather innocuous American visions of Paris that had predominated during the fifties—in movies like *An American in Paris* (1951), *Sabrina* (1954), and *Funny Face* (1957)—the late sixties brought far more sedate renderings of Paris life from Hollywood, and by the early seventies, European filmmakers were exporting a distressingly somber and critical vision of French gastronomic excess. Buñuel's dark comedy *The Discreet Charm of the Bourgeoisie* (1972) suggested that the French preoccupation with dining and food was an appalling manifestation of bourgeois decadence, doing so by constantly frustrating its characters' desire to sit down to a meal. Marco Ferreri's *La Grande Bouffe* (1973), meanwhile, was even more caustic, presenting the story of four disappointed middle-aged men who decide to get together and eat (and fuck) to their deaths. But perhaps the most depressing of all was Bernardo Bertolucci's *Last Tango in Paris* (1972), the story of a boorish, grief-stricken American widower who initiates an anonymous affair with a nineteen-year-old girl, then rapes and sodomizes her using a stick of butter as lubricant. Denounced in the United States as "pornography disguised as art," the film's bleak vision of Paris would haunt the city for decades to come.

American disillusionment with Paris had other sources as well. Jacqueline Kennedy's decision to marry Greek shipping magnate Aristotle Onassis did little to help Franco-American relations, for the two settled into the Sixteenth Arrondissement a few months after their wedding. When André Fontaine, shortly to become editor of *Le Monde*, noted that "Jackie . . . chooses to shock [the world] by marrying a man who could be her father and whose career contradicts—rather strongly, to say the least—the liberal spirit that animated President Kennedy," he was comparatively gentle in his criticism. The American media was much more savage, and its disapproval of "Jackie" spilled over into broader denunciation of Paris and its decadent luxuries. *Time* magazine noted that "in the days after Jack Kennedy's death, millions grieved for the widow . . . [but now] Jacqueline Kennedy seem[s] brusquely to [have] abdicate[d] the throne that Americans had made for her. . . . When she was asked once to decide where and in what era she would have preferred to live, Jacqueline Kennedy picked 18th century France. The unfettered universe of Aristotle Socrates Onassis comes closer to the kingdom of Louis XV . . . than any other around." The article then went on to suggest that the former First Lady's continued "delight in candlelit tête-à-têtes . . . [featuring] French cuisine" were a cruel betrayal of her recently deceased husband, for this was an unduly fancy sort of food "for which he had little gusto."[4] Under the Kennedy administration just a few years earlier, French food, fashion, and decorating had epitomized freshness and sophistication, but now all Americans who cared for such things—such as Jackie Onassis, living in grand luxury in her ugly new husband's fifteen-room penthouse on the avenue Foch—were instead seen as debauched and immoral.

Cost then became another issue that made Paris less and less appealing to the average American. President Richard Nixon was forced to acknowledge that American currency was overvalued in August 1971, and when he took the United States off the gold standard, the dollar experienced an immediate (and steep) drop in value. With American money buying less abroad, European travel was far less of a bargain, and Paris, which had always been considerably more expensive than most other European travel destinations (in part because of its limited hotel space), seemed particularly overpriced. The situation worsened in October 1973, when the Organization of Petroleum Exporting Companies (or OPEC) declared an oil embargo, causing the price of oil to quadruple and travel costs to rise yet again, even as the United States and France were hit with both recession and inflation. This oil embargo slowed the world economy through the end of the 1970s, after which a second oil crisis initiated yet another cycle of panic and recession. According to French historians and economists, it was with the oil crisis that *les Trente Glorieuses*—the thirty glorious years of French social and economic expansion—came to its own crashing end.

⚜

Meanwhile, back in the United States, new fashions, trends, and social aspirations were bringing cuisines other than French into the limelight, including Italian, Chinese, Japanese, and Indian. Most of these cuisines made better sense to the younger generation, since they featured fresher, lighter flavors, cheaper food costs, and more healthful ingredients. They also had a liberal cachet, for in many instances they were the foods of oppressed or third-world nations—and America was just then experiencing a social (if not political) swing to the left.

Dieting concerns also made them popular, for most of these cuisines were better suited to the calorie-conscious home cook. With the advent of the 1960s, the buxom, well-fed screen goddesses of the 1950s were no longer the feminine ideal. The new starlets and fashion models of the late 1960s and 1970s tended instead to be small-breasted and slim-hipped. With top designers creating fashions for this newly slender, elongated, and uncorseted female form, women were compelled to adjust their eating habits. French specialties such as butter, cream, cheese, pâté, foie gras, pastries, breads, *viennoiseries*, and rich desserts were all now seen as enemies of beauty. Cottage cheese, green salad, and diet sodas were the new order of the day.

The best American French restaurants, meanwhile, were increasingly stigmatized by their own painstakingly cultivated aura of elegance and privilege. The ostentatious displays of wealth, power, and class that had long taken place in these service-oriented, white-napkin temples of gastronomy were now no longer considered "cool" among the young and the hip, who tended to favor eateries that were less formal, less expensive, and more fun. In New York in particular, playfully themed restaurants now captured the public's attention. Joe Baum and his company, Restaurant Associates, oversaw many of the most popular of them: La Fonda del Sol, the Forum of the Twelve Caesars, the Hawaiian Room, Quo Vadis, and Tavern on the Green each had their own wacky charm. When another restaurant impresario, Warner LeRoy, opened Maxwell's Plum, a fancifully decorated restaurant cum singles bar, the menu was irreverent and highly eclectic, featuring something for just about everybody. Rather than being shot down for such madness, the restaurant received a four-star rating from *The New York Times*.

But nowhere was the widespread shift in public opinion away from *haute cuisine* more evident than when the *New York Times* food critic Craig Claiborne traveled to Paris in November 1975 for a meal so heinously pretentious that it was ultimately denounced by the Pope. In an article entitled "Just a Quiet Dinner for 2 in Paris: 31 Dishes, 9 Wines, a $4,000 Check,"* Claiborne described his ultimate fantasy-turned-reality of haute cuisine *gourmandise*. In doing so, however, he called down the wrath of the nation and ultimately lost his job.

The meal was not paid for by the *Times*. Rather it was a prize won in an on-air charity auction for WNET, New York's public television station. Claiborne bid $300 on a "dinner for two at any restaurant in the world" to be paid for by American Express, and upon learning he had won it, he chose Chez Denis, subsequently described by *People* magazine as "a small but ruinously expensive restaurant on Paris' Right Bank [whose] clientele includes Jacqueline Kennedy Onassis, Orson Welles, assorted millionaires, titled heads and government ministers."[5] Claiborne and his dining companion, Pierre Franey, then consulted in depth with proprietor Denis Lahana, ultimately deciding that their feast would be served up in three services spaced out over the course of four and a half hours. Initially conceived as *"un diner autour de neuf vins"* ("a dinner built around nine wines"), the meal was in fact a fine wine–lover's dream.

On the appointed day, the meal began with fresh Beluga caviar and a vintage Champagne, Comtesse Marie de France 1966. A 1918 Château Latour[†] was poured to accompany a parfait of sweetbreads, a mousse of quail in a small *tarte*, and a *tarte* of Italian ham, mushrooms, and truffles. Then a trio of soups: *consommé Denis* (a *consommé* of wild duck), *velouté Andalou* (a cream of tomato soup with Spanish flavors), and a cold *potage Germiny*. The fish course followed: Belon oysters, broiled quickly and served with a beurre blanc; lobster in a *sauce cardinal*;[‡] and "a Provençale pie" made with red mullet, tomato, black olives, and herbs. All were accompanied by a 1969 Montrachet. Chicken blended in a cream sauce of wild mushrooms followed; then a classic *chartreuse* of partridge; and then a *filet de boeuf Olga Palinkaš*—a

---

* That amount of $4,000 is equivalent to about $17,500 today.

† At the time of the meal, Claiborne recounted in the *Times*, "it was necessary to open three bottles of the 1918 Latour in order to find one in proper condition."

‡ A fish-stock-based béchamel featuring truffles, lobster *coulis*, and a touch of cayenne pepper.

tenderloin of Limousin beef with a truffle sauce.* These last three dishes were served with a 1928 Château Mouton-Rothschild. A trio of sherbets (orange, lemon, and blackcurrant) concluded the first segment of the meal.

Next came dainty little ortolans served *en brochette*. ("As fat as butter and an absolute joy to bite into because of the succulence of the flesh," Claiborne wrote. "Even the bones, except for the tiny leg bones, are chewed and swallowed.") Next a *salmis* of wild duck; next a roasted boned loin of veal wrapped in puff pastry with fresh black truffles about the size of golf balls, accompanied by *pommes Anna* and *purée Rachel*.† Several cold meat delicacies followed: a fresh foie gras in aspic, a "breast meat of woodcocks that was cooked until rare and served with a natural chaud-froid," and "another aspic of cold pheasant with fresh hazelnuts." The wines included a 1917 Château Lafite-Rothschild, a 1961 Château Pétrus, and then what Claiborne described as "the most magnificent wine of the evening," a 1929 Romanée-Conti. This second service ended with three rather simple desserts: a cold glazed charlotte with strawberries, *île flottante*,‡ and *poires Alma*.§ The dessert wines included a 1928 Château d'Yquem, an 1835 Madeira, an 1865 Calvados, and a Cognac *hors d'âge*.¶ After a short break came the third and final service, consisting of a variety of decorated confections, *friandises*, candies, preserves, and fruits.[6]

Not content simply to enjoy his *grande bouffe* in private, Claiborne wrote it up in detail for *The New York Times*, where editors made it a front-page story. The journalist and critic was so delighted with himself that apparently he did not stop to consider that others might think so public a display of gluttony in poor taste. A thousand letters of outrage soon taught him otherwise. In dreaming up this meal so reminiscent of Belle Époque excess, Claiborne had failed to realize that *haute cuisine* was already being negatively perceived as the food of

---

* The dish was named after Orson Welles's girlfriend, who used the stage name Oja Kodar.
† Puréed artichoke hearts.
‡ A soft meringue poached in milk, then served in a pool of *crème anglaise*.
§ Pears poached in port and orange zest, placed in a timbale, sprinkled with powdered praline, and topped with whipped cream.
¶ A Cognac so rare, fine, or old that it is considered to be outside of standard Cognac age classification.

privilege, of decadence, even of villainous overindulgence. "It is almost unbelievable that *The New York Times*, the employer of Mr. Claiborne, saw fit to publicize this vulgarity at length on its front page," one letter to the editor ran. "Is the *Times* reduced to pandering to the tastes of those who thrive on tales of extravagance, wasteful luxury and extreme frivolity?"[7] Even people within the luxury hospitality industry were repelled by the article: Jacob Rosenthal, the former president of the Culinary Institute of America, wrote that Claiborne's article had been "in execrable taste . . . [a display of] reprehensible gluttony [and] a disservice to gastronomy and the restaurant profession . . . [as well as] a desecration of great wine and food."[8] Julia Child expressed a different opinion, but only privately: "What a to-do, really," she wrote Claiborne. "I can see no reason for all that indignant uproar—does anyone object when some rich-bitch buys a $4,000 mink coat, or a $35,000 Rolls Royce?"[9] Maybe not, but Claiborne had made the fatal mistake of bragging about it on the front page of *The New York Times*—something Child herself was far too circumspect ever to do.

⚜

Child had been steadily moving away from luxury foods ever since returning to the United States, where her television programs and her writing were now addressed to the average American housewife. No longer so completely devoted to French cuisine, she was beginning to trust her own tastes and preferences, many of which were American. Although she had once told *Time*, "I will never do anything but French cooking," and once wrote Avis DeVoto, "I am half French, and that is all there is to it,"[10] and even declared in her memoirs, "I must *be* French!," *From Julia Child's Kitchen*, the cookbook that followed the second volume of *Mastering the Art*, was clearly an all-American production.

Originally intended as a compilation of the recipes used in the seventy-two episodes of *The French Chef*'s second series, the book eventually grew and expanded into a fine, hefty, Franco-American tome of 687 pages, one that ultimately made no apologies for being American. *"It's more than just French this time,"* Child wrote:

After all, though my formal culinary training was entirely French . . . I remain very American indeed. I always look at French cuisine from an American point of view. . . . But now, in addition to French concerns, I feel free to delve into New England chowders . . . personal fruit cakes, curries, pastas. I've gone into experiments with the pressure cooker, . . . the microwave oven, and the electric super-blender-food-processor. . . . In other words, [I am] putting my cooking vocabulary to work in all directions.[11]

Like *Mastering the Art*, this new book was a collaborative endeavor. But in this instance Child's collaborators were not two upper-class Frenchwomen. Instead they were six very practical Americans* who were doing behind-the-scenes kitchen work on the *French Chef* television program—and they felt, as many American home cooks do, that many convenience products were perfectly all right for home cooking. Child incorporated their helpful suggestions into her finished cookbook manuscript, and one typical incorporation—abandoning a classic (but labor intensive) *sauce brune* for a can of beef bouillon thickened with cornstarch—made clear that Child's undying allegiance to Escoffier and *La Belle France* had now officially run its course. So too would Child's enthusiasm for commercial mayonnaise and partially hydrogenated vegetable shortening, two longtime staples of the American pantry. In all these instances, Child was reaching for something more practical, realistic, and affordable for the time-pressed American home cook. Nonetheless, *From Julia Child's Kitchen* clung to its French mystique: along with its many French recipes, the book was filled with photos of the Childs' years in France, including a title-page photo of a far younger Julia, standing at the window of her Marseille apartment twenty-two years earlier.

Child's switch from French to American cooking had been going on for some time. With the publication of *Mastering the Art of French*

---

*Child's associate cooks were Bess Coughlin, Liz Bishop, Bess Hopkins, Mary O'Brien, Rita Rains, and Edith Seltzer. Child also thanked her friend and associate Rosie Manell; her secretary, Gladys Christopherson; her adviser, Avis DeVoto; and her editor, Judith Jones.

Cooking Volume II in 1970, both Julia Child and Simone Beck knew their professional collaboration had reached its end. As Beck later wrote in her memoirs, "I consider [*Mastering Volume II*] to be more [Julia's] book than mine. For the first book, I feel I was the prime mover, more of an authority on French food, more of a 'boss.' For Volume II, Julia had gained confidence and authority, especially as she was the one living in America, with instant access to the American food mentality and knowledge of products available there."[12] Beck tactfully abstains from further observing that the second volume features showy, fanciful dishes better suited to television presentation than home consumption—such as a large pumpkin stuffed with cheese, then baked and served whole at table; a whole filet of beef Wellington; and a whole roast stuffed suckling pig—all of them much more elaborate than the relatively simple French home cooking that Beck had first focused on in her original draft of *Mastering the Art of French Cooking Volume I*.

Child had also pushed much of *Volume II* toward two kinds of food preparation few French homemakers would care to undertake: charcuterie making and the home baking of breads and *viennoiseries*. As the book's flap copy explained,

> The most remarkable achievement of this volume is that it will make Americans actually more expert than their French contemporaries in two supreme areas of cookery: baking and charcuterie. In France the housewife can turn to the local bakery for fresh and expertly baked bread, brioches, croissants, petits-fours and pastries—or to the neighborhood charcuterie for pâtés and terrines and sausages. Here, most of us have no choice but to create them for ourselves . . . Now any American cook worth her (or his) salt can make specialities that have hitherto been obtainable only from France's professional chefs and bakers.

The idea of cooking authentic French bread was surely an attractive one to Americans, and Child's twenty-page recipe for a baguette is surely a tour de force—but as all Frenchmen know, an authentic

French baguette goes stale within three hours of emerging from an oven, and is practically inedible within a day, making such work largely useless to the practical home cook. Upon reading it, Elizabeth David (who was writing her own book on bread) would write James Beard (who also wrote a 1973 classic volume on breadmaking):

> I am *not* trying to tell people how to make French bread, but I *do* have to tell them why they can't—whatever Julia says—(but don't quote me)—and really I don't know why they would want to. They wouldn't want to bake it fresh four times a day would they? (Or would they?) I was much amused by the reaction of one or two Frenchwomen to whom I mentioned baking bread at home. *"Ah, non, pas possible—le pain, chez soi? Quelle idée"*—etc which was what I expected.[13]

The book's section on home charcuterie contained a number of equally far-out recipes, including one for making *confit d'oie* out of a whole goose, a process requiring twenty-four hours of salting, forty-five minutes of rendering fat, then ninety minutes of roasting the goose, and then the packing away of the preserved goose into large jars or crocks, utilizing the rendered goose fat as a preservative—an operation better suited to a nineteenth-century farm wife than to the contemporary suburban homemaker.

Of course, the real difference between the two women was not in their recipe preferences, but rather in their career trajectories. Child was now hitting her stride as a television celebrity in the United States, and Beck was simply not part of that world, nor did she want to be. The two women would always remain close, but as Child's American friend and adviser (and now employee) Avis DeVoto observed on a visit to Bramafam in late 1966, there was often a very basic tension in the kitchen when the two women cooked together:

> Simca is a creative genius . . . [but] stubborn as a mule. Julia . . . can be just as stubborn as Simca is, and will plug away trying to convince Simca until suddenly Simca changes her position, and from then on [Simca] will talk as if it

were her own idea all along. I have seen her do this on a number of occasions . . . I am sure that deep down Simca just has never been convinced that all that accuracy and measurement is anything but a crazy American idea.

. . . I would hear Simca's voice going on and on, in floods of French, Julia saying *oui, oui, oui,* at intervals, Simca's voice rising. . . . Simca is excitable, very verbal in any argument. She waves knives, clashes pans about. So does Julia sometimes . . . [but] Julia always won in the end, because she keeps her head.[14]

At Bramafam, Beck had a home-court advantage in these kitchen encounters, but that advantage was not particularly good for their collaboration. Although Child would always adore Beck as "*la Super-Française,*" she also liked doing things her own way, and at heart she seems to have resented Beck's firm belief that Child, because an American, would always have a great deal yet to learn about French cuisine. As Child would note in a letter to M.F.K. Fisher in 1969, "I did want to underline one of the great remarks about the French that I have encountered: 'Every Frenchman is convinced he is a connoisseur who has nothing to learn from the experts.' . . . It has taken me fifteen years to realize that this is, in a nugget, exactly what has been bugging me in my collaboration, and why I can't take any more of it."[15]

In coming into her own as a writer and television star, Julia Child seems to have outgrown her earlier interest in learning from French cooking instructors, cookbook authors, and food experts. And indeed she was now held in such high regard in the United States that she saw little reason to defer to them. Richard Olney, who was much more a part of France's gastronomic community, was bemused by Child's resentment of these French authors, instructors, and experts, since many of them (including Simone Beck) were close friends. Through his own years in and among the French, Olney had come to think of French cooking as a vast and constantly evolving practice that, while rooted in national, regional, and ethnic identities, was nevertheless subject to perpetual reevaluation, reinterpretation, and reinvention, and over which no one person—not even the great Escoffier—could ever dare claim absolute authority or expertise. Moreover, and far more important, he was fully receptive to the idea that French cooking really does belong to the French, and always will—that while a sympathetic American can participate in it, he or she will always be, to some extent, an outsider. Child and Olney would always remain cordial—since both were very close to Beck—but in the end they did not much like each other. At Christmas 1975, after spending several days at Bramafam (as Beck's guest and fellow cook), Olney had basically reached his limit with Paul and Julia Child's pronouncements on French cuisine, writing his brother James, "The Childs appear to be more bitter, more destructive, and more irrationally anti-French than ever—[saying that] 'Only Americans' (guess who) 'understand French cooking.' [They were] very bitchy about Odette.* . . . [I] am sick to death by now of Julia's sugarcoated barbed tongue. Most of the barbs are directed (although with careful indirection) at me."[16]

Olney was not wrong in this observation. For whatever reason, Child's antipathy toward Olney was strong enough that during the 1970s she went out of her way to advise Time-Life's editors against hiring him as general editor for its *Good Cook* series. (But they did so anyway.) Even as late as 1999, in Olney's obituary in *The New York Times*, Julia Child would apparently have the last, sugarcoated word about him, telling the journalist R. W. Apple, "I think [Richard Olney] enjoyed being difficult. But on the other hand, he could be absolutely charming if you treated him like the genius he considered himself to be."[17]

⚜

With Julia Child no longer banging a drum on behalf of French cooking—and, to the contrary, often making gently derisive comments on television about *la nouvelle cuisine*—French fine dining fell even further in the American estimation. Its champions in the press were now few: Craig Claiborne was in eclipse due to his $4,000 *faux*

---

*Odette Kahn, having started out as Madeleine Decure's assistant, became editor of *Cuisine et Vins de France* and *Revue du Vin de France* after Decure's death, in 1968. She was also author of *La Petite et la Grande Cuisine* (1977).

pas, and Mimi Sheraton, who was about to replace him as the *New York Times* food critic, was quick to point out that thanks to "a growing interest in diet and health and the resultant disaffection from the overpoweringly rich and complicated meals of classic French cookery, nouvelle cuisine [really] owes much [of its popularity] to its timeliness." She also felt very strongly that *nouvelle cuisine* was at heart something of a public relations scam, since so much of the fanfare surrounding this new style of cooking came not from diners themselves, but from "a barrage of trans-Atlantic press agentry, food critics desperate for something new to write about, and superstar chefs in search of profit and publicity."[18]

Looked at on paper, the precepts of *nouvelle cuisine* are entirely reasonable, because they emphasize seeking out the freshest and most local ingredients, then treating them creatively but with the utmost respect. It calls for a return to simplicity; a new attention to health and fitness issues; and a rediscovery of the light, bright tastes of herbaceous, garden-fresh foods. In presenting this sensible "new" philosophy of cooking in top restaurants across France, however, chefs such as Paul Bocuse, Michel Guérard, the Troisgros brothers, and Roger Vergé necessarily created dishes that were fussy, theatrical, and labor intensive—such "simplicity" in a restaurant requires a good deal of razzle-dazzle to make it worth the price. Americans diners and critics quickly branded it heavy on hype and meager on portion size: a gastronomic case, in other words, of the emperor's new clothes. But by the mid-1970s there was no stopping it in France: Paul Bocuse received the Légion d'Honneur from President Valéry Giscard d'Estaing, signaling the official dawn of a new era in French gastronomy, one that would predominate throughout the 1970s and 1980s. "Bocuse preaches in favor of provincial simplicity in the tradition of the *bonne femme* who relies more on basic ingredients than complicated technique," *Time* magazine noted of that great Lyonnais showman in 1973. "The point, as Bocuse sees it, is to 'render unto a chicken that which is its due, and nothing more.' "[19]

But American gastro-tourists did not come all the way across the Atlantic to eat roast chicken. Moreover *nouvelle cuisine*'s fussy, service-intensive, less-is-more philosophy—based on Japanese *kaiseki*, which favors tiny, exquisite portions of food given a highly artistic presentation—was basically antithetical to the American way of eating, which favors large portions of good food, well prepared. To make matters worse, the rich French foods that had traditionally made American gourmands most happy in France—highest-quality butter, cream, cheese, foie gras, pastries, breads, and dazzling confections— were largely absent from the menus of *la nouvelle cuisine*.

❖

In 1974, in the midst of this culinary turmoil, Richard Olney published *Simple French Food*. Despite America's growing distance from France and French cuisine, the book was instantly recognized in the States as a classic of gastronomic prose, one that appealed in particular to that new generation of home cooks who were attempting to live (and eat) in closer harmony with nature. Olney's special interest in fresh, local produce and herbs, preferably those gathered through scavenging or else from one's own garden, spoke to younger home cooks inspired by popular back-to-the-land authors such as Euell Gibbons, whose writings (starting with the 1962 *Stalking the Wild Asparagus*) sought to reconnect contemporary city dwellers with the simple pleasures (and foods) available to them through the great outdoors. Nika Hazelton, a European-born and -educated author of thirty cookbooks, was among the first to salute the quiet brilliance of Olney's new book. "Aside from Elizabeth David, the greatest of all food writers and author of *French Provincial Cooking*, there is no writer I know who so brings to life the uncomplicated French food we are all nostalgic about, the food the French cook in their homes and small country restaurants," she wrote. "What's more, [his] is food that can be reproduced over here [in the United States]; admittedly, it will not be as flavorful here as Provence, but it will still be the best French home cooking there is. (Only fools attempt haute cuisine in their home kitchens.)" She then went on, as many others would, to praise the clarity and spare elegance of Olney's recipe writing and "his way of teaching you to cook really French without affectation."[20]

Olney helped launch *Simple French Food* with a modest book tour that involved cooking demonstrations around the country, starting in New York. The book, which has since become a cult classic, had been acquired by Alfred "Pat" Knopf, Jr., at Atheneum, and then edited by its poetry editor, Harry Ford. Since both Knopf and Ford were great French food and wine enthusiasts as well as connoisseurs of language, they immediately grasped Olney's unique genius as a writer-cook, and encouraged rather than criticized his distinctive, slightly idiosyncratic, prose style. Olney enjoyed himself on his American travels, even as he realized that the American food-writing community was not one he cared for, and that America was not a place he wanted to live. He found James Beard unethical, self-centered, and creepy; Craig Claiborne, a mean-spirited alcoholic. But he made many new friends while giving presentations on his book, particularly in California. As he later remembered,

> In March 1975 I was in the Bay Area for the first time to promote *Simple French Food*, which had appeared in November 1974. After a demonstration in San Francisco at "Williams-Sonoma," Alice [Waters] and Jeremiah [Tower] introduced themselves. Jeremiah was then alternating with Alice as chef at Chez Panisse.* That night, Alice invited me to dinner at Chez Panisse with Kenneth Anger who, she had learned, was a friend of mine. Jeremiah was in the kitchen. Both became good friends and visited me later that summer in Solliès-Toucas, when I introduced them to my friends, the Peyrauds, at Domaine Tempier. . . . Alice [subsequently] became an adopted and much beloved member of the Peyraud family.
>
> Alice told me that *The French Menu Cookbook* and Elizabeth David's books were her two principal sources of inspiration at Chez Panisse. In London two years later, where I had begun to work on the Time-Life *Good Cook* series, I was very pleased to be able to bring her and Elizabeth [David] to-

---

* The influential (and now legendary) Berkeley restaurant had been founded four years earlier, in 1971.

gether. Elizabeth loved both Alice and Jeremiah, who had settled then in London to work with me on the early volumes of *The Good Cook*, before moving on and eventually opening [his own restaurant,] Stars.[21]

After Tower came to stay at Solliès-Toucas for Christmas, Olney wrote his brother James, "Quite mad he is—his gods are Escoffier, Ali-Bab, Elizabeth David and me—but he is not so simple as all that and will probably be a star in the food world before too many years have passed."

What both Waters and Tower responded to in Olney—first in his books, and later in his little garden-home at Solliès-Toucas—was the idea that really fine, simple cooking should be based on fresh local ingredients, with the best of those ingredients serving as a starting point for an imaginative, improvisational menu. While this concept may seem ridiculously simple today—and is also, in retrospect, the central ideology of *nouvelle cuisine*—it was radical enough for Americans of the early 1970s, many of whom had been brought up on convenience cooking, low-grade supermarket produce, and industrially processed foods. Most American restaurants, meanwhile, relied upon showy effects, culinary novelties, and rich, filling ingredients to justify their expense. But among those who cared passionately about the aesthetic pleasure inherent in fine "simple" cooking, Olney and his book had made the case for change, and that change was crossing the Atlantic, thanks in part to the imaginative responses of chefs like Waters and Tower.

A number of food journalists perceived the direct link to French culinary culture in this new notion of "simple" food. "To my knowledge, Elizabeth David and Richard Olney are the only well-known writers [in English] who remain true to the most elementary and classic [French] flavor principles," Karen Hess wrote in *The Atlantic* when *Simple French Food* was published. "The greater part of America's 'gourmet' cuisine is at best second-rate Escoffier . . . [and American] books and schools promising to turn you into a French chef are a fraud."[22] Through Olney, "simple" French provincial cooking became the new starting point, rather than the grandiose Parisian restaurant cuisine that had so amazed and inspired Julia Child during her years in residence there, 1949 to 1953.

Shortly after returning to France, Olney was asked to write and edit the new twenty-eight volume series of Time-Life cookbooks known as *The Good Cook*. At first he doubted his ability to work within Time-Life's corporate structure—and doubted, as well, Time-Life's ability to produce a good cookbook series. "[A friend] who had worked for *Time* Magazine during the 1940s likened the Time-Life Machine to a vast meat grinder into which the editors packed the finest talents available before turning the crank and reducing them to anonymous mince," he later recalled. "I told him the machine would clog if they tried to crank me through."[23] Yet the project itself attracted him, for Time-Life wanted to produce the book in Great Britain, using mostly European talent. Even more intriguingly, the aim of the new series would be twofold: first, to teach readers the basics of cooking through the use of clear, step-by-step photo demonstrations, and then, second, to encourage readers to improvise by presenting them with a variety of imaginative recipes drawn from a broad range of cookbooks, both European and American. Because this was a type of free-form, improvisational cooking instruction Olney had always believed in (and had always wanted to write about), he decided to give it a try. As he wrote Elizabeth David,

> It was difficult to explain to you what the Time-Life business is all about [when we met]—mostly because Time-Life does not know itself, and the project is only now beginning to take on some sort of conceptual form. . . . I was terrified at the notion of working with a vast machine like Time-Life, as I imagined it, but, in fact, the London staff [for the project] is very small, very young, mostly English, innocent, brimming with enthusiasm, hard-working and cooperative—If New York can be kept out of our hair, it promises to be quite amusing work—and if the whole thing works out, I shall presumably make some money for the first time in my life which will, in itself, be a grand experience.[24]

Around 1975 Olney had a telephone, and then a newly developed fax machine, installed at Solliès-Toucas to aid communication with the London office. He also grudgingly agreed to visit that city periodically to work in close, hands-on collaboration with the various researchers, photographers, stylists, and copyeditors based at the Time-Life studios. Happily, he was also allowed to hire a number of fine, internationally based fellow writers as consultants on the project, many of them his friends, among them Michel Lemmonier, Sybille Bedford, Jeremiah Tower, and Jane Grigson. While making these extended visits to London he was also able to see his brother James on a regular basis, as well as Elizabeth David (who had warily declined to be drawn into the Time-Life project), and to get to know many other fine British writer-cooks and restaurateurs (including Simon Hopkinson of Bibendum and Nico Ladenis of Chez Nico in Dulwich), cooks who admired Olney's writing and philosophy, just as, in time, he would admire their thinking and cooking. Being in London also enabled Olney to purchase a number of vintage fine wines at British auctions—wines he subsequently shipped home to his waiting *cave* at Solliès-Toucas.

British appreciation of Olney and his writing has remained strong to this day. Jill Norman, perhaps the most influential British cookbook editor of her generation, was typically enthusiastic about his sensibility, since many Francophile U.K. residents were delighted with his knowledge of French cuisine, wines, language, culture, and dining habits. "Richard was esteemed by the French . . . even as his American counterparts were playing him down as a lightweight," she once observed in an interview. "Any of the 3 star [restaurants in France] would welcome him gladly at short notice, the food and wine writers respected him and asked his advice; the wine producers filled his cellar with some of the finest wines France produces."[25] Her friendship with Olney deepened during the course of the six-year, twenty-eight-volume Time-Life project, to the extent that she made him godparent to one of her children. The series, meanwhile, proved a lasting international success.

A number of other cookbook projects followed, many of them emphasizing the proper pairing of French foods and wines. Olney also wrote definitive histories of both Château Yquem and the Domaine de la Romanée-Conti, doing so first in French, then English. Later still he collaborated with his good friend and neighbor Lulu Peyraud on *Lulu's Provençal Table* (1994), a cookbook that explored her classic Provençal home cooking in the context of her life and work at the domaine once owned by her father and now run by her husband. While working on these various projects, Olney continued to host family, friends, and guests in Solliès-Toucas on a regular basis. His nephew John came for an extended visit, became interested in wine-making, and returned to the States, ultimately joining Ridge Vineyards in California. James and Byron Olney, meanwhile, purchased Richard's home *en viager** as a way of assuring their brother's financial security. Olney's last years were spent painting and writing a memoir. When he died, peacefully and alone in his garden in the summer of 1999, the memoir had not yet been completed. *Reflexions* ultimately found small-press publication through the combined editorial efforts of James Olney, Byron Olney, and Jill Norman.

❖

Like Olney, Alexis Lichine ultimately chose life in France to life in America. He lived out his last years peacefully in the Médoc. As difficult as it had been for him to sell his name and business and to leave the wine trade, doing so was ultimately good for him financially: the Bass Charrington deal not only made Lichine rich, but also shielded him from the catastrophic Bordeaux wine crash of 1972.[26] Many of Lichine's friends, neighbors, and former competitors lost their properties and businesses in that monumental crash, but Lichine came out of it sitting pretty: with plenty in the bank, his winemaking at Prieuré-Lichine could continue without concern or interruption. When his daughter married a minor French nobleman, he was able to give her a grand wedding at St. Patrick's Cathedral, and his wedding present to them was a little inn for them to run, not far from the

---

* A *viager* is a French business agreement whereby the owner of a property sells it on a reverse annuity basis, receiving both a lump sum for the property and a yearly stipend from the buyer which continues until the seller's death.

Prieuré.[27] His son, Sacha, also eventually joined him in Bordeaux, there to take up the wine business. Though the two would not always see eye to eye, Sacha Lichine ultimately found great success of his own as a *négociant* and winemaker, most recently through his high-end Provençal rosés from Château d'Esclans, located in the hills just above Ste.-Maxime.

During the last fifteen years of his life, Lichine had plenty of time to oversee winemaking at the Prieuré, and plenty of time, as well, for a final writing venture. In *Alexis Lichine's Guide to the Wines and Vineyards of France* he recycled the best material from *Wines of France* into a tourist guide to the nation's most glorious and seductive wine regions. The new book took a far less combative tone toward the French *négociants*, for times had changed. Practical and useful as well as highly readable, the guide sold well not only in the United States but also in Britain, Germany, Denmark, Japan—and, finally, in France.

Although Lichine did not remarry after parting ways with Arlene Dahl, he never lacked for company. Often seen out and about with various professional women, celebrities, and socialites in New York, Palm Beach, and elsewhere, he was also relatively open, even among reporters, about his penchant for "*les demoiselles*."* The financial comfort of his later years also allowed him to welcome a great many interesting people to his home in the Médoc—not to sell wine to them, but simply to enjoy their company. "I have found [more] time [in Bordeaux] to enjoy congenial talk among friends," Lichine wrote in his last book. "Over the years, love of wine has attracted writers, musicians, painters, statesmen, politicians and some of France's great chefs to the Prieuré, where I manage at last to leave the overworked world of wine behind. After all, it is only by appreciating civilization in its many expressions of art, lively company, and good food that we develop our senses and understand the role that fine wine can play in life."[28] While his underfurnished fourteen-room duplex on Fifth Avenue had never really suited him—he was, after all, a retired divorcé with grown children, with no real reason to maintain so grand

---

* A French word meaning "young ladies," it often has ironic connotations, as in Picasso's *Les Demoiselles d'Avignon* (1907), set in a brothel.

an establishment—the Prieuré (which is in truth a very modest châ-teau) became ever more homey. "He spends more and more time in the Médoc," Frank Prial wrote of his cantankerous old friend in *The New York Times*, "proclaiming to everyone, including the Mayor of Bordeaux, that though the French themselves leave much to be desired, their food, their wine and France itself, are superb."[29]

In the early 1980s, anticipating ruinous French death taxes, Li-chine tried to find a buyer for the Prieuré who would allow him to retain both a lifetime tenancy and lifelong control over the château's wine production. But no one would accept his price on those terms, and as a result the Prieuré remained in his hands until he died of lung cancer in June 1989. In observance of his last wishes (and in vio-lation of French law), his twenty-nine-year-old son buried him on the grounds of the château. While Sacha Lichine sold Prieuré-Lichine just a few years later to begin his new life elsewhere, Alexis Lichine would stay put: just as the name Lichine has remained attached to the Prieuré, so too have Lichine's mortal remains, becoming a small part of its *terroir.*[30]

Afterword

In researching and writing this book over the past ten years, and in thinking about the writers I have profiled, I find myself coming back, again and again, to a volume that sits here beside my computer: Prosper Montagné's *Larousse Gastronomique*, a book of more than a thousand densely printed pages explaining French cooking terms, procedures, recipes, ingredients, and, most of all, French culinary and gastronomic history. A constant and reliable companion to me in my work, the *Larousse Gastronomique* embodies the great French desire to comprehend French cuisine in its entirety—not merely as a series of recipes, but rather as a manifestation of French culture, history, society, and national character. When it was first published in 1938, French cuisine was the most celebrated in the Western world; and even Escoffier, who read through the manuscript shortly before his death, had lauded the massive work as "the history of the table of a nation [and] a reflection of the civilization of that nation . . . presented in the form of a dictionary."[1] His amazement with Montagné's research and writing on the vast subject of French gastronomy was entirely justified, for the project is a wonder of scholarship, comparable in scope and ambition to Diderot's Encyclopedia of Enlightenment thought.

But as fine as the book may be, and however much I may admire it, the *Larousse Gastronomique* is in no way an introduction to French cuisine for Americans, except perhaps as a severe warning that the subject is far more complicated than any curious and well-meaning American could ever imagine. It is most certainly not a book for beginners, for it does not give people from outside of French culture an easy way in. And it doesn't do much to advance the average American's own gastronomic wisdom and practice, since its focus is so insistently upon France, French culture, and specifically French cuisine. Perhaps as a result, it is not a book Americans have ever shown much interest in: only in 1961, a full twenty-three years after its debut, was it even translated into English. No; what Americans needed in order to begin to comprehend the art, craft, science, and history of French cuisine— and, from there, to begin thinking about America's own ever-evolving gastronomic tradition—was in fact something no Frenchman had ever offered them: a warm and welcoming American introduction to a maddeningly complicated French subject. And Americans needed some other things as well: someone to offer them a nibble, a sip, or a night out on the town, to help make all these descriptions and explanations and histories into something vivid, palpable, and immediate.

Before 1945, French cuisine did not translate easily to the American table. In the years before World War II, most Americans thought of French cuisine (if they thought of it at all) as the overly rich, somewhat indigestible high-class hotel and restaurant fare through which the wealthy indulged themselves and their friends, usually with pomp and ostentation. But that perception changed significantly in the years following World War II, and it changed in large part because of the six writers I have written about in this book, as well as the others I have mentioned in telling their stories. Through them, Americans began to learn about the many different types of French cuisine, about the wisdom that informs its enjoyment, and also, in some cases, about the organizing principles that give modern French cooking practice its structure and logic. They also learned about wine and its relation to food, and also, more specifically, about what makes good wine good. And in the end they learned how to eat and drink more thoughtfully: to consider the relation of what they were eating and drinking to the place that it comes from, and also its relation to the world as a whole—

something that the French have been doing, to some greater or lesser extent, for hundreds of years.

In the decades since these writers published their various accounts of French food and wine, the traditional French respect for ingredients, for artisanal production, and for *terroir* has become an integral part of American food awareness. The reportage, memoirs, fictions, essays, and cookbooks these writers created all helped Americans to understand that fine food and wine were things that could be enjoyed with pleasure on this side of the Atlantic too—and not only by the rich, but by everybody, and even at home, through the relatively simple (but mindful) cooking practices that the French have long considered an essential aspect of their collective identity. Each in his or her own way, these six American writers democratized, explained, and celebrated French food and wine even as they made the key principles of eating well more accessible, enjoyable, and fun. While none of these six writers invented French cooking, and while none could be called a definitive authority on the subject, each did his or her readers an extraordinary service by introducing them to the genius of French gastronomy. As a result, many French ideas, concepts, and understandings entered American culture so completely that we no longer think of them as French. In the space of a generation or two, they had simply been incorporated into America's own various culinary practices.

⚜

When I moved to Paris in 2009 to research the Left Bank American literary and intellectual avant-garde of the 1950s, I found myself drawn back, again and again, to this group of much loved midcentury American writer-gourmands. While their work had interested me informally for years, it was now connecting me to French culture directly, and in a way that writings by other Paris-based Americans did not. The food and wine I was experiencing daily in Paris (and subsequently elsewhere in France) also drew me back to them, because I was now sharing their discoveries and their pleasures, as well as their good company. My vague awareness that each of these writers had at some point lived and learned in Paris, just as I was doing, also made me more curious about them. Yet even so I had no very concrete sense of their Parisian experiences, or of how those Parisian experiences might have shaped their understandings, their worldviews, and, ultimately, their destinies. My curiosity about it was strong enough that, in the end, I decided to write this book.

That very pleasant task led me, in time, to read the major French writers on French cooking who they learned from. French novels, cookbooks, newspapers, and magazines had all had an influence on these six writers as well; so too had French friends and mentors. But a lot of information had simply come to them, as it now came to me, through the everyday discussion of food and drink that is so much a part of French life, and that takes place literally every hour of every day in France's restaurants, food shops, street markets, and wine cellars, as well as at gatherings both public and private. As an everyday home cook and would-be gourmand, I found French gastronomic literature to be a very welcome point of entry into French culture, particularly since (as I quickly found out) the French really do love to discuss their food and wine with anyone who takes a serious and informed interest.

In retrospect, I consider the Americans in this study a good cross section of mid-century American responses to France and to the French, at various levels of engagement and intelligence. They present French gastronomy to American readers through different formats, and all of them engage with French culture in their writing, albeit to varying degrees. All are unconventional and innovative in their approach, and all make the experience of France and its dining traditions vivid and immediate to the general reader. No one had ever written about food as joyfully as A. J. Liebling, or as romantically as M.F.K. Fisher (and though I have frequently questioned her veracity in this book, I would never dispute her talent for spinning a fine and compelling tale of gastronomic adventure). No one had demystified *cuisine bourgeoise* as Julia Child did in her landmark collaboration with Simone Beck and Louisette Bertholle. No one had ever managed to explain the genius of a perfectly thought-out French menu as beautifully or as well as Richard Olney. No one had ever written about French wines more seductively or comprehensibly than Alexis Lichine. And finally, no one had ever written a more brilliant, entertaining, or ultimately more moving cookbook-memoir than Alice Toklas. Working independently of one another, each in his or her own way, these six American writers collectively brought their American readers to a higher level of understanding about the choosing, cooking, and eating of good food and/or wine, and they did so not only by writing about the French, but also by sharing a great deal about themselves.

Writing about them in a group biography was at first a challenge, but ultimately it made good sense, since all these writers had undertaken their projects in roughly the same place and time. Charting the respective progress of each proved far more meaningful in the context of the others' (often sharply contrasting) experiences. And I, being freed of the biographer's usual duty of isolating and praising the accomplishments of a single individual (in what can so often turn into a kind of secular hagiography or, alternately, celebrity puff piece), was able to look at each writer's particular accomplishments far more critically. I also came to realize that as each achieved his or her own unique success, each did so on his or her own terms, and that each of these very different kinds of successes were not simply feats of professional accomplishment, but rather (and more important) feats of self-realization. Paris to some extent transformed them, or at least helped them realize their inner potential. Through their experience of that city, all came to understand who they were and what they wanted to make of themselves.

Finally, as I came to realize during the researching and writing of this book, it takes the help of all kinds of people (with all kinds of ambitions) to begin to comprehend a subject as vast, fascinating, and complicated as French cuisine—which is why I am profoundly grateful to each of these writers for all they wrote and did. No American reader (however assiduous, however Francophile) can absorb gastronomic wisdom simply by leafing through a reference book—not even if that book is the brilliant *Larousse Gastronomique*. Rather, we must be introduced to France and its food culture gradually, and lovingly, and in a variety of ways. The six gourmands in this study started me on this adventure in learning—and it is one I fully intend to continue with, quite happily, for the rest of my days.

Notes

Full citations for most of the books indicated in these notes can be found in the selected bibliography that follows.

1. LIEBLING AND THE LION OF BELFORT

1. A. J. Liebling, *Between Meals*, p. 45.
2. A. J. Liebling, *Normandy Revisited*, in *World War II Writings*, ed. Pete Hamill (New York: Library of America, 2008), pp. 844–46.
3. Raymond Sokolov, *Wayward Reporter*, p. 167.
4. Ibid., p. 168.
5. Ibid.
6. Ibid.
7. Ibid., p. 167.
8. Liebling, *Normandy Revisited*, pp. 845–46.
9. Ibid., p. 986.
10. Sokolov, *Wayward Reporter*, p. 135.
11. Ibid., p. 107.
12. Liebling, *Between Meals*, p. 51.
13. Ibid., pp. 55–57.
14. Sokolov, *Wayward Reporter* p. 132.
15. Ibid., pp. 87–88.
16. Liebling, quoted in Sokolov, *Wayward Reporter*, p. 140.
17. Liebling, *Normandy Revisited*, p. 974.
18. Ibid., p. 988.
19. Ibid., p. 990.
20. Ibid., p. 984.

21. Ibid., pp. 990–91.
22. Ibid., p. 991.
23. Liebling, *Between Meals*, p. 155.
24. Ibid., pp. 163–64.
25. Liebling, *Normandy Revisited*, in *World War II Writings*, p. 992.

2. THE FRANCO-AMERICAN (KITCHEN) ALLIANCE

1. Dione Lucas, *The Cordon Bleu Cook Book*, p. viii.
2. Julia Child, *As Always, Julia*, ed. Joan Reardon, p. 251.
3. Lucas, *The Cordon Bleu Cook Book*, p. x.
4. Jane Stern and Michael Stern, *American Gourmet*, p. 103.
5. Geoffrey Hellman, "Very, Very Cordial," *The New Yorker*, Feb. 19, 1955, p. 38.
6. Ibid., p. 38.
7. Craig Claiborne, "Now It's Philippe of Le Pavillon," *The New York Times*, Jan. 17, 1967.
8. Hellman, "Very, Very Cordial," p. 38.
9. Virgil Thomson, *Virgil Thomson* (New York: Knopf, 1966), p. 289.
10. Sybille Bedford, *Pleasures and Landscapes*, pp. 25–26.
11. Joseph Wechsberg, "The Finest Butter and Lots of Time," *The New Yorker*, Sept. 3, 1949, p. 40.
12. Alexis Lichine, *Alexis Lichine's New Encyclopedia of Wines and Spirits*, p. xix.
13. Knopf to Lichine, June 20, 1950, Alfred A. Knopf, Inc. Records (Series II), Lichine file, Harry Ransom Center, University of Texas at Austin.
14. Joseph Wechsberg, "A Dreamer of Wine," *The New Yorker*, May 17, 1958, p. 62.
15. Ibid., p. 67.
16. "J. P. McEvoy's Americana: We Came Home On Our Elbows," *The New York Journal American*, Sept. 9, 1950.
17. Clementine Paddleford, "Estate-Bottled Burgundies Now Available Here," *The New York Herald Tribune*, Nov. 6, 1950.
18. Knopf's quote can be found on the dust jacket of the first edition of Alexis Lichine's *Wines of France*.

3. ALICE TOKLAS STARTS OVER

1. Toklas to Gallup, Mar. 11, 1947, *Staying On Alone*, ed. Edward Burns, p. 54.
2. Toklas to Rogers, Oct. 28, 1947, *Staying On Alone*, p. 88.
3. *The Alice B. Toklas Cook Book*, p. 157.
4. Toklas to the Daniels, 1956, *Staying On Alone*, p. 566.
5. *Alice B. Toklas Cook Book*, p. 31.
6. Ibid., p. 85.
7. James R. Mellow, *Charmed Circle*, p. 545.
8. Toklas to the Daniels, 1956, *Staying On Alone*, p. 566.
9. *Alice B. Toklas Cook Book*, p. 223.
10. Ibid., p. 168; see also p. 132.
11. Remembrances of that first day, including this quote, come from Toklas, *What Is Remembered*, pp. 24–25.

12. Maurice Grosser, "Visiting Gertrude and Alice," *New York Review of Books*, Nov. 6, 1986; http://www.nybooks.com/articles/1986/11/06/visiting-gertrude-and-alice/.
13. For the specific articles and their publication date, see *The Letters of Gertrude Stein and Thornton Wilder*, ed. Burns and Dydo, p. 314n.
14. Toklas, *What Is Remembered*, p. 170.
15. Mellow, *Charmed Circle*, pp. 547–48. Mellow is paraphrasing Hemingway's letter to Rogers on the subject.
16. Simon, *The Biography of Alice B. Toklas*, p. 247. (A privately printed copy of the entire will is also available in the collection of the Morgan Library, New York.)
17. For more on 1947 Paris food prices, see Don Dresden, "Paris Report," in *Endless Feasts*, ed. Ruth Reichl, from which these figures are taken.
18. Sybille Bedford, *Pleasures and Landscapes*, p. 25.
19. Toklas to Rogers, Sept. 27, 1947, *Staying On Alone*, p. 76.
20. Toklas to Taylor, Sept. 4, 1948, ibid., p. 141.
21. *Alice B. Toklas Cook Book*, p. 37.
22. Ibid., p. 29.
23. Ibid.
24. Ibid., p. 91.
25. Ibid., p. 30.
26. Mellow, *Charmed Circle*, pp. 530–31.
27. Toklas to Rogers, Jan. 6, 1950, *Staying On Alone*, p. 185.
28. Gertrude Stein, *The Autobiography of Alice B. Toklas*, p. 252.
29. Toklas to Gallup, March 23, 1948, *Staying On Alone*, p. 108.
30. Toklas to Isabel Wilder, Mar. 16, 1950, ibid., p. 190.
31. Toklas to L. Elizabeth Hansen, July 19, 1949, ibid., p. 171.
32. Mellow, *Charmed Circle*, p. 562.
33. Toklas to Thornton Wilder, Apr. 5, 1949, *Staying On Alone*, p. 149.
34. Mellow, *Charmed Circle*, p. 564.
35. Toklas to Samuel Steward, May 27, 1949, *Dear Sammy*, ed. Samuel Steward, p. 171.
36. Toklas to Steward, Oct. 15, 1950, ibid., p. 185.
37. Toklas to Taylor, Feb. 11, 1951, *Staying On Alone*, p. 222.

4. *GOURMET*, BRILLAT-SAVARIN, AND *PARIS CUISINE*

1. Julia Child, *As Always, Julia*, ed. Joan Reardon, p. 96.
2. M.F.K. Fisher to Eda Lord, Feb. 5, 1952, *A Life in Letters*, ed. Norah K. Barr, Marsha Moran, and Patrick Moran, pp. 102–5.
3. Joan Reardon, *Poet of the Appetites*, p. 185.
4. Ibid., p. 186.
5. Ibid., p. 166.
6. Alan Brien, quoted in ibid., pp. 241–42.
7. Carolyn See, quoted in ibid., p. 428.
8. Brien, quoted in ibid., pp. 241–42.
9. Reardon, *Poet of the Appetites*, p. 186.
10. *The Heritage Club Sandglass*, number 6n, p. 1, Mary Frances Kennedy Fisher Papers, Schlesinger Library, Harvard University.

11. Child, *As Always, Julia*, pp. 73–74.
12. Ibid., p. 74.
13. Jane Stern and Michael Stern, *American Gourmet*, pp. 44–45.
14. Evan Jones, *Epicurean Delight*, p. 145.
15. Ibid., p. 165.
16. Ibid., p. 147.
17. Ibid., p. 148.

5. OUT ON THE TOWN WITH PAUL AND JULIA

1. Phila Cousins, quoted in Bob Spitz, *Dearie*, p. 87.
2. Julia Child to Avis DeVoto, Feb. 3, 1953, *As Always, Julia*, ed. Joan Reardon, p. 59.
3. Noël Riley Fitch, *Appetite for Life*, p. 166.
4. Julia Child and Alex Prud'homme, *My Life in France*, p. 31.
5. Fitch, *Appetite for Life*, p. 163.
6. Julia Child to DeVoto, Jan. 19, 1953, *As Always, Julia*, p. 48.
7. Child and Prud'homme, *My Life in France*, p. 54.
8. Ibid., p. 92.
9. Julia Child to Paul Child, Apr. 15, 1950, in Fitch, *Appetite for Life*, p. 185.
10. Child, *As Always, Julia*, p. 48.
11. Fitch, *Appetite for Life*, p. 181.
12. Ibid., p. 169.
13. M.F.K. Fisher to Eda Lord [n.d.; 1975?], Mary Frances Kennedy Fisher Papers, Schlesinger Library, Harvard University.
14. Child, *As Always, Julia*, p. 90.
15. Ibid., p. 123.
16. Ibid., pp. 91–92.
17. Paul Child to Charlie and Freddie Child, May 2, 1951, Julia Child Papers, Schlesinger Library.
18. Child and Prud'homme, *My Life in France*, p. 114.
19. Child, *As Always, Julia*, p. 44.
20. Julia Child to "FSKI" (Charlie and Freddie Child), Mar. 11, 1950, Child Papers.
21. Child and Prud'homme, *My Life in France*, pp. 93–94.
22. "Food: Everyone's in the Kitchen," *Time*, Nov. 25, 1966.
23. Child and Prud'homme, *My Life in France*, p. 68.
24. Ibid., p. 68.
25. Paul Child, interview with Gilbert Cross, Child Papers.
26. Paul Child to Charlie and Freddie Child, Mar. 17, 1950, Child Papers.
27. Fitch, *Appetite for Life*, p. 185.

6. RICHARD OLNEY STARTS OUT

1. James Olney, "Remembering Richard Remembering Mlle. Marty," *The Cincinnati Review* 3, no. 1 (Summer 2006), pp. 65–85.
2. Richard Olney, *Reflexions*, pp. 11–12.
3. Olney, *Reflexions*, pp. 12–13.

4. Julia Child, *As Always, Julia*, ed. Joan Reardon, p. 98.
5. Olney, *Reflexions*, pp. 25–26.
6. Richard Olney, *Simple French Food*, pp. 12–13.
7. Ibid., p. 6.
8. Richard Olney Papers.
9. Marcel Rouff, *La Vie et la Passion de Dodin-Bouffant, Gourmet* (Paris: Dellamain Boutelleau, 1924).
10. Olney, *Reflexions*, p. 26.
11. James Beard and Alexander Watt, *Paris Cuisine*, pp. 43–44.
12. Olney, *Reflexions*, p. 31.
13. Janet Flanner, Oct. 20, 1952, *Paris Journal (1944–1965)*, ed. William Shawn, p. 181.
14. Olney, *Reflexions*, p. 37.
15. Richard Olney Papers.
16. Olney, *Reflexions*, pp. 34–35.

7. BECOMING JULIA CHILD

1. Ali-Bab (Henri Babinski), *Encyclopedia of Practical Gastronomy*, pp. 14, 19, and 34.
2. Auguste Escoffier, *Ma Cuisine* (London: Hamlyn, 1965), p. 10.
3. Susan Friedland, note to author, Aug. 2016, citing an unpublished interview with Ébrard's daughter-in-law. Ébrard published only after her husband's death made doing so financially necessary—and she did so pseudonymously.
4. The information in this section comes from an oral history given Oct. 20, 1998, at Amherst College, and kept in the special collections department of Frost Library, Amherst, Massachusetts. Turgeon was interviewed by Jack W. C. Hagstrom, a friend, Amherst alumni, and bibliophile.
5. Jane Nickerson, "News of Food: Famous Classic of French Kitchen at Last Makes Its Debut in English," *The New York Times*, May 7, 1949, p. 9.
6. Noël Riley Fitch, *Appetite for Life*, p. 181.
7. Paul Child to Charlie Child, Dec. 20, 1951, Julia Child Papers, Schlesinger Library, Harvard University.
8. Julia Child, *As Always, Julia*, ed. Joan Reardon, p. 238.
9. Fitch, *Appetite for Life*, p. 182.
10. Julia Child and Alex Prud'homme, *My Life in France*, pp. 100–101.
11. Ibid., p. 98.
12. Ibid., pp. 94–96.
13. Ibid., p. 110.
14. Simone Beck and Suzanne Paterson, *Food and Friends*, p. 91.
15. Julia Child, preface to ibid., p. xv.
16. "Le Cercle des Gourmettes," drafted by Child "6/24/1963" for an editor at *Promenade* magazine, Child Papers.
17. Beck, *Food and Friends*, pp. 151–52.
18. Child, *As Always, Julia*, p. 238.
19. Beck, *Food and Friends*, p. 161.
20. Child and Prud'homme, *My Life in France*, p. 115.
21. Fitch, *Appetite for Life*, p. 192.

22. Christopher Petkanas, "Mastering the Art of Simca," in *At Home in France* (New York: Rizzoli, 1990), pp. 92–99.

23. Paul Child to Charlie Child, Nov. 3, 1951, Child Papers.

24. Paul Child to Charlie Child, Dec. 12, 1951, Child Papers.

25. Child and Prud'homme, *My Life in France*, p. 119.

26. Ibid., p. 89.

27. Ibid., p. 119.

28. Fitch, *Appetite for Life*, p. 190.

29. Paul Child to Charlie Child, Feb. 5, 1952, Child Papers.

30. Child and Prud'homme, *My Life in France*, p. 123.

31. Ibid., p. 79.

32. Ibid., p. 117.

33. Ibid., p. 132.

34. Julia Child to DeVoto, March 4, 1953, *As Always, Julia*, p. 91.

35. Child and Prud'homme, *My Life in France*, pp. 127–28.

36. Child, *As Always, Julia*, p. 73.

37. Beck, *Food and Friends*, p. 163.

38. Child, *As Always, Julia*, p. 74.

39. Child and Prud'homme, *My Life in France*, p. 133.

8. "AS IF A COOK BOOK HAD ANYTHING TO DO WITH WRITING"

1. *The Alice B. Toklas Cook Book*, p. 199.

2. Toklas, *What Is Remembered*, p. 164.

3. James R. Mellow, *Charmed Circle*, p. 535.

4. Ibid., p. 538.

5. Gertrude Stein, *The Autobiography of Alice B. Toklas*, p. 7.

6. Ibid., p. 8.

7. *Alice B. Toklas Cook Book*, p. 189.

8. Ibid., p. 158.

9. Mellow, *Charmed Circle*, p. 520.

10. Toklas to Louise Taylor, Aug. 14, 1952, *Staying On Alone*, ed. Edward Burns, p. 262.

11. Toklas to Brion Gysin, Feb. 26, 1952, ibid., p. 252.

12. Toklas to Taylor, Jan. 23, 1951, ibid., p. 221.

13. Toklas to Taylor, Feb. 11, 1951, ibid., p. 222.

14. Toklas to Carl Van Vechten, May 7, 1952, ibid., p. 256.

15. Toklas to Van Vechten, Feb. 13, 1950, ibid., pp. 186–87.

16. Toklas to Van Vechten, May 7, 1952, ibid., p. 257.

17. Toklas, *What Is Remembered*, p. 129.

18. Ibid.

19. Naomi Barry, "A Memory of Alice B. Toklas," in *Remembrance of Things Paris*, ed. Ruth Reichl, p. 227.

20. Toklas to Isabel Wilder, Sept. 25, 1952, *Staying On Alone*, p. 264.

21. Toklas to Samuel Steward, Oct. 24, 1952, *Dear Sammy*, ed. Samuel R. Steward, pp. 199–200.

22. Toklas to Van Vechten, Nov. 24, 1952, *Staying On Alone*, p. 268.

23. Toklas to Taylor, Mar. 14, 1953, ibid., pp. 274–75.

24. *Alice B. Toklas Cook Book*, p. 1.

25. Toklas to Steward, June 28, 1953, *Staying On Alone*, p. 203.

26. *Alice B. Toklas Cook Book*, p. 3.

27. Toklas to Taylor, Mar. 14, 1953, *Staying On Alone*, pp. 274–75.

28. Carlton Lake, "Summer Reading: How the Aspic from Topeka Won the Heart of Alice B. Toklas," *The New York Times*, June 5, 1988.

29. *Alice B. Toklas Cook Book*, p. 265.

30. Ibid.

31. Ibid., p. 266.

32. Ibid., p. 280.

33. Toklas to the Daniels, Jan. 16, 1967, *Charmed Circle*, p. 477.

34. Toklas to Janet Flanner, July 8, 1953, *Staying on Alone*, p. 280.

35. Toklas to Lawrence Strauss, July 11, 1953, ibid., p. 284.

36. Toklas to Steward, Aug. 2, 1954, ibid., p. 208.

37. Toklas to Steward, Jan. 28, 1954, *Dear Sammy*, pp. 205–6.

38. "People," *Time*, Oct. 4, 1954.

39. Simon Michael Bessie to Toklas, Dec. 9, 1954, Bradley Literary Agency Papers, Harry Ransom Center, University of Texas at Austin.

40. Toklas to Dilkusha de Rohan, Feb. 1, 1954, *Staying On Alone*, pp. 296–97.

41. Simon Michael Bessie, "A Happy Publisher's Note to the 1984 Edition," in *The Alice B. Toklas Cook Book* (1954; repr., New York: Harper & Row, 1984), pp. vii–viii.

42. Toklas to Donald Gallup, "October 12-19-21" 1954, *Staying On Alone*, p. 310.

43. Toklas to Steward, Nov. 20, 1954, *Dear Sammy*, pp. 209–10.

44. Rex Stout, "To Cook Is to Cook," *The New York Times*, Nov. 21, 1954.

45. Jane Nickerson, "Two New Cookbooks Give Contrasting Views of Gourmet Fare," *The New York Times*, Nov. 22, 1954.

46. "A Dish Is a Dish Is a Dish," *Time*, Nov. 22, 1954.

47. Unsigned ("Eustace Tilley") review, *The New Yorker*, Feb. 5, 1955, p. 116.

48. For more on the subject, see Jane Stern and Michael Stern, *American Gourmet*.

49. Janet Malcolm, *Two Lives*, pp. 3–5.

50. Joe Barry, "Cooking as Culture," *The New Republic*, Nov. 29, 1954, pp. 17–18.

9. "I AM A MERCHANT OF PLEASURE"

1. *Alexis Lichine's New Encyclopedia of Wines and Spirits*, p. xxv.

2. Joseph Wechsberg, "A Dreamer of Wine," *The New Yorker*, May 17, 1958, p. 60.

3. Lichine, *Encyclopedia*, p. 38.

4. Leslie Hennessy, *The Pope of Wine*, p. 57.

5. Ibid., p. 59.

6. Quoted in ibid., p. 141.

7. Closely paraphrased from Wechsberg, "Dreamer of Wine," pp. 76–78.

8. Hennessy, *The Pope of Wine*, p. 118.

9. *Alexis Lichine's New Encyclopedia*, p. xix.

10. Ibid., pp. xix–xx.

11. *Alexis Lichine's Guide to the Wines and Vineyards of France*, pp. 23–24.

12. Lichine, quoted in Joseph Wechsberg, "A Dreamer of Wine (Part Two)," *The New Yorker*, May 24, 1958, p. 54.
13. Ibid., p. 57.
14. Ibid., p. 38.
15. Hennessy, *The Pope of Wine*, p. 120.
16. Wechsberg, "Dreamer of Wine (Part Two)," p. 38.
17. James Beard to Helen Evans Brown, Jan. 23, 1955, *Love and Kisses and a Halo of Truffles*, ed. John Ferrone, p. 86.
18. Beard to Brown, Jan. 20, 1956, ibid., p. 144.
19. Ibid.
20. Lichine, *New Encyclopedia*, p. xxi.
21. Ibid.
22. Closely paraphrased from Mark Goodman, "Alexis Lichine Is the Hustler Known as 'the Pope of Wine,'" *People*, April 7, 1975.
23. Ibid.
24. Frank Prial, "Wine Talk," *The New York Times*, Aug. 7, 1996.
25. Goodman, "Alexis Lichine Is the Hustler."
26. Hennessy, *The Pope of Wine*, p. 104.
27. Lichine, *New Encyclopedia*, p. xxi.
28. Hennessy, *The Pope of Wine*, pp. 38–39.
29. Goodman, "Alexis Lichine Is the Hustler."

10. *AROMAS AND FLAVORS OF PAST AND PRESENT*

1. Poppy Cannon, introduction to *Aromas and Flavors of Past and Present*, by Alice Toklas, p. xi.
2. Poppy Cannon, quoted in Laura Shapiro, *Something from the Oven*, p. 114.
3. Alice Toklas, *What Is Remembered*, p. 146.
4. Poppy Cannon, *A Gentle Knight*, p. 14.
5. While in later life Cannon implied in various interviews and press releases that she had graduated from Vassar (or, alternately, Barnard), only Vassar has any record of her matriculation, and then only for freshman year, and with no record of her completing that year. (Author inquiries to Vassar and Barnard Colleges, conducted by phone, 2015.)
6. Cannon, *A Gentle Knight*, p. 115.
7. Shapiro, *Something from the Oven*, p. 95.
8. Ibid., p. 96.
9. Poppy Cannon, *The Can-Opener Cookbook*, pp. 1–4.
10. Poppy Cannon, *The Bride's Cookbook*, p. 137.
11. Ibid., p. 371.
12. Ibid.
13. Shapiro, *Something from the Oven*, p. 100.
14. Joan Gage, "Letter to the Editor," *Dag News*, The Daguerrian Society, "06-29-1999," accessed online at www.daguerre.org.
15. *Kirkus Reviews*, Nov. 10, 1952.
16. Alice Toklas to Louise Taylor, May 30, 1954, *Staying On Alone*, ed. Edward Burns, p. 302.

17. Toklas to Dilkusha de Rohan, June 13, 1955, ibid., pp. 321–22.

18. Toklas to Ralph Church, Jan. 25, 1955, ibid., p. 313.

19. Toklas to Bernard Faÿ, Dec. 19, 1956, ibid., p. 340.

20. Toklas to Carl and Fania Van Vechten, Mar. 16, 1956, ibid., p. 335 (*"Herbs and Spices* has been my delight since it came on Monday").

21. Toklas to John Schaffner, Apr. 18, 1955, John Schaffner Papers, Columbia University Special Collections Archive.

22. Linda Simon, *The Biography of Alice Toklas*. p. 235.

23. Toklas to Samuel Steward, Sept. 21, 1956, *Dear Sammy*, ed. Samuel M. Steward, p. 216.

24. Paraphrased from Simon, *Biography of Alice Toklas*, p. 235.

25. Shapiro, *Something from the Oven*, p. 118.

26. Toklas to W. G. Rogers, May 26, 1958, *Staying On Alone*, p. 359.

27. Paraphrased from James R. Mellow, *Charmed Circle*, pp. 568–89.

28. Simon, *Autobiography of Alice Toklas*, p. 246.

29. Toklas to Schaffner, July 5, 1958, Schaffner Papers.

30. Toklas to Steward, Apr. 3, 1958, *Dear Sammy*, p. 226.

31. Cannon, introduction to *Aromas and Flavors*, pp. vii, ix.

32. Ibid., p. xx.

33. Ibid., pp. xx–xxi.

34. Ibid., p. xix.

35. *Alice B. Toklas Cook Book*, p. 131.

36. Naomi Barry, "Alice Toklas Hits Tin-Can Type of Cook," *Paris Herald Tribune*, Dec. 11, 1954.

37. Toklas files, Harper Publishers Papers, Columbia University.

38. James Beard to Helen Evans Brown, Sept. 14, 1958, *Love and Kisses and a Halo of Truffles*, ed. John Ferrone, p. 230.

39. Janet Flanner, "Recipes of Alice B. Toklas," *The New Republic*, Dec. 15, 1958, p. 20.

40. Charlotte Turgeon, "Favorite Dishes of Gertrude Stein and Others," *The New York Times Book Review*, Dec. 7, 1958, p. 60.

41. Shapiro, *Something from the Oven*, pp. 119–20.

42. Nora Ephron, "Critics in the World of the Rising Soufflé (or Is It the Rising Meringue?)," *New York*, Sept. 30, 1968, p. 35.

11. "A DREAMER OF WINE"

1. Alexis Lichine to Alfred A. Knopf, Jan. 24, 1957, Alfred A. Knopf, Inc. Records (Series II), Lichine file, Harry Ransom Center, University of Texas at Austin.

2. Lichine to Knopf, Feb. 19, 1957 (sent from Lichine's offices at 35-02 Northern Blvd., Long Island City 1, NY), ibid.

3. Lichine handed in several sloppy drafts of the book and failed to present a production-ready manuscript. Knopf then undertook the creation of the nine maps wanted by Lichine for the book but never commissioned or paid for by Lichine, as per his contractual obligation. Knopf also remonstrated with Lichine over his habit of handing out "free" copies of the book for promotional purposes, ultimately insisting that Lichine pay for them himself. Knopf–Lichine correspondence, Knopf Records, Harry Ransom Center, University of Texas at Austin.

4. Edgar Kanarik to Knopf, Jan. 27, 1957, ibid.

5. Quoted in Leslie Hennessy, *The Pope of Wine*, p. 156.

6. Knopf to Lichine, Apr. 9, 1957, Knopf Records, Lichine file.

7. Knopf to Lichine, Apr. 15, 1957, ibid.

8. Hennessy, *The Pope of Wine*, p. 126.

9. Lichine to Knopf, July 16, 1957, Knopf Records, Lichine file.

10. Joseph Wechsberg, "A Dreamer of Wine," *The New Yorker*, May 17, 1958, p. 48.

11. Wechsberg, "A Dreamer of Wine (Part II)," *The New Yorker*, May 24, 1958, p. 37.

12. Ibid., p. 58.

13. Wechsberg, "Dreamer of Wine" (Part I), p. 49.

14. Wechsberg, "Dreamer of Wine (Part II)," p. 57.

15. *Alexis Lichine's Guide to the Wines and Vineyards of France*, p. 69.

16. Ibid., p. 70.

17. Associated Press, "Tax Fraud Is Charged to Philippe," *The* [Spokane] *Spokesman-Review*, Oct. 3, 1958, p. 28.

18. "Taxes: Better Than 15%," *Time*, Oct. 13, 1958; "Ex-Waldorf Aide Fined in Tax Case: Philippe, Former Banquet Head, Admits Evasion—Gets $10,000 Penalty," *The New York Times*, Sept. 20, 1960; "Ex-Executive of Hotels Becomes a Consultant," *The New York Times*, Aug. 6, 1964.

19. "Philippe Is Leaving Zeckendorf to Direct Summit Hotel Here," *The New York Times*, Jan. 10, 1961.

20. Mark Goodman, "Alexis Lichine Is the Hustler Known as 'the Pope of Wine,'" *People*, Apr. 7, 1975.

21. Hennessy, *The Pope of Wine*, p. 155.

22. Ibid.

23. Associated Press, "Arlene Dahl Weds Fourth in Barbados," Dec. 24, 1965. See also the local Barbadian coverage in *The Bridgetown Morning Record*, of the same date, p. 6.

24. Quoted in Hennessy, *The Pope of Wine*, p. 157.

25. Quoted in Goodman, "Alexis Lichine Is the Hustler."

26. *Alexis Lichine's Guide to the Wines and Vineyards of France*, p. 24.

27. Hennessy, *The Pope of Wine*, p. 153. For the wine cellar, see Goodman, "Alexis Lichine Is the Hustler."

28. Goodman, "Alexis Lichine Is the Hustler."

29. Hennessy, *The Pope of Wine*, p. 130.

30. *Alexis Lichine's Guide to the Wines and Vineyards of France*, p. xxiii.

31. William Grimes, "Ab Simon, Chairman of Seagram Wine Unit, Dies at 88," *The New York Times*, Jan. 4, 2011.

32. Hennessy, *The Pope of Wine*, p. 158.

33. Ibid.

34. Robert J. Misch, "A Fine Bouquet," *The New York Times Book Review*, Dec. 3, 1967, p. 50.

12. A CHANGING OF THE GUARD

1. "France: Pebbles in a Pond," *Time*, Feb. 7, 1964.

2. Quoted in Thomas McNamee, *The Man Who Changed the Way We Eat*, pp. 154–55.

3. Julia Child, foreword to *French Provincial Cooking*, by Elizabeth David, p. 11.

4. McNamee, *The Man Who Changed the Way We Eat*, p. 97.
5. A. J. Liebling to Mitchell, quoted in Raymond Sokolov, *Wayward Reporter*, p. 175.
6. Brendan Gill, *Here at the New Yorker* (New York: Random House, 1975), p. 345.
7. Sokolov, *Wayward Reporter*, pp. 306–7.
8. Gill, *Here at the New Yorker*, p. 347.
9. Ibid., p. 344; see also Sokolov, *Wayward Reporter*, pp. 230–31.
10. Sokolov, *Wayward Reporter*, p. 232.
11. Ibid., pp. 238–39.
12. Ibid., p. 271.
13. David Roberts, *Jean Stafford* (Boston: Little, Brown, 1988), p. 347.
14. Sokolov, *Wayward Reporter*, p. 298.
15. Ibid., p. 299.
16. Ibid., p. 309.
17. Ibid., p. 320.
18. William Shawn, "A. J. Liebling," *The New Yorker*, Jan. 11, 1964, pp. 107–8.
19. Edwin Gilbert, "Where Food Was King," *The New York Times Book Review*, Nov. 11, 1962.
20. Julia Child, *As Ever, Julia*, ed. Joan Reardon, p. 149.
21. Ibid., p. 349.
22. Ibid., p. 350.
23. "Food: Everyone's in the Kitchen," *Time*, Nov. 25, 1966; accessed online at http://content.time.com/time/magazine/article/0,9171,843114,00.html.
24. Julia Child to Elizabeth David, Apr. 14, 1964, Elizabeth David Papers, Schlesinger Library, Harvard University.
25. Child to David, Feb. 6, 1965, David Papers.
26. James R. Mellow, *Charmed Circle*, p. 570.

13. OLNEY STAYS ON

1. Richard Olney, *Reflexions*, pp. 61–62.
2. Ibid., pp. 70–71.
3. Ibid., p. 73.
4. Ibid.
5. Simone Beck and Suzanne Paterson, *Food and Friends*, pp. 275–77.
6. Olney, *Reflexions*, p. 68.
7. Naomi Barry, "Heritage of Alexandre Dumaine," *Gourmet*, Feb. 1964.
8. Olney, *Reflexions*, p. 83.
9. Richard Olney to Guy Griffin, May 10, 1998, Richard Olney Papers.
10. Closely paraphrased from Olney, *Reflexions*, p. 80.
11. Ibid., p. 80.
12. Ibid., p. 71.
13. Richard Olney to James Olney, Oct. 30, 1963, Richard Olney Papers.
14. Michel Lemmonier, "*La Lettre Gourmande*," *Cuisine et Vins de France*, Mar. 1968, p. 16.
15. Byron Olney to Krystyna, Feb. 14, 2001, Richard Olney Papers, Collection of Byron Olney, Rochester, Minn.
16. Olney, *Reflexions*, pp. 78–79.

17. Sybille Bedford to Elizabeth David, May 11, 1967 (from Les Bastides, La Roquette-sur-Siagne), Elizabeth David Papers, Schlesinger Library, Harvard University.
18. Sybille Bedford, *Pleasures and Landscapes*, p. 150.
19. Sybille Bedford, "La Vie de Château," in ibid., pp. 151–52.
20. Olney, *Reflexions*, pp. 97–98.
21. Ibid., p. 102.
22. Richard Olney, *Simple French Food*, pp. 9–10.
23. James Olney, "Remembering Richard Remembering Mlle. Marty," *The Cincinnati Review* 3, no. 1 (Summer 2006), pp. 65–85.
24. Olney, *Reflexions*, p. 88.
25. Ibid., p. 92.
26. Ibid.

14. M.F.K. FISHER AND *THE COOKING OF PROVINCIAL FRANCE*

1. M.F.K. Fisher to Eleanor and Donald Friede, Apr. 22, 1962, *M.F.K. Fisher: A Life in Letters*, ed. Norah K. Barr, Marsha Moran, and Patrick Moran, p. 180.
2. Joan Reardon, *Poet of the Appetites*, p. 256.
3. Ibid., p. 327.
4. M.F.K. Fisher, "Two Kitchens in Provence," *The New Yorker*, Aug. 27, 1966. pp. 29–36. See also Reardon, *Poet of the Appetites*, p. 328.
5. "Marietta Voorhees: Tough Old Bird," *St. Helena* [Calif.] *Star*, Oct. 11, 2007; accessed online at http://napavalleyregister.com/star/news/opinion/columnists/marietta-voorhees-tough-old-bird/article_d105fc51-c6cf-5bbc-82a0-5788121e091f.html.
6. Reardon, *Poet of the Appetites*, p. 262.
7. Ibid., pp. 270, 280.
8. Ibid., p. 285.
9. Ibid., pp. 285–86.
10. Ibid., p. 121.
11. Ibid., p. 307.
12. Ibid., p. 315.
13. Ibid., pp. 321–22.
14. Time-Life, "Foods of the World" press release, Mary Frances Kennedy Fisher Papers, Schlesinger Library, Harvard University.
15. Quoted in ibid., pp. 332–33.
16. Time-Life promotional material, "Meet Your Chef Hosts," Mary Frances Kennedy Fisher Papers, Schlesinger Library, Harvard University.
17. M.F.K. Fisher, foreword to *The Alice B. Toklas Cook Book* (1954; repr., New York: Harper & Row, 1984), p. ix.
18. Ibid., p. x.
19. Ibid.
20. Ibid., p. xi.
21. Reardon, *Poet of the Appetites*, p. 337.
22. Fisher Papers, Schlesinger Library, Harvard University.
23. Fisher, foreword to *The Alice B. Toklas Cook Book*, p. x.
24. Reardon, *Poet of the Appetites*, p. xi.

25. Ibid., p. 435.

26. Julia Child, *As Always, Julia*, ed. Joan Reardon, p. 398.

27. "Michael Field, Food Writer, Dies; Once Duo Pianist," *The New York Times*, Mar. 24, 1971, p. 46.

28. Reardon, *Poet of the Appetites*, p. 337.

29. Ibid.

30. Sybille Bedford to Elizabeth David, Sept. 21, 1963 (from Les Bastides), in Artemis Cooper, *Writing at the Kitchen Table*, p. 228.

31. Elizabeth David, *French Provincial Cooking*, p. 4.

32. Julia Child, foreword to *French Provincial Cooking*, by Elizabeth David (1960; repr., New York: Penguin, 2000), pp. 12–13.

33. Richard Olney, *Reflexions*, p. 145.

34. Untitled article about Elizabeth David by Sybille Bedford, Elizabeth David Papers, Schlesinger Library.

35. M.F.K. Fisher to Julia Child, June 16, 1966, *M.F.K. Fisher: A Life in Letters*, pp. 230–31.

36. Reardon, *Poet of the Appetites*, p. 338.

37. Julia Child to Judith Jones, Sept. 1, 1966, Alfred A. Knopf, Inc. Records (Series II), Harry Ransom Center, University of Texas at Austin.

38. Reardon, *Poet of the Appetites*, p. 342.

39. Ibid., p. 343.

40. Ibid.

41. M.F.K. Fisher, *The Cooking of Provincial France*, p. 9.

42. Ibid.

43. Ibid., p. 97.

44. Ibid., p. 132.

45. Ibid., p. 133.

46. Ibid., p. 156.

47. Ibid., p. 10.

48. Ibid., p. 14

49. Ibid., p. 19

50. Ibid., p. 24.

51. Ibid., p. 30.

52. Reardon, *Poet of the Appetites*, pp. 343–44.

53. Ibid., p. 354.

54. Ibid., p. 347.

55. Ibid., p. 345; see also supporting documentation in Fisher Papers.

56. M.F.K. Fisher to Arnold Gingrich, Nov. 5, 1966, *M.F.K. Fisher: A Life in Letters*, pp. 241–42.

57. Craig Claiborne, "Debut for a Series of International Cookbooks," *The New York Times*, Feb. 19, 1968, p. 46.

58. Nora Ephron, "Critics in the World of the Rising Soufflé (or Is It the Rising Meringue?)," *New York*, Sept. 30, 1968, pp. 34–39.

59. Hebe Dorsey Paris, "Cookbooks Debut in Empty Les Halles," Mar. 20, 1969, *International Herald Tribune*, Fisher Papers, Box 108, Folder 12.

60. "A Gastronome's Revenge," *Newsweek*, Apr. 28, 1969, p. 53.

61. Fisher, *Cooking of Provincial France*, p. 17.

62. Robert J. Courtine, *The Hundred Glories of French Cooking*, pp. 63–66.
63. Fisher, *Cooking of Provincial France*, p. 121.
64. "A Gastronome's Revenge," *Newsweek*, Apr. 28, 1969, p. 53.
65. John L. Hess, "Time-Life Cookbook: It's Self-Roasting," *The New York Times*, Apr. 15, 1969.
66. Bedford to David, Aug. 2, 1970 (from La Roquette), David Papers.
67. Richard Olney to James Olney, Dec. 18, 1970, Richard Olney Papers.

15. OLNEY IN THE VAR

1. Richard Olney, *Reflexions*, p. 87.
2. Richard Olney, *The French Menu Cookbook*, p. 5.
3. Richard Olney to Greg Drescher of the American Institute of Wine and Food, Oct. 10, 1986 (outlining a presentation he hoped to give in Dallas), Richard Olney Papers.
4. Ibid.
5. Michel Lemmonier, *"Lettre Gourmand: 'L'Américain en France' et Ses Trois Talents,"* *Cuisine et Vins de France*, Mar. 1968, p. 16 (translation by the author).
6. James Olney to Sybille Bedford, Dec. 13, 2000, Sybille Bedford and Eda Lord Papers, Harry Ransom Center, University of Texas at Austin.
7. Jane Wilson, email to author.

16. THE END OF THE AFFAIR

1. "France: Battle of the Sorbonne," *Time*, May 17, 1968; accessed online at http://content.time.com/time/magazine/article/0,9171,838353,00.html.
2. Henry Pillsbury interviewed by Jason Weiss; accessed online at http://www.itinerariesofahummingbird.com/american-center-paris.html.
3. Judith Pillsbury, interview with author, summer 2009.
4. "From Camelot to Elysium (Via Olympic Airways)," *Time*, Oct. 25, 1968; accessed online at http://content.time.com/time/magazine/article/0,9171,900374,00.htm.
5. Rudi Chelminski, "He Can't Believe He Ate the Whole Thing!," *People*, Nov. 24, 1975.
6. Details drawn from Craig Claiborne, "Just a Quiet Dinner for 2 in Paris: 31 Dishes, 9 Wines, a $4,000 Check," *The New York Times*, Nov. 14, 1975, p. 1. See also Thomas McNamee, *The Man Who Changed the Way We Eat*, pp. 205–9, and Chelminski, "He Can't Believe He Ate the Whole Thing!"
7. Letters to the Editor, *The New York Times*, Nov. 20, 1975. Endnote from McNamee, *Man Who Changed the Way We Eat*, p. 210.
8. Jacob Rosenthal, "The Four Thousand Dollar Dinner Controversy! The Wrong Reason . . . ," *Taste*, Winter–Spring 1976, quoted in McNamee, *Man Who Changed the Way We Eat*, p. 225.
9. Julia Child to Craig Claiborne, Jan. 7, 1976, in McNamee, *Man Who Changed the Way We Eat*, p. 211.
10. Julia Child, *As Always, Julia*, ed. Joan Reardon, p. 239.
11. Julia Child, *From Julia Child's Kitchen*, p. i.
12. Simone Beck and Suzanne Paterson, *Food and Friends*, p. 226.

13. Elizabeth David to James Beard, Oct. 28, 1974, James Beard Papers, NYU/ Fales Special Collections Library.

14. "Some Scattered Notes on a Visit to Bramafam–Pitchoune Dec 17, '66 to Jan 3, '67," Avis DeVoto Papers, Schlesinger Library, Harvard University.

15. Julia Child to M.F.K. Fisher, Sept. 1, 1969, Mary Frances Kennedy Fisher Papers, Schlesinger Library.

16. Richard Olney to James Olney, n.d., quoted in Richard Olney, *Reflexions*, p. 196.

17. R. W. Apple, "Richard Olney, 71, A Writer of the Joys of French Cooking," *The New York Times*, Aug. 4, 1999.

18. Mimi Sheraton, "Nouvelle Cuisine's 10 Commandments and Many Heroes," *The Chicago Tribune*, Dec. 3, 1979.

19. "Modern Living: The Simple Lion," *Time*, Apr. 9, 1973; "Ship of Drools," *Time*, May 19, 1975.

20. Nika Hazelton, "Delectations: French Home Cooking," *The National Review*, n.d., Richard Olney Papers.

21. Richard Olney to Patric Kuh, July 5, 1999, ibid.

22. Karen Hess, "The Gourmet Plague," *The Atlantic* 234, no. 2 (August 1974), pp. 60–62.

23. Olney, *Reflexions*, p. 213.

24. Richard Olney to David, May 12, 1976, Elizabeth David Papers, Schlesinger Library.

25. Guy Griffin, "A Charmed Life: Richard Olney Is One of the World's Great Food Writers," *Australian Gourmet Traveler*, Oct. 1994, pp. 18–19.

26. For more on this subject, see "Bordeaux Modern History," by Edmund Penning-Rowsell, in *The Oxford Companion to Wine*, ed. Jancis Robinson, p. 127.

27. Leslie Hennessy, *The Pope of Wine*, p. 147; see also "Count Is Fiancé of Miss Lichine," *The New York Times*, Oct. 11, 1981.

28. *Alexis Lichine's Guide to the Wines and Vineyards of France*, p. xxiii.

29. Frank Prial, "Wine: In Possession of His Fortune," *The New York Times*, June 21, 1987.

30. Hennessy, *The Pope of Wine*, p. 150.

AFTERWORD

1. Prosper Montagné, Dr. Gottschalk, Auguste Escoffier, and Philéas Gilbert, *Larousse Gastronomique*, pp. 5–6.

Selected Bibliography

Adair, Arthur H., X. Marcel Boulestin, and Marie Laurencin. *Dinners, Long and Short.* London: Victor Gollancz, 1928.

Andrieu, Pierre. *Les Vins de France . . . et d'Ailleurs: Comment Les Choisir—Les Servir—Les Déguster et Les Utiliser en Cuisine.* Paris: Flammarion, 1939.

———. *Fine Bouche: A History of the Restaurant in France.* London: Cassell, 1956.

Arbellot, Simon. *Guide des Touristes Gastronomes.* Paris: Taride, 1958.

———. *La Gastronomie.* Paris: Hachette, 1962.

———. *Tel Plat—Tel Vin.* Paris: Éditions Amphora, 1963.

———. *Curnonsky, Prince des Gastronomes.* Paris: Les Productions de Paris, 1965.

Arndt, Alice. *Culinary Biographies: A Dictionary of the World's Great Historic Chefs, Cookbook Authors and Collectors, Farmers, Gourmets, Home Economists, Nutritionists, Restaurateurs, Philosophers, Physicians, Scientists, Writers, and Others Who Influenced the Way We Eat Today.* Houston: YES Press, 2006.

Association des Amis de Curnonsky. *Curnonsky et Ses Amis.* Paris: Librarie Edgar Soete, 1979.

Babinski, Henri [Ali-Bab, pseud.]. *Gastronomie Pratique: Études Culinaires Suivies du Traitement de l'Obésité des Gourmands.* Paris: Flammarion, 1907.

———. *The Encyclopedia of Practical Gastronomy.* New York: McGraw-Hill, 1974.

Baldwin, James. *Go Tell It on the Mountain.* New York: Dial Press, 1953.

———. *Notes of a Native Son.* Boston: Beacon Press, 1955.

———. *Nobody Knows My Name: More Notes of a Native Son.* New York: Dial Press, 1961.

———. *Another Country.* New York: Dial Press, 1962.

———. *The Fire Next Time.* New York: Dial Press, 1963.

———. *Going to Meet the Man.* New York: Dial Press, 1965.

———. *Giovanni's Room.* New York: Dial Press, 1966.

———. *Tell Me How Long the Train's Been Gone.* New York: Dial Press, 1968.

Barry, Naomi. *Paris Personal.* New York: Dutton, 1963.

——. *Gourmet: Paris à Table.* New York: Gourmet Books, 1971.

Baudelaire, Charles. *Les Paradis Artificiels.* Paris: Michel Lévy, 1869.

Beard, James. *Hors d'Oeuvres and Canapés, with a Key to the Cocktail Party.* New York: Granger, 1940.

——. *Cook It Outdoors.* New York: M. Barrows, 1941.

——. *The Fireside Cook Book: A Complete Guide to Fine Cooking for Beginner and Expert.* New York: Simon & Schuster, 1949.

——. *Jim Beard's Barbecue Cooking.* New York: Maco, 1954.

——. *James Beard's Fish Cookery.* Boston: Little, Brown, 1954.

——. *The Complete Book of Outdoor Cookery.* With Helen Evans Brown. New York: Doubleday, 1955.

——. *Jim Beard's Casserole Cookbook.* New York: Maco, 1955.

——. *The James Beard Cookbook.* New York: Dell, 1959.

——. *Delights and Prejudices: A Memoir with Recipes.* New York: Atheneum, 1964.

——. *James Beard's American Cookery.* Boston: Little, Brown, 1972.

——. *Beard on Bread.* New York: Knopf, 1973.

——. *James Beard's Theory and Practice of Good Cooking.* New York: Knopf, 1977.

——. *The New James Beard.* New York: Knopf, 1981.

——. *Beard on Pasta.* New York: Knopf, 1983.

——. *Love and Kisses and a Halo of Truffles: Letters to Helen Evans Brown.* Edited by John Ferrone. New York: Arcade, 1994.

Beard, James, and Gino Cofacci. *How to Eat and Drink Your Way Through a French (or Italian) Menu.* New York: Atheneum, 1971.

Beard, James, and Alexander Watt. *Paris Cuisine.* Boston: Little, Brown, 1952.

Beck, Simone. *Simca's Cuisine.* New York: Knopf, 1972.

Beck, Simone, Louisette Bertholle, and Julia Child. *Mastering the Art of French Cooking.* New York: Knopf, 1961.

Beck, Simone, and Julia Child. *Mastering the Art of French Cooking Volume II.* New York: Knopf, 1970.

Beck, Simone, and Michael James. *New Recipes from Simca's Cuisine.* New York: Harcourt Brace Jovanovich, 1979.

Beck, Simone, and Suzanne Patterson. *Food and Friends: Recipes and Memories from Simca's Cuisine.* New York: Viking, 1991.

Bedford, Sybille. *The Sudden View: A Mexican Journey.* London: Victor Gollancz, 1953.

——. *A Legacy.* London: Weidenfeld & Nicolson, 1956.

——. *A Compass Error.* London: Collins, 1968.

——. *A Favorite of the Gods.* New York: Obelisk/Dutton, 1984.

——. *Jigsaw: An Unsentimental Education.* New York: Knopf, 1989.

——. *Pleasures and Landscapes: A Traveler's Tales from Europe.* New York: Counterpoint, 2003.

——. *Quicksands: A Memoir.* New York: Counterpoint, 2005.

Bemelmans, Ludwig. *La Bonne Table.* New York: Simon & Schuster, 1964.

Berne, Victoria [M.F.K. Fisher and Dillwyn Parrish, pseud.]. *Touch and Go.* New York: Harper & Bros., 1939.

Bertholle, Louisette. *Secrets of the Great French Restaurants.* New York: Macmillan, 1974.

Boulestin, X. M. *Simple French Cooking for English Homes*. London: William Heinemann, 1923.

——. *The Conduct of the Kitchen: How to Keep a Good Table for Sixteen Shillings a Week*. London: William Heinemann, 1925.

——. *A Second Helping: Or, More Dishes for English Homes*. London: William Heinemann, 1925.

——. *What Shall We Have To-Day: 365 Recipes for All the Days of the Year*. London: William Heinemann, 1931.

——. *Having Crossed the Channel . . . {an Account of Travel on the Continent, with Special Reference to Food and Cooking.}* Illustrations by J.-E. Laboureur. London: William Heinemann, 1934.

Brillat-Savarin, Jean-Anthelme. *La Physiologie du Goût, ou Méditations de Gastronomie Transcendente*. Paris: Gabriel de Gonet, 1848.

——. *The Physiology of Taste; or, Transcendental Gastronomy*. Translated by Fayette Robinson. Philadelphia: Lindsay & Blakiston, 1854.

——. *Gastronomy as a Fine Art, or, the Science of Good Living*. Translated by R. E. Anderson. London: Chatto & Windus, 1877.

——. *Brillat-Savarin's Physiologie du Goût. A Handbook of Gastronomy*. London: Nimmo & Bain, 1883.

——. *The Physiology of Taste: Or, Meditations on Transcendental Gastronomy*. Foreword by Frank Crowninshield. New York: Boni & Liveright, 1926.

——. *The Physiology of Taste: Or, Meditations on Transcendental Gastronomy*. Translated by M.F.K. Fisher. New York: Heritage, 1949.

Campbell, James. *Talking at the Gates: A Life of James Baldwin*. New York: Viking, 1991.

——. *Exiled in Paris: Richard Wright, James Baldwin, Samuel Beckett, and Others on the Left Bank*. New York: Scribner, 1995.

Cannon, Poppy. *The Can-Opener Cookbook*. New York: Crowell, 1952.

——. *The Bride's Cookbook*. New York: Henry Holt, 1954.

——. *A Gentle Knight: My Husband, Walter White*. New York: Rinehart, 1956.

——. *Unforbidden Sweets: Delicious Desserts of 100 Calories or Less*. New York: Crowell, 1958.

——. *The ABC's of Quick and Glamorous Cooking*. Garden City, N.Y.: Dolphin Books, 1961.

——. *Eating European Abroad and at Home*. Garden City, N.Y.: Doubleday, 1961.

——. *The Electric Epicure's Cookbook*. New York: Crowell, 1961.

——. *The Fast Gourmet Cookbook*. New York: Fleet, 1964.

——. *The Frozen-Foods Cookbook*. New York: Crowell, 1964.

——. *Poppy Cannon's All-Time, No-Time, Any-Time Cookbook*. New York: Crowell, 1974.

Carême, M. A. *French Cookery: Comprising L'Art de La Cuisine Française, Le Pâtissier Royal, et Le Cuisinier Parisien*. Translated by William Hall. London: John Murray, 1840.

Chamberlain, Samuel. *France Will Live Again: The Portrait of a Peaceful Interlude, 1919–1939*. New York: Hastings House, 1940.

——. *Clémentine in the Kitchen*. New York: Hastings House, 1943.

——. *Bouquet de France: An Epicurean Tour of the French Provinces*. New York: Gourmet, 1952.

Chaney, Lisa. *Elizabeth David*. London: Macmillan, 1998.

Chelminski, Rudolph. *The Perfectionist: A Life and Death in Haute Cuisine*. New York: Gotham, 2006.

Child, Julia. *The French Chef Cookbook*. New York: Knopf, 1968.

———. *From Julia Child's Kitchen*. New York: Knopf, 1975.

Child, Julia, and Avis DeVoto. *As Always, Julia: The Letters of Julia Child and Avis DeVoto.* Edited by Joan Reardon. Boston: Houghton Mifflin Harcourt, 2010.

Child, Julia, and Alex Prud'homme. *My Life in France*. New York: Knopf, 2006.

Claiborne, Craig. *The New York Times Cookbook*. New York: Harper & Row, 1961.

———. *A Feast Made for Laughter*. Garden City, N.Y.: Doubleday, 1982.

Clark, Robert. *The Solace of Food: A Life of James Beard*. New York: HarperCollins, 1993.

Cooper, Artemis. *Writing at the Kitchen Table: The Authorized Life of Elizabeth David*. London: Penguin, 2000.

Courtine, Robert J. *La Vraie Cuisine Française*. Verviers, France. Gérard et Cie, 1963.

———. *The Hundred Glories of French Cooking*. New York: Farrar, Straus & Giroux, 1973.

———. *Feasts of a Militant Gastronome*. New York: William Morrow, 1974.

———. *Balzac à Table*. Paris: Robert Laffont, 1976.

———. *Guide Courtine: A Guide to Paris Restaurants*. Secaucus, N.J.: Lyle Stuart, 1976.

———. *The Master Chefs of France Recipe Book: Recipes from 300 Great Restaurants of France*. New York: Everest House, 1981.

Courtine, Robert J., and Céline Vance. *The Grand Masters of French Cuisine: Five Centuries of Great Cooking*. New York: Putnam, 1978.

Cuisine et Vins de France [periodical]. Paris: Compagnie Française d'Éditions Vinicoles, 1947–1975.

David, Elizabeth. *A Book of Mediterranean Food*. London: John Lehmann, 1950.

———. *French Country Cooking*. London: John Lehmann, 1951.

———. *Italian Food*. London: Macdonald, 1954.

———. *French Provincial Cooking*. London: Michael Joseph, 1960.

———. *Summer Cooking*. Harmondsworth, U.K.: Penguin, 1965.

———. *English Bread and Yeast Cookery*. London: Allen Lane, 1977.

———. *An Omelet and a Glass of Wine*. New York: Penguin, 1986.

———. *South Wind Through the Kitchen: The Best of Elizabeth David*. Boston: David Godine, 2006.

Davidson, Alan, ed. *The Oxford Companion to Food*. New York: Oxford University Press, 1999.

Diat, Louis. *French Cooking for Americans*. Philadelphia: Lippincott, 1946.

Dumaine, Alexandre. *Ma Cuisine: Souvenirs Culinaires et Recettes Recueillis par Henri Clos-Jouve*. Paris: Éditions de la Pensée Moderne, 1972.

Dumas, Alexandre. *Alexandre Dumas' Dictionary of Cuisine*. Translated by Louis Colman. London: W. H. Allen, 1959.

Dutourd, Jean. *Au Bon Beurre*. Paris: Gallimard, 1952.

Ébrard, Evelyn. *La Bonne Cuisine de Madame E. Saint-Ange*. Translated by Paul Aratow. Berkeley, Calif.: Ten Speed Press, 2005.

Escoffier, Auguste. *Guide Culinaire: Aide-Mémoire de Cuisine Pratique*. Paris: Imprimerie de Lagny, 1903.

———. *Ma Cuisine*. Translated by Vyvyan Holland. London: Hamlyn, 1965.

———. *The Complete Guide to the Art of Modern Cookery*. London: William Heinemann, 1979.

———. *Memories of My Life*. New York: Van Nostrand Reinhold, 1997.

Farmer, Fannie. *A New Book of Cookery.* Boston: Little, Brown, 1912.

Ferraz, Corréspondant de l'Institut. "Brillat-Savarin et M. Lucien Tendret." *La Revue du Siècle.* Paris: Bureau de la Revue, 1896, pp. 75–95.

Field, Michael. *Michael Field's Cooking School: A Selection of Great Recipes Demonstrating the Pleasures and Principles of Fine Cooking.* New York: William Morrow, 1965.

———. *Michael Field's Culinary Classics and Improvisations.* New York: Knopf, 1967.

———. *All Manner of Food.* New York: Knopf, 1970.

Fisher, M.F.K. *Serve It Forth.* New York: Harper & Bros., 1937.

———. *The Gastronomical Me.* New York: Duell, Sloan & Pierce, 1943.

———. *The Art of Eating: Five Gastronmical Works of M.F.K. Fisher.* Cleveland: World, 1954.

———. *Map of Another Town: A Memoir of Provence.* Boston: Little, Brown, 1964.

———. *The Cooking of Provincial France.* New York: Time-Life Books, 1968.

———. *With Bold Knife and Fork.* New York: Putnam, 1969.

———. *Among Friends.* New York: Knopf, 1971.

———. *Two Towns in Provence.* New York: Vintage, 1983.

———. *Long Ago in France: The Years in Dijon.* New York: Prentice Hall Press, 1991.

———. *Stay Me, Oh Comfort Me: Journals and Stories 1933–1941.* New York: Pantheon, 1993.

———. *M.F.K. Fisher: A Life in Letters, Correspondence 1929–1991.* Edited by Norah K. Barr, Marsha Moran, and Patrick Moran. Washington, D.C.: Counterpoint, 1998.

———. *From the Journals of M.F.K. Fisher.* New York: Pantheon, 1999.

Fisher, M.F.K., with David Lazar. *Conversations with M.F.K. Fisher.* Jackson: University Press of Mississippi, 1992.

Fitch, Noël Riley. *Appetite for Life: The Biography of Julia Child.* New York: Doubleday, 1997.

Flanner, Janet [Genêt, pseud.]. *Paris Journal (1944–1965).* Edited by William Shawn. New York: Atheneum, 1965.

Franey, Pierre. *A Chef's Tale: A Memoir of Food, France, and America.* New York: Knopf, 1994.

Fussell, Betty. *Masters of American Cookery: M.F.K. Fisher, James Andrews Beard, Raymond Craig Claiborne, Julia McWilliams Child.* New York: Times Books, 1983.

———. *My Kitchen Wars.* New York: North Point Press, 1999.

Gallup, Donald. *Pigeons on the Granite: Memories of a Yale Librarian.* New Haven: Yale University Press, 1988.

Gallup, Donald, and Gertrude Stein. *The Flowers of Friendship: Letters Written to Gertrude Stein.* New York: Knopf, 1953.

Geiger, John. *Nothing Is True, Everything Is Permitted: The Life of Brion Gysin.* New York: Disinformation Co., 2005.

Haight, Mary Ellen Jordan. *Walks in Gertrude Stein's Paris.* Salt Lake City: Peregrine Smith, 1988.

Harvey, Peggy. *Great Recipes from the World's Great Cooks.* New York: Gramercy, 1964.

Hellman, Geoffrey. "Very, Very Cordial," *The New Yorker,* February 19, 1955, pp. 37–75.

Hemingway, Ernest. *A Moveable Feast.* New York: Scribner, 1964.

Hennessy, Leslie. *The Pope of Wine.* San Francisco: Montrachet Publishing, 2012.

Hess, John L., and Karen Hess. *The Taste of America.* New York: Grossman, 1977.

Hesse, Jean-Pascal. *Maxim's: Mirror of Parisian Life.* New York: Assouline, 2011.

Horowitz, Helen Lefkowitz. *A Taste for Provence.* Chicago: University of Chicago Press, 2016.

Huber, Inge. *Curnonsky—à la carte . . .* Munich: Edition Curnonska, 2007.

———. *Curnonsky—en route . . .* Munich: Edition Curnonska, 2007.

———. *Curnonsky—souvenirs gastronomiques . . .* Munich: Edition Curnonska, 2007.

———. *Curnonsky: Oder das Geheimnis des Maurice-Edmond Sailland.* Munich: Edition Curnonska, 2010.

Johnson, Hugh. *Wine.* New York: Simon & Schuster, 1966.

———. *The World Atlas of Wine.* New York: Simon & Schuster, 1971.

Jones, Evan. *Epicurean Delight: The Life and Times of James Beard.* New York: Knopf, 1990.

Jones, Judith. *The Tenth Muse: My Life in Food.* New York: Knopf, 2007.

Kahn, Odette. *La Petite et la Grande Cuisine: 300 Recettes, 60 Menus, 60 Fiches Techniques.* Paris: Calmann-Lévy, 1977.

Kamman, Madeleine. *The Making of a Cook.* New York: Atheneum, 1971.

———. *When French Women Cook: A Gastronomic Memoir.* New York: Atheneum, 1976.

Kamp, David. *The United States of Arugula: How We Became a Gourmet Nation.* New York: Broadway, 2006.

de Knight, Freda. *A Date with a Dish.* New York: Hermitage Press, 1948.

Knopf, Alfred A. *Portrait of a Publisher 1915–1965.* New York: Knopf, 1965.

Kuh, Patric. *The Last Days of Haute Cuisine.* New York: Viking, 2001.

Lang, George. *Nobody Knows the Truffles I've Seen.* New York: Knopf, 1998.

Leibenstein, Margaret. "MacAusland and Gourmet: The Magazine of Good Living 1941 to 1980." In *Cooks and Other People: Proceedings of the Oxford Symposium on Food and Cookery,* edited by Harlan Walker. Totnes, U.K.: Prospect Books, 1986.

Leeming, David. *James Baldwin: A Biography.* New York: Knopf, 1994.

———. *Amazing Grace: A Life of Beauford Delaney.* New York: Oxford University Press, 1998.

Lichine, Alexis. *Wines of France.* New York: Knopf, 1951.

———. *Encyclopedia of Wines and Spirits.* New York: Knopf, 1967.

———. *Alexis Lichine's New Encyclopedia of Wines and Spirits.* New York: Knopf, 1974.

———. *Alexis Lichine's Guide to the Wines and Vineyards of France.* New York: Knopf, 1979.

Liebling, A. J. *The Road Back to Paris.* New York: Doubleday, Doran, 1944.

———. *Normandy Revisited.* New York: Simon & Schuster, 1958.

———. *Between Meals: An Appetite for Paris.* New York: Simon & Schuster, 1962.

———. *The Most of A. J. Liebling.* New York: Simon & Schuster, 1963.

———. *Liebling Abroad.* New York: Playboy Press, 1981.

———. *Liebling at the New Yorker: Uncollected Essays.* Albuquerque: University of New Mexico Press, 1994.

———. *World War II Writings.* Edited by Pete Hamill. New York: Library of America, 2008.

Lord, Eda. *Childsplay.* New York: Simon & Schuster, 1961.

———. *A Matter of Choosing.* New York: Simon & Schuster, 1963.

———. *Extenuating Circumstances.* New York: Knopf, 1971.

Lucas, Dione. *The Cordon Bleu Cook Book.* Boston: Little, Brown, 1947.

———. *French Cookery.* Chicago: Smith College Scholarship Fund, 1953.

———. *The Gourmet Cooking School Cookbook: Classic Recipes, Menus, and Methods as Taught in the Classes of the Gourmet Cooking School.* New York: B. Geis Associates, 1964.

Lucas, Dione, and Marion Gorman. *The Dione Lucas Book of French Cooking.* Boston: Little, Brown, 1973.

Lucas, Dione, and Rosemary Hume. *Au Petit Cordon Bleu: An Array of Recipes from the École du Petit Cordon Bleu, 29 Sloane Street, London.* London: J. M. Dent, 1936.

Lynch, Kermit. *Adventures on the Wine Route: A Wine Buyer's Tour of France.* New York: Farrar, Straus & Giroux, 1988.

———. *Inspiring Thirst: Vintage Selections from the "Kermit Lynch" Wine Brochure.* Berkeley, Calif.: Ten Speed Press, 2004.

Malcolm, Janet. *Two Lives: Gertrude and Alice.* New Haven: Yale University Press, 2008.

Marshall, Lydie. *Cooking with Lydie Marshall.* New York: Knopf, 1982.

Mathiot, Ginette. *Je Sais Cuisiner: 2,000 Recettes, Plats Exquis, Recettes Simples, Conseils Rationnels.* Paris: Albin Michel, 1932.

———. *Je Sais Faire la Pâtisserie.* Paris: Albin Michel, 1938.

———. *La Cuisine pour Tous.* Paris: Albin Michel, 1955.

———. *À Table avec Édouard de Pomiane.* Paris: Albin Michel, 1975.

McCoy, Elin. *The Emperor of Wine: The Rise of Robert M. Parker, Jr., and the Reign of American Taste.* New York: Ecco, 2005.

McNamee, Thomas. *Alice Waters and Chez Panisse: The Romantic, Impractical, Often Eccentric, Ultimately Brilliant Making of a Food Revolution.* New York: Penguin Press, 2007.

———. *The Man Who Changed the Way We Eat: Craig Claiborne and the American Food Renaissance.* New York: Free Press, 2012.

Mellow, James R. *Charmed Circle: Gertrude Stein and Company.* New York: Praeger, 1974.

Mendelson, Anne. *Stand Facing the Stove: The Story of the Women Who Gave America "The Joy of Cooking."* New York: Henry Holt, 1996.

Mengelatte, Pierre. *Buffets & Receptions.* London: Virtue Press, 1978.

———. *Buffets & Réceptions.* Paris: Vilo, 1977.

Montagné, Prosper. *Larousse Gastronomique: The Encyclopedia of Food, Wine and Cooking.* Edited and translated by Charlotte Turgeon and Nina Froud. London: Hamlyn, 1961.

Montagné, Prosper, Dr. Gottschalk, Auguste Escoffier, and Philéas Gilbert. *Larousse Gastronomique.* Montrouge, France: Larousse, 1937.

Montagné, Prosper, and Prosper Salles. *Le Grande Livre de la Cuisine.* Paris: Flammarion, 1929.

Muhlstein, Anka. *Balzac's Omelet.* New York: Other Press, 2011.

Norman, Remington. *Grand Cru: The Great Wines of Burgundy Through the Perspective of Its Finest Vineyards.* London: Kyle Cathie, 2010.

Oliver, Raymond. *Gastronomy of France.* London: Wine and Food Society, 1967.

———. *La Cuisine: Secrets of Modern French Cooking.* New York: Tudor, 1969.

Olney, James. "Remembering Richard Remembering Mlle. Marty." *The Cincinnati Review* 3, no. 1 (Summer 2006), pp. 65–85.

Olney, Richard. *The French Menu Cookbook: The Food and Wine of France—Season by Delicious Season—in Beautifully Composed Menus for American Dining and Entertaining by an American Living in Paris and Provence.* New York: Simon & Schuster, 1970.

———. *Simple French Food.* New York: Atheneum, 1974.

———. *Yquem.* Paris: Flammarion, 1985.

———. *Yquem.* Boston: David Godine, 1986.

————. *Ten Vineyard Lunches.* New York: Interlink Books, 1988.

————. *Romanée-Conti.* Paris: Flammarion, 1991.

————. *Provence, the Beautiful Cookbook: Authentic Recipes from the Regions of Provence.* San Francisco: Collins, 1993.

————. *Lulu's Provençal Table: The Exuberant Food and Wine from Domaine Tempier Vineyard.* New York: HarperCollins, 1994.

————. *Romanée-Conti.* New York: Rizzoli, 1995.

————. *The Good Cook's Encyclopedia.* London: Quadrille, 1997.

————. *Richard Olney's French Wine and Food.* New York: Interlink Books, 1998.

————. *Reflexions.* New York: Brick Tower Press, 1999.

Olney, Richard, series ed. *The Good Cook: Techniques and Recipes Series.* 28 vols. Alexandria, Va.: Time-Life Books, 1981–1990.

112 Gripes About the French. Fontenay aux Roses, France: Imprimerie Bellinand, 1945.

Pellaprat, Henri-Paul. *L'Art Culinaire Moderne: La Bonne Table Française et Étrangère.* Paris: Comptoir Français du Livre, 1937.

————. *Good Food from France.* Translated and Adapted by Charlotte Turgeon. New York: Barrows, 1951.

————. *Modern Culinary Art: {"L'Art Culinaire Moderne"}, French and Foreign Cookery.* Prefaces to the English edition by Margaret Weddell and Doris H. Glasson; French edition prefaced by Maurice Sailland [Curnonsky, pseud.]. Paris: J. Kramer, 1955.

————. *The Great Book of French Cuisine.* New York: World, 1966.

————. *Modern French Culinary Art: The Pellaprat of the 20th Century.* Translated by John Fuller. London: Collins, 1967.

————. *Everyday French Cooking for the American Home.* New York: World, 1968.

Pépin, Jacques. *A French Chef Cooks at Home.* New York: Simon & Schuster, 1975.

————. *La Technique.* New York: Times Books, 1976.

————. *La Méthode.* New York: Times Books, 1979.

————. *The Apprentice: My Life in the Kitchen.* Boston: Houghton Mifflin, 2003.

Point, Fernand. *Ma Gastronomie.* Introduction by Joseph Wechsberg. Wilton, Conn.: Lyceum Books, 1974.

de Pomiane, Édouard. *Good Fare: A Code of Cookery.* Edited by Doris Langley Moore. Translated by Blanche Bowes. London: Gerald Howe, 1932.

————. *La Cuisine en 10 Minutes. Conférences Faites à l'Institut d'Hygiène Alimentaire de Paris.* Étampes, France: Imprimerie La Semeuse, 1934.

————. *Cooking in Ten Minutes; Or, the Adaptation to the Rhythm of Our Time.* Translated by Peggie Benton. Los Angeles: Pacific Press, 1948.

————. *Radio-Cuisine: Chroniques Gastronomiques Diffusées par T.S.F.* Paris: Albin Michel, 1949.

————. *365 Menus, 365 Recettes: Précédées d'une Étude sur le Régime Alimentaire de Chacun.* Paris: Albin Michel, 1951.

de Pomiane, Édouard, and Henri Babinski. *Bien Manger pour Bien Vivre: Essai de Gastronomie Théorique.* Paris: Albin Michel, 1922.

Reardon, Joan. *Poet of the Appetites: The Lives and Loves of M.F.K. Fisher.* New York: North Point Press, 2004.

Reichl, Ruth, ed. *Endless Feasts: Sixty Years of Writing from "Gourmet."* New York: Modern Library, 2002.

————. *Remembrance of Things Paris: Sixty Years of Writing from "Gourmet."* New York: Modern Library, 2004.

Rigaux, Jacky, and Aubert de Villaine. *Le Réveil des Terroirs: Défense et Illustration des Climats de Bourgogne.* Messigny-et-Ventoux, France: Éditions de Bourgogne, 2010.

Robinson, Jancis, ed. *The Oxford Companion to Wine.* New York: Oxford University Press, 1994.

Rogers, W. G. *When This You See Remember Me: Gertrude Stein in Person.* New York: Rinehart, 1948.

Rombauer, Irma. *The Joy of Cooking: A Compilation of Reliable Recipes with Casual Culinary Chat.* St. Louis: privately printed, 1931.

————. *Joy of Cooking.* Indianapolis: Bobbs-Merrill, 1936.

Root, Waverley. *The Food of France.* New York: Knopf, 1958.

————. *Paris Dining Guide.* New York: Atheneum, 1969.

Rose, Sir Francis Cyril. *Saying Life: The Memoirs of Sir Francis Rose.* London: Cassell, 1961.

Rouff, Marcel. *The Passionate Epicure: La Vie et La Passion de Dodin-Bouffant, Gourmet.* New York: Dutton, 1962.

Rowlands, Penelope, ed. *Paris Was Ours: Thirty-Two Writers Reflect on the City of Light.* Chapel Hill, N.C.: Algonquin Books of Chapel Hill, 2011.

Sailland, Maurice [Curnonsky, pseud.]. *Gaietés et Curiosités Gastronomiques.* Paris: Delagrave, 1933.

————. *Six Gastronomic Portraits.* London: Écu de France, 1938.

————. *À Travers Mon Binocle.* Paris: Albin Michel, 1948.

————. *La Table et l'Amour; Nouveau Traité des Excitants Modernes.* Paris: La Clé d'Or, 1950.

————. *Bon Plats, Bon Vins: 3,000 Recettes et Conseils de Cuisine Bourgeoise.* Paris: Maurice Ponsot, 1950.

————. *Cuisine et Vins de France.* Paris: Larousse, 1953.

————. *Souvenirs Litteraires et Gastronomiques.* Paris: Albin Michel, 1958.

————. *Larousse Traditional French Cooking.* Introduction by Pierre Troisgros. New York: Doubleday, 1989.

Sailland, Maurice [Curnonsky, pseud.], and Pierre Andrieu. *Les Fines Gueules de France.* Paris: Typographie Firmin-Didot, 1935.

Sailland, Maurice [Curnonsky, pseud.], and Austin de Croze. *Le Tresor Gastronomique de la France.* Paris: Delagrave, 1933.

Sailland, Maurice [Curnonsky, pseud.], and Marcel Rouff. *La France Gastronomique: Guide des Merveilles et des Bonnes Auberges Françaises.* 13 vols. Paris: Rouff, 1921–1928.

Saint-Ange, Mme. E. *La Bonne Cuisine de Madame E. Saint-Ange.* Translated by Paul Aratow. Berkeley, Calif.: Ten Speed Press, 2005.

Saintsbury, George. *Notes on a Cellar-Book.* London: Macmillan, 1920.

de Saligny, Marc. *Précis des Nouveaux Usages.* Paris: Éditions Prisma, 1948.

Schoonmaker, Frank. *Come with Me Through France.* New York: R. M. McBride, 1928.

————. *Dictionary of Wines.* New York: Hastings House, 1951.

————. *Frank Schoonmaker's Encyclopedia of Wine.* New York: Hastings House, 1964.

Schoonmaker, Frank, and Tom Marvel. *The Complete Wine Book.* London: G. Routledge & Sons, 1935.

Shapiro, Laura. *Perfection Salad: Women and Cooking at the Turn of the Century.* New York: Farrar, Straus & Giroux, 1986.

———. *Something from the Oven: Reinventing Dinner in 1950s America.* New York: Viking, 2004.

———. *Julia Child: A Life.* New York: Lipper/Viking, 2007.

Simon, André L. *A Wine Primer.* London: Michael Joseph, 1950.

———. *A Concise Encyclopaedia of Gastronomy.* New York: Harcourt, Brace, 1952.

———. *The Commonsense of Wine.* New York: Bonanza Books, 1965.

———. *Wines of the World.* New York: McGraw-Hill, 1967.

Simon, Linda. *The Biography of Alice B. Toklas.* Garden City, N.Y.: Doubleday, 1977.

Sokolov, Raymond. *Wayward Reporter: The Life of A. J. Liebling.* New York: Harper & Row, 1980.

Souhami, Diana. *Gertrude and Alice.* New York: Pandora/Harper, 1991.

Spitz, Bob. *Dearie: The Remarkable Life of Julia Child.* New York: Knopf, 2012.

Spring, Justin. *Secret Historian: The Life and Times of Samuel Steward.* New York: Farrar, Straus & Giroux, 2010.

Stein, Gertrude. *Three Lives.* New York: Grafton Press, 1909.

———. *The Autobiography of Alice B. Toklas.* New York: Harcourt, Brace, 1933.

———. *Wars I Have Seen.* New York: Random House, 1945.

———. *Blood on the Dining Room Floor.* Pawlet, Vt.: Banyan Press, 1948.

Stein, Gertrude, and Alice Toklas. *Dear Sammy: Letters from Gertrude Stein and Alice Toklas.* Edited and with an introduction by Samuel M. Steward. Boston: Houghton Mifflin, 1977.

Stein, Gertrude, and Thornton Wilder. *The Letters of Gertrude Stein and Thornton Wilder.* Edited by Edward M. Burns and Ulla Dydo. New Haven: Yale University Press, 1996.

Steinberger, Michael. *Au Revoir to All That: Food, Wine and the End of France.* New York: Bloomsbury, 2010.

Stern, Jane, and Michael Stern. *Square Meals: A Cookbook.* New York: Knopf, 1985.

———. *American Gourmet.* New York: HarperCollins, 1991.

Taride, Alice Marie. *Tante Marie's French Kitchen.* Translated by Charlotte Turgeon. New York: Oxford University Press, 1949.

Tendret, Lucien. *La Table au Pays de Brillat-Savarin.* Belley, France: L. Bailly Fils, 1892.

Thurman, Judith. *Secrets of the Flesh: A Life of Colette.* New York: Knopf, 1999.

Toklas, Alice. *The Alice B. Toklas Cook Book.* Illustrated by Francis Rose. New York: Harper, 1954.

———. *Aromas and Flavors of Past and Present.* New York: Harper & Bros., 1958.

———. *What Is Remembered.* New York: Holt, Rinehart and Winston, 1963.

———. *Staying On Alone: The Letters of Alice B. Toklas.* Edited by Edward Burns. New York: Liveright, 1973.

Tower, Jeremiah. *California Dish: What I Saw (and Cooked) at the American Food Revolution.* New York: Free Press, 2003.

Turgeon, Charlotte. *Time to Entertain.* Boston: Little, Brown, 1954.

———. *Creative Cooking Course.* New York: Weathervane, 1975.

de Toulouse-Lautrec, Mapie. *La Cuisine de France et du Monde.* Paris: Hachette, 1958.

———. *365 Jours de Cuisine.* Paris: Fayard, 1959.

———. *La Cuisine de France.* Translated by Charlotte Turgeon. New York: Orion, 1964.

———. *Good French Cooking.* Translated by Charlotte Turgeon. London: Hamlyn, 1966.

————. *La Cuisine de Mapie*. Paris: Tallandier, 1967.

Villas, James. *The French Country Kitchen: Undiscovered Glories of French Regional Cuisine*. New York: Bantam, 1992.

————. *Between Bites: Memoirs of a Hungry Hedonist*. New York: Wiley, 2002.

————. *Stalking the Green Fairy: And Other Fantastic Adventures in Food and Drink*. Hoboken, N.J.: Wiley, 2004.

Waters, Alice. *The Art of Simple Food: Notes, Lessons and Recipes from a Delicious Revolution*. New York: Clarkson Potter, 2007.

Watt, Alexander. *Paris Bistro Cooking*. New York: Knopf, 1955.

Wechsberg, Joseph. *Blue Trout and Black Truffles: The Peregrinations of an Epicure*. New York: Knopf, 1953.

————. *Dining at the Pavillon*. Boston: Little, Brown, 1962.

————. *Trifles Make Perfection: The Selected Essays of Joseph Wechsberg*. Boston: David Godine, 1999.

Wharton, Edith. *French Ways and Their Meaning*. New York: Appleton, 1919.

White, Max. *How I Feed My Friends*. New York: Duell, Sloan & Pearce, 1946.

Wickes, George. *Americans in Paris*. Garden City, N.Y.: Doubleday, 1969.

Williams, Roger. *Lunch with Elizabeth David*. London: Little, Brown, 1999.

Wineapple, Brenda. *Genêt: A Biography of Janet Flanner*. New York: Ticknor & Fields, 1989.

VIDEO AND AUDIO

The French Chef. WGBH, Boston, 1963–1973.

The French Chef with Julia Child. 3 DVDs. WGBH Boston Video, 2005.

The French Chef 2 with Julia Child. 3 DVDs. WGBH Boston Video, 2005.

Lichine, Alexis. *Alexis Lichine's The Joy of Wine*. New York: MGM Records, 1968

ARCHIVES AND PRIMARY SOURCES

The James Beard Foundation, New York, N.Y.
James Beard Library Collection

Beinecke Rare Book and Manuscripts Library, Yale University, New Haven, Conn.
Gertrude Stein and Alice Toklas Collection
Samuel M. Steward Papers
Carl Van Vechten Papers
Walter White and Poppy Cannon White Papers
Thornton Wilder Papers

Columbia University Special Collections Archive, New York, N.Y.
Harper Publishers Papers
John Schaffner Papers

Cornell Special Collections Archive, Ithaca, N.Y.
A. J. Liebling Papers

New York Public Library Archive, New York, N.Y.
The New Yorker Magazine Archive
NYPL Menu Collection Index
NYPL Gastronomy and Food History Archive

NYU/Fales Special Collections Library, New York, N.Y.
James Beard Papers.
Cecily Brownstone Cookbook Collection and Papers
Noël Riley Fitch–Julia Child Papers
Voices from the Food Revolution Oral History Collection

Harry Ransom Center, University of Texas at Austin
Sybille Bedford and Eda Lord Papers
Bradley Literary Agency Papers
Allanah Harper Papers
Alfred A. Knopf, Inc. Records (Series II)
Carlton Lake Manuscript Collection
Alice Toklas Papers

Schlesinger Library, Radcliffe Institute, Harvard University, Cambridge, Mass.
Simone Beck Papers
Narcisse Chamberlain Papers
Julia Child Papers
Elizabeth David Papers
Avis DeVoto Papers
Mary Frances Kennedy Fisher Papers
Dione Lucas Papers

Tisch Library, Tufts University, Medford, Mass.
Waverley Root Papers

University of Michigan Special Collections Library, University of Michigan, Ann Arbor, Mich.
Janice Bluestein Longone Culinary Archive

Papers Still in Private Hands
Lydie Marshall Papers, Nyons, France
Richard Olney Papers and Cookbook Collection, Solliès-Toucas, Var, France
Richard Olney Papers, Collection of Byron Olney, Rochester, Minn.

Interviews Conducted by the Author
James Fox, Susan Friedland, Helen Lefkowitz Horowitz, Jennifer Josephy, Marc Lanza,
    Lydie Marshall, Jill Norman, Byron Olney, Elizabeth Olney, James Olney, Marilynn
    Olney, Judith Pillsbury, Helen Rattray, Elliott Stein, Thomas A. Stewart, Jeremiah
    Tower, Kit van Tulleken, Amanda Vaill, Jean Vallier, James Villas

Acknowledgments

For help and advice in the researching and writing of this book, I have many people and institutions to thank.

This project was made possible financially through assistance that came to me from three institutional fellowships: a Schlesinger Library Fellowship at Harvard, a Brown Foundation Fellowship at the Dora Maar House in Ménherbes, and a Leon Levy Center Biography Fellowship at the CUNY Graduate Center. I'd particularly like to thank the Levy Center's executive director, Gary Giddins, and its program director, Michael Gately, for their friendship and support throughout the fellowship and after. I should add that my initial research into the life and writings of Alice Toklas was also supported by a fellowship at the Beinecke Library—this, more than fifteen years ago.

I'd also like to thank several mentors who encouraged my interest in food writing over the past decades. Early on, my work as a freelance editor for Robert and Susan Lescher at Lescher & Lescher literary agency gave me my first exposure to this special and somewhat idiosyncratic world. Wine expert and gourmet Louis Broman, meanwhile, first introduced me to Richard Olney's *Simple French Food*. Our early adventures in cooking from that book helped me to see its unique synthesis of fine writing and fine cooking instruction, and to start thinking about cookbooks and gastronomic writing in a new way. Film producer and director Ismail Merchant also encouraged my interest in food, cooking, and its literature, teaching me by example what it was to be a gourmand; in time, Madhur Jaffrey did the same, only this time by showing me what it was to research and collect recipes the world over. Laura Shapiro was an early believer in my writing and helped me find my way to the Schlesinger Library. Her own writing on food has been a decade-long inspiration. Jennifer Josephy, who edited my *Itty Bitty Kitchen Handbook* at Broadway Books/Random House, was also very encouraging. Along with introducing me, firsthand, to the challenges of writing and publishing a cookbook, she was kind enough to share reminiscences of her relatives Alfred, Blanche, and Pat

Knopf. Francine Maroukian, a true professional in the food world, has been a constant source of sound advice to me for decades. Throughout the researching and writing of this book, however, my most important mentor has been Susan Friedland, who has freely shared her extraordinary experience and knowledge of cookbook editing with me, as well as her many firsthand recollections of the individuals I write about in this book. Through the years she has become a trusted friend as well as a revered guide and source of information.

Several other people in the culinary and publishing worlds have helped and/or advised me in my research. First among them is my agent, Alia Hanna Habib, at McCormick Literary, who was a constant source of encouragement throughout the long process of taking the book from original idea to finished work. The journalist and cookbook author James Villas gave me writing advice along with his recollections of James Beard, Alexandre Dumaine, Richard Olney, and Jeremiah Tower. Paula Wolfert was also enormously helpful in sharing her recollections of Paris in the 1960s and '70s, and in describing her friendships with Dione Lucas, James Beard, Louisette Bertholle, and Richard Olney, among many others. Jeremiah Tower likewise shared many recollections of his earlier days, doing so with his characteristic good humor. Jill Norman was gracious in sharing her recollections of Richard Olney, Sybille Bedford, and Elizabeth David. Though we have never yet been able to meet in person, Guy Griffin in Australia offered his advice and support throughout the researching and writing of the book. Additional help and advice also came to me from Kit van Tulleken, David and Maggi Gordon, Jane Sigal, and Helen Lefkowitz Horowitz. The painter Jane Wilson, a beloved friend, colleague, and fellow cook, shared her early, Iowa memories of Richard Olney with me, and gave me one of his cooklbooks. Jean Vallier, former head of the Alliance Française, introduced me to Elliott Stein just a few months before Stein's death; during a memorable afternoon in Brooklyn, both men shared their extraordinary memories of Paris in the 1950s and '60s with me. James Fox, meanwhile, helped me find my way through the legal department of HarperCollins Publishers. Lydie Marshall not only shared her reminiscences with me but granted me access to her extraordinary archive of *Cuisine et Vins de France* magazines, as well as to her own private library, both at her home in Nyons. She also gave me a bed for the night, and a very good meal!

This book could not have been written had not my subjects, their families, and their estates made their papers available to qualified scholars and researchers. For permission to review the M.F.K. Fisher Papers I would like to thank literary agent Michael V. Carlisle and the estate of M.F.K. Fisher. The Olney family gave me unlimited access to the papers of Richard Olney. The Julia Child Papers, Alice Toklas Papers, and A. J. Liebling Papers are open to all qualified researchers.

For photo permissions, the Julia Child Foundation, through its administrator, Lauren Salkeld, was kind enough to grant permission for the reproduction of Paul Child's 1951 valentine. The Schlesinger Library allowed me to reproduce the photographs of Paul and Julia Child, Dione Lucas, and M.F.K. Fisher. Château Prieuré-Lichine and Château Lascombes allowed me to include their photographs in the book, as did the restaurant Le Grand Véfour. Sacha Lichine graciously gave me permission to reproduce photographs in his family collection, as did Claudia Franey Jensen, Diane Franey, and Jacques Franey. Michael Williams kindly allowed me to reproduce the Alice Toklas photographs of Samuel M. Steward. Byron and Marilynn Olney were extraordinarily generous in allowing me unlimited access to Richard Olney's papers in Solliès-Toucas and in Rochester, Minnesota, and for allowing me to reproduce many of Richard Olney's personal photographs from those papers in this book. James Olney, though I met him only once, was enormously supportive of my writing; since then, Byron and Marilynn Olney have been fine hosts, helpful and informative sources, and, ultimately, good friends to me.

I'd also like to thank several important special collections libraries and their librarians: the Schlesinger Library, Harvard, particularly my contact there, Diana Carey; Fales Special Collections Library at NYU, particularly its director, Marvin Taylor; Smith College Special Collections Library; the Beinecke Library, Yale, particularly curator (and friend) Timothy Young; the Ransom Humanities Center at the University of Texas at Austin; Cornell University Special Collections Library; Columbia University Special Collections Library; Harvard Imaging Services; and the Amherst College Special Collections department at Frost Library.

Thanks are also due to the biographers, scholars, and editors who have written and published significantly on the writers featured in this book. My thanks to Edward Burns, Noël Riley Fitch, Leslie Hennessy, Janet Malcolm, James R. Mellow, Alex Prud'homme, Joan Reardon, Linda Simon, Raymond Sokolov, Bob Spitz, Samuel M. Steward, and Brenda Wineapple.

During my year in France, and on subsequent return visits, I experienced extraordinary kindness and hospitality from a number of people, first among them Estrellita and Dan Brodsky. Estrellita's love of Paris and of France has been an ongoing inspiration to me; so too, her enthusiasm for roll-up-your-sleeves research and scholarship. Gertrud Ingigliardi was an extraordinary source of information about all things Parisian and French, particularly relating to the domestic arts and the French home. Rachel Stella offered friendship as well as wisdom, as did her partner, the poet Jacques Demarcq, and her daughter, Rebekah Edmonde Aubrey. Jean Paul Beaujard was a genial host; Pepita Dupont a kindly writer-colleague. Lulu Peyraud was generous and charming in her recollections of Richard Olney. Marc Lanza was equally hospitable during my residency at Solliès-Toucas. Jean Silvy-Leligois was extraordinarily kind to me during my afternoon with him in Bilignin. Judith Pillsbury was a fine and helpful next-door neighbor to me in Paris as well as an incredible source of firsthand information. My good friend Mélanie Facchetti was very helpful to me in understanding the Parisian point of view, as were Caroline Spitzer and Emmanuel Delaunay. Brooks Adams and Lisa Liebmann helped me to understand the many challenges faced by Americans living in France, as well as the many joys. So too did Robert Parker, Beatrice Philippe and Zoltan Hankofsky, Jean Coyner, Féderica Matta and Todd Brandow, and the great Darthea Speyer. During my residency in Ménerbes, Gwen Strauss, director of the Dora Maar House, became an extraordinary friend as well as adviser.

In England, I'm particularly grateful to the following friends and colleagues: Sir Roderic Wood, Sandra Korner, Charles Darwent, Julie Lawson, Angela Huxley Darwin, Norma Wasserman-Miller, Tabitha Estabrook Claydon, Judith Unwin, and Georgina Paul. In Austria, Andrew and Gabriele Braunsberg, Miryam Charim, and Lisa Ungar. In Germany, my sincere thanks to Anya Hatzfeldt for her friendship and hospitality at Sommerberg.

A number of friends here in the United States helped me with the researching and writing of this book. They include Patricia Mason Beaury, Cam Beaury, and Bob Beaury; Martin and Mary Puris, Jason Puris, and Katie Riccio Puris; Loren and Nancy

Dunlap; Noami Marks and Vernon Taylor; Jean Vanderbilt; Steve Harvey and Perry Sayles; Wendy Vanderbilt Lehman; Laura Donnelly; Idoline Scheerer and Tom Scheerer; Valerie Smith; Amanda Vaill and Tom Stewart; Honor Moore; Blake Bailey; Mary Jo Kline and Ted Crackel; Dr. Edward Goldberg; James Zajac; George Shackelford; Alison de Lima Greene; Julie Saul; Pari Stave; Elizabeth Easton and James Traub; Anne and Alain Goldrach; Sok Song; Alexander Horwitz and Ben Heisler; Lisa Chase Tatham; Christopher Gardner and Gary Tinterow; Rick Kinsel; Leslie Camhi; Karl Willers; Lucia Guimaraes; Darren Walker and David Beitzel; Alexandra Anderson; Bob Smith; Sarah and Andy Spongberg; Helen and Alexander Philon; and Edgar and Eileen Koerner. Also Robert Boynton, Brad Gooch, Fernando Salles, Anne Cantacuzene, Isabel Carden, Edith Aronson, Diana Festa, Greil Marcus, Rudi Dundas, Robert Kushner, and Max and Joyce Kozloff.

At Farrar, Straus and Giroux, I have many people to thank, first among them Ileene Smith, whose astute and compassionate editing made the experience of being edited so very pleasant. Jonathan Galassi saw the book's potential and gave it his blessing. Trent Duffy was the book's copy editor extraordinaire, understanding exactly what I hoped to write, even as he suggested various ways of writing it better. I am particularly grateful to him for his meticulous attention to every last detail in this detail-filled book. Jonathan Lippincott did a beautiful job designing the text and photographic layout, and Pier Gustafson made its two brilliant, beautiful maps. Debra Helfand, Katie Hurley, and Nina Frieman saw the book through production, and Jackson Howard kept everything in order, doing so with admirable patience and good humor. Laura Ogar wrote a thoughtful index for the book, and Karen Ninnis and Christopher Caines did exceptional work proofreading the manuscript. Stephen Weill, who handled publicity for my previous book, has once again made the process of publishing and promoting this new book a pleasure.

I'd like to thank my family for their years of goodwill and support: my sister, Margaret Spring, and her husband, Mark Bunter; my brother, Arthur Spring, his wife, Rosalind, and their son, Kelby. Also my stepfather, Richard Johe. My late father, Justin M. Spring, lived long enough to read this book in draft form, and I'll always remember the kind and encouraging things he said to me about it in our last conversations. Most of all though, I'd like to thank my mother, Sharon Johe, whose lifelong enthusiasm for good cooking and good writing has inspired me from childhood onward. So too has her incredible work ethic, both as a career professional and homemaker.

Finally, I'd like to thank my partner of many years, Tony Korner, whose encouragement, enthusiasm, and sense of adventure have made the researching and writing of this book such a pleasure. Tony, how lucky I have been to know, to love you, and to be with you—both here and there!—this last quarter century.

Index

A NOTE ABOUT THE AUTHOR

Justin Spring is the author of two previous biographies: *Fairfield Porter: A Life in Art* and *Secret Historian: The Life and Times of Samuel Steward*, the latter a finalist for the National Book Award. His writing on visual art includes monographs and museum catalogues, most recently *Andy Warhol: Fame and Misfortune* and *Paul Cadmus: The Male Nude*. He is a recipient of fellowships from the Guggenheim Foundation, the Leon Levy Center for Biography, and numerous universities.

Printed in the USA
CPSIA information can be obtained
at www.ICGtesting.com
LVHW040729150724
785511LV00002B/236

9 780374 538019